IN CAMERA

BY THE SAME AUTHOR

Caught in the Act

IN CAMERA

An Autobiography Continued

RICHARD TODD

HUTCHINSON

London Sydney Auckland Johannesburg

This edition first published in 1989 by
Hutchinson

Century Hutchinson Ltd, Brookmount House,
62–65 Chandos Place, London WC2N 4NW

Century Hutchinson Australia (Pty) Ltd
20 Alfred Street, Milsons Point, Sydney NSW 2061, Australia

Century Hutchinson New Zealand Limited
PO Box 40–086, Glenfield, Auckland 10, New Zealand

Century Hutchinson South Africa (Pty) Ltd
PO Box 337, Bergvlei, 2012 South Africa

Set in 11/12½pt Baskerville by Input Typesetting Ltd, London

Printed and bound in Great Britain by
Butler and Tanner Ltd, Frome and London.

British Library Cataloguing in Publication Data
Todd, Richard, 1919–
In camera
1. Acting, Todd, Richard, 1919–
Biographies
I. Title
792'.028'0924

ISBN 0–09–173534.3

TO VIRGINIA WITH MY LOVE

Contents

1   Getting My Act Together   1

2   Caught On a Hot Tiled Roof   9

3   It's a Boy!   19

4   A Disney World   26

5   Per Ardua Ad Elstree   30

6   Enter Miss World   35

7   A Highland Fling   40

8   Disneyland   49

9   Heathcliff Takes French Leave   55

10 Roman Holiday   59

11 Bombs Gone!   66

12 A Kind of Miracle   75

13 Good Queen Bette   84

14 The Dam Busters Take Off!   89

15 Back to Front   96

16 A Chinese Puzzle   104

17 A Moving Period   111

18	A-Farming I Did Go	131
19	Shooting A Mixed Bag	138
20	A Blank Check	151
21	A Trilogy of Films	168
22	Flying Visits	183
23	D-Day Plus Seventeen Years	194
24	Here, There and Everywhere	200
25	How Not To Get On When Really Trying	207
26	All Work and No Pay	221
27	A Farewell to Farms	234
28	There Is Life After Debt	251
29	Moving Moments	263
30	A Perfect Stranger	279
31	A Triumphant Beginning	293
32	An Heir-Raising Experience	305
33	By Road, Rail and Air	312
34	Oh, For a Quiet Life!	332
35	Home Is Where You Make It	340
36	Another Heir Apparent!	348
37	Here Endeth the Second Volume	359

Illustration Credits

1 National Film Archive
2 J. Arthur Rank Organisation
4 RKO Radio Pictures
12 Bob Martin
14 Norman Greville
16 BFI
17 Kobal Collection
20 Kas Heppner
21 *New York Times*
22 Flair Photography
23 Warner-Pathé
24 Millar and Harris
27 Kobal Collection
28 Rex Features
29 Kobal Collection
30 Rex Features
32 Popperfoto
33 Edward Quinn
34 Rex Features
36 Popperfoto
37 Robert Hawkins
40 Keystone Press
43 Roger Allen
44 Bill Kenwright

1

Getting My Act Together

From my bird's-eye view, as I circled gently a few hundred feet above it, the great United States warship sparkled like a profusion of glittering jewels set in a sapphire sea. Dressed overall, with flags flying and hundreds of electric bulbs strung about her, she was a memorable sight and well worth my aerobatic venture, the most ambitious that I had ever attempted.

I decided to take a closer look, banked steeply to my left and swooped down in a shallow dive that would take me right over her from stem to stern, my head lowered a little and my arms closer to my sides, quite forgetting that I would now be clearly visible to those on deck – a mistake that was to be my undoing.

My power of flight depended entirely on confidence and belief: I had to *know* that I could do it, or I couldn't even take off. Anything that undermined that certainty was disastrous for me.

So here I was, soaring along quite happily, until I caught sight of the incredulous look on a matelot's face as he yelled out, 'Jesus, I don't believe it! There's a guy up there flying.'

That did it . . . Suddenly I didn't believe it either and crumpled like a well-shot pheasant, heading straight for the sea. Just before the moment of impact I woke up, sweating, as I generally did at the end of one of these flights of fancy.

I had had a similar dream several times, though usually I found myself winging my way around film sound-stages or other familiar large indoor spaces. I believe that such sleeping hallucinations are not uncommon and mine may have had their provenance in my wartime service as a parachutist. That was a period of my life which I described at some length in *Caught in the Act*, the first volume of my memoirs, little thinking that it would have some slight repercussion on my behaviour years later during a visit to the South of France.

My wife Kitty and I had landed at Nice airport in the early afternoon on our way to Monte Carlo, where I was to film *24 Hours of a Woman's Life* with Merle Oberon.

If I had ever hankered after a glamorous film location, my hopes were surely now fulfilled. The weather was brilliant, the Côte d'Azur scenery quite gorgeous and our temporary home was the opulent Hôtel de Paris in Monte Carlo. All very different from my last film location on *Robin Hood* in a dank and dripping woodland area near Denham Studios, where our arrows went zinging in the rain.

Although I was here to work, I regarded this stint as something of a holiday. Who could arrive in the South of France in August without responding to the sunshine, the salty tang of the air and the relaxed atmosphere? In any case I enjoyed my job, there would be a certain amount of free time and I was actually being well paid too. I still had not got quite accustomed to my change of fortune. It was all a very different world from the seven-day week of my slog not so long ago in repertory theatre.

Our room at the Hôtel de Paris overlooked the Casino and the Grande Place, and we joined the film's producer Ivan Foxwell and its director Victor Saville for dinner later in the dining room. I remember being startled by the prices on the menu, and wondering if I should choose the more modest dishes.

I was on an expenses-paid contract, which was always embarrassing, since one was never sure exactly which expenses were allowable. Even our laundry bills staggered me, and my conscience pricked me every time I decided to change my shirt. But one thing I was quite certain about: allowable expenses did not include gaming in the Casino!

However, being in Monte Carlo without having an occasional flutter on the tables would be like visiting London without ever going to a theatre, so that first evening, Ivan led me across to the Casino. As residents of the Hôtel de Paris we had *entrée* cards to the Salle Privée, the Valhalla of the place, and we were properly impressed by the ornate grandeur of it all. Fortunately, I am not a gambler by nature: I was quite content to buy a pile of chips small enough not to strain my personal finances and when it ran out on the roulette tables I never went back for more. But I was agreeably surprised to see no noticeable flicker of disdain when I purchased my little ration of chips.

Next morning I met my co-star Merle Oberon when I visited the film unit as they worked on a scene on the beautiful two-masted sailing yacht *Valrosa*, chartered complete with Russian skipper from an Italian family, the Cicognas of Venice. Merle was then at the peak of her career, with a gorgeous figure and enchanting Eurasian features. I realised that if I was to be believably the lover of this alluring creature as the story demanded, I would need all the help I could get from the script, the director, the cameraman and my Cyril-Castle-cut suits.

Filming with Merle that day was Leo Genn, actor and barrister-at-law, with whom I was to enjoy a warm rapport during our weeks of work. Also on board as a guest was Henry Cotton, the golf maestro, who had a golf school in Monte Carlo and was then still the British Ryder Cup team captain. I took an immediate liking to this great sportsman and his jolly South American wife and stepdaughter Nellie, and we became close friends.

Sunday was Kitty's birthday, and we celebrated with lunch at La Reserve at Beaulieu, joining our great friends Derek and Maggie Hall-Caine, who were staying there. Later that day a group of us which included Kieron Moore, the Irish actor, dined at Château Madrid, a restaurant stunningly placed high on the corniche overlooking Beaulieu and the Mediterranean. From our table on the low-walled terrace literally carved out of the cliff we had a perfect view of an American warship on a courtesy visit, twinkling its festoons of lights about a mile away.

Our celebratory feast had been generous to say the least and we were all in high spirits in every sense. At the coffee and brandy stage I recalled my recurring dream of being able to fly by simply taking a deep breath, flapping my arms and taking off, and was sorely tempted to test if I could achieve lift-off from such an ideal vantage point. The derisive comments of my friends soon quelled my self-confidence, fortunately, but that night in my dreams I re-enacted the scene, with the nightmarish result I have already described.

Anyone who might accuse me of having a pretty cushy time on that film would be right! I did no work at all for the first week, but simply made the most of our glamorous location.

Indeed that week was idyllic. I spent most days reading my script on the beach and wandering round Monte Carlo. No great hardship in that! There was plenty to look at, both human and scenic . . .

The following Sunday we joined Ivan, Merle, the Genns, British film producer John Wolff, pretty Jill Clifford-Turner and others on *Valrosa*. We cruised to Antibes, where we anchored and spent a beautiful day swimming and eating scrumptious *bouillabaisse* prepared by the yacht's cook.

The next day I finally started filming with Merle in scenes on the Casino terrace. These took all that week, and the following weekend the unit moved to Grasse, a town in the Provençal hills above Cannes. Kitty stayed on in Monte Carlo.

We were all quartered in a large, gloomy hotel where the only other residents were a group of Italian film-makers busy on their own picture. It was a miserable place altogether, and none of us ever took our meals there. I did spend a few evenings indoors before going out to dinner, but this was because I enjoyed playing table-tennis with a delectable little Italian girl called Gina, in tight jeans and even tighter T-shirt, who was working with the other film group. I presumed she was a wardrobe or make-up assistant, but she spoke no English and I spoke no Italian, so our acquaintanceship was pretty stilted and never progressed beyond the games room. Besides, she was usually under the watchful eye of one of her companions who was a terrific player. I much preferred playing with her. Her chaperone invariably slaughtered me at the table.

Most of our location shooting that week was at Gourdon, a fascinating hamlet high in the rugged hills with a little stone-built castle, a couple of narrow streets of plaster-peeling cottages and a small restaurant, the Eagle's Nest, perched on the edge of a cliff. The views were over valleys that seemed mostly covered in lavender bushes, their scent pervading everything. We also did some work at a simple little church at Maqagnosc, whose priest for our purposes was Stephen Murray – with whom I had worked on my first film, *For Them That Trespass*. He and I and Jacques Brunius, a very pleasant French actor, supped some evenings together in a little café in Grasse, since Merle apparently preferred to have food brought to her room in our dreary hotel.

I did get to know Merle quite well eventually. She was a witty, sophisticated and very articulate lady, and a great raconteuse. A couple of times I took her to dinner in Cannes at my favourite restaurant, D'Aboutot's, which I knew from a previous holiday there with Kitty. The grubby plastered walls were covered with the signatures of celebrities, written in lipstick – hers and mine were added to those of Rita Hayworth and Prince Ali Khan.

On another evening we had drinks with Frederick Lonsdale the playwright, a friend of Merle's and, to me, the archetypal wit and bon viveur of the 1930s with his repartee, natty suiting, bow tie and 'corespondent' brown-and-white shoes.

It might be thought that our main exertions on this film location were eating and drinking, but in fact we worked long hours from early morning in rather steamy conditions. On one occasion, too, the whole project nearly ground to an abrupt halt when the horse pulling the *fiacre* that I was driving in one scene, with Merle as my passenger, took fright on passing the camera and bolted along the twisting *haute corniche* road high on the mountainside. There was only a low stone wall between us and a fearsome drop, and for some distance we careered along crazily until I managed to regain control after sawing the bit and pulling back for all I was worth. Just in time, too, as the offside wheel turned out to have been badly damaged in one clash against the parapet.

I was glad to get back to Monte Carlo, especially as we were now starting to film a sequence that I knew would be fascinating: actual gaming scenes in the Sporting Club. This was a second Casino that was not open to the public at that time of year, and Ivan had rented the whole place and some of the staff, including croupiers, so that we could create the typical atmosphere with busy tables and the usual throng of onlookers.

Word had got around Monte Carlo that for this sequence Ivan needed several hundred paid extras, but I don't think the money attracted the queues which turned up to sign on so much as the fun of being filmed. We needed, in film parlance, a smart evening-dress crowd, and that's just what we got. It became almost the chic thing at that time in Monte Carlo; to appear in this British picture carried a certain cachet and glamorous women and well-groomed men of all ages arrived in droves. British, French, Germans, Scandinavians – they were all represented.

Each day, as the gambling sessions started, all those involved at the tables including myself were issued with a stack of chips for which we had to sign and which had to be handed back at the end of the day. The chips (or *plaques*) were bona fide Casino currency and could otherwise have been exchanged for actual money. As each scene was filmed the play was conducted exactly as authentic gambling, and even when separate scenes or close-ups were being shot, the background extras played continuously, since all the sights and sounds of a genuine Casino were needed. Real gambling fever seemed to have gripped everybody – and for good reason, all the exits were locked.

Amongst the absorbed crowd artistes, the elderly, opulent-looking ladies were the people whom I found the most bizarre. Splendidly gowned and festooned with jewellery, they and their escorts seemed to be taking their play on the tables deadly seriously, each making copious notes and referring to what must have been predetermined systems, scarcely listening to directions called out by our film assistant directors. Totally intent, they clawed in their winnings and placed their bets. Day after frenetic day they fell to. So great was their excitement that one or two of them actually became involved in noisy rows as they accused croupiers or fellow-gamblers of cheating.

A croupier explained to me that many of these old people were the casualties of the Monte Carlo syndrome. They had probably come to the place long ago, and had fallen to the lure of the Casino. Perhaps once quite wealthy, now most of them would be eking out a penurious existence which allowed them only a very occasional visit to the tables, so that the chance both to earn a little money and to play with a nice pile of borrowed chips was an illusory temporary resurrection for them.

Kitty left for home ten days before me, so I had a while on my own to work and drift around. Most evenings I had supper with Merle or Ivan or the Genns, but one night the Henry Cottons took me to a magic little place they had discovered. It was a simple cottage high in the hills somewhere near Menton, from which one could see a small fishing-boat drifting in the light of the setting sun as its owner caught our meal. The young fisherman and his wife catered for a handful of patrons who sat in the garden drinking local wine and waiting for the catch to arrive. She was a typically gifted French cook who baked the fresh-caught fish in earth over a wood fire and garnished it with herbs. Nothing can quite describe the flavour of that simple but mouth-watering food, eaten al fresco under the stars. I wished I had known about it before.

24 Hours of a Woman's Life – titled *Affair in Monte Carlo* in America – was my ninth picture in three years, and I had begun to get the 'feel' of a film whilst shooting was in progress. I realised quite early on, therefore, that this current movie was not going to break any records; the story was twee and slow-moving, and charming and beautifully-set though it was, gorgeous backgrounds are not the only requisite for a successful box-office picture. I was in a very competitive profession, where your last picture was the one by which you were judged and if, like me, you were just a plain actor and not an internationally bankable star, there was always the fear that there would be no *next* picture.

My last two films to be released – *Lightning Strikes Twice* (made in Hollywood) and *Flesh and Blood* – had received moderate reviews and done reasonable business, but the euphoria of my 1950 Oscar nomination for *The Hasty Heart* had begun to pale.

So during my last few days alone in France I began to take stock of my professional prospects, hoping desperately that my latest Robin Hood film, not yet released, would get me back on course. I think the easygoing opulence of my weeks on location had started to frighten me a little, and I was quite glad to fly out from Nice on 2 October. At Northolt airport in London I was welcomed by Kitty and Baron, our much-loved great Dane, and as I came through the customs barrier Kitty could not hold on to him – he lunged towards me, grinning hugely. Such homely affection was a wonderful relief after the glitter of Monaco.

We had now lived for a year in Wayside House, our pretty old home at Pinkneys Green in Berkshire, and our plans for the house and garden were slowly taking shape. We had still not managed to restore and furnish the big drawing room, but the rest of the house was gradually filling up. Kitty had a flair for picking up good things at local country-house auctions – everything from garden implements to glassware – but many pieces were bought from Julius Winestone, a benevolent Glasgow antiques dealer who seemed to have taken us under his wing, even lending us pictures, furniture and silver that we could not yet afford to buy.

Incidentally, the name of the house belied its situation: it was nowhere near a main road, but was approached by a single-track lane that led through National Trust grassland and woodland. The garden, only about an acre, walled on three sides and overlooking a large area of well-wooded common land on the fourth, was now quite tidy: every spare moment we had was spent in it, scrubbing out the pool, rolling the tennis court or planting, cutting and clearing.

Rutland, our chauffeur-handyman, had done a great deal of the initial heavy work, but now we also had a retired local gardener who came in daily and took charge, helped by a part-time postman who spent his evenings with us.

I now had quite a household to support: Rutland and Mrs Rutland, our cook; two daily women; two part-time gardeners; George Reeve, who had buttled for us on occasions in London and now ran a school for butlers, and came down every two weeks to do my clothes and the silver; and of course Bridget Piercey, my secretary. Bridget left to get married in October and her replacement was Jill Paul, who moved in with us soon after my return from France. There was not only Jill but our whole canine family: two corgis, one enormous great Dane and one cross-eyed bull terrier. I had good reason to hope that my gainful employment would not dry up!

For the next few weeks, therefore, I spent most of my spare time involved in discussing and reading a lengthy list of possible subjects.

I had meetings almost daily with Robert Lennard, the casting director and my mentor at Associated British, Fritz Gotfurt, the very Germanic head of the scenario department, and Leslie Frewin, the publicity direc-tor. And quite a list of potential subjects had cropped up: a script about Gilbert and Sullivan; a project to shoot a film based on Ibsen's *A Doll's House* to be made in France; and a bagful of scripts from America and elsewhere. I had also decided to buy an option on a very funny spoof-spy novel called *Mr Blessington's Imperialist Plot* by John Sherwood, and Mr Cross, the ABPC lawyer, drew up the contract for me.

Most importantly Robert Clark, the ABPC executive director of productions, had bought Paul Brickhill's book *The Dam Busters* as a vehicle for me, which I instantly raved about.

I had meanwhile met Olga Horstig-Primuz, a very prestigious French agent who handled a small but exclusive group of actors and actresses in Paris, including Brigitte Bardot. To my surprise and delight, Olga agreed to represent me in France.

So out of all this something would surely crystallise, I hoped.

The first few days of November were partly taken up by rehearsals for the annual Royal Film Show with its usual posse of American stars, who this year included Burt Lancaster, Jane Russell, Fred MacMurray, Van Johnson and Dan Duryea. At the party afterwards we were joined by Sharman Douglas, a charming girl whose father Lewis Douglas was the then American Ambassador in London.

The following two days were spent travelling by special train to Birmingham and Newcastle for further Royal Film Performances, which also involved civic balls afterwards, and from Newcastle I had to dash to Brighton for a St John Ambulance bazaar. Film personalities were much in demand for charity functions in those days. A couple of weeks later I was back in Birmingham for a newspaper carnival ball where I had the pleasant but demanding task of choosing the beauty queen. Leslie Frewin piloted me through my various duties and made sure that I was briefed about all the local dignitaries. And the next evening we attended the Pathfinders Ball in London where we shared a table with Mickey Martin, the fabled bomber pilot who had been Guy Gibson's 2 i/c with 617 Squadron. I took the chance to find out all I could about Gibson.

Surprisingly, we also managed to have a pretty busy social life with our friends and neighbours, particularly the Hall-Caines, and Freddie and Ann Weil. Since we had first met Freddie in America, we had become close friends and I spent more and more time at his nearby stud farm and racing stable.

As the year drew to its close I was obliged to stay at home and work long hours with Jill Paul on a backlog of mail and book-keeping. But then, in December, Kitty's doctor confirmed that she was pregnant, so 1951 went out with a flourish for us. Soon Wayside House would be a proper family home. Even the Bentley was no longer alone: I had bought Kitty a small Ford estate car, so Henrietta Ford and Algy Bentley shared the garage.

2

Caught On a Hot Tiled Roof

By the first day of 1952, I had been beavering away for weeks at my self-imposed task of drumming up projects for my film future; and was spending most of my free time writing a film treatment of *Mr Blessington's Imperialist Plot*. But then, on that day, a film script arrived from an unexpected source. It was *Venetian Bird*, a thriller by the well-known author Victor Canning, set in Venice, and it came to me from Betty Box and Ralph Thomas. They were the very successful producer-director duo who had made a series of popular pictures, mostly comedies. They worked through the Rank Organisation at Pinewood and it was unusual that they should approach a contract player like myself from the great Rank rival, Associated British.

However, I was not concerned with the niceties of studio politics. I read the script that same day, liked it, and decided that this should be the next job for me. The covering letter told me that filming was due to start in Venice in eight weeks' time, and that most of the casting had already been decided except for the two leads.

Two days later I met Betty and Ralph at Les Ambassadeurs restaurant to discuss the script, and we got on marvellously. They were a fun team and we spent as much time giggling together as we did eating and talking. I had a few observations to make about the script and they agreed with me. We decided to meet again in a couple of weeks, after they had discussed the terms of my loan-out with Robert Clark and Robert Lennard of Associated British.

Well, that was a load off my mind! At last I knew that very soon I would be filming again with a really good story and script. And to further overfill my brimming cup of fortune, my former agent, and now my friend and adviser from Hollywood, Milton Pickman, arrived a few days later at Heathrow airport where I met him and Harry Koernitz, the American screenwriter, and drove them to Claridges Hotel.

They were only in London for two days and had various ideas for

my next American film that they wanted to discuss. But then so had
Ken Harper, a British producer, Jack Dunfee (an agent and film-
packager) and my old friend Anatole de Grunwald. And Robert Lennard had to be kept informed, of course. So on the second day we had
a seven-handed pow-wow in Pickman's suite while we crammed in
smoked salmon sandwiches and coffee before I had to rush him back
to Heathrow.

I drove home rather dazed by all this high-powered wheeling and
dealing. The prospects were perhaps too good to be true. So many
carrots were being dangled before my nose that I gloomily supposed I
would inevitably choose the wrong one. One such project was Terence
Young's script of *The Red Beret*. I did not like this script, probably
because I was still rather serious-minded about anything to do with the
Airborne Forces and thought it an over-fictionalised treatment.

During that week there came the sad news that King George VI had
died. We all mourned his passing.

Meanwhile, Betty Box and Ralph Thomas had gone to Italy to choose
from a short-list of actresses the star to play opposite me in *Venetian
Bird;* they were particularly interested in Gina Lollobrigida, a very
exciting newcomer to the movie scene. They had already agreed my
suggested amendments to the script, so apart from suit-fittings there
was nothing I could do in the way of preparation for the picture.

On their return from Rome I went to Pinewood Studios to meet them
and Betty greeted me with: 'I thought you said you didn't know Gina
Lollobrigida.'

'I don't.'

'That's not what *she* said!'

'But I've never even seen her.'

'No? Then what about all that table-tennis you played with her in
Grasse last year?'

So *that* was the little, delectable Gina who never strayed far from the
watchful eye of her 'minder' – not surprisingly: he was her husband.

Betty and Ralph had found her enchanting too, and she had wanted
very much to do the film with us, but sadly her English was then still
pretty sparse. My leading lady was to be Eva Bartok, who was at that
time living in Italy.

So there would be no more indoor games on this next location . . .

Looking back on those early years of my film career, I am reminded
how lucky I was. During the fifties and until midway through the sixties,
the film industry worldwide was at its peak, with a huge output that
varied from undistinguished pot-boilers to some great and memorable

pictures. The major studios had long lists of actors, directors, producers and technicians under contract and, while occasional disagreements would arise, those lucky enough to be in this position did enjoy the support of absolutely enormous resources.

The two most important British film conglomerates were the Rank Organisation, based on Pinewood Studios, and the Associated British Picture Corporation at Elstree Studios. Each of these companies not only had their own production facilities, but between them they also owned over one thousand theatres on prime sites countrywide.

I started my initial seven-year contract with Associated British in 1948. The chairman of the Corporation was Sir Philip Warter, the managing director was C. J. Latta – an American who represented the Warner Brothers' interest in ABPC – and my immediate boss was the executive director of productions, Robert Clark, a taciturn Scot with the power of veto or approval over almost everything I did.

My confidant and closest supporter in the Corporation was Robert Lennard, the casting director who had given me my first chance of a screen career by offering me the original test for *For Them That Trespass*, my début film.

For years I had all the power and resources of this huge organisation behind me and benefited in many ways beyond the reach of less fortunate actors.

For example the scenario department, a group of grey-faced, rather untidy academics under the leadership of Fritz Gotfurt, were constantly seeking suitable subjects for me. Gotfurt was a German/Jewish refugee whose fractured English gave me seriously to doubt his ability to assess the qualities of dialogue in any script, yet he had already persuaded Robert Clark to buy the screen rights to *The Dam Busters* for me. He and his team were in fact readers rather than writers, and I believe that only one original screenplay ever came from this department.

Then again, the astute and ebullient Leslie Frewin's publicity and public relations department had a sizeable staff of very experienced and able men and women working on the image of the Corporation, its productions and its contract actors. Scarcely a week went by, even when I was not filming, without my appearing in some newspaper or magazine article, or on a radio or TV programme. There were civic balls too, gala premières, charity affairs and various other public functions to which I was accompanied by a PR man, with a chauffeured Rolls-Royce always available.

Frewin even opened a fan-mail office which dealt with my daily post, only sending on to Jill and me those letters which needed a personal

reply. The two girls in this office also set up a Fan Club for me, and
coordinated its activities such as visits to the studios, the issuing of
membership cards and a Fan Club magazine which was for years
printed and distributed.

I mention all this to illustrate what was entailed in being a contract
actor in the heyday of the film industry. And I must admit I revelled
in it. The rewards were great and more than compensated for any
pressures. It was all a far cry from the Workmen's Hall in Ebbw Vale,
or the Byre Theatre in St Andrews.

My spare time meanwhile was becoming more and more involved
with visits to Freddie Weil's stud farm and racing stable, only a mile
or so from Wayside. Although I had never been any sort of gambler,
the breeding and training side of racing really began to interest me,
and soon I had registered my colours and leased three of Freddie's
horses. All three were fillies – Hoity-Toity, Profitless and Chou-Chou
– and they had just started their training as two-year-olds to race during
the coming season. Of my three hopefuls the best-bred was Profitless,
so I trusted she would not live up to her name. She was by High Profit
by the great Hyperion out of a mare called Primness.

With this new interest in the racing world I even got up early enough
on many mornings to ride out with the second string on road work and
training gallops, and became quite proficient as an equine pilot, though
not as yet trusted to handle the green two-year-olds. Kitty, now some
four months pregnant, wisely stayed at home. When there was time I
did my share of mucking-out, feeding and grooming, gradually learning
some of the wrinkles of horse-management. It was a joy to see a horse
rolling vigorously in the sand-pit after a training session, and I was
intrigued to discover that a bottle of a well-known brand of stout was
added to the feed of many of the horses just prior to racing.

On numerous afternoons, too, a large horse-box would park on the
green outside Wayside House and three or four two-year-olds would be
decanted and allowed to nibble happily on the grass, while the stable
lads in charge were given tea and cake from the house. The purpose
was to get the younger, unraced horses accustomed to being boxed and
trundled around the countryside.

Then, to my delight, in mid-February I found myself in the rare
position for an actor of knowing what my next assignment was to be
before I had even started on my current one. A letter arrived from Perce
Pearce, the producer of Disney's *Robin Hood* picture, offering me the
leading role in Walt's next film to be made in England, starting in

August. Its American title was *When Knighthood was in Flower*, but this was changed to *The Sword and the Rose* for the UK.

The script soon followed, and fortunately I really liked this rollicking story about Charles Brandon, a swashbuckling courtier who married Henry VIII's sister Mary and was created Duke of Suffolk. I could be sure that the Disney company would put all their expertise and financial strength behind the picture, as they had done with *Robin Hood*. Even if I had felt any doubts about the screenplay I would probably have agreed to do the movie anyway – after all, this was a major Walt Disney product made for worldwide viewing.

Very quickly I got Robert Clark's approval for the project and arranged that Robert Lennard would negotiate for me and Associated British. This he did with gratifying results. In fact, from the first year of my original seven-year contract with the Corporation, ABPC never had to pay me a salary, as their revenue from loan-out agreements was many times more than my basic contract payments. No wonder I was quite popular with Robert Clark and the board!

By the time I left London to fly to Venice for the Victor Canning film, the year had rosy prospects for me: I had no immediate worries either personal or professional. Above all, Kitty had never felt better. We had been advised by her doctor that her previous ill-health – due largely to a persistent anaemic condition – would probably be put right by pregnancy, and this now seemed happily to be proving the case.

My journey to Venice was memorable for its awfulness.

Southern Europe was shrouded in fog and at our first stop, Nice, it was decided that the conditions were unfit for flying. Passengers on my British European Airways flight were told that special facilities had been arranged for us to travel by train to Milan and thence by air the following day to Venice.

We bumped through the murk from the airport to the station in an ancient, wooden-seated charabanc. The train we were herded on to must have come from some railway museum. Packed with tired, chilled unfortunates like myself who had been stranded at the airport, its compartments had been designed for five people on each side, with little wooden flanges at head-height separating the stalls. We were six on my slatted bench and I finished up with one of these projections in the back of my neck as I sat hunched and miserably cold for the rest of the journey.

We clattered through the night inexorably except for an unexplained two-hour stop in Genoa, arriving soon after dawn in Milan. There the weather was bitterly cold but bright and by some miracle of efficiency I was then carried on smoothly and comfortably to Venice and our hotel, the Bauer Grunwald.

For the rest of that day and on the next we had a chance to look round Venice. The wintry sunlight gave a pellucid water-colour clarity to the lagoon, the canals and the buildings of this uniquely beautiful city. As this was an out-of-season period it was all very quiet, and we were spared the usual hordes of tourists as we wandered around. Even the thousands of pigeons which descended on St Mark's Square at feeding time behaved tactfully and didn't seem to expect handouts at other times.

Venetian Bird was a mystery-thriller film with a story involving politicians, international assassins, shady thugs and, of course, an intrepid detective – me! It entailed lots of shadowy observation, roof-top chases and some violence – very mild by today's standards – and also, inevitably, a few romantic moments in gondolas.

On my third evening in Venice I started filming night sequences, which involved me and the shadier characters and lots of hanging about in the freezing darkness on some of the minor, very narrow canals. This sequence of work is not my pleasantest memory of my weeks there.

Our lighting was all powered by our big generator mounted in a barge, and we had constant (and understandable) complaints from local residents who couldn't understand that the diesel-engine of a generator was an essential if nerve-jangling feature of all-night location shooting in films.

Our powerful lamps illuminated more than just the cast. Those back waterways were not a pretty sight at night as dead cats, dead dogs, sewage and other hideous flotsam and jetsam floated sluggishly along, together with an all-pervading ghastly stench. How it was all cleaned up by daylight I don't know. Perhaps the tides had something to do with it.

To add to my nausea, the make-up assistant had forgotten to include theatrical blood in his box of tricks, and made up for his slip by daubing my supposedly damaged person with dollops of reeking tomato ketchup. To this day the sight of a famous variety of sauce bottle evokes evil memories of nights spent along the odoriferous backwaters of Venice.

Once those night location sequences had been completed our work became much more agreeable.

Of my co-star, Eva Bartok, I saw very little except when we were filming together. She was undergoing some kind of emotional crisis and her spare time seemed to be spent either locked in her hotel room or engaged in endless stormy telephone conversations.

Nor did I see a great deal of John Gregson, Walter Rilla or George Coulouris, the other leading actors, who were all staying in different hotels.

But I did form a close and lasting friendship with a remarkable Venetian, Contessa Anna-Maria Cicogna, and her children Bino and Marina. Anna-Maria was then a handsome, middle-aged patrician lady, separated from Count Cicogna and living in a small astonishingly beautiful palazzo by the Chiesa de la Salute, a house which she had commissioned to be built by leading craftsmen and artists of the day, architects, plasterers, masons, wood-carvers, sculptors and painters.

The Contessa was, and still is, probably the most erudite and knowledgeable woman I have ever known, and a leading advocate of the 'Save Venice' appeal which helps to preserve and restore the architecture and character of the city. The Cicogna family were the owners of the lovely yacht *Valrosa* which we had used on *24 Hours of a Woman's Life* in Monte Carlo the previous year, and subsequently – during my weeks in Venice and for years after – we became great friends and I spent almost every evening with Marina and Bino Cicogna. They were a most attractive pair of youngsters, witty, intelligent and totally extrovert. Marina was a good deal more practical than her brother. Pretty, vivacious and surrounded by admirers, her main concern was how to be sure eventually that she was wanted for herself and not for her wealth. In fact she never married, but went on to become one of Italy's leading independent film producers.

Victor Canning's script took in all the well-known sights of Venice, and soon we were really familiar with the city and its surrounds. The Grand Canal, the Doge's Palace, the Bridge of Sighs and St Mark's Square all figured in our scenes. As the weather got warmer, so we enjoyed our exterior work that much more – except for one sequence, in my case . . .

A part of the story had me chasing the chief villain along the roof-tops on one side of St Mark's Square. To be at that height with no parapet or guard rail was bad enough, with my awful reaction to heights, but to be scrabbling along half-way up a steeply-sloping scree of red pantiles was stomach-turning. Below there was nothing between me and the paving of the Square dozens of feet below except a crumbling gutter, and every move dislodged broken tiles which clattered down and bounced over the edge. I sweated on that tiled roof as though it were midsummer, and was mightily relieved when my quarry reached the famous clock, where he was swiped away by the figure that pops out when the hour is struck. Even watching the substituted dummy sailing through space and smashing on to the paving was a nightmarish experience.

I much preferred trying to blow glass in one of the famous works on the island of Murano where Marina and I went one day.

I had one special cause for celebration while in Venice. Disney's *Robin Hood* picture was premièred in London and New York and received mostly rave reviews. So to celebrate I ordered a christening robe, cap and pillow cover to be made by some lace-makers recommended by Contessa Cicogna, ready for the baptism of our baby who was due in July. Almost every day I spent a few minutes watching the progress of the pieces, having chosen the designs.

Before long our film unit was an accepted part of life in Venice, and we had a daily gallery monitoring our progress. On one occasion we had set up to film a small riot sequence and had hired as many extras as the budget would allow, but by a stroke of good fortune we found ourselves virtually alongside a rather heated union meeting where tempers frayed and led to some quite ugly scenes. Naturally, our camera crew pointed their lens in this direction, and soon were photographing really good crowd-work that would have cost a fortune in England.

Even out of season, Venice was a lovely city to be in. Visits to the Lido, Murano and other scenic places were made all the more memorable by the loan of the Cicogna motor-boat with its smartly uniformed crew, and very often by the company of one or both of my young friends.

Harry's Bar is probably the most famous of Venetian restaurants, and it was here one day that I met once again the Duke and Duchess of Windsor, whom I had first encountered on the old *Queen Elizabeth* liner during our first trip to America. For some reason which I cannot remember I found myself at their lunch table at Harry's. At one point the Duke – with his surprisingly booming voice – was happily describing his prowess on a nearby golf course earlier that morning, when his soliloquy was sharply cut short by the Duchess complaining of a draught from a window above the table. Without even asking a waiter to help, the Duke immediately scrambled up on to the table and wrestled with the rather stiff frame. The Duchess was, in fact appropriately, wearing trousers on that occasion.

Perhaps my most amusing meeting in Venice was with an absolutely charming, disarming and zany lady from America, Frances Carpenter; she and her little retinue were also staying in the Bauer Grunwald Hotel. Frances was a Dupont and outrageously wealthy, but she contrived to enjoy her position by making a joke of it, so that it was impossible to be offended by her displays of affluence.

She was very health- and figure-conscious – so much so that she had arranged for Gaylord Hauser, the international expert on dietetics and author of tomes on that subject, to accompany her for part of her European jaunt as her food-watcher, surely a very expensive way of keeping off the pasta!

She was tremendous fun to be with, but I never learned quite how to take some of her more bizarre statements. For example, a group of us were walking through St Mark's Square after dinner on a particularly balmy, starlit night when Frances stopped, gazed around the great quadrangle and said, 'Do you know what I'd like to do? I'd like to have a great glass roof built over here so that I could give a terrific party. Wouldn't that be wonderful!'

Nothing like thinking big!

Then there was the day when Frances asked me to join her in a visit to a jeweller's. Intrigued to see what her extravagance would lead her to, I went along. I was surprised to find that her choice fell on several rather heavy, chunky baubles, made of bright blue stones encrusted in some gold-like material. A bit flashy and ornate, I thought. Then she explained that they were to hang from the collars of her three little silver poodles back home. I could just imagine the yaps of joy as the three thrilled toys received their gifts from Italy. 'Just what I've always wanted!' they would twitter.

When my filming in Venice was completed I was anxious to get home as quickly as possible, but could not get an airline reservation, so the head porter at the Bauer Grunwald booked me a sleeper on the Orient Express that very night. It was a change of plan that would keep my guardian angel quite extraordinarily busy.

My farewells made, I settled into the comfort of my compartment. I had a delicious dinner on board, and when we arrived in Milan decided to buy a bottle of wine from the platform trolley as an aid to sound sleep. Perhaps thirty minutes after we left Milan, therefore, I opened my bottle before undressing and turning in. I had just finished a glass when the train seemed to be running over a particularly rough stretch of track. As we bumped and swayed I grabbed my bottle in case it should topple over. The swaying and bumping increased to violent juddering and sounds of grinding and smashing. For what seemed like ages I clung to my wine bottle as the compartment seemed to disintegrate around me. Then the floor began to splinter as the carriage ploughed along over the tracks, finally lurching to a standstill on its side at the bottom of an embankment.

My bottle abandoned now, I scrambled to my feet – on what remained of the door into the corridor. I didn't have a scratch on me, but I could hear cries for help and moans of pain all around me in the sudden eerie silence of the night.

I clambered up the berth and managed to slide open the window which was now over my head. It was very narrow, but I wriggled my head and shoulders through and looked about. From what I could see in the moonlight it appeared that on a bend the last three carriages had somehow broken loose from the rest of the train, which had carried on and disappeared into the night. Mine was the middle of the three carriages and the front one had suffered the worst damage, having hit a small house by the railside.

As I wriggled to get clear of the window I was suddenly aware of a man in pyjamas climbing similarly out of the next compartment. We caught each other's eye and immediately started speaking simultaneously. As we struggled for words of Italian it must have dawned on us both that we were having trouble with a foreign language. So I tried English and so did he – we were Britons. The realisation seemed so incongruous in that bizarre situation that as we laboured to get clear we broke into nervous giggling. But it soon stopped once we reached the ground and began to help the less fortunate.

Other people appeared from the surrounding countryside and soon there was a crowd of willing helpers working in the light of cars parked nearby. In a very short time ambulances arrived, casualties were tended and taken away; while the rescue work was going on, those of us who were unhurt were helped to collect our belongings, and given blankets to huddle in and copious supplies of coffee.

Eventually a railway official told us that replacement carriages would soon be arriving from Milan to be attached to our train, which had now reversed back to the scene of the accident. Those who wished to do so could continue their journey.

I decided to carry on, and boarded the sleeping-car when it arrived. But I have to admit that I had difficulty in getting to sleep. Every little wobble of the train had me lying in tense anxiety, and I didn't finally doze off until after we had cleared customs at the Swiss frontier.

3

It's a Boy!

Once back from Venice, despite that city's splendours I had no doubt where my heart really lay: in my own home, in the warm half-timbering of Wayside House, with its surroundings of grassland and woodland, the bulbs now in flower and green spring coming to life.

Filming of interiors at Pinewood Studios did not start for a few days, so Kitty and I had time to spare together. She had never looked better, and we spent hours at the stables watching training gallops, and even managed to enjoy a singularly unprofitable day's racing at Kempton Park. We also gave a home to Trigger, a gun-shy pointer bitch who would have been put down if Ann Weil had not heard about her and rescued her. When we first saw Trigger she was in a very poor state. Skinny, trembling, dreadfully nervous, she curled her lips and bared her teeth at me, but, fortunately, I realised that she had the same endearing characteristic as Baron, our great Dane, and was merely grinning uncertainly. Within days she had settled down and was a loving, affectionate dog, although for years she was always a bit neurotic and became an inveterate wanderer until middle age slowed her down.

So now we had a great Dane, a bull terrier, two corgis and Trigger pointer. And bitches outnumbered Baron by four to one. I used to wonder if the giant great Dane might develop some sort of complex about his sexual segregation. Here he was, some three years old and in his prime, hardly ever encountering one of his own gender and surrounded by a harem of what must have seemed to him to be miniature pygmies, quite unsuited to any amorous advances from him. But it didn't seem to bother him at all. Good-natured toleration was his attitude, and his female followers obviously adored him. So gentle was he that Tinkerbell corgi as a puppy had contracted the habit of munching the tips of his ears when he lay down. His only reaction was an occasional yelp of pain and a vigorously shaken head when she drew blood, with consequent spattering of our panelling and carpets, which

19

had to be washed more than once. For some months Baron needed plasters on his ears.

I took Baron to the studios with me so regularly now that he became more or less my black shadow. One cartoonist actually published a drawing of me showing my shadow as being four-legged and dog-like.

For several weeks until the end of May we worked steadily completing all the interior scenes on *Venetian Bird*. The rushes of all we had shot in Venice were excellent, the backgrounds were most impressive, and the film was taking shape nicely. It was going to be a good, fast-moving thriller, years before its time with a story about a terrorist setting out to assassinate a politician.

While *Venetian Bird* was nearing completion other developments were taking place. In mid-May I had lunch with Perce Pearce and Maud Spector, who was casting *The Sword and the Rose*. They told me, to my joy, that Glynis Johns and James Robertson Justice were to be my co-stars on the picture, and we talked about all the other main casting. I was also given the latest shooting script.

I had worked with Glynis briefly a couple of years earlier on *Flesh and Blood*, and had liked her enormously. She was a delectable little creature with china-blue eyes, tip-tilted nose and husky voice. I had been entranced by her kittenish mermaid (could there be such a piscatorial feline hybrid?) in *Miranda*, and was thrilled by the prospect of working with her again.

Jimmy Justice had, of course, been Little John in *Robin Hood* a year ago; we were good friends and had a lot in common outside the film world, especially in field sports. This large, bearded brigand was a very amusing companion, knowledgeable about many topics and able to discuss them in several languages. He had first won my admiration when he turned up at the Dorchester Hotel for a script conference driving an old Rolls-Royce converted to an estate car which contained several squealing piglets running loose in the back, and nonchalantly handed the whole thing over to a doorman for parking.

This was one of those busy periods for me. That same week MGM approached me through Irving Lazar, an agent in Hollywood, with an offer for me to film with Ava Gardner in *Mogambo*, a picture to be made in Africa, subject to my being free at the right time. I immediately told Robert Lennard about it and phoned Milton Pickman, my friend and former agent in California, asking him to keep an eye on the project for me. Sadly, within a couple of weeks it was clear that I would not be free in time to do the MGM movie owing to their need to bring their schedule forward a month or two in order to get suitable weather conditions in Africa.

So I never got to meet the glamorous Ava Gardner . . .

Even when at home at weekends I was not exactly indolent. It was my only time for private business meetings and a succession of friends and associates came to spend weekends at Wayside. Perce Pearce came down to go over the Disney script with me, and to chat in general about our film due to start shooting in August; and practically every spare daylight moment that I had was spent at the stables watching the horses in training and learning a little about racing management. I also started riding out with the second string again on Saturday mornings, under the watchful eyes of our trainer and the wise old head lad.

During this time Kitty was thriving as she prepared for her baby due in July. We had already arranged for Ben Fick, a London interior designer, to work out plans for the nursery suite and my office, which was to move to the sun-room downstairs. The only problem was that age-old question: Should the nursery colours be basically blue or pink?

At the end of May I finished work on *Venetian Bird*, my tenth film, subsequently to be titled *The Assassin* outside the UK in deference to the Americans' preference for hardline titles. I had enjoyed working on it, particularly with the exuberant Ralph Thomas as director. He was always ready to see the funny side of things, and I can well understand how he and Betty Box made such a success of their later series of comedy 'Doctor' movies with Dirk Bogarde and James Robertson Justice.

Temporarily free of daily studio commitments, I was now able to follow my normal routine, especially on Thursdays, which were the days when The Variety Club of Great Britain held its frequent big charity luncheons, usually at the Savoy Hotel. I had been one of the original founder-members of the London Tent No. 36 (the Variety vernacular for the first British branch of this great charity organisation) at its inception, organised by two American Variety Club officers, C. J. Latta of Associated British, and Bob Woolf, head of RKO Pictures in London. Since then the Variety Club has flourished in Britain and raised millions of pounds for needy or underprivileged children.

I had at this time a good reason to spend a couple of days with Kitty roaming around parts of Wessex where I had spent most of my boyhood and also my wartime army training. I had been invited to open an exhibition at Salisbury connected with the history of that great cathedral city, so drove down a few days in advance, staying at the old White Hart Hotel near the Cathedral Close. I had last lunched there a few days prior to D-Day 1944, and nothing had changed much since then – except the food!

On the day of my public function, after the official luncheon at the Assembly Rooms attended by the mayor, the local MP and Sir Thomas Berney, one of the organisers, we were ushered to a specially-constructed stand in the Market Square from which I and the mayor were loud-speakered to the crowd. My opening ceremony duly performed, we toured the exhibition, had tea, dropped Sir Thomas at his home in Downton and drove home after a very pleasant and, for me, nostalgic few days.

This period of comparative freedom epitomised for me the difference between the film and live theatre worlds. True, I was involved in preparations for my next picture and with almost daily PR, but I *could* have gone off on holiday for a few weeks if Kitty and I had so wished, and even during the actual shooting of a movie there were occasional breaks and no weekend working.

By contrast, if I had been appearing in a successful, long-running play I would be engaged in an unremitting, six-days-per-week grind, with no weekend breaks and little chance for normal family holidays or activities. Furthermore, while the stage actor's every fault or slip-up is there for his audience to see and judge, shooting a major well-budgeted cinema film is a comparatively relaxed and easygoing exercise for all concerned, especially when it has been as meticulously prepared as those Disney movies were. Problems do arise, of course, but most mistakes are discarded on the cutting-room floor, and a screen actor usually has the chance to re-shoot anything less than satisfactory.

I have had no experience of working to the cut-to-the-bone schedule of a TV series, but I can well imagine that the pressures must be hard on actors who try to maintain reasonable standards in the face of the driving need to speed along regardless. However, such series clearly have a very salutary effect on the casts' financial standing . . .

Although we were not due to start filming until early August, by mid-June I was already almost daily involved with preparations for *The Sword and the Rose*. There were frequent script conferences, in which every set-up was planned, sketched and photocopied into albums for each of us. Our production team was exactly as it had been for *Robin Hood* – Ken Annakin, director, Larry Watkin, screenwriter, Carmen Dillon, art director, and Geoffrey Unsworth, director of photography – so we were all very used to working together. Every location scene had been scouted and planned, and the indoor studio sets were already being built.

I had also started working in a miniature gymnasium set up at Pinewood by Paddy Ryan and Bob Simmons, the stunt men, and was being coached in swordplay by Rupert Evans, as I had been for *Robin Hood*. With Bob Simmons (a brilliant young stunt artist who years later did much of the stunts on the 'Bond' series) I had to practise a wrestling sequence in which he would double for my opponent. Within a few weeks I was also practising dancing *La Volta* with Glynis Johns for a sequence featuring that particularly energetic Tudor ballroom prance.

There were also fittings for my wardrobe, which included some tremendously handsome costumes designed by Valles and made by Bermans, and riding sessions at the stable which was to supply the horses for the film.

One way and another, Perce Pearce saw to it that I would not go into the picture unprepared!

A welcome break from this routine came when Gina Lollobrigida and some other Italian artistes arrived in London for a festival of Italian films and I met her at the annual *Sunday Pictorial* Film Garden Party. This time I made no mistake in recognising my former table-tennis opponent and we were delighted to see each other. By now she spoke some halting English and I a smattering of Italian after my weeks in Venice, so after we had lunched together in Wimbledon I and the Associated British publicity team made sure that she stayed close to me for the whole of the open-air function at Merton Park. Each time I was jeeped to another area of the Garden Party she went with me, much to the delight of the crowds who may not have known who she was at that time, but certainly knew they were looking at a really beautiful woman. Even Jacob Epstein, the great sculptor, had recently asked to model a bust of her. How I wished that she had been able to do *Venetian Bird* with me!

Towards the end of June I was due to go to Paris with Veronica Hurst to represent Associated British at *La Kermesse aux Étoiles*, an outdoor fête in a central Paris park, similar to the London Film Garden Party but lasting for three days. On the morning before my evening flight to Paris Kitty and I went to Windsor races to see my colours (cherry and white hoops) run for the first time, carried on Profitless by a young lad – I think he was about fifteen years old – named Lester Piggott.

Naturally it was an exciting afternoon for us, even though we did not

expect much of Profitless. The little filly had never raced in public
before and her trainer Tommy Farmer told Piggott not to force her too
hard. The boy merely nodded in the collecting ring and said not a
word. He was certainly taciturn, and I was struck by his pallor and
stony-faced silence. But what I was seeing was the dedication and
determination that were to make Lester Piggott one of history's greatest
race-riders.

As expected, Profitless did not show in the frame after her race and
Piggott, when asked how she had run, merely said, 'She needs time.'
However, our afternoon turned out to be a good one. To begin with,
even before the first race Tommy Farmer took me to the Jockeys' Room,
a visit that would not be allowed today. They were all there busily
changing for work, from the great Gordon Richards down to the freshest
apprentice jockeys. I was fascinated to meet so many famous sportsmen
– and also it was probably the only occasion in my life when I would
be the tallest man in a crowded room. And then Kitty and I backed
the winners of the first four races.

I had to leave Kitty for the airport before the last two races, and
eventually arrived in Paris at about 9.30 that evening. As our baggage
had gone astray we did not reach our hotel – the Trianon Palace at
Versailles – until about 11.30. It had been quite a day.

Next day I lunched at the Georges V Hotel and then launched into
the maelstrom of *La Kermesse aux Étoiles*, a seething mass of Parisians
having a high old time at their annual fête, the kind of gathering of
fans that no longer exists except perhaps at rock festivals.

I broke away during the evening and went back to Versailles to
change and phone Kitty. She was in great form and just leaving with
her parents, who were now staying at Wayside, to go out for dinner.
So I plunged back into the frenetic activity of *La Kermesse* until the small
hours, and didn't get to bed until about 5 am, by then almost beyond
feeling tired.

I was awakened by Kitty's mother phoning to say that the baby
seemed imminent and Kitty had been driven to the maternity home at
27 Welbeck Street in London. It was a month or so early, but perhaps
the excitement of Windsor Races the day before had precipitated things.

I dressed hurriedly and phoned John Parsons to arrange for me to
fly back to London if need be. It seemed awful that I should be rushing
around in Paris when Kitty was so near to being in labour, but her
parents had assured me that there was nothing to worry about. I then
lunched in Paris with the popular and very charming French singer
Line Rénaud and her husband, and learned that I was expected to do

a broadcast in French with her the next day. Later, back in Versailles, I phoned home for the latest news. Kitty was fine and there was no need to fly home at once, although there was no doubt that the baby was due very soon.

I then went through much the same routine as the previous evening, but this time I excused myself from joining the others for supper and returned to the hotel soon after midnight.

Next morning, 30 June 1952, Kitty's father phoned me to say that Peter Grant Palethorpe Todd had been born at 27 Welbeck Street at 9.30 am, prematurely and very small, but hale and hearty, and that Kitty was well.

John Parsons managed to get a flight reservation for me, and on my arrival at London airport, I was met by an ABPC car and driven to London. There I changed and cleaned up, dashed out to buy an armful of roses and then went to see Kitty and to meet my son for the first time.

Kitty was a bit weak – it had not been easy for her – and Peter was very pink and still quite wrinkled, but with a lusty pair of lungs.

I suppose my reaction to the tiny scrap was typical of that of most first-time fathers. When a smiling nurse placed him in my arms I had a momentary sense of panic lest I should hold him too hard or, even worse, too loosely and drop him. And then I was totally tongue-tied. All I could think of to say was 'Hello!', which seemed somewhat inadequate on such an auspicious occasion.

4

A Disney World

It now seemed that I would be working for Walt Disney for the next year or more, and I could not have wished for a pleasanter prospect. The reason for my extended contract with the Disney organisation was that I had been offered the lead in his next major film, which was to be the story of Rob Roy MacGregor, to start shooting in April 1953. With work on *The Sword and the Rose* extending to the end of 1952, and all the usual preparations for *Rob Roy* beginning at the start of 1953, there would be virtually no break between the two movies.

I was well aware of my good fortune. In less than five years I would have starred in twelve first-feature films, six of them American-made (although five of these were shot in the UK) and therefore getting major distribution in the international market.

Jill Paul, my secretary, was now not only working all hours with me, but also keeping the house running smoothly and looking after the dogs while Kitty spent a couple of weeks in the maternity home. She seemed to be gathering strength, and Peter was thriving. During that time I wrote to enrol him for a place at Eton, an approach which had already been prepared by his godfather Tim Reeve who had been our best man and was himself an Old Etonian. Peter was assured of a definite place in J. D. R. McConnell's house, much to my joy.

Walt Disney himself visited London for a couple of days and we lunched together twice, once at Pinewood and once at the Dorchester. Typically, he sent Kitty a magnificent bouquet of flowers.

Finally Kitty and Peter arrived home on a Sunday morning, accompanied by Sister Anne Cullinan. Kindly, sensible Anne Cullinan was a most reassuring addition to the household: quiet, humorous and supremely efficient, her tall, spare frame always immaculate in crisp white dresses, she ruled her domain unquestionably without any fuss.

Meanwhile my routine continued at Pinewood Studios with daily fencing, wrestling and riding sessions interspersed by wardrobe fittings and various meetings.

Our costumes for the film were numerous and elaborate. The court of Henry VIII certainly was not to suffer from any scrimping. Bermans, the theatrical costumiers, did sumptuous work to the designs of Valles in rich brocades, encrusted with beads and coloured 'gems' and collared or lined with furs.

The great theatrical dress houses had always fascinated me: room after room packed with railed rows of costumes, regalia and weaponry, from Roman togas to Edwardian morning dress; from halberds to rapiers; from blunderbusses to ivory-handled pistols; from rows of medals and orders to bishops' rings and ladies' lorgnettes. The historical knowledge of the advisers had to be immense, backed up by pictures, fashion plates and weighty reference books: not a medal must be mounted in the wrong order, not a bodice or a hemline must be out of date. Boxes and drawers full of rings, costume jewellery, watches, fobs and seals had been collected – some of them in themselves of considerable beauty and value.

Two of the leading costumiers were Bermans and Nathans, each a few yards from Leicester Square. Later these two firms joined forces and moved to Drury Lane. Another London establishment well known to the acting and dancing professions is Gamba's, who make shoes, boots and ballet pumps of all descriptions and all periods. They made all my footwear for the picture.

I seemed by now to have built up quite a following in Europe, particularly in France, greatly aided by frequent articles and photographs in *Ciné Revue*, a Belgian-owned film magazine. On the advice of my French agent I engaged a Paris-based publicity agent, Pierre Chambord, and my French connection was pleasantly strengthened in July when a small party of British film celebrities attended a reception to mark the opening of General Ridgeway's new NATO Air Headquarters at Fontainebleau.

At last, after weeks of rehearsal, training and planning, we started shooting on *The Sword and the Rose* at Pinewood on 5 August. We opened with a wrestling contest between myself and Michael Gough which involved quite a lot of crowd scenes and took the whole week to complete. Fortunately, neither Michael nor I was any the worse for our exertions.

I also received my first 'Good Luck' telegram from Peter, which I thought very thoughtful of him considering he was only five weeks old!

On the Friday evening I drove to London for a meeting with Robert

Clark of Associated British and Fred Leahy, Walt Disney's representative, at which my contractual terms for *Rob Roy* next year were agreed and it was further agreed that the film should be made at ABPC's Elstree Studios, with two sound stages to be rented from April to August 1953. So in a way I had been instrumental in securing a lot of employment for the Associated British staff and also a nice fat payment for the corporation itself.

I soon found that working again on a Disney film, as with *Robin Hood*, had a special quality about it quite unlike the atmosphere on any other production. There was very much a family ambiance, a feeling of harmony partly engendered by Perce Pearce's avuncular presence, partly arising from the fact that most of us had worked together before and knew each other well – but mostly perhaps due to the smoothness with which the schedule rolled along as a result of the careful preplanning of previous weeks. Everybody involved knew what was expected of them, from the director down to the dressers. Even the crowd artistes were kept informed and in good humour by our wonderful first assistant director, Peter Bolton.

A particularly close bond was formed between those of us who worked together most closely and frequently: Ken Annakin, Jimmy Justice, Glynis and myself. Ken was the kind of quiet, coaxing director who understood his actors and gentled the best from them; Jimmy was wonderful fun to work with; and Glynis and I formed a rapport that held us as close and affectionate friends for many years.

I look back on those Disney days with great warmth – they were such *fun*! Although we all worked hard and well together, we also laughed a lot – especially Glynis and myself, the two worst gigglers in the business. Indeed, on days when I was not in the sequences being filmed Ken still called me to the studios for part of the day, ostensibly to rehearse or prepare something but actually to keep Glynis in good spirits over lunch or while she waited for a set-up to be organised. I don't think she had ever looked more delicious than in her tight-waisted, bejewelled gowns as Mary Tudor, sister to King Henry VIII.

An arrangement had been made between Associated British and Walt Disney for me to attend a few days of the annual Venice Film Festival, so towards the end of August I flew to Italy. When I arrived at the Hotel des Bains on the Lido, I found messages from Bino and Marina Cicogna and also a list of appointments which were going to keep me pretty busy. I had a quick meal in my room, bathed and changed, and had done two TV interviews, seen a Norwegian film entered for the Festival and given several press interviews before I met the Cicognas for a drink at the Excelsior Hotel at midnight. We then took their motor launch from the Lido to Venice, and spent an energetic night at the Roof Club of the Bauer Hotel and the Martini Club. The boat returned me to my hotel at 5 am.

After a couple of hours in bed I was up quite early for some newsreel pictures and publicity shots, and by midday had recorded radio interviews in French, Italian and English.

I lunched at the Excelsior with Marina, after which we did a very good newsreel tour all afternoon in the Cicogna boat with its two white-uniformed attendants. This was followed by a press conference at 5.30, a change of clothes, then dinner at Harry's Bar. Finally, after a round of visits to some of my old haunts such as Ciro's, I again arrived back at my hotel at 5.30 am!

I mention this itinerary in detail because, looking back now, I realise what enormous stamina one needed on such occasions!

After another couple of hours in bed, I left Venice airport at 8.45, spent an interesting few hours shopping in Milan, visited the cathedral and had a splendid lunch at a restaurant recommended to me by Contessa Cicogna, before leaving for Paris in the afternoon. I changed planes at Orly airport and arrived at Heathrow in time to be home soon after 10 pm. And since I would be leaving the house by 6.30 the next morning for an early call at Pinewood I went straight to bed.

5

Per Ardua Ad Elstree

During my most active years as a film actor, the 1950s and 1960s, I was fortunate to spend many busy weeks in all the major motion picture studios in England, several in the United States and a couple in France. Though they all had one common purpose – making films – they varied greatly in size, layout and working practices.

Some have since been lost to the film industry, such as the MGM Studios at Borehamwood and the Rank Organisation's Denham Studios in Bucks; some have dwindled, with large areas given over to building development; some, such as ABPC's Elstree Studios, have actually increased in size and scope for picture-making; others have become centres for TV production.

The three main studios where I worked in America – Warner Brothers, Twentieth Century-Fox and Metro-Goldwyn-Mayer – were vast in comparison with their counterparts in Europe. Through decades they had developed into sprawling complexes of whole streets lined with great hangar-like sound stages, office buildings, stores, commissaries (restaurants), dressing-room blocks, make-up centre, garages, cutting-rooms, stores, viewing theatres and gardens, and with back-lots covering many acres, some with entire faded lath-and-plaster villages used over and over for different film scenes.

Some of the companies also owned ranches a few miles from Hollywood where much of the location filming was done. At the Fox Ranch there were wood-and-plaster fortresses, stockades, mining townships and ranch buildings used again and again in Westerns, an Indian village left over from a Tyrone Power film, a Mexican village and what looked to me like part of a medieval English hamlet. The Californian climate made it possible for these flimsy structures to remain intact for years, something that would have been impossible in Europe.

In America I made three films at the Twentieth Century-Fox Studios, spending off and on a total of something like a year in this town-within-a-city, so I knew it better than the other major movie centres. It was vast. The heart of the complex was a large office and administrative building where Darryl Zanuck had his plushy inner sanctum. Twentieth had a flock of producers, directors, writers and executives on the permanent payroll, some of whom had their quarters in this main building while others occupied bungalows in the grounds.

There were groups of enormous sound-stages (where the interior filming was done) all neatly aligned along wide, tidy streets – virtually boulevards – which in turn led to the other main buildings. The back-lot, with its scattering of ramshackle street scenes, houses and a small lake, was never still: even if no exterior scenes were being shot, there was always the light squeak and thudding of 'nodding-donkeys', the small pumps above miniature oil wells. Twentieth, it seemed, was also in the oil business!

When I arrived for a day's work, I would drive through the security check at the main gate straight to my dressing-room suite, change into my film clothes and then board the waiting car to be driven to the make-up centre. Walking was never a Hollywood habit: fleets of cars were buzzing around all day with studio drivers. From the make-up centre the studio car would take me to the stage where I would be shooting. Lined up outside the stage were the caravans or trailers where we spent our time when not actually shooting; they were very comfortable and had all the usual toilet and washing facilities.

Once in my trailer my first visitor might be the dialogue coach, a functionary peculiar to Hollywood. I believe a lot of artistes were actually schooled by him in the delivery of their lines before facing the director. For myself, I found him helpful in hearing my lines to be sure I was word perfect for the day's shooting.

For each of the three pictures I made at Twentieth I was allotted the same dressing-room suite consisting of an outer sitting room; a large drawing room with pleasant furniture, a sofa-bed and a generously stocked bar; a dressing room and a shower-room with toilet. And somebody had decorated the walls, possibly especially for my sake, with coloured prints of old English coaching inns.

In England, ABPC's studios at Elstree were most familiar to me, as I was under contract to the corporation for about twelve years. Purpose-built in 1948, Elstree was a thoroughly efficient and well-laid-out film factory, initially composed of four big sound-stages designed in pairs, back to back, each pair having its own set of dressing rooms and make-up rooms, with the usual office and admin block which included a canteen and an executive dining room, and ancillary workshops, cutting rooms and still-photography studio.

The back-lot was several acres in extent and had a large concrete lake where, for example, parts of *Moby Dick* were shot. The wind machines on the lakeside – used to create 'ripples and waves on the water and to simulate storm scenes – were two Rolls-Royce Merlin engines stripped from a wartime Mosquito fighter-bomber. Per Ardua Ad Elstree!

In comparison with the American movie centres, Elstree was spartan as well as being much smaller. For example, each set of so-called 'star' dressing rooms – only four to each stage – were small rooms equipped with a wash-basin, a divan, a chair and a small wardrobe, and of course a tiny toilet. Having seen the Hollywood versions, I knew that visiting American stars would not be immensely impressed with their quarters. In America one could entertain and even live quite comfortably in the average suite.

I did manage to persuade Robert Clark, our head of productions, to install refrigerators and also screens behind which an actor could decently change and clean up while perhaps being interviewed by a journalist.

The great attribute of Elstree, despite occasional union squabbles, was the enthusiasm and spirit of the workforce. As at all major studios, there were workshops for the many technicians and tradesmen who built and maintained the scenery and sets: electricians, carpenters, plasterers, plumbers and camera specialists. About the only building tradesmen not represented were bricklayers – film bricks were made of plaster. In 1949, I had even had a smart new canvas hood made by Elstree specialists for my open Railton sports car.

The most attractively placed studio was Pinewood, near Iver in Bucks, the centre of the Rank Organisation productions. It was all in the grounds of what had been a large stately home, and had still fine gardens and wooded policies. The rambling main house was the administrative headquarters and also contained a large dining room which had probably been the original ballroom, with a cosy bar opening off it. There was almost a club atmosphere in this panelled setting. It gave on to the gardens and was the place to be seen in for young hopefuls and their agents. I first set eyes on a youthful and very striking Joan Collins among the tables there.

In recent years one of the biggest stages in the world, similar to the one at Elstree erected for *Star Wars*, was built at Pinewood for the James Bond films.

Shepperton had a country-house atmosphere too, and my dressing room when I was filming there was a large bedroom in the old house, still with its huge bed and Edwardian bathroom.

The two major studios where I worked in France were only a short drive out of Paris and rather shabby compared with those in America and England. However, there were compensations in the splendid eating and drinking facilities available to all throughout the day and, above all, in the very civilised working practices.

In France shooting started at midday and went on non-stop until just before 8 pm, with none of the statutory lunch and tea breaks which disrupted production in Britain and America.

This meant that the entire workforce, including actors, was able to drive to the studios without the need for early-morning calls and rush-hour journeys. Thus one could return to Paris for a pleasant social evening, including theatre and dinner, without the fear of not getting enough sleep. I could leave my apartment or hotel at 10.30 next morning and still be in good time for make-up and wardrobe calls.

The technicians usually arrived at the studios at about 11 am and immediately sat down to a hefty brunch-meal before starting work. Thereafter, anybody who wanted a snack or a coffee during the day could slip into the canteen when they were not on call.

Another very sociable little touch was the frequent end-of-day board set up in the stage announcing that all and sundry were invited to *prendre une verre avec* whoever was the host for the day, and stars and others took turns to provide this friendly service of wines. Very amiable and very French!

The only practice that took a bit of getting used to in France was the use of female dressers for both male and female leading actors. However, my lady never turned a hair as, on one film, I had to strip completely while she helped me to tug on the ballet strap which I wore under my tights. Again, very amiable and very French!

As I rose bleary-eyed after late nights, whether social or official, and hurried to English or American studios, I often yearned for the civilised Gallic way of doing things.

Sadly, on the evening of the very day I wrote the above I was contacted by the BBC, inviting me to appear that night on their TV 'Newsnight' programme to comment on the announcement a few hours earlier that Pinewood was closing as a producing studio with a permanent staff of technicians and other employees. Henceforth that great symbol of the aspirations and past glories of the British film industry was to be simply

a four-walls hire centre for any who wished to rent space, equipment
and part-time personnel to make a movie – just as Elstree had become
a few years earlier under its EMI management.

Sic transit gloria movie . . .

6

Enter Miss World

Any sluggishness which I may have felt after my activities at the Venice Film Festival was soon jolted out of me on my return to the *Sword and the Rose* production as we started several energetic days on location at Wilton Park, near Beaconsfield. The sequence we were shooting entailed my being on horseback nearly all day, and at last I had the use of a real quality animal, unlike my *Robin Hood* nags.

Even more enjoyable were the couple of days which I spent the following week filming at Chapman's Pool, near Corfe Castle, set in the lovely scenery of the Purbeck Hills and the Dorset coast.

While I was still filming at Pinewood I had two of my previous pictures premièred in London: in September *24 Hours of a Woman's Life* opened at the Empire, Leicester Square, and at the beginning of October *Venetian Bird* opened at the Leicester Square Theatre. The reviews were mixed, but at least I was in the enviable position of having two movies running concurrently at major cinemas facing each other across the Square!

On 15 September I drove Algy Bentley home from Pinewood, garaged the lovely, sleek car and fondly kissed it good night. I was to take delivery of a Rolls-Royce the next day – a hard decision to make, as I really loved that Bentley, but it was getting long in the mechanical tooth and would soon be showing serious signs of old age. The replacement Rolls was a much more sedate model, henceforth to be known to us all as Agatha.

Agatha's first official duty came the following Saturday when she conveyed Kitty and me and Peter to our local church at Stubbings, where Peter Grant Palethorpe Todd was christened on a glorious day and in the presence of all our friends including Fay, his new young nanny, who had been trained by the redoubtable Sister Cullinan. Among his godparents were Ann Weil and our former best man, Tim Reeve.

Church ceremonies seemed to proliferate during that beautiful summer. A couple of weeks later my new grey morning suit had its first outing in Kent at the wedding of Bridget Piercy, my previous secretary, and the following day we were at the christening of Jasper Booty's son – my godson – in Sussex.

We were by now about half-way through the *Sword and the Rose* schedule, and these very active weeks were punctuated by a stream of late-night engagements which left little time for proper rest: three film premières, the annual Royal Film Performance, the ABPC Staff Ball, the Variety Club Ball, the Cesarewitch Dinner Dance given by the Racehorse Owners' Association and various private and professional dinners and weekend parties. Kitty and I rented the Weils' London flat at Berkeley House for a couple of weeks to ease the strain for both of us.

Our few free days and weekends at Wayside House were equally energetic either socially or in the garden, with frequent shuttles to Castleman's Stud Farm where I now had four horses in training.

One weekend is particularly clear in my memory . . .

We had Glynis with us for the Saturday night and that evening gave a small dinner party. Glynis was in the main spare suite, the bathroom of which was above the dining room. Now that bathroom contained a rare and much-prized appliance, which, because of its occasional waywardness, could hardly be described as antedeluvian. One of the earliest water toilets ever installed, it consisted of an armchair seat of almost Chippendale proportions and grandeur, obviously designed by its famous makers for rest and contemplation as much as for the other needs of nature. To flush it one had to stamp on a metal raised stud on the floor nearby. We had learned to treat it with respect as it was inclined to over-react if operated too vigorously and to carry on flowing – and flooding – until one fiddled with a valve inside the tank behind. We usually instructed guests in the proper procedure, but in Glynis's case we had unfortunately forgotten.

Our little dinner party had gone very pleasantly and enjoyably up to the moment when the ladies left the room and the men got down to the serious business of lighting their cigars and passing the port (Taylor's '27, which I had found stored and seemingly forgotten in a local vintner's cellar). Then I heard it, right above where I sat – a series of clanking thuds from the bathroom which I knew betokened Glynis in some trouble with our self-willed antique.

Nobody else seemed to have noticed or, if they had, they were far too polite to comment. So I settled down again, hopeful that things had righted themselves. It was only when I heard the resounding plop of drips of water beside me on the floor and looked up to see the tell-tale damp patch on the ceiling that I realised all was definitely not well. However, I reckoned that this was a domestic crisis which Kitty and the staff would cope with. Even when the urbane and unruffled George Reeve (who was buttling for us that evening) quietly placed a plastic bucket beside me, not an eyebrow was raised nor a remark made by my guests.

I could imagine Glynis's cry for help and the mopping-up operation that had taken place behind the scenes, but everything carried on quite normally in the dining room until we left to rejoin the ladies. I felt that it said much for British *savoir-faire*!

After the same thing had happened a few weeks later however, when my aunt and uncle FitzPatrick came to spend a weekend with us, it was time for action: on the Monday I contacted the makers in London and described the appliance and its eccentricity. The head of the firm was astonished and delighted to hear that such a museum piece was still in use, and immediately dispatched a technician to inspect the apparatus. Within days a new valve had been specially made, and I would like to think that this most favourite of my antiques is still in operation to this day.

By the beginning of November there was a distinct end-of-picture feeling at Pinewood. James Robertson Justice had finished his stint, as had most of the others, and just Glynis and I were left doing odd pick-up shots and stills photography sessions. This period in the making of a happy film is always rather sad, as a group of actors who have worked together for months begin to drift apart.

I saw several rough-cut sequences and was pretty pleased with them. Whatever its merits as a box-office success, and whatever the reviews might be, the picture had the look of quality about it.

Even after my last shot on the film I was still involved with the cameras and with Alex Bryce, the second-unit director, as we compiled a TV publicity film for Disney about its making. Alex and I spent some time at the stud farm preparing for a sequence that would be shot there with Glynis and myself, and at Wayside House which would also figure in the TV picture. And meanwhile Glynis and I had been invited to join the panel of judges for the Miss World beauty competition at the Lyceum Theatre.

The format for this annual event is now too well known to need description. From personal experience I can say however that the method of adjudication is totally fair, that the results are genuinely compiled from marks given independently by each judge. Naturally the members of the panel have their own standards of classification but the marks they award, when totted up, give a true cross-section of their opinion.

My own particular fancy was for Miss Sweden, a dazzling blonde who flashed her glittering smile at us with telling effect, and I was not alone in my choice because she was crowned Miss World of 1952. I had obviously found favour with the organisers of this contest, since I was invited to join the judging panel four more times over the coming years, a form of jury service which I thoroughly enjoyed!

Happily for me and everybody concerned, I had finished all my work at Pinewood and was just doing my last shot at the stables for Alex Bryce's TV film when Hoity-Toity, my little two-year-old filly, decided to live up to her name. I had been riding her as part of a group of youngsters going through a light training session. After some easy walking and cantering round the track, it was decided that we should line up in the starting gate and have a final scurry round.

Green young horses always get pretty excited when lined up for a racing start, and our little band of fillies and colts was no exception. It was not easy to get them all pointed in the right direction as they skittered about, the other lads and I doing our best to get them into some sort of order. Finally, when they were more or less in line, the tapes went up and we were off! Hoity-Toity went away like a rocket, preceding her flat-out dash with an enormous plunging rear which dislodged me from the saddle so that I ended up bumping crazily on her hindquarters like a circus acrobat, desperately trying to pull myself forward again into my proper place on her back. We were well ahead of the others and I suppose I could eventually have regained the saddle; but I was afraid of unbalancing her and riding her into the rails, so I decided to bale out.

Trying to remember my old parachuting training for hitting the ground hard, I disembarked curled up as much as possible with my arms tightly locked to my sides, forearms across my chest. I thumped to earth and rolled over and over. It could have been worse: I broke a lower rib and tore some ligaments in my chest.

After my journey to the local hospital in Maidenhead and the usual X-ray, I was heavily strapped up and sent home. Those who have experienced a similar injury will know that it is nothing serious but bloody painful. I had a couple of very sore days in bed until our local GP, himself a keen follower of the local Garth Hunt, decided that I would be better off without the strapping.

He was right – it was much more comfortable and within four or five days I was up and about again.

Thank goodness this had not happened during the making of the film! From then on my Film Producer's Indemnity insurance policies all stipulated that I should not take part in any hazardous sports and pastimes.

In December baby Peter was quite seriously ill with a stomach disorder. For days he was fed only distilled water and looked very frail and wan. As soon as I got home each evening I rushed up to see him and I think that time really crystallised my attachment for him. Thank God he soon recovered, but it had been a nasty fright for us.

The year 1952 ended on a celebratory note, and all in the Todd world seemed well. Kitty was fitter than ever before, Peter was back to form and I had completed a busy professional period. I took Colonel Weil as my guest to a Variety Club lunch at which the Duke of Edinburgh was the chief speaker; Richard and Sheila Attenborough came to spend a day with us and we found a corgi pup for them to take home; and Christmas was spent with a series of parties. The snow fell at just the right time, and Wayside and the surrounding woods looked beautiful under its sparkling white mantle. I was grateful for what God had given me – and prayed for a little more.

7

A Highland Fling

1953 was to be a memorable year for me. It began with my first experience of domestic strife. Kitty and I had driven to London and we returned home in the early evening to find that there had been some nasty squabbles amongst the household staff, with my secretary Jill doing her best to keep the peace.

Apparently the trouble centred around the Rutlands, the couple who had been with us for some two years as cook and chauffeur/gardener. That morning there had been scenes between them and Peter's new nanny and Peggy, our daily help. Mrs Rutland had retired to bed, Peggy had gone home and the nanny said she was afraid to go into the kitchen quarters.

I spoke to Rutland that evening and he was in a very black and abusive mood. Obviously this could not be allowed to continue, so I gave him notice to quit within the month, told him I would help as far as I was able and offered him the use of Kitty's Ford to look around for jobs.

What a start to the New Year. The atmosphere was pretty bleak and the strain began to tell on Kitty's nerves. To cap it all, Nanny became unwell and took to her bed also. So now I was back to stoking that bloody boiler and carrying trays of food, aided by Jill, who had plenty of her own work to do.

Meanwhile, although I didn't like leaving the house for any longer than was absolutely necessary, I had to be away quite often for meetings with Perce Pearce for *Rob Roy* and script readings with Harold French, who was to direct the picture.

After a week Kitty collapsed one evening, and then again a few days later, and was ordered to bed by the doctor. However, by then Mrs Rutland was prepared to do some cooking and arrangements were made for Nanny and Peter to go and stay with the Weils.

After three very fraught weeks Rutland started a new job locally and they moved out. Peace at last returned to our home. I even managed to arrange for Peggy's husband and a local part-time postman, Goddard, who had already been helping us, to take over the boiler and the garden.

This had all been a salutary lesson for me: the glamorous image of a newly-established film star's public life was soon deflated when he had to be a domestic dogsbody in private. I had at least learned some new skills such as changing nappies for a baby, much to Peter's obvious consternation as I bundled him up and tried to avoid sticking the pins into him.

By now preparations were in full swing for the film, with all the usual meticulous pre-planning typical of the Walt Disney organisation. I started physical training sessions with Paddy Ryan, the stunt man, and – as with *Robin Hood* and *The Sword and the Rose* – sketches of every set-up were made, copied and distributed so that we all knew exactly what was required of us. Also, to my great joy it soon became apparent that we were to have almost the same team for *Rob Roy* as for the previous films. The production team was nearly identical, the main changes being Harold French as the director and Guy Green as director of photography, both eminent in their fields.

Many of the cast, too, had worked with me on the two earlier Disney films. Above all Glynis Johns was again to be my partner, and with me once more were to be James Robertson Justice, Michael Gough, Archie Duncan, Ewen Solon and my two trainers and stunt men, Paddy Ryan and Rupert Evans. We had become almost a cinema repertory company . . .

Once our domestic scene at Wayside had been sorted out, I was able again to spend a lot of time at Freddy Weil's Castleman's Stud and Racing Stables, where I had acquired a new young two-year-old whom I called Red Beret – aptly, as it happened, for he was a fiery chestnut with a temper to match and very difficult to train and handle.

I was also sitting for a young artist, Michael Francis, for my portrait as Rob Roy in full Highland costume complete with broadsword. I had by then grown my hair longish and had a full, bushy beard, both now dyed to a rich auburn-red colour. I even managed to spend several hours in the BBC Record Library choosing music for a recording of 'Desert Island Discs' with Roy Plomley.

I had taken the lease of a London flat in Nell Gwynn House, a large block in Sloane Avenue, so Kitty and I were busily choosing furniture, carpets and curtains for that. And meanwhile, Jill had arranged rooms for us in a hotel in Scotland a few miles from where we would be filming.

I had chosen the Buchanan Arms at Drymen, a very pleasant country hotel which I remembered from an excellent meal there a few years before. Jill had booked three rooms for us by phone – one for Kitty and me, one for Peter and Nanny, and one for me to use as a dressing room with the bed removed to make room for extra hanging space for my voluminous Rob Roy costumes. This was all agreed until Jill mentioned that I would also have two dogs with me. At this the receptionist baulked, saying no dogs were allowed in the hotel. So Jill cancelled the reservations.

Half an hour later Mr Charles Guy, the proprietor of the Buchanan Arms, phoned to say that *of course* I could bring my dogs. The only reason they had a no-dogs rule was because they had some of their own and had found visitors' dogs frequently a nuisance, but he was *sure* that mine would be no trouble at all. Little did he know that one of them was an enormous great Dane! So the hotel booking was confirmed . . .

On 14 March I set out in Agatha Rolls with Baron and our cheerful little corgi Wendy for my journey to Scotland. It was a fine bright day and I enjoyed a leisurely drive north, with Wendy beside me and Baron stretched out on the back seat. We stopped for the night at the Scotch Corner Hotel, where the dogs were welcome, and set off next morning over Bowes Moor to Carlisle and across the Border.

Arriving at the Buchanan Arms, we were greeted in the car park by the kilted Mr Guy himself who faltered only momentarily as Baron lumbered out of the car. Our baggage was unloaded – it included Peter's cot and most of Kitty's luggage – and we were shown to our rooms; they were together at one end of the hotel and were excellent except that my dressing room, contrary to my request, had a large bed in it. When I pointed this out, Mr Guy said, 'Oh, but Mr Todd, where would the dogs sleep?' A man after my own heart!

The following day I drove the few miles to the Forest Hills Hotel overlooking Loch Ard, a most beautiful spot, the water shimmering in the bright early-morning light surrounded by a green-mantled panorama of mountain and forest. Harold French and all the senior members of the unit were staying there, and I spent most of that day with Alex Bryce looking over our location areas.

The centrepiece of our film was to be a splendid, rugged-looking and utterly believable simulation of a highland fortress, built to Carmen Dillion's design as Inversnaid Fort, on a high plateau in Corrie Glennan with stunning views over Loch Ard and the surrounding stream-scarred heather uplands. Held by English troops, it was soon to be the scene of much of the fighting between Rob Roy's force of Highlanders and the Red-coats. The setting was breath-taking. As Alex and I surveyed the wild landscape from the fort on that bright, crisp day I could already imagine the horde of plaid-clad Highlanders streaming across the heather in their battle charge.

After dinner that evening I sorted out all my Rob Roy clothes and kit and readied myself for the opening shots on the morrow. Yards of tartan plaid, sword, skean-dhu (dagger), targe (a round leather shield, metal-studded), bonnet, belt and buckles were all laid out. My beard was by now luxuriantly red and bushy, and after my weeks of earnest training and preparation I felt I could do justice to the doughty Rob Roy MacGregor, the Highland rogue.

I had hired a Land Rover to get to and from the location sites and at a very early hour on 17 March a hirsute Rob Roy and his two faithful followers, Wendy and Baron, clattered along to the meeting place, the last point reachable by ordinary wheeled transport, well below the level of Inversnaid Fort. Here a motley collection of men and machines was ready and waiting. Army 3-ton lorries, film trucks, cars, food wagons and buses were drawn up in a grassy clearing. Army ambulances too, I noticed.

The most memorable and colourful sight of all at that moment was the rows of several hundred soldiers of the Argyll and Sutherland Highlanders, part of a battalion of that great regiment recently returned from the war in Korea. By arrangement with the army, this unit was to be our fighting manpower for the film, both as Red-coats and as Highland rebels. Tanned, tough and craggy, they looked the part ideally. That they entered into the fray with a will would be an understatement. I was soon to see why the medical unit and ambulances had been provided!

Presently a bus arrived bringing a posse of actors from the Glasgow Citizens' Theatre Company who had been hired to play the leading crowd parts and some small speaking roles. Sallow and mostly exposing white, knobbly knees beneath their kilts, they looked ill-at-ease and were in weedy contrast with their military compatriots. One gravel-voiced Argyll and Sutherland Highlander was heard to say to his neighbour, 'Hey, Jock – will ye look at our effing ancestors!'

The Argylls were dressed as clansmen and soldiers in roughly equal proportions and were obviously ready and eager to join battle, although it was explained to them via their officers that while we naturally wanted as much realism as possible on the screen, they were not to get too enthusiastic. This they cheerfully accepted and behaved like real gentlemen. At the end of the first day the medical unit had dealt with a mere 120 casualties, a high proportion of them being NCOs.

The first set-up of the picture was a long shot of me leading a fierce charge of clansmen in a yelling, sword-brandishing onslaught on the red-coated fencibles over a rough, heathery expanse of ground some few hundred yards square.

All keyed up for the start on this lovely, crisp spring day I took my place in the line after the first camera rehearsals, ready to show these real Highlanders what a mere Sassenach could do when a bit of action was called for. Supremely fit and trained to the hilt, my ego was even further stimulated by a liberal application of dark tan make-up on my legs, arms and torso which was shirtless under my plaid. Even the Argylls' Korean suntan was by now faded to a paler hue than my Max Factor bronzing.

'Action!' came loud and clear over the tannoy loudspeakers, so I set off like a rocket, whirling my sword and shouting encouragement to my clansmen. But I had run only about twenty yards when my right foot disappeared down a concealed rabbit hole and I collapsed in a heap.

From the instant pain in the back of my thigh I knew that I had badly pulled a hamstring and the muscles in the back of that leg, which within an hour or so had turned blue-black. I was stretchered out of the fray and spent the rest of the day in Glasgow having physiotherapy treatment, which consisted mainly of sitting for an hour or so in a sweat-box with only my head popped out of the electrically-heated contraption, then massage, then rest and then the whole process over again.

And so ended my first stirring entry into the story of Rob Roy MacGregor: rogue, rebel, cattle rustler, fighter and hard man of the Highlands.

Much to my relief the leg responded quite quickly and, although next day I again spent hours in Glasgow being alternately cooked and kneaded like dough, within two days I was able to hobble back up to Inversnaid and do some shots.

A few days later Kitty and Peter and his nanny came to join me at Drymen and we were once more together as a family, while Wendy went to Glasgow to stay with Kitty's parents. A couple of weeks later Glynis joined us and Jill, my secretary, came up for a week. By now my leg was fully recovered and I was filming busily every day.

Fortunately no production-time had been lost by my mishap as there were lots of set-ups in the battle scenes which did not include me. In fact, we moved quite quickly as the weather for the first week was brilliant and there were no hold-ups. Within days the large-scale battle scenes had been filmed and those hardy Argyll and Sutherland Highlanders departed for a more sedentary and peaceful life.

That was just as well because the climate became more typical of that time of year in the Trossachs. Between spells of sunshine the elements threw everything at us: snow, sleet, hail, pelting rain and high, bitter winds. For hours we would huddle miserably in what shelter we could find, then for minutes we would hurriedly scramble about and take advantage of a brief snatch of good light. Matching light and weather conditions is always a problem on location. Obviously, a sequence which takes only a couple of minutes' screen-time cannot be filmed in different lights, with moments of rainy background suddenly switching to clear skies. Occasionally close-up shots can be matched with the use of big arc-lights, but even then the actors have to be quickly dried out and tidied up after a sudden rain-squall. Windy conditions, too, are always a problem. In a film sequence shot out of doors, you can't have the characters ruffled and buffeted by a gale and then suddenly still and tranquil. Occasionally wind machines are brought into action on an unsettled day, and even simulated rain may have to be sprayed over a scene to keep up continuity.

These, then, were some of the problems with which we battled for several weeks, yet we kept right on schedule largely due to the hard work and cheerful willingness of the film crews, technicians and back-up staff.

This eagerness to get on with the job is something which seemed to be universal and which I always admired about film units on location. I have worked in widely differing areas and conditions: in the sweltering heat of the Mojave Desert in California; on the Skeleton Coast bordering the Kalahari Desert in Namibia; in the animal-, snake- and insect-infested stifling bush near Murchison Falls in Uganda; and in the swamps of Zululand; but none called for more dogged spirit than some of those days in the Highlands of Scotland. Occasionally even lashed by ropes to some rock-face, the camera crew seemed concerned about only one thing – to keep their precious equipment weatherproof, and to get their shots whenever an opportunity occurred. Manhandling their heavy and awkward lamps and cables over very rough terrain, the electricians slogged away together with the sound-men and the props men, each helping the others. There were no union demarcation disputes, nor any real grumbles.

I was not exactly feather-bedded myself on this Scottish location. Due to my insistence that I should not be doubled by a stunt specialist except where absolutely necessary, I had to undertake some fairly hairy enterprises. Two particular sequences still stick in my memory. In the first I was leashed to a horseman, my arms loosely pinioned behind me by a stake across my back, and I had to break my bonds and snap the stake (aided by a judicious nick already cut in it!) during a river-crossing with the water almost up to my neck. I then dived under the belly of the horse and swam under water for some distance before scrambling up the bank and legging it into the woods. Mercifully, we did this shot at the first take, because I didn't fancy chancing the horse's reactions a second time! Besides, the water was icy, literally newly-melted snow and absolutely freezing.

A second part of this escape sequence was even more exciting and involved me diving into the Lynn Dhu (the Black Pool), a notoriously dangerous water hole. Creeping along the line of a mountain stream now in spate where his pursuers were unable to follow his tracks, Rob had reached this barrier, a waterfall some 30 feet high dropping into the pool, and had decided to go over the edge. It was like going down the neck of a chianti bottle and finishing up in the bulbous body, its sides eroded and rounded out by years of the rush and undertow of water. The suction in there was very strong and on my first dive I thought I was never going to reach the surface again. Weighted down by yards of sodden plaid, I was near suffocation when I suddenly emerged into daylight. A rope was thrown to me and several pairs of willing hands pulled me to the bank and heaved me on to dry land. As I stood gasping and swaddled in towels I was shivering like a pneumatic drill, my teeth chattering a drum-roll on the mug of rum held to my mouth.

That pool sequence took two days to shoot and during all this Baron, who was always with me, watched anxiously. Somebody had thought-fully put him into my old duffle coat, with his front legs in the arms of it, and had wrapped a muffler round his neck and put the cowl over his head. But still the dog worried and groaned. I'm sure that if I had cut myself, Baron would have done the bleeding. He was much loved by everybody, especially at the Buchanan Arms, where every evening after dinner when we were sitting in the hotel lounge he would go upstairs and fetch my slippers like a fussy old aunt, then take my shoes back to my room.

Another sequence I will always remember, but for its haunting beauty rather than for its dangers, was the scene picturing the funeral of Rob Roy's mother, Lady Glengyll, a kinswoman of the Duke of Argyll. The burial took place on an island in Loch Ard, where there already existed an ancient family cemetery, a walled circle of old tombs. The cortège set out from the rocky shore in a group of boats led by the funeral long-boat, a line of men at the oars, the coffin on a wooden platform and the piper at its bow playing a lament. Standing in that long-boat on a still afternoon, the waters hardly rippling and the early-spring light steely-bright, I felt a genuine sadness as the oars thudded and splashed in time to the lament.

We met a number of people whose ancestors appeared in our story: Sir Malcolm MacGregor of MacGregor, the clan chief, the then Duke and Duchess of Argyll and the Duke and Duchess of Montrose, whose estate was near Drymen. The Argylls invited us for a weekend at Inveraray Castle, their magnificent seat on the shores of Loch Fyne, and we also dined with the Duke and Duchess of Montrose at Auchmar House, where the Duke showed us letters of Rob Roy's and relics of his ancestor the great Marquis of Montrose, soldier and patriot.

Another pair who were most hospitable to us were Brigadier and Mrs Ewing-Crawford, who lived nearby at Auchentroig House. Mrs Ewing-Crawford had converted the ancient original manor house of the estate into a wool mill, from which she produced rolls of real vegetable-dyed tartan plaid material. She in fact supplied our tartan clothing for the film, probably the biggest order she had ever had.

There were lighter moments too, as when on one occasion I was taken (in all my Highland finery) by a PR man to visit Inversnaid Farm, which had once been in the possession of Rob Roy's family. When my companion knocked on the door, it was opened by an elderly woman who had evidently been baking, judging by her flour-covered hands. With a sweeping gesture towards me the PR man announced in needlessly melodramatic tones, 'Rob Roy MacGregor has come to visit you!' Taking one look at me, the old lady let out a piercing screech, threw her apron over her face and had hysterics. It took us quite a while to calm her down and assure her that she had not seen a ghost.

During some of the action sequences I had been very impressed with the sturdy agility and good temper of Damson, one of the horses. I found that she was by a good steeplechaser called Apple Sammy out of a Connemara mare, a real tough sort that I reckoned would make a useful and sensible addition to our family for Kitty or me to ride, and particularly for me to get some jumping experience. Accordingly, I bought Damson and arranged for her to be transported south when we had finished in Scotland.

Kitty had also arranged for an addition to the Wayside circle: a very nice young Scots girl, Elsie Barr, who was to join us in due course as housemaid.

Peter also contributed to our memories of our Rob Roy location by cutting his first two teeth at the Buchanan Arms.

By the end of April we had nearly finished our location work. Kitty and Peter flew home and I followed a few days later in Agatha Rolls accompanied by the dogs and my stand-in, Freddie Gayton. And for all the magnificence of the Highland scenery, it was nice to be back at tranquil old Wayside.

But not for long. I had a single day's break and then started studio work at Elstree where, amongst other things, Glynis and I had a short, intensive course in Highland dancing ready for the celebrations at Rob Roy's wedding.

8

Disneyland

Apart from a hurried flight to Scotland one weekend to shoot some pick-up scenes which the weather had previously made impossible, the rest of the *Rob Roy* schedule followed a routine studio pattern at Elstree.

It was nice to be back working at Elstree. I was now spending the weekdays in the London flat and thus saving myself a lot of late-night and early-morning driving. My only problems were household ones. Kitty was none too well again and I was anxious to make things as easy as possible for her, but with mixed results. We had at last found a good cook – a rather fiery and moody Hungarian, heavy on the paprika with a temper to match, and neither the nanny nor Elsie from Scotland got on with her, nor with each other.

Damson, the horse I had bought in Scotland, arrived at Euston Station and was met by Bob Armstrong, the stud manager at Knowl Hill, and boxed down to the farm. She had not enjoyed her travels and was very nervy. However, she and I soon found a rapport so that the next day Kitty rode her quietly and the two of them got on well. From then on I rode Damson most weekends and started jumping her under Bob Armstrong's tuition.

Bob was a grand chap. One of England's most famous farriers, he accompanied most of our international show-jumping and three-day-event teams on their trips abroad. He was himself a fine horseman and a useful trainer of steeplechasers.

By the end of May London was a-flutter with flags and decorations in preparation for the Coronation of Queen Elizabeth II. It was a time of high hopes throughout the country and all over London crowds enjoyed the lights and the celebrations amidst scenes which I had not witnessed since the war.

Just before Peter's first birthday his new nanny arrived, and at least one of our problems was solved. Nanny Pitcher was one of the real old school: middle-aged, she had spent a lifetime as a children's nurse and was very proud of her calling. Rarely do you see her sort any more: always uniformed in grey, with white starched cuffs, collar and belt, and with a grey coat and brimmed hat for outdoors, she was a real professional and devoted to her job – as she was also to Peter. Within weeks he had become the centre of her life and caring for him was her joy. A great believer in the benefits of fresh air for a child, she would walk miles pushing his pram every day. We had a nursery suite of two rooms and bathroom at Wayside and that was her unassailable territory, especially as she had there a little electric cooker on which she prepared all his meals. Despite her independence, Nanny Pitcher fortunately always got on with the rest of the staff and there never seemed to be any resentment of her privileged position in the house. She stayed with us for years and still kept in touch with us until recent times.

We had all got used to my bearded, apostolic appearance. In fact Elsie Barr, the housemaid, had never seen me without my face fur. On the day after I had finished all my photography for the film and removed my beard, she came into our bedroom with the morning tea, took one look at the clean-shaven stranger sharing my wife's bed, gasped and fled, taking the tray with her.

My thirty-fourth birthday was marred by the news from Kitty's doctor that she might need an operation. Never very robust, she was going through a rather poor time with gynaecological troubles partly due to a tendency to anaemia, with consequent depression. That evening we went to a party at the Nepalese Embassy, but had to leave early. A week later she had her operation at a London nursing home, where she stayed for a week before coming home with strict orders to stay in bed for some days. Mercifully she gradually picked up, after plenty of rest.

My work on the picture completed, on 25 July I flew to New York for an extensive promotional tour in America arranged by the Disney organisation, preparing the run-up to the release of *The Sword and the Rose*.

I was greeted at Idlewild Airport by Charlie Levy, Disney's head of PR in New York, a jovial, friendly man who made me very welcome and who made my formidable list of appointments seem like a pleasant prospect. I was billeted in a sumptuous apartment in the Waldorf Towers, part of the Waldorf Hotel complex but consisting only of private suites with their own separate elevator and even a 'home kitchen', where two old dears prepared special meals for the residents with a simple but delicious menu.

The only drawback was the heat. The suite at that time was not air-conditioned for some reason, and I sweltered. One evening I even contemplated climbing into the enormous refrigerator. New York can be steamy in August and I had hit town at one of the most humid periods.

Walt Disney really gave me regal treatment during my stay. God knows how much I must have cost his organisation, but I certainly worked hard singing for my suppers. In 23 days I did 26 TV and radio broadcasts; 48 press and magazine interviews; spent a day in Boston and another in Cleveland; managed to see three theatre shows and had several other luncheon and dinner appointments.

My flight to New York from London had been my first in a Boeing Stratocruiser. How different were trans-Atlantic flights in those days from the cramped supersonic swoops of a modern Concorde – and how much more pleasant if you could spare the time! The Stratocruiser was a large, fat-bellied aircraft with a separate compartment under the fuselage, the rear of which was for cargo and the front a small, cosy cocktail or coffee bar for first-class passengers. After the evening take-off from Heathrow (then still largely a shambles of Nissen huts and plain sheds), we were asked to go downstairs for a while to give the cabin staff time to lay up our tables for dinner. Then a splendid meal was served with plenty of space and no rush at all.

After dinner we again went downstairs for coffee and liqueurs and a smoke (everybody seemed to smoke in those days), before returning to the main deck to find our sleeping bunks all made up ready. They were in two tiers, and curtained, rather like some sleepers on railways. Some were even doubles. And there was time for a full night's sleep too, since depending on the wind conditions, the crossing from London to New York could take as much as twelve hours.

Well before landing, we were wakened with tea or coffee and had enough time for a wash and shave in roomy toilets before breakfast was served. Never one to enjoy rushing around, this form of travel suited me completely.

After three weeks Kitty flew from London to join her bloated husband in New York (regular daily luncheon and dinner meetings had not improved my shape) and the next day we flew to California. Walt Disney himself came to meet us there at the Beverly Hills Hotel, and was as genial and kindly as ever. He did not think much of the modest car I had hired and insisted that from then on I should use one of his Cadillacs. He asked us to spend the next day with him and his wife at their home in the Holmby Hills nearby.

Walt's home reflected the nature of the man himself. It was a pretty, rambling house set in large grounds with immaculate gardens, not at all glossy or flashy but solidly comfortable and homely, and with cabinets full of the objects that he loved: tiny things; miniatures of all sorts in china, wood or metal. And the real heart of his domain was his barn and workshop, with his miniature railway.

Walt had been born and raised on a small farm out in the Mid-West, and soon after he moved into the Holmby Hills house he had gone to visit his boyhood farmstead home and bought the timber barn; he had it dismantled, then re-erected it in the centre of his grounds as a remembrance of his humble start in life, and as a get-away den for his own very personal and practical hobbies. In there were his train-shed, his lathe and work-bench and, especially, the Disney Stove Works.

His warmest memory of childhood was the pot-bellied stove round which he and his family had clustered in their living room during the long winters. Now one of his great delights was to turn out little models of that stove, complete with riddle and lid, as gifts for his friends. I still have the one he gave me that day, a beautiful little thing about six inches high, painted in white, green and gold.

Even his trains, which he engineered and maintained himself, were put to good use. Rail tracks went all round the garden, and as we trundled round for a little trip he explained to me that the gardeners used the trucks to move refuse, leaves and plant pots.

Such was the simple generosity of this man that every Christmas afterwards for many years he sent a crate of gifts to my own children, each present carefully chosen according to the child's age and with a label: 'With love from Uncle Walt'. The last one had been shipped a few days before he died.

After a busy few days in California, meeting lots of old friends from our time there in 1950, we flew home to England for the première of *The Sword and the Rose* at the Gaumont Cinema in London. We just had time to drive home, unpack and then dash up to town for the gala opening.

We were in fact quite lucky to be there at all. During the flight across the Atlantic, I awoke momentarily and peered out of the window beside our double bunk. I noticed that the inboard propeller was still. I was too sleepy to think much about it and dozed off again. As we later had breakfast while flying over Ireland I saw that the engine was still shut off, but as there had been no announcement about it I concluded that it was probably some fuel-economy measure. It was not until we finally touched down at London Airport and I saw the line of fire engines and ambulances near the runway that I realised there had indeed been an emergency. The evening papers were full of the reports of a giant airliner which had limped across the Atlantic on three engines.

That September Kitty and I had our first real rest and break in many months. It was a fine summer so we used the pool, played tennis, I rode and jumped Damson nearly every day and we also went to a few race meetings to see our horses run – some with a fair degree of success. It was about then that we were given the marvellous news that *Rob Roy* had been chosen for presentation at the annual Royal Film Performance on 26 October. To be in the Royal film at any time was an honour, but to be the star of the film in that Coronation year of Queen Elizabeth II was something extra special.

Our leisure period was rounded off during the first week of October with evenings at the Horse of the Year Show at Harringay Arena. I had become a member of the British Show Jumping Association, so we had dinner each evening in the Members Restaurant and some very convivial sessions afterwards in the various caravans where competitors and their families lived during the show.

In mid-October I was approached by Laurenz Marmstadt, a Swedish film producer, about a film he was shortly to make in Paris. The film, *Le Lit*, was to be in four episodes telling the history of a bed – a story with many possibilities obviously, especially in a French film! The co-star in my episode was to be that marvellous actress Jeanne Moreau.

I was given a script, had a discussion about the project with Bob Lennard and then met Marmstadt for dinner. I liked him enormously and we had a very friendly meeting during which he agreed various suggestions that I made about the screenplay.

The next day I worked out details of the deal we wanted with Bob Lennard and then went to Paris to meet Henri Decoin, who was to direct my episode.

Next morning I had a meeting with my French agent to discuss my contract, then flew home in time for lunch at Wayside.

I then barely had time to work on a speech I was to make the following evening at the Mansion House in London. One of the City Livery Companies, the Worshipful Company of Upholders, had invited me to be guest of honour at their Coronation banquet. Apparently their surprising choice of speaker was a result of their wish to mark the Coronation of our youthful Queen by picking somebody reasonably young who had achieved some measure of public success in recent years. They surely had a lengthy list of potential qualifiers and why they settled for me I will never know. I had gratefully accepted the invitation before its full implications really dawned on me.

Perhaps I should have appealed to the scenario department at Elstree for inspiration! Instead, I trusted to my oft-used ability to ramble on at length about nothing in particular. But I certainly sweated over my basic notes that Sunday evening . . .

Sitting in the ornate splendour of the Mansion House, surrounded by all manner of distinguished personages, I can't say that I enjoyed either the excellent food or the fine selection of wines. Rigid with nervous tension, I'm afraid that Kitty and I must have been dreary company for our neighbours. Besides, it was a warm evening and being bundled up in my bemedalled tail-coat, starched shirt and stiff wing collar did nothing to cool my apprehension.

Then came the speeches and finally the awesome moment when the toastmaster prayed silence for Mr Richard Todd. It was all over in about five minutes, I suppose. God knows what I said. I can only remember that I managed without referring to any notes, got a few good laughs (intentionally, I hasten to add) and sat down to what seemed to be a pretty good curtain-call reception. Thankfully I gulped down the glass of port that I had carefully saved for that moment.

The rest of that week was partly taken up by rehearsals and preparations for the Royal Film Performance. The stage show was to be a brief one, much to my relief. Tony Kimmins, who had directed me in *Flesh and Blood*, was in charge of it and contrived to present each of the British, American and foreign stars with a minimum of fuss.

The Royal Film Performance was a success and much to my relief the reception for *Rob Roy* seemed genuinely enthusiastic. Leicester Square was thronged with thousands of cheering people, there to see the Queen and Prince Philip and the dozens of film personalities. And after the presentations to the Royal party the huge do at the Savoy Hotel was a tremendous affair which we all thoroughly enjoyed, dancing the hours away till dawn.

9

Heathcliff Takes French Leave

Feeling pretty groggy after my almost sleepless night following the Royal Film Performance, I tried to sound as sensible as possible at lunch next day as I listened to a proposal from two of the heavyweights of BBC Television, Michael Barry and Rudolph Cartier.

The subject we discussed was the forthcoming BBC live television production of *Wuthering Heights* which Barry was to produce and Cartier to direct. It was to be probably the most ambitious TV drama ever attempted by the BBC – at that time, of course, the sole TV channel in Britain. I was invited to star as Heathcliff, with Yvonne Mitchell playing Cathy.

Nothing then was pre-recorded, so it was quite a daunting proposition: two live performances, on Sunday and then the following Thursday, each of one and a half hours. Rehearsals would start in November and the play would be screened in December.

I could just fit in my French film to which I was now committed.

I decided to accept the challenge.

The following day I and several other American and British screen personalities set off on the replica Royal Film Performances, to be held that year in Bournemouth and Bristol, which were great money-raisers for the Cinematographic Trade Benevolent Fund. The programme was always the same:

> 6.30 Press Cocktail Party
> 7.30 Civic Reception
> 8.30 Replica Royal Film Performance
> 10.30 Dinner
> 11.30 Civic Ball
> 2 am Bed, rather the worse for wear

On this occasion we were accompanied by The Royal Canadian Air

Force Pipe Band, who contributed lustily to the Scottish air of the proceedings.

The only thing lacking was a haggis!

On my return to London from Bristol I went with Rudolph Cartier and Michael Barry to see a production of *Wuthering Heights* at the Royal Academy of Dramatic Art, then had a lengthy discussion about plans for the TV production before thankfully settling for a quiet weekend at home.

Since our *Rob Roy* celebrations in London Kitty had not been feeling too well – and for good reason. Within days she was rushed into the London Clinic for an emergency appendix operation. Her surgeon finally pronounced that all was well, and after a slow start she recovered very well. Her hospitalisation turned out to be right on cue, because once again I had to dash off to France for meetings with Marmstadt and de Coin.

My episode in *Le Lit* was the story of a young British officer in the last war billeted for the night in a small isolated farmhouse in northern France whose sole occupant was a young Frenchwoman, Jeanne Moreau, very *enceinte* and rather *distraite*. Dog-tired after a long jeep drive, the officer is only too glad to have a light supper and then collapse in to bed. Almost immediately, his slumber is shattered by a piercing scream from another room. Scrambling out of bed, he is horrified to find that the young woman is in labour and about to give birth at any moment. With no telephone available he dare not leave her to seek help and so perforce becomes acting midwife for the rest of the night, insisting that she has his bed which seems to be the only large one in the little cottage.

It may not sound very amusing in the telling, but with a neat script and Decoin's adroit direction it promised to be a really funny and slightly dotty little cameo.

I didn't have to act – I *was* that harassed young man. Like him, I had never encountered such a situation and had only the vaguest notion what to do. And I got little help from the girl herself who was equally panic-stricken. Decoin had me scuttling about with bowls of boiling water and towels and desperately trying not to be sick.

Relative calm having been restored by dawn, the officer finally gets help from the nearest village and, tottering with fatigue and delayed reaction, goes to retrieve his jeep from the barn, only to find that the farm cat has had a fine litter of kittens on his driving seat . . .

We had ten days of great fun shooting our episode in both French and English versions. My French was still good enough, despite having got pretty rusty.

On my return to Wayside House I was very glad to find Kitty much stronger and in quite good spirits, especially since I had to start the very next day on rehearsals for *Wuthering Heights*.

During the rehearsal period I stayed at the London flat. We had just two weeks to prepare this very difficult and complex TV production, and we needed every moment.

TV drama was still in its infancy and most shows were pretty static, rather like a stage play being filmed. But *Wuthering Heights* was to break new ground: far from being static with few camera angles, we had over 70 different set-ups to contend with and several cameras to shoot them. Furthermore, the actors had to become word-perfect in the short rehearsal time.

We started in the usual way in a large hall with the confines of each set marked out by tapes on the floor, and a few essential props to work with – including a stuffed horse in the stable scene!

On the second Saturday of our rehearsal period we had our first camera rehearsal at Lime Grove Studios, and I realised what I had let myself in for. It was utter chaos!

How Rudolf Cartier managed to handle the frenzy from his control room I couldn't imagine . . .

Studio E was a huge space which had taken on the appearance of a Heath Robinson cranky invention. The sets were all ranged around the walls like cubicles – about forty of them, I think. The middle of the floor – what was left of it – was crammed with cameras, sound booms, technicians and a forest of other equipment, with twisted ganglions of cables and wires cluttered everywhere. Over all hung the lighting, lamps of all shapes and sizes.

Getting from one set to the next was like negotiating an obstacle course, and the director, scriptwriter and set designer must have had nightmares after working out how to get the actors from one scene to another without any hold-up. Each of us had a floor-assistant guiding us from set to set and hurriedly telling us what to do next.

The opening shot on me was of the aged Heathcliff, bewigged and bewhiskered, leaning out of a window staring across painted snow-swept moors while somebody scattered soap flakes between me and the camera. From there I had to change in seconds to a young Heathcliff, revealed with Cathy, grooming that moth-eaten stuffed horse in the stable on the other side of the studio. Stripping off my top-coat, wig and whiskers, wiping my face clean of age make-up, I darted across to

Cathy through the equipment jungle, trying not to appear too breathless when I got there. Hopefully, my heavy breathing would be taken for romantic excitement.

Next day, Sunday, at 8.40 pm, *Wuthering Heights* was broadcast live. After a day of sheer panic at Lime Grove, we got through somehow – quite well, in fact, with no major disasters.

During the next few days I was glad to be home. Kitty was again not too well, so I was able to spend time quietly with her. One thing that cheered us both up was the arrival of a new and marvellous cook, Miss Murray-Hamilton. A Scots girl, she had trained at the Cordon Bleu School of Cookery and was splendid both as a person and as a *cuisinière*. She remained in charge of our kitchen for years and I reckon we had the best cook in England in a private house. I think she enjoyed being with us too, particularly as we entertained quite a lot so she had frequent chances to display her skills.

The re-broadcast of *Wuthering Heights* on the Thursday evening went much more smoothly than the first and both shows got very good reports.

Apart from a couple of days spent in Paris seeing a rough-cut of *Le Lit* and preparing the script for more scenes in it to be done next year in Rome, I spent the rest of the month at home, reading scripts and having a few meetings in London. For Christmas, Peter's second, we gave him a swing and a toy pony and he had another case of gifts from his Uncle Walt Disney. He had a great time sitting by the Christmas tree tearing off the wrapping paper.

1953 had been a busy year, and now 1954 gave me something special to look forward to – *The Dam Busters*. For nearly two years research and scripting had been progressing on that subject and within a few months, all being well, we would be in production. I was tremendously excited at the prospect of getting started on what we were all sure would be a great film.

10

Roman Holiday

The New Year opened for Kitty and me in Rome. I was to do about three days filming on *Le Lit* and we decided to spend a week after that seeing as much as possible of the Eternal City, which neither of us had visited before.

My filming was done at Ciné Cita, then the main studio in Rome and certainly the most chaotic movie centre I had ever experienced. Filming on the first day started at 10 am and went on until 1 am the following morning, during which time we managed just three set-ups. My impression was that there was some sort of strike or go-slow in progress, but apparently this was quite the normal pace of work. Everybody seemed to spend hours arguing or swigging wine in the bars, shouting and gesticulating vehemently. And my second and third days at Ciné Cita were similar, each ending well after midnight.

One consolation was the presence of Vittorio de Sica, who was working with me, and did not seem at all impatient about the delays. I found him a very courteous, interesting man.

Thereafter Kitty and I spent our days trying to take in as much of Rome's splendours as we could: St Peter's, the Vatican, the Colosseum, Villa Borghese, a car tour to Tivoli and the Villa d'Este – and of course we threw coins into the Trevi Fountain for luck!

We were sad to leave Rome – a sadness that soon turned to shocked distress.

I had tried to book seats on a Comet flight to London en route from the Far East, but had been told that the plane was completely full, so I had to settle for a return later that day on a Viscount, that sturdy old work-horse of British European Airlines.

We took off from Ciampino airport in the late afternoon, and after about half-an-hour in the air I asked a stewardess if there was an evening paper available. 'Sorry, Mr Todd,' was her reply, 'but we are not giving any out . . .' she paused, assessing me, then made up her

mind '. . . because of the news. But you can have mine for a while, if
you like.' I thanked her and took the covertly-proffered paper. The front
page headline was 'COMET DISASTER'.

The morning flight on which I had tried to get seats had ended in
tragedy. Over the sea somewhere just off the Italian coast the Comet
had disintegrated and crashed with the loss of all on board. It was
horrible news.

Once again, my skin had been narrowly saved on a journey from
Italy: first the train crash near Milan in 1952, and now this . . .

The rest of that trip was thoroughly alarming. Over the Alps we ran
into the most almighty electrical storm. Our little Viscount was bounced
about sickeningly, and from the windows lightning flashes in the evening
gloom gave momentarily terrifying glimpses of snow-capped mountains.

My flurry of filming ended a few days later in Paris, where Jeanne
Moreau and I finished our stint on *Le Lit*. Apart from the three days
at Ciné Cita it had been great fun working with the French.

While in Paris I found Michael Wilding staying at the Prince de
Galles, and he and I spent a couple of evenings together. He was then
married to Elizabeth Taylor and living in California. She was in
England making a picture, but for tax reasons he had to ration his time
there – so where better to be in exile than Paris?

Mike was always a most amusing and relaxed companion and after
dinner we went to a club notorious for its largely lesbian clientele but
also celebrated for its excellent cabaret, which included the brilliant
young Eartha Kitt. Mike and I sat at a small table for two, watching
the floor-show and the antics of the female customers dancing together.
Perhaps we too should have danced together, just to keep up
appearances . . .

My return home was saddened by the news of two deaths: the splendid old Duke of Montrose, who had been so kind to us in Scotland;
and Kitty's grandmother, the grand matriarch of the family. Next day
I took Kitty to the airport at the start of her journey to her old home
on the Isle of Bute.

We had had a dinner party arranged for that evening, and Jill stood
in very efficiently for Kitty. Alone for a few days I took Peter and
Nanny Pitcher for several drives, including my first visit to my father's
grave at Brookwood Military Cemetery in Surrey. As I stood by the
simple headstone among thousands of similar stones in the huge tree-
girt plot so many memories flowed through my mind, especially his last
words to me in 1942, when he knew he would never see me again:
'Goodbye, old chap. Good luck,' as he saw me off at Euston Station on

my journey into the unknown, laden with Arctic equipment. Fortunately, my destination turned out to be Iceland, and not Russia.

Only a few days later, I too was travelling north, catching the night-sleeper train to Glasgow, but for a happier reason: the Scottish première of *Rob Roy*.

The Scots gave the film a tremendous reception and the whole evening was a gala of kilts, bagpipes and best Highland malt whisky.

During that visit I had the pleasure of meeting John Rollo, a Scottish industrialist who had been instrumental in setting up the Highland Fund, a quasi-governmental agency dedicated to encouraging a back-to-the-land movement in the Highlands where crofters trying to eke out a living on their hilly smallholdings needed help and encouragement. John Rollo himself had designed and was building at his factory a mini-tractor suitable for use on the steep, cramped steadings, and he and Lord Malcolm Douglas-Hamilton invited me to present the first of these tractors to the Fund, which I was only too happy to do, in a ceremony marking the opening of a public fund-raising campaign.

At dinner that evening John Rollo told me how he had accepted safe-keeping of the Stone of Scone for a period after it had been spirited away from Westminster Abbey by a group of Scottish Nationalist students. This legendary slab lies under the Coronation Chair in the Abbey and is synonymous with the kingship of Scotland, having been brought to London from Scone Palace. There had been a great furore when it disappeared, but it was eventually restored and the adventurous students pardoned. It was while they were treating for its return and their pardon that the group had asked John, whom they trusted, to keep it safe for a while. It had already suffered slight damage, and they were anxious that it should remain intact, as it did for some time under the floor of John's office!

Home again, I collected from Robert Lennard the latest screenplay for *The Dam Busters*. It was magnificent – taut, gripping and totally realistic. Even so I knew that further revisions were to be made, partly for technical reasons.

During the next couple of months before we actually started filming in April I spent many days involved with preparations for the picture and in discussions with those concerned, including the screenwriter Robert Sherriff, the playwright and film writer, whose credits included the play *Journey's End*, and films such as *The Invisible Man, Goodbye Mr Chips, The Four Feathers, Lady Hamilton, Odd Man Out, Quartet* and *No Highway*.

In one meeting I had had with Robert Clark, who was the executive producer of *The Dam Busters* and who had bought the subject for me, he announced that he intended to give direction of the film to a complete unknown (at least, to me). 'Damn!' I thought. 'Typical cheese-paring. He's going to spoil the ship for a ha-porth of tar.'

However, he said that he wanted us to meet so that I could form my own opinion. And so it was arranged: I was to have dinner with Michael Anderson.

Here I give full credit to Robert Clark for his inspired choice. In all my years of filming I have never met and worked with a more charming, sensitive and quietly-efficient director than Michael. Within half an hour of our meeting I had total confidence in his talent and in his attitude to the making of *The Dam Busters*. He conceived the picture almost as a documentary, shot in black and white partly to create that aura of reality, partly to avoid the romantic prettiness of colour photography, and partly so that he could use certain stock shots already in the archives. Thus it was that *The Dam Busters* turned out to be one of the finest, most realistic war films ever made in Britain, thanks also to Paul Brickhill's original book and to Robert Clark, Robert Sherriff, Michael Anderson and a superb crew.

Together Michael and I saw footage of the special effects photography that had already been shot and which was crucial to the making of the film. Without believable shots of the actual demolition of the dams there could be no picture, and I was amazed how realistically the special effects boys had contrived the explosions, the collapse of the two enormous stone dams and the release of vast torrents of water. No wonder Michael was quietly confident.

And together we also met and talked with many of those who had been connected with the famous raid, including the pilot Guy Gibson's widow, Eve, and his frail old father; Mickey Martin, his 2 i/c, and other survivors; and above all Dr Barnes Wallis, inventor of the 'bouncing' bomb. Sherriff, too, had met them and there was not a line of dialogue or a single incident enacted on the screen which was not true to the events.

Meeting Barnes Wallis had been a special treat for me. I had heard so much about this great man and his achievements. Inventor, mathematician, engineer and head of research at Vickers; designer of the R100 airship and the Wellington bomber – his contributions to aviation and his country had been immense. God knows why it was only near the end of his distinguished life that he was honoured by a knighthood. He was already elderly when I met him, lean, pink-faced, smooth-skinned and white-haired, but his enthusiasm, keenness of mind and plans for future aircraft development belied his years. He had received nothing but his salary for his war work and after the war, when he received a grant from a special fund established to compensate those such as he who had bestowed their gifts so selflessly, he gave every penny of this grant to establish a nursery at Christ's Hospital School for the orphans of RAF personnel. He was not a rich man, and had struggled to educate his own and adopted children, so he had genuine sympathy for the needy.

The last time I was with Barnes Wallis he was in his late seventies, but still head of research at Vickers and bursting with ideas for new departures in aviation development. He had just invented the swing-wing aircraft and was currently engaged on a project which he described as making conventional aircraft look like hansom cabs. It had something to do with vertical take-off straight up into the stratosphere, using the revolution of the earth to boost the speed of the aircraft. I didn't really understand what he was getting at, but perhaps others of his kind understood and are even now working on it. 'It will mean London to Sydney, Australia, in six hours,' he told me.

He was also enthusing over his discovery of a revolutionary submarine propellant based on the use of simple paraffin. 'It will drive a sub faster and for longer than any nuclear engine.' I wonder what happened to that.

I asked him if he was not thinking of retiring and taking a rest. He twinkled at this and said he had enough on the drawing board to keep him going for the next nine years. He had worked out his life expectancy, based on his health and his parents' longevity, and reckoned he would carry on until he was eighty-nine. 'After all,' he smiled, 'I think you get a bit senile when you reach ninety.'

The scripting, special effects work and the preparation of the necessary aircraft for *The Dam Busters* had been worked on for nearly two years before shooting started in April 1954. Vickers, the aircraft manufacturers, had put together five Lancaster bombers fit to fly for us, and RAF crews were standing by to operate the Lancs and the camera aircraft.

Meanwhile I kept pretty busy. There was the usual succession of meetings with various producers and agents wanting to discuss their projects, and a steady series of film premières, charity events and dinner engagements in London. I tried to compensate by riding out at the stud farm as often as possible and going for daily runs with Baron through the woods and grassland of Maidenhead Thicket, which surrounded Wayside House. I puffed along clad in my old Airborne athletics sweatsuit, now faded from maroon to a grubby pink, while the enormous dog barely had to break into a trot.

Kitty and I also toured round antique shops and auctions looking for furniture and paintings, encouraged by a couple of legacies which had been left me by my dear old Granny Todd and her older sister, Clara Chatwin. Granny, my most staunch supporter for years, had died when I was in America and was the last occupant of the Todd family vault in Co. Tyrone.

At the end of March another diversion took me away from home for a few days: the Cannes Film Festival. This was my first visit to this much-publicised shindig. I learned pretty quickly about the pleasures and the pitfalls of such international movie get-togethers, having already tested the water at the Venice Festival, and was eventually to become a sort of hardy annual at the event as the main banner-waver for Associated British.

While the core of the Festival was the wheeling and dealing of the movie marketeers, the majority of those attending were there to push themselves into the public eye (and the producers' attention) by whatever means at their disposal – and the many would-be starlets displayed a startling variety of means. That was what the media wanted, and if shocks and scandals were not readily available they were not beyond cooking something up themselves. Cameras and scribble-pads were everywhere.

One picture that caught the world notice was obtained when a well-endowed young actress was posed in conversation with Robert Mitchum and ensured instant notoriety for herself by dropping her pectoral guard suddenly and displaying a mountainous vista to the startled Mitchum. This was long before the ubiquitous topless beaches came into being.

The urbane and laconic Robert soon recovered his composure and most of the photographs caught him with a 'Very nice, but put them away' look on his face.

But there was a semi-serious side to the occasion for most of us, and for actors, directors and producers there was the all-important exercise of making contacts and just being *seen*. In addition for me there was the job of spokesman for Associated British at many of the receptions which the corporation held, since I was the only one who spoke reasonable French.

I was quite luxuriously quartered at the Carlton Hotel and most of my photographic forays were organised and controlled by the intrepid Leslie Frewin. These included the compulsory running along the beach hand-in-hand with a pretty girl, a fixed 'It's all such fun!' grin on one's face, or lolling about on hired yachts and milling around in the foyer of the main cinema. As to the films themselves, we went to those almost as an afterthought.

On the day before I left I became the subject of one of the press set-ups. A popular movie magazine asked me to do a photo session with a charming and very pretty young French actress, which was all quite innocuous. It was then arranged that I should escort her to the film show that evening, which I did with pleasure.

Neither of us realised that this was all part of a contrived 'romance' until the next day, when a shot of me lighting her cigarette appeared in all the papers, captioned with an implication of very close intimacy. That day was the end of the festival and although it was pure coincidence that Nicole Courcel and I had booked on the Blue Train to Paris that evening, both of us drew the line when we arrived at the station to find that our reservations had been changed to a double sleeping-compartment and that a posse of photographers was hanging around there.

11

Bombs Gone!

My work on *The Dam Busters* started in early April on location near Skegness, on the Lincolnshire coast. The sequences we were shooting were the tests and trials of the 'bouncing' bombs, at first dismal failures and then, after Barnes Wallis had hurriedly made alterations to his calculations, final heart-stopping success. For a week I filmed on the bleak Gibraltar Point with Michael Redgrave, who was to give such a memorable performance as Wallis. He and I, and my bomb-aimer and various Ministry officials, were shown watching the trials, which were carried out with a specially adapted Wellington bomber, fitted to carry the huge, round, flat-sided prototype bombs. Wallis knew that this aircraft could carry this weird load.

He had had trouble in getting the use of the plane, which was then the RAF workhorse most in demand. After various abortive requests, he finally waited for hours in the office of a harassed Air Ministry official to put his plea.

'What possible reason could I put to the Minister for you to have the use of a Wellington?'

'Well, perhaps if you said that I designed it?' was the mild reply.

He got his wish!

The actual shots of the Wellington bomber dropping its huge dam-busters were cleverly contrived by Michael Anderson from some rather poor-quality archive film shot in 1943 during the original tests. He framed it in such a way as to make it appear that it was seen by us through our binoculars, which explained the difference in quality of the 1943 material.

Michael Redgrave was a joy to work with. A shy, quiet and private man, I saw little of him away from our work but on the set he was such a professional and a marvellous actor. We got on splendidly together.

From Skegness we moved to Lincoln, which was to be our base while we worked at the nearby airfields at Hemswell and Scampton, the original wartime home of 617 Squadron RAF – the Dam Busters, formed and led by Wing-Commander Guy Gibson, DSO and bar and, later, VC for the raid on the dams. Scampton had not changed much since Gibson's days there, except that the Lancasters were gone, replaced by Lincoln and Vulcan bombers. The hangars, briefing rooms, living quarters, messes and offices were more or less unchanged.

I spent many days with all sorts of people who had known Gibson because I was anxious to make my portrayal of him in the film as accurate as possible. I learned his mannerisms, stance and walk and discovered that he wore a German Mae West life-jacket instead of a British one, and wore a Boy Scout badge on a narrow leather wrist-band. He was an inveterate pipe-smoker and enjoyed his mug of beer. Fortunately, he was short and stocky, so I had no height problems on this movie!

I and Michael Anderson and others stayed at the old White Hart Hotel close to the great Lincoln Cathedral, and on my first day there I was joined by a most important member of the cast: the dog who was to play Nigger, Guy Gibson's beloved black Labrador.

The dog we were using was a highly-trained Army dog whose task was sniffing out land-mines. Nigger – for that, strangely enough, was his official Army name too – arrived complete with his corporal handler. Now, I knew enough about trained dogs to know that they will only work for one person, and that if his handler remained with us Nigger would always look to him for orders. So Bill Whittaker, our company manager and associate producer, managed to get approval from his Army base for Nigger to be left with me, and the corporal returned to his unit.

From then on it was up to me to gain the dog's complete confidence and liking and for the next couple of weeks he scarcely ever left my side. This meant getting the hotel's permission for him to become a resident, which was given somewhat dubiously and only on condition that he stayed in my room and did not enter the public rooms. This was no problem for me, and for his bed I gave him my old duffle coat which I always carried in my car for Baron. Nigger settled down very contentedly on this.

I must admit to some trepidation about Nigger's house-training, especially as he snuffled territorially at all carpets he had never seen or walked on before. After all, he was a kennel dog, and had never been indoors. But that intelligent animal made not a single mistake the whole time he was with me. To be sure I walked him out as frequently and as late as possible and put his bed in my tiled bathroom when I was downstairs dining, but I need not have worried. He never let me down.

Nigger was brilliant to work with – a lot of actors could have learned from him. Shown by me what to do at one rehearsal for a shot, and he was always dead on cue with his reactions and movements. There was never a re-take for any fault of Nigger's.

Except once. . . .

We were filming a very atmospheric and gripping scene at Scampton which showed all the aircrews clustered in groups on the grass outside Gibson's office immediately prior to take-off. Some were standing around chatting, some sprawled on the grass, some played with a cricket ball. It was a moment of great tension in the story.

I as Gibson was scheduled to walk with Nigger amongst the crews, having a word here and there. Nigger refused point-blank to go near a particular spot, and cowered back. Even when I put him on a leash, he still would not budge and we had to leave him out of the scene. Did some instinct tell him that the spot was in fact where Gibson's actual dog was buried? There had been a memorial stone to mark the place, but we'd removed it for the duration of the film-making.

Our first morning at Scampton was memorable particularly for the arrival of the five Lancaster bombers which had been reconstructed for our use. When they appeared, droning specks in the distance gradually increasing their sound to a shattering roar as they passed low overhead in perfect wing-tip to wing-tip V-formation, not only ourselves but every RAF officer and man turned excited eyes to the sky.

The black war planes wheeled several times as they 'beat-up' the airfield within feet of the hangar roofs, obviously showing off to the cheering, waving crowd below. Then, scorning the runway, they landed still in V-formation on the grass. What a display; what a moment!

As we only had five operational Lancasters, five was the maximum that could ever be seen in the air together, but for ground shots on the airfield the Lancasters were parked in the foreground and the background was filled in by Lincoln bombers, very similar aircraft.

When the Lancasters were not required at Scampton they were off with the second unit flying over Lake Windermere and another lake in Wales, either with cameras in the aircraft showing a plane's-eye-view or being photographed from our camera-aeroplane.

All this on a budget that would hardly suffice for a home movie today!

We were lucky with the weather and our location work in Lincolnshire came in under schedule. I loved every day of our time there – especially when, after some rudimentary instruction, I was allowed to start up the four motors for one shot and drive the aircraft round the perimeter track and on to the runway, winding the speed up to the beginning of take-off. I must admit, however, that there was a RAF instructor crouching by my seat and telling me what to do.

After a few days' break at home, mostly gardening, in mid-May I started studio work at Elstree.

My first few days in the studios were spent strapped into the pilot's seat in a Lancaster fuselage. The whole contraption was mounted on a metal pedestal to which it was fixed by a sort of ball-and-socket device powered electrically so that the aircraft canted upwards, downwards and sideways in response to my control column and steering, exactly as if we were airborne. It was all very ingenious and realistic.

The greatest difficulty for me and for other crew members who had to be photographed in the aircraft was lack of space. The Lancaster fuselage was cramped and bristling with instrumentation at any time, but with the addition of the camera, lights, cables, microphones, camera and sound crews there was scarcely room to breathe. And it was dreadfully hot, too, as we sweated in our helmets and Mae West jackets.

It was I, perforce, who spent most of the time in these conditions. Once I was in my seat, there was no means of getting out again until all the equipment had been removed, so for days on end I was strapped in by about 8.15 am, released for lunch and re-incarcerated from about 2 pm until the end of shooting at 6 pm. The needs of nature occasionally caused total chaos and a lengthy hold-up.

However, I was saved from boredom during the long waits between set-ups by the presence of a RAF flying instructor who was there mainly to ensure that I carried out all the right procedures as we took off, climbed, dived or dodged searchlights during the long low-level flight to and from the dams.

Between takes the instructor patiently taught me as much as he could about the business of flying a four-engined plane, and, once I began to get the hang of it, he would present me with various situations and check my responses.

'Right, you are ten minutes from base. What do you do now?' I would then try to do what he had taught me, including reporting my position over the radio, losing height, probably banking around the airfield, giving my flight engineer instructions regarding the flaps and speed, and so on up to the moment of landing. It was really interesting for me and passed the time wonderfully. I reckoned I could have almost taken over in an emergency – at least, in a studio mock-up emergency!

Filming *The Dam Busters* was a very happy experience. For a start, we all knew we were making a fine picture and the rushes each day confirmed that knowledge. We had a marvellous script, a tremendous true story, a good cast and a great director – plus a fine director of photography, Erwin Hillier. The Elstree technicians working with us were a grand bunch, and there was never any discord during the entire period of shooting.

The younger actors, especially the air-crews, had nearly all (like me) seen some kind of military service, either during the war or on National Service, and between us all we created some of the breezy, friendly atmosphere of an actual RAF squadron. One possible exception was Robert Shaw, who played my sergeant flight-engineer. He was a curt, morose sort of chap – at least at that time – and rather distanced himself from the others.

I lived at the flat during the week, Kitty joining me always on Thursdays when we usually dined out with friends. I supped most evenings at some restaurant or other, and my list of favourite haunts was lengthy: Chez Luba, the Caprice, the Mirabelle, Les Ambassadeurs, Don Juan and the Milroy Club were just a few of the places where I had accounts.

I was also nearing the last year of my seven-year contract with Associated British, and discussions with Robert Clark and Robert Lennard had already started about my future with the corporation. Then, at the end of May, I received a phone call from Darryl Zanuck, President of Twentieth Century-Fox and one of the last great moguls of the movie industry. I practically stood to attention as I spoke to him.

He told me he was sending me a book named *A Man Called Peter*, written by Catherine Marshall about her late husband the Rev. Peter Marshall, Chaplain to the Senate and pastor of the famous Presbyterian so-called Church of the Presidents in Washington DC. He wanted to know if I would play Peter Marshall in the film then being scripted, based on the book. My reaction to the idea was to be discussed from then on with Lew Schreiber, the head of the Fox Studios in California.

Naturally, I could scarcely wait to get my hands on the book!

The next day it was handed to me by Basil Litchfield, who was in charge of the Fox offices in London. The following Sunday I spent nearly the whole day reading *A Man Called Peter*.

The book, a hugely successful best-seller in America, was an account of the life and work of Peter Marshall, who had started his teenage earning days as a shipyard apprentice in Scotland and then, as the result of a near-fatal accident, realised that his vocation was in the

Church and went to America to work his way through a religious seminary, taking on all manner of manual jobs such as road-making. He was to become perhaps the most famous and loved churchman in the United States. He was a warm, down-to-earth man and a magnificent preacher. Such was his oratorical power that his sermons, preached each Sunday to a packed congregation, were relayed by loudspeaker to the crowds outside who were unable to find seats in the church.

It was a fascinating and gripping story told very much through the eyes and heart of a woman, his widow, but perhaps tending to be a little sugary and sentimental.

There was certainly a potential film in it, but I was rather apprehensive about the attitude that the screenwriter would take to it. It could easily become a schmaltzy love story rather than the hard-hitting tale of an earthy realist with the gift of great, almost poetic oratory.

I phoned Lew Schreiber and told him of my doubts. He responded by sending me the latest screen treatment of the book. This turned out to be even longer than the book itself and gave no indication of what form the screenplay would take. Again, I phoned to say that I was not persuaded. It was not the only time that I had practically talked myself out of a job. I had once, when first approached, said that I didn't think I could properly play the Scot in *The Hasty Heart*!

Then the producer assigned to *A Man Called Peter*, Sam Engel, had a bright idea. He sent me a package of recordings of Peter Marshall's sermons, actually made at church services.

I listened to these enraptured, especially by one, 'Were you There?', a description of the Crucifixion and the reactions of all those present at Calvary. I had never heard anything so inspiring, moving and graphic as those sermons, not even Churchill's greatest wartime speeches. To this day I occasionally pick one out and listen enthralled, fearful lest I should wear the record away by too-frequent use. They must be unique.

I then put a call through to Sam Engel to ask if any of the sermons were to be included in the proposed film. He assured me that the script was scheduled to include about twenty minutes of Peter Marshall's oratory in the pulpit.

That was enough for me: to be privileged to speak Marshall's words in public was a bait few actors would resist. I told Sam that in that case I would do the film unseen – in other words, never mind the screenplay so long as some sermons were in it.

But I still added one proviso: I was unsure of my ability to capture the fine and rhetorical power of the original speaker, or to emulate his lilting, slightly Americanised Lowland Scottish burr. I wanted to test myself on film, and only then would I give an affirmative answer. To this the rather surprised Engel agreed. It must have been the first time he had heard of a film actor demanding a screen test before accepting a plum role.

So it was that I asked Elstree for the use of an empty sound-stage, a lectern, a camera crew and a sound crew, plus a few electricians with some very basic lighting equipment, and one evening after the day's work on *The Dam Busters*, I and my little group gathered in the gloom of an unused stage.

I merely told the crews that I was going to read something from the lectern and that I wanted to be filmed in a medium shot simply picking me out in the surrounding darkness. None of the men had any idea what I was going to talk about – in a sense, they were to be my congregation.

In a short time all was ready, and I began to read my half-learned sermon. I had chosen a very moving excerpt from one of Peter Marshall's orations, which lasted about three minutes.

As I reached the end, there was absolute silence for some moments and then I noticed that the focus-puller and the boom-operator had tears running down their faces. 'Christ! That was marvellous,' said one of them. 'What's it for?'

I then explained what I had been trying to do. They were all unanimous in assuring me that it had worked.

To the cameraman I said there was no need to print what had been filmed. Why waste money? I knew now that I could do it, and what my next film was to be.

By the time we finished filming *The Dam Busters* at the end of July I had signed my contract for *A Man Called Peter* with Twentieth Century-Fox, and had even filmed some of the Scottish sequences in the picture with Jill Esmond (who played my mother), directed by George More O'Ferrall.

While I had so much to look forward to, I was really sad when work ended on *The Dam Busters*. There was an end-of-schooldays feeling amongst those of us who had worked so long and happily together. Above all, I hoped to work with Michael Anderson again. While we knew that we had made a good picture, we little realised what a classic British film *The Dam Busters* would become when it was completed. Even 'The Dam Busters March' by Eric Coates is still a familiar and stirring piece of music today.

During all this activity at Elstree there were occasional breaks for me when I was either at home, mostly gardening or working in my office with Jill, or was involved in multifarious interests elsewhere.

One such was an evening when I presented Marlene Dietrich to her adoring audience at the Café Royal. She turned her talents to cabaret and was singing, dancing, and chatting her way through a programme that drew capacity audiences. Each night she had arranged to be introduced by one of her many friends and admirers. The first had been Michael Wilding, and she chose me to be the second. After the show we all went in a gay party to the Milroy – I use 'gay' in its traditional sense!

Whenever I was free to do so I went racing with Freddy Weil and in July we attended our first International Horse Show at the White City arena. This and the Horse of the Year Show in October became annual occasions for our calendar of events.

In the White City days members were able to book tables on the terraces and dine while watching all the excitements of the show. On the first evening we were invited to have coffee with Prince Bernhard of the Netherlands and his two daughters, who were apparently great fans of *Robin Hood*; and on the second Kitty and our guests, the Hall-Caines, were thrilled by a wonderful competition for the King George V Cup which was finally won by a German, narrowly beating one of my equestrian heroes, Alan Oliver.

We also made several trips to view houses and farms, since I had decided I wanted more land, land I could actually work. Some properties were as far afield as Sussex, but none was right; either the house did not attract us or the land was not suitable. But I was intent on farming somewhere eventually.

When my work on *The Dam Busters* was finished, Leslie Frewin and I flew to Belgium for a film and music festival at Knokke-le-Zoute, where *Le Lit* (now called *Secrets d'Alcove*) was screened. After a couple of hectic days of receptions, dinners, parties and press and TV interviews there, I was driven on to Paris where I had dinner in the charming old Abbey restaurant at Feucherolle with Henri Decoin and Nicole Courcel, flying home the next day in time for lunch at Wayside.

Soon after this Kitty and I flew to Norway as the guests of the Norwegian Jockey Club. I had been asked if I could run one of my horses in the Polio Cup, the big event of the meeting which was to benefit charity, but I did not have a horse suitable for the race. However, I was still invited to come to Oslo and present the cup.

We landed at Fornebu airport, where we were each presented with a large bouquet of flowers by girls in national costume. Apparently it is a Scandinavian custom to garland men as well as women, and a very delightful one too. We were met by Kaare and Mabel Anderssen, friends of the Hall-Caines, and they escorted us to the Grand Hotel where we were to stay and then on to a press reception. After the local première of *Rob Roy*, which was a great success, we then all had dinner at the Queen Restaurant.

Next day we enjoyed a splendid day's racing and saw the Polio Cup won by a horse appropriately called Norse.

On the following day we visited the Kon Tiki raft and some Viking ships, and lunched at the restaurant set at the head of the spectacular Olympic Ski Jump. Finally we left Norway and arrived home to be greeted by the latest additions to our family: five pups that our corgi bitch Tinkerbell had produced that morning!

The next week or so was spent in preparing for my departure for America to make *A Man Called Peter*. Visas had to be arranged for Kitty, Peter and his nanny, who were to follow me out as soon as I had found a suitable home to rent in California, and I also had to secure my work permit.

On Sunday 25 August, I flew out to New York en route for Hollywood.

12

A Kind of Miracle

After a one-day stop in New York – perhaps the Polar flight direct between London and Los Angeles was not yet operating at that time – I took the all-night flight to LA and was met by Milton Pickman who drove me to his home, where my advance baggage sent off by sea three weeks before had already arrived.

During a pleasant few days with Kay and Milton he introduced me to a particularly American phenomenon: a business management company. I don't know if such organisations exist elsewhere in the world, but certainly mine took most of the problems from my temporary stay in California. I wanted to find a house to rent for nearly four months and already this company had a list of properties for me to see and a cook-housekeeper standing by ready to start work the moment I settled on a place.

The business management company also arranged my car rentals, credit cards, accounts at various stores, shops and restaurants. It paid my bills and, finally, submitted my tax return just before my departure. I'm sure if I'd had trouble sleeping or learning my lines they'd have done that for me too.

I looked at a number of properties and settled for 708 North Rodeo Drive. It had a nice garden ('yard' to Americans) and a concrete tennis court which Kitty and I could use and which would make a secure playground for Peter. I spent a weekend sorting out our heavy advance baggage and then was joined there by Sarah Quigley, our cook-house-keeper. English-born, she was a good cook and very competent, although she and Nanny were rather wary of each other.

Meanwhile I had also been to Twentieth Century-Fox studios to meet the producer, Sam Engel, and the director Henry (Bobby) Koster. I could not have been more fortunate in my two guides and mentors. Sam and his sweet wife Ruth became good friends of mine and Bobby, who had an impressive list of film credits, was perhaps the kindest and most gentle director I would ever know.

Sam gave me a copy of the final screenplay and I soon found that he'd kept his word: Peter Marshall's sermons were the central theme of the whole script. We also went through the schedule, which was to begin on location work in Atlanta, Georgia, and the cast list. Jean Peters was to be my co-star as Catherine Marshall.

I was also shown my dressing-room suite at the studio: once again somebody had tried hard to make me feel at home. The two main rooms had some very English-looking chintz covers, while the walls were hung with prints of 'Olde Worlde' English pubs and inns. The previous occupant had been Victor Mature and I wondered what motif had been chosen for him – a Roman-villa-look, probably.

I had three weeks in Hollywood before we were due to start our location-shooting, and most of the days were spent in preparation for the picture: script conferences, wardrobe fittings and all the usual pre-production activities. I had also been able to get everything ready for the family's arrival. We now had a house, a cook, a daily and two cars all laid on, and a nice stay in California for Kitty and Peter to look forward to. When I met them at the airport Peter was bouncing around excitedly, but Kitty and Nanny were tired out after their long journey.

Within a few days I was flying to Atlanta, convinced that we were about to make a movie which could not only be successful in a material sense but also help and inspire a lot of people. And from the very first day our unit seemed to be a particularly harmonious one. Although a film sound stage is not normally a venue for piety, nor is a film unit usually noted for an air of serenity, as the shooting progressed to the Hollywood studio interiors, so the air of general good nature increased.

The subject matter of *A Man Called Peter* seemed to have cast a spell over everybody concerned with the picture. Shooting was by no means leisurely, but we were all imbued with a team spirit even greater than was usual on the studio floor. Even the extras abandoned their card games, their knitting and their habitual bored detachment during the inevitable periods of inactivity. They watched, they listened – they were interested.

Word got about, too, that something was happening. Every day actors, technicians and staff from all over the huge Fox studio complex stood around our sound stage, quietly watching and listening. Marilyn Monroe, working on a nearby stage, was often amongst them and was once seen to be crying during one of Marshall's sermons.

And unknown to most people, a real-life human drama was being played out as well . . .

One of the principal characters in the film was that of an autocratic lady, an unbending pillar of Peter Marshall's church in Washington. To play it, Twentieth Century particularly wanted a certain well-known actress ideal for the part. However, when she was approached she refused the offer, pointing out that she was now badly handicapped: as the result of a dreadful motor accident, injuries to her pelvis and legs made it impossible for her ever to walk again.

It was suggested that she could perfectly well play the part in her wheelchair, but she again refused. She felt she had neither the stamina nor the confidence to tackle the task.

One day Sam Engel invited her to visit our set as a guest; it was at a time when one of Peter Marshall's sermons was being filmed.

The lady sat in her chair amongst the litter of studio paraphernalia, her handsome features and vivid blue eyes composed, totally absorbed. When the long master shot of the sermon had been completed she turned to Sam and told him that her faith and her will to work had been restored to her. She *would* play the role, but not in a wheelchair; she would walk.

And she did, at first haltingly and painfully with the aid of two sticks, then finally moving confidently and briskly with only a light cane.

For Marjorie Rambeau a moment of a movie had brought faith and the determination to overcome her handicap.

From people I have met all over the world, and from letters I have received, I know that Miss Rambeau has not been the only one stirred and aided by *A Man Called Peter* and the example and preaching power of Peter Marshall.

At a time when there is so much disquiet and discussion about the influence of films, TV and theatre on the activities and attitudes of the public, perhaps this one instance may serve as a reminder that the effects are not always detrimental.

My flight to Atlanta, Georgia, with the rest of the unit was in a chartered plane, and I was surprised that Jean Peters – my co-star whom I had not yet even met – was not with us, since I knew we were starting work together the next day. Bobby Koster and Sam Engel were already there.

I arrived at the hotel in the afternoon and in the early evening I was told that Jean had arrived by special plane on her own with just a female companion. What I didn't know was they had been the sole occupants of a large TWA Constellation provided for them by Howard Hughes, who owned the airline. But then, nobody had thought to tell me about Jean's relationship with the eccentric tycoon.

As a normal courtesy I phoned her suite to ask if she would like to have dinner with me so that we could meet, but her companion, who took the call, told me that Miss Peters was very tired and would not be leaving her rooms that evening. This I quite understood and thought no more about it.

We finally met in the morning at our location at Covington, where Peter Marshall had been the pastor of his first little country church and where he had met his future wife, Catherine.

I found Jean to be a lovely young woman, ravishingly pretty, intelligent and great fun to be with, though we rarely chatted except when we were actually rehearsing or shooting. She and her rather formidable and taciturn female companion took themselves off to their trailer, and never sat with the rest of us.

Everything went well with our first day's exteriors, and the weather was lovely.

That evening I again phoned to ask if Jean would care to dine with me, but got the same response as the previous day. By then the message was quite clear: Miss Peters wanted to be alone. And this was to be the pattern throughout our filming. Jean never left her trailer-caravan, even for meals, except when actually working on set.

Three days later I and the unit flew to Washington DC, and I moved into the old Mayflower Hotel. Years later I was to discover that Washington was one of the most impressive and beautifully-laid-out cities in the world, but on that trip I had no chance to explore it. What I *did* discover was that the climate there can be horrendously hot and steamy. The area was then in the throes of a heat-wave, for some reason or other the air-conditioning at the hotel was not working, and I spent miserable nights sleepless and pyjama-less in a virtual pool of sweat, gulping jugs of iced water.

On my first evening there I was visited by a charming, good-looking Englishman who told me that he was either the First or Second (I forget which) Secretary at the British Embassy and that if I needed anything while in Washington I should call him. We had a drink together, and I have since often wondered, could he have been the infamous McLean who later defected to Moscow?

When I got to our first location site in the morning I was staggered to see a look-alike for Jean Peters, wearing Jean's film clothes and all ready to start filming with me. I was then told that Jean would not be joining us in Washington at all, but that her double would take her place. Jean had no dialogue in the Washington location scenes, so this was quite feasible, but to my mind pretty extraordinary.

Then the mystery was explained to me:

Jean had been briefly married to a young Washingtonian whom I was told she had met in Rome when making *Three Coins in the Fountain*, but now she had come under the spell of the fabulously rich and powerful Howard Hughes whom she eventually married. That was the reason for the TWA planes, for the ever-present female 'minder', for her solitariness and for her non-appearance in Washington. Mr Hughes was evidently a persistent and demanding wooer; he was also pretty formidable.

So I got on with my work in Washington without Jean.

On my first Sunday there I met Catherine Marshall, and together we went to a service at the New York Avenue Church, scene of Peter Marshall's thrall over his parishioners. It was an eerie experience for me in some ways, to be with the widow of the man that I was trying to portray and to be in his church where so many of the congregation would probably still hear the echo of his voice. Catherine, a pretty woman, was charming and soon put me at my ease.

Once back in California I had a two-week break before we started filming again, so Kitty, Peter and I were able to spend time with some of our old friends, especially Milton and Kay Pickman and Walt and Lillian Disney.

By now Nanny Pitcher had got to know her way round Beverly Hills and set off daily on her determined walks with Peter. We had feared that she might be lured to stay there when she learned of the enormous salaries that English nannies could command, but we need not have worried – she was far too devoted to Peter.

Our first scenes at the Twentieth Century-Fox studios were location shots on the back-lot where the young Peter Marshall was preaching and holding an open-air service, his pulpit a farm-cart and his congregation clustered on wooden 'bleachers'. A hundred or so extras, mostly young people, made this a pleasant introduction for me into the task of delivering a sermon, since this was my first attempt with a live audience. They were so attentive and receptive they were for all the world exactly like a real congregation. They actually applauded spontaneously at the end of the first master take. As I was leaving at the end of the day, one young chap came up to me and said, 'Mr Todd, you know what I like about you? You got balls!' I had never had any reason to doubt this, but it was nice to have it so enthusiastically confirmed . . .

It was also the first day I had met dear Harry Baum, my stand-in, who was to remain my friend and confidant for years.

Harry was something of a fixture at the Fox studios, almost a permanent employee and known and liked by everybody. He worked mainly because he loved the studio atmosphere and hated to be idle, even though he was reasonably well-off from the income he derived from a small apartment block, in which he had invested when property had been cheap, and from a generous disability pension he had as an Army veteran. He had contracted severe arthritis during his service, and walked with a limp. Divorced, he shared his own apartment with a pretty young daughter whom he worshipped, and was the sweetest, kindest of men. His talisman and his greatest pride was always his glossy next-year's Cadillac. In 1954 he was already driving the latest 1955 model.

Harry did not see his job as simply standing in for me on the set when a scene was being lit, but reckoned that his whole day was at my service as companion, friend and general factotum. He became expert at brewing tea English-style, and saw that I was never without a good strong 'cuppa' when I needed it. He kept my dressing-room suite stocked with drinks and cold snacks, and would rush there as soon as work finished to have a long, iced vodka-and-tonic ready for me. During some of his unavoidable away-from-the-studio errands, Harry arranged a stand-in to stand in for *him*, with no demur from the production manager. When Kitty arrived he even took her shopping and showed her the layout of the Beverly Hills district.

On later films, at times when I was alone in Hollywood, he would always ask me if I was alone that evening and would I like him to keep me company at dinner? Several times when I had invited a girl to dinner, he came along too, as a sort of chaperon against the inquisitive prying of columnists' legmen who abounded in every main restaurant in the area.

Harry was also well-versed in some of the least salubrious activities that were not uncommon in Hollywood . . .

At the end of that first day's filming, as I was leaving the set, an assistant director gave me my call-sheet for the following morning and then asked me if there was any one of the extras that I particularly wanted called back.

'No. Why?'

He seemed quite pained by my dumbness. 'I mean, is there any broad that you fancy? Would you like someone to have a drink with you in your room now?'

A few minutes later, as I changed and downed the drink that Harry had prepared, he told me that this was a common practice at all the studios. They liked to keep their leading actors happy and there were lots of girls who were prepared to ensure their continued employment by being accommodating. Perhaps if I had been playing a pirate and not a parson my response might have been less incredulous.

Filming continued happily right on schedule, and eventually the day approached for me to work on one of the most crucial moments of the picture: Peter Marshall's sermon to the US Navy cadets at the Naval Academy at Annapolis. We had spent a day there during our stay in Washington DC, and I had counted myself most fortunate to have visited this beautiful place with its vast layout of grand Georgian-style buildings, pretty adjoining township, lovely grounds and parkland and the immense chapel. I suppose I am the only layman ever to have preached to a huge congregation of intent, serious-faced, crop-haired, uniformed cadets in that unforgettable place.

Peter Marshall had been invited to deliver a sermon there on the day that chanced to be the eve of Japan's attack on Pearl Harbor. As he watched from the vestry door and saw this blue-clad horde filing in to the chapel and then scanned the sea of young faces, he had a premonition of something dreadful. He saw death there.

He felt impelled to change the text of his sermon and asked the chaplain's permission to do so. This granted, he delivered a marvellous, spontaneous, unhesitant and uplifting peroration on the meaning of death. One of the moving stories he told concerned an ailing little boy who asked, 'Mummy, what is it like to die? Does it hurt?'

His sermon covered five pages of closely-typed script and took nine minutes to deliver. I was told that it was probably the longest single speech in the history of motion pictures. At Annapolis I did not have to learn it by heart but read it from the pulpit as nearly as possible in the way I would eventually speak it in the studios, when the camera would be on me only. At the Naval Academy we had three cameras rolling, one facing straight on to the congregation, one at a side angle and one long shot of me. It was an unforgettable occasion for me.

The studio scene had been left until the end of shooting and, because of the length of the sermon, it was scheduled to take three days. I spent several evenings learning it, aided by a tape recording that I made and which I listened to even when having supper, last thing at night in bed and first thing in the morning. I believe that Kitty too would have been word-perfect if tested!

On the morning when we started shooting on this sermon, I managed to get through the master shot of the entire speech without a fluff or a hesitation, much to Bobby Koster's amazement. Hollywood was perhaps not used to theatre actors who could learn large chunks of dialogue. My nervous tension and total concentration may have contributed to the realism that came to the screen. After all, for Peter Marshall himself it had been a spontaneous, unrehearsed speech.

Then we filmed excerpts from different angles and in close-up. These were easy for me as none was very long. By early afternoon we had completed the entire sequence. So I then had two days off, since nothing else had been scheduled. I think I must have been quite popular with everybody except the extras, who lost two days' work!

By the end of November we had completed all the main work on *A Man Called Peter*. On the last day of shooting Bobby Koster gave an end-of-picture party at his house for the entire unit and most of the cast. We were all surprised but quite delighted when Jean Peters turned up. We had a very jolly supper but then on the stroke of ten o'clock, long before anyone else was thinking of leaving, a large black limousine hove up to the front door and she was whisked away.

A week later, after doing some post-synching sessions and still photos, I flew to Washington again for some added scenes, arriving back in Los Angeles just in time to greet my Associated British boss Robert Clark, who had come to California for discussions with Twentieth Century-Fox about a proposal that studio chief Lew Schreiber had put to me.

On his first evening Mr Clark had supper with us at the house, and the next morning I took him to the studios to meet Lew.

I had already been told that Fox wanted me back next year to play Sir Walter Raleigh, with Bette Davis as Queen Elizabeth, in *The Virgin Queen*, subject to the consent of Associated British. Not only this, but Fox was prepared to enter into a four-picture deal with me over the next four years.

To my great relief Robert Clark agreed to the proposal, and the deal was confirmed. Imagine my excitement! I now had the guarantee of four major American films over the next few years in addition to any I would make for ABPC or others in Europe. I was indeed a most happy fellah . . . Moreover I also had the prospect of working with Bette Davis, whom I had always regarded as being the greatest of them all. There was great jubilation in the Todd household that day!

That same night I had still further cause for celebration. At 3 am Sam Engel phoned me to say that he had just had a call from Darryl Zanuck, who had seen a rough-cut of *A Man Called Peter* and was raving about it. I even had a congratulatory note from the great man himself the next morning.

I spent a few more days dubbing sound at the studios and having talks with Lew Schreiber about my Fox contract before we left for New York on our way home. We lunched there with a delighted Milton Pickman before boarding our BOAC night flight for London, with just a few days left to organise our Christmas at home.

I scarcely needed any presents myself – I had been given so much already that year.

13

Good Queen Bette

During the first week of 1955 I signed my contract for *The Virgin Queen* in Bob Lennard's office and on the same day we took Peter to his first Bertram Mills Circus at Olympia. He had a marvellous time. Our seats were rather prominent ring-side ones and the clowns paid a lot of attention to him. This was fine for him, and the Olympia Circus became an annual event for us. We all loved it – except that in later years, when Peter insisted on spending time in the fun-fair after the show, I felt it necessary to accompany him for his safety, and after half an hour of carousels, big wheels, dodgem-cars and chairoplanes I invariably came away feeling decidedly air-sick.

The next day I had a meeting with Basil Stebbings to discuss my finances, future contracts and the purchase of a farm. With my income expanding annually, I was more than ever anxious to buy land and launch into an agrarian life. It was a deep-felt yearning in me; I had spent most of my boyhood on my grandfather's land at Brecart in Northern Ireland, and since that place did not come to me – just as well, probably, since the legendary curse of Brecart might have fallen upon me – I was determined to buy my own farmland.

In this project I was guided by Paul Rosewarne, a charming and wise Henley estate agent who agreed to act for me in the sale of Wayside and the purchase of a property and, later, to act as my land agent. We visited a number of possible places but there was no time to make a decision, and I decided to leave things until later in the year.

I also had to be in London almost daily, getting my work permit and our visas for America, also having meetings to discuss the possibility of making *The Man Who Never Was*, an intriguing wartime story, with André Hakim, a producer, his wife Susan (Darryl Zanuck's daughter) and Ronald Neame, the director.

Three days before I left for California, I was asked to join Robert Clark, Michael Anderson and some RAF chiefs at Elstree to see a running of *The Dam Busters*. What a marvellous film! The modest Mickey Anderson was overwhelmed with congratulations from the entire, professionally critical audience.

So I flew from Heathrow Airport content in the certainty that I had one good picture yet to be premièred.

In Los Angeles I was met by Harry Baum complete with his latest gleaming new Cadillac convertible. It seemed only a few days since he had seen us off at the same airport in December, and here he was again, smiling delightedly and once more taking complete charge of my welfare. There could not have been a more unique stand-in than Harry, and Twentieth Century-Fox seemed to have given him *carte blanche* as a kind of roving ambassador.

This time I was booked into a suite at the Beverly-Wilshire Hotel until a suitable house to rent could be found for me, and in the morning I drove to the studios to meet Bobby Koster – who to my great joy was to direct *The Virgin Queen* – and Charles Brackett, the producer, a delightful and learned man with a remarkable record as writer and producer who was currently the President of the Motion Picture Academy. So I was in good hands!

We went through the script together and I was told who was to be in the cast. To my surprise Walter Raleigh's wife was to be Joan Collins, who had just been put under contract by Fox to play the part. I had never seen her on the screen and knew her only from brief glimpses of her quite startling vital statistics in the restaurant at Pinewood Studios or at film premières. Not at all my idea of a demure English rose and scion of an ancient and noble family.

I should have had more regard for Charles Brackett's wisdom and good taste. In the event, Joan was splendid: a real professional, a very competent actress, a nice person and excellent in the role of Mistress Throckmorton.

Others in the cast were Herbert Marshall, Robert Douglas, Dan O'Herlihy – who had recently scored a great success as Robinson Crusoe – and as many expatriate British actors as Fox could unearth.

Evidently Charles Brackett considered that I did not entirely have the ideal features for the adventurous Raleigh, for it was decided that I should have a kind of reverse nose-job done on me by the make-up department. My rather insignificant hooter was to be built up, and after various tests a number of small rubbery falsies were produced, one of which was glued to my snub snout each day. They were very subtle, but did the trick and were undetectable in camera. And for the first time in my life I was able to see my nose without going cross-eyed.

I was not the only one to undergo physical alteration: Bette's hairline was shaved back an inch or two to represent the apparent near-baldness of Queen Elizabeth I, and Joan's ample bosoms were squashed into tight, ribbed bodices.

As soon as I started on the film with Bette Davis, I realised that I was working with the supreme professional. Always first on the set in the morning, after long and tedious make-up and wardrobe sessions; always word-perfect; always full of energy and never flagging even at the end of a hard day – she was exemplary. I had heard that she could be fearsome if things did not go as she wanted, but soon I found that although she certainly did not suffer fools gladly, she was never unpleasant in the way some lesser actors and actresses can be (usually through an inferiority complex). Fortunately, she and Bobby Koster and I got on splendidly together and the film raced through its tight schedule.

Two examples of Bette's good humour and professionalism occurred during the shooting of one of her most difficult and wordy scenes: a council chamber conference during which she had to deliver a long and impassioned speech. All went well except for a few seconds after the harangue when a very old English actor playing the Lord Chamberlain was supposed to interrupt with a simple line of dialogue. The poor old chap simply couldn't get it right, and either broke in too early or too late or completely forgot his line. Take after take was beginning to wear down even the ebullient Bette. After about the sixth take, Bobby Koster drew Bette and me aside and asked if we minded doing just one more shot, only this time there would be no film in the camera. He simply had not the heart to dismiss the unfortunate octogenarian or to berate him in front of everybody. Such was Bobby's kindness, and Bette's too, because she readily understood and agreed.

So we went through the sham, with the Lord Chamberlain fluffing his line as usual. It did not seem to worry Bette that she would have to do the whole thing again the next day with a different actor. At the end of the shot Koster called out 'Cut! Print!' and went up to the old man to thank him for a great day's work and to congratulate him on a fine performance. The actor beamed happily and left the stage.

Half an hour later there was a phone call for Koster from the main gate:

'Did you have an old guy called Smith working on your picture?'

'Yes.'

'Well, he's just dropped dead.'

So, thanks to Bobby and Bette, one man departed this life on cloud nine and not in misery.

The very next day, as we re-shot this scene, it was my turn to deserve Bette's fury. Just after that long take had been printed, a worried continuity girl came to me and said, 'Richard, where's your Garter chain? You had it on yesterday, didn't you, in the other takes?'

'My God – you're right! Oh, hell, I'll have to tell Bette.'

When I nervously confessed my mistake I expected a tirade, but Bette simply glared, shouted 'You bastard!' and went through the whole piece again even better than before.

I really loved working with her. In some of the dramatic scenes I was able to let fly with everything I had, knowing she would come back with even more.

A few days after we had started on the picture Kitty joined me at 917 North Rexford Drive, the very attractive and comfortable house I had rented, complete with several laden avocado trees in the garden and Alma, a huge, cheerful black lady who was our cook-housekeeper. Kitty was rather shaken after a dreadful flight from New York through electrical storms. One engine had caught fire and after an unscheduled stop at Denver they had changed planes.

The film had so far concentrated on all Bette Davis's scenes because she had to be released early to make another picture, and on the night she finished she gave a dinner party for us at her house. I then had a two-week break to leave me free to go to New York for the opening of *A Man Called Peter*, which had been rushed out at amazing speed – all part of the Hollywood expertise – to catch the Easter release nationwide.

The film was premièred at the Roxy Theatre and received quite startling reviews. Not since *The Hasty Heart* years before had I read such praise for a picture of mine and all concerned. It was a smash hit. We had sat in El Morocco Club late that night with Pickman, waiting on edge until a PR man arrived with an armful of early editions of the papers – a nerve-racking ritual in America after the first night of any show. Then we could scarce believe what we read, and a great sense of relief flooded over me. The good reviews were later repeated all over the country. To be honest, I had been nervous about the critical response and, despite Zanuck's confidence, I knew that his sales force had been somewhat at a loss to know how to sell the film. After all, a story about a parson, including some twenty minutes of sermons, was not exactly the usual fare.

They need not have worried. The film sold itself and went on to do tremendous business worldwide – except, sadly, in Britain, where it opened on the first day of a month-long national press strike and sank without trace. Men plodding around the West End with sandwich-boards could hardly make up for a lack of press and commercial radio and TV.

I don't remember leaving El Morocco that night . . .

People who have seen that movie never forget it and it is still a hardy annual offering on American TV, especially at Eastertime. Its impact on one particular man tells its own story:

A personal friend of Zanuck's, a hard-headed business tycoon who owned a mammoth department store in Texas, was shown a private screening at the studios. He returned to Texas and a few days later hired a large cinema to which one afternoon he sent his entire staff, some thousand or so people. At the entrances to his store that day, signs were erected saying, 'This store is closed. The staff have all gone to see the movie *A Man Called Peter*, and we suggest that you should do the same.'

Three days crammed with press, TV and radio interviews ended with a sumptuous dinner party at the palatial Westchester home of Spyros Skouras, president of Twentieth Century-Fox. I then flew for interviews in Chicago, Detroit, Cleveland, Washington and Atlanta, returning a few days later to New York to spend a couple of days there with Kitty before she flew home to London and I went back to Los Angeles to finish my work on *The Virgin Queen*.

For nearly a month I stayed at the house in Roxbury Drive, tended by Alma but never alone because when I had no other engagement the ever-faithful Harry Baum kept me company.

I was lucky enough to have as my companion on various occasions the lovely Dana Wynter. I had admired her in the past in London and she was now under contract to Twentieth Century-Fox. A most beautiful girl, with great charm and humour, she became a firm friend. Although of German birth, she had a great 'Englishness' about her and we thoroughly enjoyed each other's company.

On one occasion Fox had asked me to squire Sarah Churchill, Sir Winston's rather wayward daughter, to a film première, but within minutes of my leaving to pick her up someone phoned to say she was not well and couldn't go, so I joined Dana and Gregory Ratoff, Zanuck's great friend.

Finally the day came for me to shave off my Raleigh beard, discard my Raleigh noses, make my round of farewells and fly out to New York en route for London. I was seen off by Dana and, of course, by Harry Baum.

14

The Dam Busters Take Off!

Although it was to be nearly four months before I started work on another film, I was far from idle from the moment I arrived back home.

Inevitably a longish period abroad meant that there was a lot of catching up to do with purely private matters, not least trying to get some time to spend with my family, especially Peter who was now nearly three, and to get through the mass of office work which had piled up despite all Jill's efforts to cope with it.

Fortunately, I did not have to worry about being out of work. I was still under contract to ABPC, which meant that the monthly cheque kept coming in, and the previous twelve months had been pretty lucrative. There was the ever-present shadow of the tax man looming over me, especially as I had spent a fair amount on getting Wayside House in order and well-found, but Basil Stebbings always kept a beady eye on my outgoings, though even he was hard put to curb my innate extravagance – shades of my happy-go-lucky father!

The end of my seven-year contract with Associated British was in sight, and already I found waiting for me a letter from Robert Clark exercising their option on a further five-year deal, enclosing a contract for my signature on exactly the same terms and conditions which held in this my final year with the corporation.

This, I felt, was rather taking things for granted. However, knowing the wily Mr Clark's tactics, I reckoned that it was an opening gambit and I decided to argue my case.

The day after I returned home I went to London to talk things over with my agent, Al Parker, whom I felt should be the one to speak on my behalf. For years he had had literally nothing to do to earn his percentage, so now was his chance to do something constructive. His feeble response was, 'Well, what do you want me to say?'

'Hell!' I thought, '*you* should be the one telling *me*!' In the end I left, determined to look after my affairs on my own, as I had done all along.

To continue with this little saga out of sequence, a few days later Robert Clark's secretary phoned me saying that Mr Clark would like to discuss my contract with me. I made a date for a meeting, at which I told him I would like an improved deal.

I was quite clear about what I wanted: *not* a full-term contract, but a one-picture-a-year deal for exactly the same money as they were offering me for a full-year deal, and with ABPC not having first call on me, so that I would be able to make one or two independent films every year, including my remaining two under my Fox contract. Up to then the corporation in effect had never had to pay me any salary at all, as they recouped much more from their share of my loan-out deals. Even the salary which they would pay me for one picture a year was about one third of what I got for other films, so I felt that I was not being ungrateful or driving a hard bargain.

Robert Clark seemed to agree with me, if reluctantly, and within days an agreement was reached. On 14 July I signed my new one-picture-a-year contract with Associated British.

And meanwhile a lot of other things had been taking place.

First and foremost, *The Dam Busters* had opened with a Royal première at the Empire Theatre, Leicester Square – actually two premières. On the first night Princess Margaret attended, and the following night the Duke and Duchess of Gloucester came. The reception for that film and its subsequent success in Britain and the Commonwealth is now all part of cinema history. Robert Clark's good sense in buying the subject in the first place, and Michael Anderson's masterly direction gave a classic picture to the industry's archives and a lot of enjoyment to the public. Eric Coates' 'The Dam Busters March' still follows me around almost wherever I go.

On my first weekend home I went to Castleman's Stud Farm to see Damson; she was in foal to Court Nez, a great stallion who would, I hoped, get a show-jumping type. My other great pleasure at the stables that day was to see the British Three-Day Event team there in training with their lovely animals. I remember especially Colonel Frank Weldon and his great Kilbarry, and also Laurence Rooke, Diana Mason and Bertie Hill. A week later Kitty, Peter and I watched the European Horse Trials over two days in Windsor Great Park, when our team won the gold medal and Frank Weldon on Kilbarry won the individual gold. Freddie Weil's gesture in offering them stabling and training facilities at Knowl Hill, only a few miles from Windsor, had certainly paid off.

I had also been offered two films: *Loser Takes All*, by Graham Greene, and *Marie Antoinette*, a historical and very lavish film to be made in

France. Ken Annakin came down to Wayside a couple of times to discuss *Loser Takes All*, which he was to direct, and I later had a meeting with John Stafford, the producer, Fritz Gotfurt (head of the scenario department at Elstree) and Graham Greene himself in London. I agreed to do the picture, provided it went into production fairly soon and would not conflict with my next Fox contract film, whatever that would be.

I was particularly anxious not to have any problems with Twentieth Century-Fox and to find out what their plans for me were to be. Luckily I got the chance to visit Hollywood for talks with Lew Schreiber when I flew out to Canada for some personal appearances with *The Dam Busters*.

The Canadian visit began in Toronto where I did a whole series of press, TV and radio interviews before appearing at the two premières. Since these were held only minutes apart at two cinemas, to enable me to get from one theatre to the other I was given a police motor-cycle escort of three riders with flashing lights and blaring sirens, going through red traffic lights, just like in a gangster movie.

I was able to relax later with three old friends, who had all been contacted by the PR men: Eric Sievewright and Pat Comrie, from my Dundee theatre days, and Hugh Fellows, who had served with me in my old parachute unit. I managed to get to the airport in time to catch the 12.30 pm flight back to Montreal, arriving at my hotel at 3 am.

At 9.30 am I attended a civic reception, did the usual interview stints, made a personal appearance at a cinema in the evening, then after a very late dinner was driven through the night to Ottawa, where I went through exactly the same programme as before, starting at 9.30 am.

Next day I flew to Los Angeles via Toronto and Chicago. At Chicago I changed to an American Airlines flight which was absolutely packed, except for the seat next to mine which was vacant. But then after lunch had been served, one of the hostesses sat down beside me. A very pretty girl, with lovely peachy skin and dark, almost Creole beauty, she told me with that frankness so endearing about Americans that she had arranged for that seat to be kept empty because she wanted to meet me and talk with me for the rest of the trip.

I was quite sorry when we landed at Los Angeles, but delighted to be met by – guess who? – Harry Baum, who drove me to the Beverly Hills Hotel and later chaperoned me and the charming young air hostess at dinner.

My first meeting with Schreiber was inconclusive. He had no idea what my next subject was to be or when it would be in production, so

I spent the rest of the day working on Sam Engel and Charles Brackett to see if they had anything suitable in mind.

That evening I ran *The Dam Busters*, a copy of which I had managed to get hurriedly flown down from San Francisco. The audience included Darryl Zanuck, Lew Shreiber, Dana Wynter and the Alec Coppels. As the film ended Zanuck rasped, 'Gee! That's a hell of a picture! Is that a true story?'

'Absolutely,' I said.

'Then why doesn't it say so!'

I saw his point. I had always felt that *The Dam Busters* had not been properly marketed in America, where the facts of the raid were not common knowledge as they were in England. I had even suggested that General Eisenhower, who was then President, and Sir Winston Churchill would probably have agreed to write prefaces to be included in the opening titles.

The following evening I had a rather frantic phone call from Lew Schreiber, asking me to see him at the studios the next morning. He was afraid that I had already left Hollywood. When we met he told me that Zanuck was really keen to find a subject for me, but that it would have to be towards the end of the year so as to fit in with their studio programme.

So my mission had succeeded and I knew that there was time to fit in one picture in Europe.

I spent several days in New York on my way home, doing TV and radio shows, mainly about *A Man Called Peter*, including the prestigious Ed Sullivan Show.

It was a beautiful early August when I got back to Wayside, but I had little time for gardening or using the pool except when we all cooled off before turning in. I had a batch of scripts to read, and also had to withdraw from the Graham Greene project as it had been delayed.

I now concentrated on the *Marie Antoinette* picture which Robert Clark had said he would leave to me to decide upon. I had two days in Paris in talks with Delannois, the director, Bercholz, the producer, and Nancy Mitford, who was writing the English language script.

The film was to be shot in two versions, English and French, and was to star the lovely Michèle Morgan and include most of the well-known actors in France, according to the cast list. Needless to say, between them they convinced me that I should play Count Fersen, Marie Antoinette's Swedish lover.

On the second afternoon Robert Clark and Jimmy Wallis arrived for talks with Bercholz, who was angling for an Associated British Cinemas release for the film in England. Again, Mr Clark left it to me to decide and I finally agreed to be in the film. We flew back to London that evening.

My home life that summer had been pretty fragmented due to all my comings and goings, but we did manage to spend some time with our friends at weekends and I visited the stables to ride out whenever I could, usually with the second string of horses in training so that I didn't have to rise at dawn. Damson's foal, a filly called Gemini, was born in June and was a delightful wee thing.

I was also still hoping to buy a home with more land attached and had found the Haileywood estate which was owned by Christopher Mann, a leading film, theatre and literary agent. He was married to Eileen Joyce, the famous Australian-born concert pianist, which explained the three grand pianos that we had seen in the house when we visited it. We liked the place very much, and had admired the rather splendid boathouse on the Thames when we took a launch trip from Henley one day, but I had too much on my plate just then to contemplate such a major move, especially when it included setting up a farming enterprise. Luckily Christopher Mann had not yet found a suitable farm to move to, so the whole deal was put on hold.

Kitty was in the early stages of another pregnancy and, never very robust, she had to rest a good deal. We hoped that a second child would further stave off her tendency to suffer from anaemic problems.

We also drove down to Broadstairs to visit Wellesley House School, which was to be Peter's prep school before he went on to Eton. Our arrival there was less than impressive as Agatha Rolls-Royce had a major mechanical problem and, having limped the last few miles, finally expired on the school drive and was towed away to Broadstairs, leaving us to get back to London eventually by train.

For the filming of *Marie Antoinette* I had arranged to rent a large and very elegant flat in Paris, on the ground floor of a building in the Square Lamartine not far from the Bois de Boulogne, where I was sure Nanny Pitcher would find lots of space for her walks with Peter.

I took Jill with me for the first couple of days to help sort things out before the family's arrival, though we need not have worried about the condition of the place. It was immaculate and cared for by a splendid couple, Jeanne and Maurice. We would be in good hands.

I think Jill enjoyed her short time in Paris. I took her to see the leggy Lido show with its marvellous troupe of statuesque English showgirls.

I wondered how the rather proper Jill would react to it, but she loved it – I did, too, for that matter!

By the time Kitty and Peter arrived, I had started work on the film and had begun to realise what a lavish production it was to be. Certainly, no Hollywood company would have built the sets or furnished them as they were in *Marie Antoinette*.

We had been given by the French state the complete run of the Palais de Versailles and its grounds and also Le Petit Hameau, the miniature pastoral village so beloved of the royal court when they were playing at being peasants. So far as I know, no other commercial film company had ever been allowed such spectacular facilities.

All our first scenes were on location at Versailles, either shooting in the palace itself or in the gardens, and I was staggered by the magnificence – the costumes, the grand interiors and the huge numbers of extras in the state scenes. When not actually engaged in shooting I just wandered around marvelling at the splendour of it all.

Michèle Morgan was charming both as an actress and as a person, and lovely to work with – and incredibly beautiful too. All the rest of the cast were equally friendly and capable, though many of them were unable to speak English and had difficulty mouthing their lines in the English version, which would later be dubbed by English-speakers.

I could sympathise with them. My own rusty French was strained to its limits, not only when acting in the French version but also by having to speak and listen to a foreign language all day. The fact that I was playing a Swede would to some extent excuse my shortcomings, but even so I don't think I was very good in either version.

Also, Jean Delannois' style of direction bothered me. He was most meticulous and had worked out every move and gesture himself prior to rehearsal. This I found inhibiting: I didn't always feel it natural to move exactly where and when he had done, or to gesticulate as he had in his very Gallic and excitable way. I know that Michèle frequently had the same difficulty; most often we played the scenes our own way in the English version, but tried to follow his instructions in the French one. He was a renowned director and a patient, charming man, but not easy for me to work with.

Acting in another tongue is hard, but especially for an Englishman in the French language, which has no tonic syllables in its words, so that he cannot stress syllables as he normally would. Even so, I enjoyed making that film, and there were all sorts of consolations: Paris itself not least. Kitty, although beginning to bulge, thoroughly enjoyed herself, as did I. We tried many different and excellent restaurants and decided that our favourite was Laserre in the Avenue Franklin D. Roosevelt.

We also engaged a nice French maid, Bernadette – found for us by Jeanne and Maurice – who was shortly to join us at Wayside House for a year.

When the time came for Kitty and Peter to return home I had a few days free, so decided to show them around Normandy en route to the ferry at Dieppe. I showed them the old battlefields of 1944, and finally took Peter round the Airborne Cemetery at Ranville. He walked beside me, hands behind his back as mine were, subdued and intent when I pointed out the graves of old comrades in the tight-packed, orderly rows of simple crosses. Finally, with all the innocent practicality of the very young, he said:

'Daddy, why are all the graves so close together? Is it because they were such good friends during the War?'

I returned to Paris for another four weeks to finish my work on the film. In that splendid apartment, thoroughly spoiled by Jeanne and Maurice, I made the most of a very enjoyable few weeks.

The studio shooting went well after a few exterior scenes when I again had horse trouble. I had been allocated a magnificent chestnut stallion, very handsome and high-spirited. The only problem was that he was dressage-trained, and I had never attempted any *haute école* horsemanship. The slightest twitch of my leg or my hand gave some signal to him that was usually the opposite of my intention, and we became a somewhat confused partnership. How I often wished that I could again team up with Reno, my sage and willing little cow-pony in America on *Lightning Strikes Twice* years before!

Just before I finished in France, I had a phone call from Lew Schreiber telling me that I would be starting work in Hollywood in November with Robert Taylor and my dear friend Dana Wynter on *D-Day, the Sixth of June*. So, mercifully, the rest of my year was preordained.

15

Back to Front

By the end of the year I was once again in Hollywood working on *D-Day, the Sixth of June*.

Our female star was Dana Wynter, as lovely and charming as ever, and the leading man was Robert Taylor, still as handsome as he had been before the war with Greto Garbo in *Camille*.

The film's producer was Charles Brackett and the director was dear Henry Koster, with whom I had already made two pictures, so once again I was part of a friendly team. The story concerned the preparations for a commando-style beach landing on the French coast on D-Day by a combined force of British Commandos and American troops. The operation was commanded by me as Lt-Colonel John Winter, with Robert Taylor as second-in-command. Not surprisingly my fiancée in the story, an ATS officer played by Dana, meets Taylor and is greatly taken by him, with consequent doubts about her relationship with me. The triangular problem had been resolved in the original script, with Taylor going back to his wife and children in America and me being left to pick up the pieces with a rather crestfallen ex-fiancée.

I didn't see it this way at all, and persuaded Brackett and Koster to alter the ending so that John Winter was killed by a land-mine in the last few seconds of the film, thus leaving it open to question what the outcome might have been had he lived. They both liked the idea.

The actual explosion of the mine was very ingeniously contrived: A canister containing some explosive material with a mild blast effect was buried in the sand and detonated electrically by remote control. Also in the canister on top of the explosive was some smoke-dust, some Fuller's earth and a handful of flash-powder. As I walked over the spot, clad in flame-proof trousers and sturdy jock-strap (my idea, the latter!), the blast was just enough to pick me up and pitch me forward, engulfed in a bright flash and lots of smoke, dust and sand. The shock effect at the end of the film was splendid. I sustained no noticeable damage, and honour was preserved all round.

The D-Day setting of the story was pretty familiar to me, and Brackett and Koster allowed me to devise the beach assault scenes and even to direct parts of them. I became a sort of unofficial military adviser and enjoyed every moment. Dear Harry Baum had a tea-mug specially decorated for me captioned 'Lt-Col John Winter, DSO, MC', which I have to this day.

I had a merry time altogether. Because Kitty was heavily engaged in her own production I had rented an apartment on Santa Monica Boulevard and on the rare occasions when I was alone, Harry kept me company.

There were lots of parties, especially around Christmas and New Year. One of these I particularly remember:

It was at Alec and Myra Coppel's house, and the guests included Robert Newton, Trevor Howard, Reggie Gardiner, Elizabeth Taylor, Michael Wilding, Mary Preminger, Valerie French and Robert and Sue Douglas. It was a pretty bibulous evening and it was not long before Bob Newton, Trevor and Reggie were firing on all cylinders in an imaginary Shakespearian scene, declaiming at the tops of their considerable voices in a gibberish of their own invention which made excellent sense to those of us who were no less pie-eyed than they!

My own high spot that night came at a time when I found myself in a corner sitting on the floor with Elizabeth Taylor, Mary Preminger and Reggie's lovely Russian-born wife, Nadia. For some reason our conversation got round to fashion models, and I complained that most of them were too skinny and had scrawny, hollow thighs. Thereupon Mary, herself a beautiful ex-model, drew up her skirts and stretched out her shapely shanks. 'Call those hollow! Go on, feel them!' I obliged, Liz and Nadia followed suit and there I was comparing all three, prodding like an old farmer at the cattle market. It has to be said that Liz Taylor had the most rounded limbs . . .

Despite my enjoyment while making *D-Day, the Sixth of June* I was anxious to get home as quickly as possible lest I again be absent when the latest family addition arrived. I worked until the last moment and was finally rushed to the airport by Harry Baum and Mary Preminger, reaching London just in time to be at Wayside House when Fiona Margaret Palethorpe Todd was born there, at 2.25 pm on 8 February 1956.

Kitty had hated being in a nursing home for her first-born so her gynaecologist, Dr Hannay, had agreed that she should have her second at home. He and our family GP, Dr Pallot, and the splendid Sister Cullinan were all in attendance at the birth.

Wayside was now in every sense a family home filled almost to capacity with Kitty and me, Peter and Fiona, four living-in staff and five dogs, together with as many guests as we could manage from time to time. We had been fortunate in our seven years of marriage and had seen many changes for the better.

From our original flat in London we had moved into a considerable country house, now totally restored and decorated thanks to Granny Todd's legacy and my new-found earning power; we had our comfortable little *pied-à-terre* in Chelsea, and I now owned a couple of horses and leased others from Freddie Weil. Agatha Rolls-Royce was beginning to feel her years, so I bought a new car, a very sleek blue James Young Bentley, whom we christened Belinda. In a material sense our world was glowing and I kept my fingers crossed and hoped for more.

The only shadow that ever clouded our outlook was Kitty's continual health problems. Fiona's birth took a lot of her strength, and it was some three weeks before she was on her feet again. I decided that a holiday would be the best thing for her as soon as I was free from dubbing *Marie Antoinette* at Elstree and from various meetings which I had to attend in London regarding future films and my unsatisfactory relationship with my agent, Al Parker.

With the advice and help of my solicitor, Laurence Harbottle, my agency agreement was finally rescinded and henceforth I had no agent for several years, my film contracts being prepared and vetted by Harbottle and my accountant Basil Stebbings. At Basil's suggestion several future film payments were not made in single lump sums but spread over five years in order to ease the tax burden in any one year. I had good reason to be thankful for this arrangement eventually . . .

Our holiday was spent on Capri and was idyllic, with lovely spring weather and lots of luscious pasta. We also had a few days in Rome, our favourite city, and Kitty was soon back to good form.

Once home again I was soon immersed in a series of meetings with Robert Lennard, Robert Clark and various producers regarding proposed movie subjects. The film industry was then at its peak in England and America, and a large number of major pictures was always in full production or in the planning stages. The studios were humming with activity and both the big corporations and independent producers were scrambling for floor-space and competing for their actors. It was not so much a case of looking for work as of deciding which proposition to choose.

I also had several sessions discussing my purchase of Christopher Mann's Haileywood estate, which I eventually agreed to take over the following year. Wayside had been a lucky house for us and was an ideal home in many ways, but I was keen to get into farming – that had always been my greatest desire, ever since my childhood in Ireland. Even at Wayside, my first tentative step towards animal husbandry had been the establishment of a useful flock of laying hens and geese, the latter being the terror of the neighbourhood and almost better house-guards than the dogs themselves. As commoners we were allowed to graze on the surrounding grassland as many birds as we could in winter, and our hen-houses were full.

At the end of April I was off to France for my second Cannes Film Festival. On the evening of my arrival there – after a day of incessant TV and radio interviews – I accompanied Michèle Morgan to the première of *Marie Antoinette*, which was rapturously applauded by the French audience, and then went on to a celebratory ball afterwards, arriving back at the Carlton Hotel at about 4 am. From my experience of the Festival the previous year I knew that one was not in Cannes for a rest cure, and sure enough I was on the beach a few hours later for a photo session with Bella Darvi.

After a press luncheon at La Napoule I did an afternoon of press photos which was much more to my liking and had been arranged by our own Leslie Frewin. My consort on this session was the gorgeous Brigitte Bardot, who was now firmly established as France's favourite young star – and I could see why! As we wandered around the Old Town for a couple of hours, cameras flashing continuously, the time passed very quickly and enjoyably and I was sorry when our publicity stint was over. As we were driven back to the Carlton I asked Brigitte if she would like to join me for tea. Much to my surprise, since afternoon tea was hardly an accepted French custom, she agreed. My last tea-party had been with the vicar, arranging Fiona's christening.

The rest of my time in Cannes followed the usual course of interviews, receptions, official banquets and film-viewing, including the British entry *Yield To The Night* and an Alfred Hitchcock picture. At the Associated British dinner I was deputed to make a speech welcoming the guests on behalf of Robert Clark, since I was the only one in our party who spoke reasonable French.

The week in Cannes had a few pleasant off-duty moments, especially a fascinating lunch with the old Aga Khan and his stately and kindly

Begum at their villa in the hills above the town. During a stroll in the large, exotic garden she pointed out the little numbered pegs which her ailing husband used as distance markers for his prescribed exercising walks. I also received an invitation to drinks aboard the yacht of Prince Bira, the famed racing driver who had settled in England. Our hostess, his South American wife Princess Chelita, insisted on driving me back to the Carlton in his Aston Martin, a trip which frightened me stiff. She was not exactly in total control of the powerful car.

Back in England again, Jill Paul had become engaged to be married and was to leave us very soon. Her replacement would be Pat Wilkie, who had been Bob Lennard's assistant secretary for some years. Because of her position in Bob's office, Pat knew all about my film career and was the ideal person to take over, especially as she was already acquainted with most of the people whom I dealt with in the industry. She had always wanted to live away from London, and took a flat in Henley, a couple of miles from us. Pat and Jill worked together for a month or so before Jill's final departure. We were sad to see her go; she had been part of the family for four years.

Just before my visit to Cannes I had received a phone call from Herbert Wilcox from California. He was in the process of setting up a production to be filmed later in the year in England based on the true story of HMS *Amethyst*, the British warship which had been trapped in the Yangtse River by Chinese communist forces and had shot her way back to sea in a gallant escape action. The script was tentatively titled *Sitting Duck*. Wilcox wanted me to play Commander John Kerans, who had taken over command of *Amethyst* and planned and led the ship's escape. A script was to follow as soon as possible.

I was very excited by this offer. Herbert Wilcox was a most successful independent producer with a long list of important films to his credit, and the subject sounded to me just the kind of thing I would enjoy: like *The Dam Busters* an authentic true action story which British movie-makers did so well.

And the months had been slipping by since my last picture. I had not been desperately keen about any of the projects that I had been offered and, to give Associated British their due, had not been put under any pressure to start work again. I still had two films completed and as yet unseen, but I was anxious to get something lined up; so far as I was concerned the holiday was over and, as with any other actor, 'resting' was not my favourite occupation.

By mid-May I had read the first draft screenplay of *Sitting Duck* and, to my relief and excitement, liked it enormously. Within a few days I and Milton Pickman, who had arrived in London, had a long meeting with Herbert Wilcox in his Park Lane flat when he told us his plans for the film. It would start in August and he hoped to shoot it at Elstree with ABC distribution and release, with Michael Anderson directing and Eric Ambler, the famous novelist and screenwriter, doing the script.

To work with Michael again had been my dream since *The Dam Busters* and I knew he was the ideal director to handle the subject. With the combination of his and Eric Ambler's skills, and Herbert's experience, I was sure this could be a great picture.

The very next day I spent the evening with Robert Clark at one of his favourite haunts, the Caledonian Club, the bastion of expatriate Scots. To my joy, after a rather hesitant start he finally agreed that studio space would be available at Elstree and that ABPC would become associated with the film.

At last I knew what my next picture was to be. I had a number of discussions with Michael Anderson and Eric Ambler about the script, and Herbert agreed several alterations and additions. John Kerans himself, now retired, was to be our technical adviser and our contact with the Royal Navy. Now I had two free months before starting work on *Yangtse Incident*, as the film was now to be called, and I felt justified in making the most of them.

Fiona's christening on a beautiful early-summer day at our local church, Stubbings, was the first event on my non-professional calendar. Her godparents were Peter Jackson, an old friend of Kitty's; Lady Palmer, our close friend and neighbour; and Marina Cicogna of Venice – and Fiona gave a lusty vocal performance at the font, which I am told is a lucky sign.

In June Kitty and I went to Stockholm for the Olympic Games Equestrian Events. The weather was quite dreadful, heavy thunderstorms and torrential rain making the cross-country course for the Three-Day-Event really hazardous, with slippery, mud-churned landing and take-off points adding to the difficulties of the enormous obstacles. I had never seen fences like those I saw as I walked the course on the evening before the competition started. It was laid out mostly on grass tracks through a hilly forest area, and the rugged timber-built jumps were frightening. The Wagnerian 'Ride of the Valkyrie' atmosphere was enhanced by the lightning flashes and claps of thunder which rent the soggy silence of the woods.

At the hotel later Frank Weldon confided to me that the cross-country fences were really formidable, but was confident that the British team could cope with them better than any other.

The atmosphere in Stockholm that week was stirringly pro-British. The Queen and Prince Philip had arrived in the Royal Yacht *Britannia*, which lay in the water almost in the centre of that city, dressed overall with flags flying and lights festooning the masts, yards and superstructure, looking magnificent. Every shop-front displayed pictures of our royal couple and Union Jacks abounded.

I had hired a car so we were able to take in some of the sights around Stockholm, including the massive, grim Drottingholm Castle, and we also visited a number of restaurants with British and Swedish friends.

The actual cross-country day was unforgettable. The weather was still appalling and the going horrendous. From my previous survey of the course I had decided that we should position ourselves by what looked to me the most dangerous obstacle of all: a wide, deep, water-filled ditch with a stout post-and-rail fence running along between the banks. It was about two-thirds round the course, and I reckoned that any horse which cleared that should go in to finish. I wasn't far wrong, since again and again riders and horses came to grief here, mainly because of not only the size of the leap required but also the treacherous condition of the ground on both sides. We yelled with joy as Frank Weldon on Kilbarry and the rest of our team sailed over in great style except for one: I think it was Bertie Hill on Countryman. The horse skidded badly on the approach and landed half across the wooden fence, teetering like a see-saw. His rider jumped off, stood in the water on the far side, got his hands under the fore-hooves and literally heaved him up till he fell kicking and struggling back in the water on the approach side. He scrambled back up the bank and was remounted, clearing the obstacle easily on his second attempt.

The final day of the Three-Day-Event went splendidly for us and Britain won the gold medal, with West Germany second and Canada third.

Sunday marked the closing ceremony and the final rounds of the showjumping competition. Again Britain did well, winning the bronze medal, but the gold medal went to Hans Winkler of Germany on Halla. Again it was a huge course, with only the greatest horses able to cope with the spreads and heights. We had not realised that Winkler had broken a collar-bone in the preliminary round, and wondered why he appeared to be riding rather loosely in the final jump-off, using mainly his legs. What we thought were shouts of encouragement to Halla were apparently in fact yells of pain at each jump, yet the great horse carried his rider round without fault.

A short while later I was flying to a city with a very different atmosphere from that of Stockholm: West Berlin. I had been invited to the Berlin Film Festival as an individual guest. Fortunately, the first people I met on arrival at my hotel were my teenage Drama School crush, Dinah Sheridan, and her husband John Davis, head of the Rank Organisation. He immediately kindly arranged for Theo Cowan, his PR department chief, to look after my press and TV appointments and to point me in the right direction at the various receptions and functions.

The Berlin Festival had none of the tinsel and glamour of its Cannes counterpart, and was a more serious-minded salesman's convention, its setting grey and cheerless. West Berlin in 1956 was hardly a frolicsome playground, even though there was an almost frenetic urgency to make the best of things in its bars and in its nightlife. I got the impression that many of its citizens, especially the younger ones, were putting on a show of exuberance to cloak their underlying isolation and insecurity. This was before the Wall finally clove East from West.

There seemed to be a military presence everywhere, mostly American and British, and even flying into Templehof airport was more like an approach to a military airfield, concrete-bound and strongly guarded.

My great good fortune was to meet Rudolf Schock, the famous operatic tenor. With him and his family I spent a pleasant afternoon in the suburbs boating on the Vansee, a large lake where numerous families were enjoying themselves relaxing in the sunshine.

Rudolf was in good standing with the Russians because he occasionally sang in East Berlin at the great Berlin Opera House; he took me for a trip into the eastern sector, and was able to show me areas where no ordinary visitor could venture.

While West Berlin still bore some of the scars of war, parts of East Berlin looked as though the conflict had never ended. Behind the newly-built façade of Stalinallee, the main street, was a wasteland of rubble where people still lived in ruined cellars. Celebratory parades of military pomp and grandeur could march along Stalinallee and present an orderly, impressive front to the world, but elsewhere I was aghast at what I saw.

16

A Chinese Puzzle

Our location work for *Yangtse Incident* was centred on a stretch of the River Orwell between Harwich and Ipswich where, according to John Kerans, the terrain was similar to that part of the Yangtse River on which HMS *Amethyst* had been trapped when Chinese communist gun-fire temporarily crippled the ship and left her fast aground while on a lawful, peaceful voyage up-river.

Kerans himself, then the Naval Attaché at Peking, had been ordered by the Commander-in-Chief, Far East, to journey to the ship, take command of her and negotiate for her release. There had been several killed, and the worst of the wounded were evacuated to a hospital of sorts ashore. When Kerans arrived morale was low and the position seemed pretty hopeless, with negotiations dragging on pointlessly, so he determined to devise a plan to free the ship from the mud and run the gauntlet of guns, booms and mines in a night-time escape to the sea. How he and his crew succeeded was an epic story of gallantry, cunning and determination.

As our contact with the Royal Navy, Kerans had managed to persuade the Admiralty to let us use HMS *Amethyst* herself, although the battered old vessel had been de-commissioned and cocooned and her main engines were not usable. But the generator and pumps were serviceable, so there was electric power on board.

The ship was towed up to the Orwell from Devonport and anchored close in-shore. We were allowed to damage her superficially but not to hole her below the waterline, and the action shots of her under way during the break-out were to feature her sister-ship HMS *Magpie*, who was to be her stand-in for one day and had once been commanded by Prince Philip, Duke of Edinburgh.

Kerans had further recruited a group of ex-Royal Navy sailors to act as a maintenance party on board *Amethyst*, and had succeeded in finding the ideal man to take charge of the ship: an Engineer-Commander,

RN, who while awaiting retirement was still in uniform. He had a distinguished war record and had been awarded the DSO. He ran the ship with great efficiency and was respected by everybody. At one stage he found some defects in the state of the engines, which were hurriedly rectified by engineers dispatched from Devonport.

For the three weeks of our location work on *Amethyst* I stayed in the Marlborough Head, a lovely old inn, all oak beams and undulating floors, in the beautiful Constable-associated village of Dedham. There was a much fancier hotel nearby, but I enjoyed the cosiness of the tavern, my evenings spent in the bar chatting with local farmers and countrymen, the good English food and the ministrations of Charlie, the general factotum of the place – a sweet-faced smiling near-midget, who cheerfully brought me my breakfast very early each day.

Working in the cramped confines of a small destroyer had its problems, but Michael Anderson and his film crew coped marvellously and we kept on schedule, using a lot of ingenuity. For instance, for one long tracking shot moving along a narrow passageway there was no room to mount the camera on its usual wheeled platform. Our technicians fixed the camera on to a pair of roller skates instead, and when the contraption was pulled by a wire the length of the passage the resultant shot was perfect.

The big moment for all of us came on the last day's work. It was the scene in which *Amethyst* – or, rather, her stand-in HMS *Teaser*, which at the last moment had replaced *Magpie* – ran the daylight gauntlet of the final stage of her escape to the sea under the guns of the shore batteries, returning the heavy fire with her own guns blazing. For this a half-mile or so of the wide river had been planted with dozens of explosive charges electrically activated by our special-effects technicians, each one to be timed as a near-miss. The ship herself had also been fitted with plastic explosive flash charges to simulate actual hits, also electrically triggered.

For all this, split-second timing was essential. We only had the use of the ship for one day, the tide had to be taken into account, and the river also had to be clear of all other shipping.

Finally all was ready and the scene, filmed by several cameras from different angles and essentially a one-off operation, was set to begin. Just as Michael Anderson was about to radio the start signal, a little Dutch freighter came chugging up the river and into camera view. She had obviously chosen to ignore all warning signals, and had wallowed past the waiting warship.

The delay seemed interminable, and when she drew level with our position on the bank Michael could wait no longer and gave the signal for action. Within seconds the warship came into distant view, guns blazing, flashes and explosions going off on her hull and superstructure and great plumes of water blowing up all around her.

The Dutchmen must have got the fright of their lives. Perhaps thinking that his freighter was the target of an angry Royal Navy, the dumpy little cargo ship's captain suddenly crammed on all speed, her bows rose and her stern went down as she scuttled up towards Ipswich like an old lady picking up her skirts and running. At least she got out of camera shot.

The scene was a great success and even Herbert Wilcox and I were amazed by the work of our special-effects men.

Those on board HMS *Teaser* must have been similarly impressed and unprepared for the reality of it all. Just as she sped out of shot she flashed a signal to us which rightly expressed her commander's feelings: 'You bastards.'

Just a few days before we left the Orwell a sad incident occurred when two plain-clothes detectives visited our unit and asked to see our splendid Engineer-Commander. After a brief interview in his cabin he was led away to a waiting police car, and was later charged with illegally wearing Her Majesty's uniform. At his subsequent trial, at which Herbert Wilcox emphasised his good work for us, it emerged that he was a motor mechanic who had never even been in the Navy but had a Walter Mitty fascination with everything about the Senior Service. His perfect bearing, his detailed knowledge of the ships on which he claimed to have served and the actions they had been in, even his descriptions of their officers, completely fooled everybody and showed that he had done his homework. He had run our ship superbly.

I had a two-week break before starting the studio shooting on *Yangtse Incident*, and needed every moment of that time to sort out various domestic problems.

The children were fine, but Kitty was not at all well. All her old troubles seemed to have recurred and on two occasions she collapsed with dreadful haemorrhages. On the second occasion our GP called in a specialist and she was rushed to hospital for an operation and blood transfusions. At times she was fine and carried on with our social life at home and in London, but she needed careful watching and for a while we had a nurse living in at Wayside.

To make matters worse, Kitty had sacked Nanny Pitcher because she felt that she was devoting too much attention to her beloved Peter and too little to baby Fiona. So for months we had a series of temporary nannies. George Reeve had retired to concentrate on running his school for butlers in London, Bernadette had finished her year with us and returned to France, her replacement was useless and without Pat Wilkie and Miss Murray-Hamilton we would have been in a pretty pickle.

I did what I could to help, but once work started at Elstree I had to be in London except at weekends. And I also kept active in other ways. One morning I took the Institute of Advanced Motorists test, a tricky two-hour ordeal under the stern surveillance of their chief examiner, George Eyles, an ex-police driving instructor who told me that he looked for a driver who could travel safely from London to Bristol in 2½ hours – and that was long before the motorway! The course took in every kind of road conditions from heavy London traffic to fast freeways, and included some searching questions. I was driving my own Bentley which I reckoned I handled efficiently enough, but I was totally surprised by the examiner's summing-up when we finished: 'Mr Todd, I can tell you right away that you've passed. You're a magnificent driver.' My motor insurers, please note!

I also bought another horse. I needed a yearling filly to run out with Gemini and keep her company. Even a donkey would have done, but a local dealer went to the Newmarket sales for me with strict instructions to pick up something cheap, and returned with a weedy little chestnut filly, Striped Quill, that had cost £100. She had come up near lunchtime, when the ring was pretty empty, and nobody had fancied her. Within days, the British Bloodstock Agency contacted me – having discovered from their sale lists what had happened – and offered me many times what I had paid. After a hurried conference with Freddie Weil I agreed to sell Striped Quill. I was only too pleased to make such a good profit, especially as she was not much to look at. I subsequently discovered that she was half-sister to Princequillo, a very successful American horse descended from the great Man-o'-War, had been bred in America, imported for breeding in England and sent to the sales by mistake. Maybe I should have kept her!

One of my interests was Masonry. My father and grandfather had been members of the Craft, and I was duly initiated as a member of the Lodge of Emulation No. 21, one of the oldest Lodges in British Freemasonry. The membership consisted almost entirely of professional men, especially doctors and barristers, and I have enjoyed many years of friendship and fellowship at the Lodge, eventually becoming Master myself and a Grand Steward of the Grand Lodge of Great Britain.

Peter was now attending a little pre-prep school class held in the Palmers' house where his five fellow pupils included the Palmers' two daughters, William Astor, Bruce Dundas and another boy. The Palmers and the Astors were close friends, and it was around this time that we had our first invitation to lunch at Cliveden, the famous and palatial home of the then Viscount Astor. Bill Astor was kindness itself and afterwards took me round the great Cliveden Stud, where we visited every box and most of the paddocks.

Bill and I subsequently became firm friends and our two boys, Peter and William, were great chums. He and I were in close touch for the next ten years until his untimely death in 1966, brought on in large measure by the shattering exposure of his connection with the Stephen Ward/Christine Keeler/Mandy Rice-Davies scandal of 1963 from which his health and his self-esteem never fully recovered.

The drama and the devastation of that affair, throughout which Kitty and I were appalled onlookers, will figure in this narrative in due course.

While we were still working on *Yangtse Incident* at Elstree, news came through about the terrific American reviews for Mickey Anderson's latest picture, *Around the World in Eighty Days*, which he had directed and which became almost an historic classic. We were all delighted for him.

My French agent made a short visit to London with her star client, Brigitte Bardot, and we had a very pleasant dinner together, followed by a while at the Milroy Club where BB showed her eye-catching paces on the dance floor. I had by now learned to act as a pivot for my partner and to let her do the showy work, which Brigitte did with considerable zest.

By the beginning of November I had finished my work on *Yangtse Incident*. At that time gathering political storm-clouds were casting a grim shadow over Europe and the Middle East. Russia had invaded Hungary, and the British and our French allies had sent a force into the Suez area spearheaded by airborne troops. The country was almost on a war footing, petrol had been rationed and convoys of sand-camouflaged Army vehicles and tanks were heading towards the ports. For those of us who remembered the build-up to the Second World War, the signs were ominous and depressing.

On the weekend after filming had finished we gave a dinner party at Wayside for ten of our closest friends. At 10 pm we took the unusual step of watching the Prime Minister's TV broadcast. Bill Astor was particularly concerned with the plight of the Hungarians and within a week or so he was at the Hungarian frontier helping refugees to escape across the border, a risky task for which he volunteered without hesitation.

I was fortunate in having a few free weeks at that time. Kitty was quite seriously ill in mid-November and had an internal operation, so I was able to lend a hand with the children and some of the house chores. I was particularly proud of my work in polishing all the panelling in the hall and newly-decorated dining room. Pat Wilkie was a great help and together we got up to date with our office work and piles of mail.

I still had to go to London quite often and I travelled mostly by train, due to the temporary petrol shortage. One of these trips was to meet Otto Preminger, the great director/producer, who was about to film Shaw's *St Joan*. He offered me the good part of Dunois and gave me a script to read. Very flattered that he wanted to include me in the galaxy of stars whom he had contracted for the picture, I rushed home clutching the script.

I was at Elstree the next day dubbing sound and doing a stills photo session, but that evening read the script and phoned Pickman in Hollywood. He was delighted, because this was to be a major movie.

So I already knew what my next job was to be in the New Year of 1957, subject to contract. This was all happily agreed with the help of Bob Lennard and Laurence Harbottle, and within days I was included in the cast that Preminger announced at a press reception at the Dorchester Hotel. I was able to break the good news to Kitty during the next of my twice-daily visits to the hospital.

Shooting was to start in mid-January, but before that we were to read and rehearse in December. Preminger was meticulous in his preparations and was adamant that we should all be thoroughly conversant with our parts before going into the studio. I also had to have several fittings for the suit of armour I was to wear throughout the picture, and had a session with Roger Furze, the designer, discussing the medieval pudding-basin haircut I was to adopt.

I found Otto Preminger very courteous in his heavily-accented Teutonic manner. Although he could be a hard taskmaster, I personally got on with him extremely well. Indeed, he was most helpful to me and took great pains to get the best out of my performance, especially in slowing down my rather clipped diction – a lesson I never forgot. Gentle John Gielgud seemed terrified of him, as did the unfortunate Jean Seberg who was reduced to tears on several occasions by Otto's hectoring ways.

Totally inexperienced and insecure, the poor girl had a dreadful time and we were all sorry and embarrassed for her. With her flat Mid-West intonation and total lack of previous acting ability, she was scarcely up to the demanding role, but Otto managed to drag some fire and power out of her by his Svengali methods, albeit by making her life utterly miserable. He did once explain to me that he had to be cruel to be kind, but I'm not sure that he didn't sometimes relish his constant badgering.

I well remember our first reading at Shepperton Studios. We were ranged around a long table in the board room like monks at a refectory table with our abbot, bald and rather sinister, at the head taking the service. It was a distinguished gathering which included Sir John Gielgud, Richard Widmark, Finlay Currie, Felix Aylmer, Francis de Woolf, Victor Maddern, Anton Walbrook and David Oxley.

I had lunch afterwards with Richard Widmark, and we both agreed that we were in for a tough few weeks in the New Year.

We rehearsed daily almost until Christmas, my journeys back and forth to Shepperton plagued by some very heavy fog.

By Christmas Day Kitty was home from hospital and we had a lovely time round the Christmas tree as the children opened their presents, which included the annual parcel from Uncle Walt Disney with special baby gifts for Fiona. In the afternoon, replete after a huge lunch, I happily spent a couple of hours on the drawing-room floor playing with their toys.

That evening we dined with Lord and Lady Palmer, starting a ritual that was to last for years. It had been a fine, clear evening, bitterly cold but dry and crisp. As we left the dining room later and went into the drawing room we found the scene outside the windows transformed. While we had been dining heavy snow had fallen, covering the surrounding garden in a silent white blanket. There could not have been a more traditional ending to Christmas Day 1956.

17

A Moving Period

Our Christmas holiday was rounded off by our annual visit to Bertram Mills Circus at Olympia. We picked up William and Nanny Astor at Cliveden and had a very jolly family lunch with them and the Palmers and their little daughter Carol; afterwards it was great to see the children (and the grown-ups!) bubbling with enthusiasm under the big top.

The next day Peter and Fiona went to a party at Cliveden. Fiona, not yet quite a year old, apparently enjoyed herself hugely. That was one of Bill Astor's great attributes: he adored children and was a great organiser of games and fun for them, spending much of his time on all fours giving piggy-back rides to the little ones.

After several more rehearsal days and armour-fittings filming started on Otto Preminger's *St Joan*. Shepperton Studios were quite near Wayside, so Baron came with me most days. The great black dog was quite happy lying around the set, looking majestic and perfectly in keeping with the medieval scenery.

It was marvellous to be working with a great, if somewhat austere, director and a group of splendid actors. My only problem was with my heavy and uncomfortable armour, which pinched me in all manner of places at every move. It had been carefully fitted but still made me wince, especially when I had to kneel. God knows how the knights of old retained their manhood in battle or on horseback! By the end of each day I was very glad to unbuckle myself out of my metal casing.

Apart from that the filming went very smoothly and Otto became almost mellow – except to the unfortunate Jean Seberg – and even asked me to join him in a TV trailer he was shooting about the making of the movie.

One evening after shooting I went to London to join Herbert Wilcox and Michael Anderson at a special private showing of *Yangtse Incident* which was attended by the heads of Associated British and the British Lion distributors. We were all three thrilled by their reactions.

On another occasion I had supper with Vincent Sherman, who had directed *The Hasty Heart* nearly ten years before. I was delighted when he told me he had at last found a subject which we could work on together again. The script of *The Naked Earth* was in its early stages: it was set in Africa and would be made later in the year. He was very enthusiastic about it and the part I would play. 'It'll bring you another Oscar nomination,' he said, and seemed genuinely to believe that. Naturally, I was agog to read the finished script. Apart from anything else, I had great affection and respect for Vince both as a director and as a person. He had already spoken to Robert Lennard about my availability and had been assured that ABPC would not raise any obstacles.

I had a fair amount of free time at this period, as my role as Dunois in *St Joan* only required about ten days' shooting and I had a long break in the middle of the schedule. I had intended to take Peter and Kitty to Switzerland for a winter sports break, but had to abandon the idea owing to insurance problems in the event of an injury. Apart from various meetings in London, I managed to spend a lot of time at home, especially for Fiona's first birthday party.

One of my discussions in London was with Vincent Sherman and his scriptwriter and a professional crocodile hunter who was to be our technical adviser eventually in Uganda. Fortunately for my peace of mind he was intact and assured me that the dangers would be minimal!

I also went to Dublin for a few days doing personal appearances at the cinema that was showing *D-day, the Sixth of June*, where I was accompanied by my friend and co-star Dana Wynter who had flown from America for the occasion. My FitzPatrick aunt and uncle met me at Dublin airport and we spent a lot of time together.

On the day of my return home dinner was served for the first time by our new houseman, White, who seemed to be very efficient and was the best polisher of furniture, floors and silver that we have ever known. Possibly his service in the Royal Navy accounted for this. I was also home in time for the wedding of Jill Paul, my former secretary.

While having regular talks with Vince Sherman about *The Naked Earth*, which was starting at the end of July, I suddenly found myself approached about yet another film project. It was then called *The Prescott Affair*, produced by Douglas Fairbanks Jnr, and to be directed by Michael Anderson. I read the script one evening over supper at the Chez Luba restaurant and loved it.

What a prospect I had before me! Here I was in the midst of filming *St Joan* and being offered two fascinating subjects which I could just fit in that year, working with two directors whom I already knew and respected. I could scarce believe my luck . . .

Immediately after the end-of-picture party for *St Joan* early in March I went straight to the Savoy Grill for supper with Michael Anderson and Douglas Fairbanks's associate producer, a delightful man called Tommy Clyde, who filled me in with the plans for *The Prescott Affair* – later to be called *Chase a Crooked Shadow*. The film was to be started in May with location scenes on the Costa Brava in Spain, then finished at Elstree Studios. The female star would be Anne Baxter, whom I had always admired since her terrific performance in *All About Eve*.

So much was happening in those spring weeks. As well as the two film prospects I was finalising our move to take over the Haileywood estate and to start farming, and I even took a couple of weeks off for a holiday in Switzerland.

We planned to spend two weeks in Arosa, a delightful little resort, and arranged to take Sister Stokes to look after Peter while Fiona stayed at home with Nanny Northwood, her new nurse. We had a lovely week there as I tried to recall some of the skiing skills learned during my wartime months in Iceland, while Peter completely outshone me after only a couple of days.

I came more into my own during the *après-ski* sessions in the late afternoon, knocking back glasses of hot punch, stuffing in mounds of Swiss patisserie and clumping around heartily on the dance floor. We met a lot of people similarly enjoying themselves, but were particularly intrigued by one couple who never seemed to join in with the general conviviality. They always stayed apart, and dining alone, and we felt rather sorry for them so we decided to invite them to dine with us one evening. They were Germans named Geissendorfer – he rather fat and pasty-faced, she very chic and handsome. They seemed only too glad to join us, and subsequently he told me that he had been one of Hitler's official war artists and had faced the Nuremberg war trials. I presumed that he had only recently been released from a term of imprisonment, which would account for his sickly appearance. On the day we were leaving he said he would like to send me one of his works and asked what subject I would like. Without any real thought I said 'horses'. Within a few weeks a lovely etching of wild horses careering across the landscape arrived, and I still have it. I have often wondered as to the truth about him.

Arosa was a beautiful spot and the view from our balcony was glorious, but unfortunately the snow began to disappear very quickly, so we decided to spend our last week at Lausanne at the Hôtel Beau

Rivage, where we were given a glamorous suite lately vacated by King Farouk of Egypt. While there, Kitty went to Professor Rochat at his famous clinic to see if he could sort out some of her internal problems. He found nothing organically wrong, but prescribed a course of injections for the next three months.

We arrived home, tanned and fit, the day before the *Yangtse Incident* première in London.

What a day that was! First, in the morning there was the press showing, followed by a reception at which there was no doubt about the reviews that would follow. Herbert Wilcox and I exultantly lunched together at the Pastoria.

Of its first public showing that evening, nothing could better describe the occasion than the description written by Franklin Gollings, Wilcox's associate producer and the man who had originally envisaged the project:

On 1st April, 1957, in front of a distinguished audience headed by His Royal Highness, The Duke of Edinburgh, *Yangtse Incident* was given a fabulous and memorable world première at the Plaza Cinema, Piccadilly Circus. Prince Philip described it as the finest naval picture he had ever seen.

Felix Barker, doyen among the film critics and reviewers, advised exhibitors, 'Mortgage your cinemas for this one!' Not surprisingly, after such a reception, which captured the world's Press next day, it remained at the Plaza for eight weeks, the only British picture to occupy a West End cinema, exclusively, for such a prolonged engagement.

I must admit that during the next few weeks, every time I rounded Piccadilly Circus I sneaked a proud look at my name up there at the top of the huge electric sign!

Negotiations for my contract for *Chase a Crooked Shadow* had now reached a rather sticky stage. Robert Clark wanted the film to count as my ABPC contract film for the year; this would have meant that I received less than 50 per cent of my salary, and would leave ABPC with no need to find another subject for me under my one-film-a-year deal with them. I was not unduly surprised at this ploy, as I knew Mr Clark hated to be caught out by having to pay me my one-picture salary even if Associated British did not succeed in finding a subject. I felt that this was not my fault, and that in any case *Chase a Crooked Shadow* was not an ABPC picture. Douglas Fairbanks and Tommy Clyde supported me in this, and Laurence Harbottle advised me that I was legally correct. So I sweated out a long period of meetings and arguments until, at a lengthy discussion at Elstree with Clark and Jimmy Wallis, it was agreed that I could make a separate deal with Fairbanks's company. Once again I had won my point, though I disliked being involved in these squabbles.

Funnily enough, Mr Clark always seemed to be equally relieved when the arguments were over. I believe he just could not help being contentious in any business deal. He was a man who had fought his way up from poor beginnings in Glasgow by working to pay his way through school and law college. At one time he drove a bus and felt he had been unfairly treated by his employers; he had bided his time, made a pile of money by playing the stock markets and eventually bought the bus company and sacked his former bosses. He became a multi-millionaire the hard way, was a tough negotiator, but was always fair in the end. He did a great deal for the film industry as President of the British Film Producers Association, yet was never honoured – God knows why. Perhaps successive governments found him too hard a nut to crack.

My contract for *Chase a Crooked Shadow* finally signed, I went through all the preliminary stages of wardrobe fittings, make-up tests and script conferences, then early in May I flew to Cannes for yet another Festival with Michael Anderson and Herbert Wilcox. We were accompanied by David Kingsley, deputy chairman of British Lion, and his wife, a very jolly lady.

This was by far my most memorable Cannes Film Festival so far, partly because my own film *Yangtse Incident* was to be screened, and partly because of the terrific public relations exercise that Herbert and the Royal Navy mounted. On the day that our picture was to be shown HMS *Birmingham*, a handsome cruiser, lay off-shore surrounded by hundreds of small craft and drawing the admiring gaze of the crowds thronging the sea-front.

There was an invitation-only reception on board before lunch and hordes of gangway-crashers had to be turned away. Herbert, Michael and I were invited to stay on board for lunch with a few others and the afternoon was taken up by a series of radio and TV interviews. HMS *Birmingham*'s presence was the centrepiece of the Festival and the day also coincided with the annual Battle of Flowers, a spectacular firework display and all the festivities of a real French gala, with the cruiser – floodlit and a-sparkle with festoons of lights – making a magnificent backdrop to the whole scene.

We entertained the ship's officers to dinner at the Carlton Hotel, and then all strolled down to the official opening of *Yangtse Incident* at the main cinema. The reception afterwards was tremendous. Altogether, it had been Britain's day at Cannes. Later, needless to say, the celebrations were continued for a while at the casino – where I finished up more or less all square with my usual modest little pile of chips – and then at a nightclub where the chief attraction was a floor-show staged with a mixture of transvestite show 'girls' mingled with numbers of seemingly female dancers. Distinguishing between the sexes was not easy; one pretty blonde had caught my eye and when the entertainers joined the customers at the bar after the show my friends dared me to test her credentials by asking her to dance with me and to join our table. Somewhat nervously I took the gamble, reckoning that I would very soon find out if I had erred in my judgement. To my great relief, she turned out to be a delightful girl who paid for her annual Riviera holiday by being a water-ski instructor by day and dancing at night.

With scarcely time to pack and get to Nice airport, Michael Anderson and I were in flight to Barcelona for the start of shooting on *Chase a Crooked Shadow*, arriving in Spain in the evening and then being driven to the Hostal de la Gavina at S'Agaro, a sumptuous small hotel set in a lovely and very private part of the Costa Brava.

We soon found that the rain in Spain did *not* stay mainly on the plain, for it interrupted our first two days' filming at Tossa, a coastal village. However, the weather then cleared and we caught up with our schedule. Our locations were partly on the beach, partly in and around a beautiful villa perched above the cliffs with glorious sea-views, but most crucially along a stretch of narrow, winding road that snaked hazardously along the coastline half-way up the cliffs, with a sheer drop to the sea on one side and a wall of rock-face on the other.

The story of the film concerns the mysterious disappearance of a racing driver who has left his sister (Anne Baxter) with considerable wealth and a few questions to answer. The character I play turns up claiming to be that long-lost brother, with impeccable credentials that Miss Baxter cannot crack despite all her suspicions and queries. Finally, she hits upon a foolproof idea: her brother, Ward Prescott, owned a powerful Lagonda sports car which he could drive along that cliff road between two points in a very fast time. The car is still in the garage in working order and ready to go; she dares me to drive it and equal that time, a challenge which I accept, with her as passenger to check the speed and time.

This is where Anne Baxter earned my wholehearted admiration. For two days we did hair-raising runs along that terrifying course, and she never once flinched or asked for a double to take her place. More than once I nearly scared myself witless, but if she was frightened she never showed it. Perhaps she was unaware how near we were to spinning over the edge at times.

Because of the speeds and the nature of the road it was not possible to have us followed or preceded by a camera car, so the cameras were mounted in different positions behind, before and beside the Lagonda, bolted to the car on tubular steel frames. Now I quite fancied myself as a skilled driver, and had learned to 'heel-and-toe' and to drift a car round corners in the days before the war when I had used a little Lagonda Rapier sports car, and later with my hairy old Railton. But what I was unprepared for was the change of balance on the car caused by the heavy camera and the steel tubes, especially when they were mounted on the front of the car. Several times I approached a sharp bend at what I reckoned was a fast but safe speed, only to find that I had a hell of a job to lug the whole caboodle round the angle, sometimes having to brake on the apex of the corner just when it was dangerous to do so.

Also I had to be careful, when the camera was stuck out at the side of the car, not to get too close to the rock-face, and was therefore unable to straighten out some of the worst bends. If that camera had hit the cliff, it would have meant a certain crash.

I was very relieved when that two-day sequence was safely in the can. It was perhaps the most exciting highlight of the picture, but Anne – who always said she had perfect confidence in me – never knew the degree of risk she took.

It was just as well that the scene was finished before Kitty arrived to join us for the last week in Spain. She would have been even more petrified than I was. Apart from that we all enjoyed our location, set in one of the most beautiful parts of Europe.

Only one other thing bothered me: I had developed an infuriating dry, ticklish cough, probably caused by the dustiness of the area. Time and again I spoiled a shot by hacking away uncontrollably.

On my first day back at Elstree Studios I contacted an ear, nose and throat specialist. Deciding that extreme measures were needed if I was to continue filming, he gave me a couple of antrum punctures, a very nasty process which entailed shoving a drill up my nostrils and boring through my upper jaws, then sticking tubes into the aperture to drain away the ghastly gunge that dripped down. It was all rather revolting, but I still managed to keep a dinner date at Chez Luba that night.

I had some discomfort from my sinuses the next day, but the cough gradually got better and an X-ray at the end of the week at St Mary's Hospital showed some slight infection still remaining but nothing serious. However, the sinus trouble had debilitated me a bit and my thirty-eighth birthday came on a day when I felt pretty wretched. Luckily a party of young Australian girls was being shown round the studio and it transpired that it was also the birthday of one of them, so on impulse I invited her to supper that evening in London. I think it made her day, and it certainly helped to cheer me up.

Filming ran very smoothly until mid-July, and from what I saw of a rough-cut of the picture it was a credit to Michael Anderson's masterly direction. I had loved working with him again and with Anne Baxter, Herbert Lom and Faith Brook, also the charming Tommy Clyde and Douglas Fairbanks.

Fairbanks was also a close friend of Bill Astor, and in mid-June Bill gave him and Mrs Fairbanks the use of Cliveden for a coming-out ball for their daughter. It was a splendid affair of a grandeur which few great houses in England could still support. The place looked magnificent – floodlit and with the wide drive from the enormous, ornate fountain to the forecourt lined with flambeaux. The interior was no less impressive, and the guests in their finery even more so.

Mrs Fairbanks acted as hostess for the occasion, and to her fell the honour of welcoming the Queen and Prince Philip and the Royal Ascot party from Windsor Castle.

The Royals left at about 2.30 am and we finally got home just in time for me to have a bath and leave for the studios at 6.30.

I certainly needed my sleep the next night, because that evening saw the première of *St Joan* with dinner after at the Mirabelle. The reviews were mixed and particularly hard on poor Jean Seberg, but I came out of them unscathed.

It was a glorious summer that year. We still hadn't moved from Wayside and we used our pool a lot. The children also spent a great deal of time in the lovely pool at Cliveden, splashing around happily with young William and their other friends. Bill always liked to see children enjoying themselves there – and other people too, at weekends, as it unhappily became widely known in later years.

It had also become a custom of ours to let the Shrewsbury School boat crews use our pool during Henley Regatta week. They always stayed at our local vicarage a short walk away from Wayside, and loved to cool off after a hard day's rowing. For years, even after we left Wayside, the Shrewsbury boys spent their spare time with us, driven

Right: What news on the Rialto? With Eva Bartok and gondolier in *Venetian Bird*.

Below: Caught on a hot tiled roof — from the same film.

Below right: With Merle Oberon in *24 Hours of a Woman's Life*. Is that sympathy or doubt on her face?

The Costume Dramas

Opposite page

Above: The British ambassador, Sir
Roger Makins, visits the Court of
Queen Elizabeth. Behind him is
William Holden, on the right Joan
Collins. Bette Davis, of course, plays
the Queen.
Below left: Rob Roy and his highland
men sharing some hairy moments.
Below right: Baron the Great Dane
and Dunois the Bastard – in *St Joan*.

This page

Right: My dear Hollywood stand-in,
Henry Baum, and I take a breather
(and a gasper) on the *Virgin Queen*
set.
Below left: A worried but well-
protected Baron watches me going
over a waterfall in *Rob Roy*.
Below right: Glynis Johns and I
dancing cheek to cheek in *The Sword
and the Rose*.

Right: What I told Juliette Greco was obviously enough to make a croc laugh.

Below: Also from *The Naked Earth*: John and I make a quick getaway from those terrifying schools of hippo.

Beauty and the beasts: Marianne Koch and cheetah during the filming of *Sanders*

Wayside House, my first country home after the war.

The household we managed to maintain in the mid-fifties. *Standing L to R*:
Peggy (daily), part-time gardener, George Reeves (butler), French maid,
Miles (gardener), postman-cum-part-time gardener. *Seated*: Nanny Pitcher,
Miss Murray-Hamilton (cook), Kitty (with Fiona), Peter, me, Jill Paul,
Sister Cullinan.

The Dam Busters

Right: As Wing-Commander Guy Gibson, V.C.

Far right: It works! Guy Gibson and Barnes Wallis (Michael Redgrave) jubilant at the first successful test of the prototype bouncing bomb.

Below: With Sir Barnes Wallis and ex-members of 617 Squadron at a Dam-Busters reunion, 14 May 1955.

My aerial view of a damn
good piece of busting.

Being presented to H.M. The Queen, under the admiring gaze of Jean Simmons.
Below: Ride him, cowboys! With Walt Disney at Coney Island.

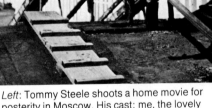

Left: Tommy Steele shoots a home movie for posterity in Moscow. His cast: me, the lovely Carole Lesley and Peter Arne.
Below: *A Man Called Peter*: Peter Marshall preaching.

in their minibus by their coach the redoubtable Peter Gladstone, himself a former Oxford Blue and Leander crew member. That year we were delighted when they broke the record for the Princess Elizabeth Cup event, even though they were beaten next day in the final. I had become a member of the Henley Regatta stewards and every year we looked forward to that week and especially to the success of the Shrewsbury crew. They were always a charming bunch of lads.

The week was usually rounded off by a dinner party at Stonor Park given by Sherman and Jeanne Stonor. Sherman's family had a long association with the Regatta and it was he who proposed me as a steward. They were old friends of ours and had in fact been instrumental in persuading us to look for a home near Henley-on-Thames when we first moved to live in the country.

That summer – when neither filming nor necessarily in London – I spent as much time as I could at Wayside and at the stables, where Damson had produced another foal. I was also often at Haileywood, trying to decide what improvements were needed to the house, the cottages and the farm buildings, and also discussing farming policy with Paul Rosewarne who was my agent and mentor.

I had agreed to take over the farming of the Haileywood land on 7 October, a week after Michaelmas Day, although it would be some weeks before we could move into the house itself because of the work to be done there. I had for years been yearning to try my hand at farming, but I had no practical experience and very little knowledge, and I faced it with some trepidation as well as excitement. For months I assiduously read the weekly *Farmer and Stockbreeder* journal and pored over books on dairy farming and arable production. That potted knowledge was the sum total of my expertise as an agriculturalist, so I relied heavily on Rosewarne's advice and knew that my first search must be for a reliable, experienced farm foreman/manager. Furthermore, I had to assemble all the necessary machinery – not to mention forming the beginnings of a herd of Jersey cows, the breed that was already at Haileywood and which I decided to stick to. I always admired a pretty face!

So there was a lot to be done, especially as I was due to go to Africa in July, and the money from Vince Sherman's film was going to be pretty crucial to me.

Finishing *Chase a Crooked Shadow* in mid-July, I spent most days of the following week with Vincent Sherman going through the script for *The Naked Earth* and having fittings for tropical kit. This was to be a Twentieth Century-Fox picture, one of my four-picture deal with them.

As I had enjoyed a busy and lucrative twelve months without making a picture for Associated British, who had been unable to find a subject of their own for me, I felt a twinge of conscience about taking their money, so proposed that they should suspend my contract for a year. That way they would not have to pay me my annual stipend; but I asked that, should they not take up all their annual options on my services before the full term of my contract, I should be compensated by a back payment for the year which had been missed out. To my slight amusement, but not greatly to my surprise, the multi-million-pound corporation jumped at the idea with alacrity and an agreement was drawn up by Laurence Harbottle, who plainly thought that I was daft. I thought I was, too, but at least my conscience was clear in the knowledge that I was not taking money for nothing.

After an exciting evening at the White City International Horse Show, I left early next morning from London airport for Entebbe, where I arrived the next day in time for lunch and a bath at the Lake Victoria Hotel before taking off again for the unit location at Murchison Falls Park, an enormous game reserve literally teeming with wildlife.

The trip in that light aircraft to the Wangkwar airstrip at Paraa was only the first of a series of hair-raising incidents in what was to be for me the most spine-tingling few days I had ever known since D-Day, 1944.

The pilot was a well-known local character famed as much for his alcohol intake as for his aeronautical skills. In other words, he was a boozy Irishman who had somehow managed to hang on to a commercial flying licence, and transported unsuspecting tourists to the Murchison Falls Park, where they would feel a lot safer than they did in his plane.

Unfortunately, I got him after what must have been a particularly heavy lunch-time session, and he really set out to give me an exciting hour or so of close-up viewing of the terrain and its four-legged inhabitants.

Chattering incessantly, he had us skimming the bush, weaving and dodging about until he spotted a herd of elephants or antelope, whereupon he would let out a whoop of glee and proceed to stampede them, ducking and diving and circling until they disappeared in a cloud of dust while he looked for more game to aggravate. It is a moot point who was the more terrified: me or the animals. However, already rather queasy from TAB and yellow fever jabs which I had been given before departure from London, I just hung on uncomplainingly to my seat, reckoning that he would probably be even more elated and reckless if he saw how much he was scaring me.

When we reached the airstrip, it was only to see a little black boy scampering about waving a stick in an effort to clear the runway of dozens of small impala that were happily grazing there. After a few circles, we eventually put down and bumped to a stop. I collected my baggage and tottered groggily to a waiting Land Rover, hoping that the next part of the trip would not be long and I would soon be able to gain the sanctuary of a lavatory.

When we reached the Safari Lodge it all looked quite civilised: a collection of huts and dining-halls and wash-rooms securely ringed by a huge wooden boma or stockade. To my consternation, however, our unit manager told me that while Vince Sherman and all the rest were living in the Lodge, I was to have the signal honour of staying with the Chief Ranger, Colonel Trimmer, and his wife a mile or so away in their bungalow somewhere in the bush. For all their hospitality and kindness, I would have much preferred to sleep in the safety of the Lodge. Frankly the prospect of a stay in the bush in an area teeming with elephant, buffalo, leopard, lion, hippopotamus and all manner of predators alarmed me. However, there was nothing I could do about it.

The Trimmers lived in a very simple wood and galvanised iron building, and I duly presented myself there. They were both charming, he quite elderly and she rather younger, and both obviously besotted with wildlife and totally oblivious to any danger. That was fine for them: they had lived like that for years and were used to it. But I wasn't, and not a day passed without something putting the wind up me.

My room opened off a balcony and had an iron bed covered with mosquito netting, the minimum amount of furniture and a stable-style door. I was told that it would be quite safe to leave the top half of the door open at night.

I was to breakfast with the Trimmers but to go to the Lodge each evening for dinner, so as soon as I had settled into my room I boarded the waiting Land Rover once more and went back to the stockade. We had travelled only a few hundred yards when my African driver suddenly stopped and switched off the engine and lights. 'Hippo,' he said. Now in the silence I could hear them grunting and munching as they made their way slowly across the track back to the river from their grazing grounds. My driver had shinned up a tree, whether for safety or to get a better view I never knew. Our conversation was restricted to a few English words. I crouched in the Land Rover hoping not to be noticed, while the school of several dozen hippopotami went by just ahead. The driver then took his place again and we reached the Lodge, much to my relief.

Every single evening that drive and the return to the bungalow scared me literally stiff. I would almost rather have walked – at least I could have heard what was going on in the night.

When I got back to the billet, Colonel Trimmer was waiting for me full of enthusiasm and Scotch whisky. 'There's a lot of activity tonight,' he said. 'Let's go down to a watering hole. You should see quite a lot.' He didn't seem to notice my sickly attempt to look excited at the prospect.

As we walked through the bush, I noticed gratefully that he carried a rifle. The night was full of sounds – bellows, screeches, grunts and animal alarm signals. They certainly alarmed me, but Trimmer kept steadily walking ahead. Then suddenly he motioned me to stop, and pointed to a spot where the moonlight glistened on a muddy pool. I crouched and waited, not knowing what to expect. We must have been there nearly an hour before anything happened, then a leopard slunk out of the shadows and slaked its thirst. It was a lovely sight and made Trimmer's day, but I must admit that my own mouth was by now bone-dry and I was counting the minutes to the moment when I could get back to the bottle that I had prudently brought from the Lodge. While the leopard was still there, some buffalo arrived and began to drink. There seemed to be a sort of eventide armistice arrangement between the species round that water-hole.

Back at last in my room, dog-tired and still nerve-jangled, I undressed, had a large scotch, then made a thorough search by torch-light all around my bed in case of any creepy-crawly nasties being there, before dossing down and tucking in my mosquito net securely around me. The last thing I remember noticing was Mrs Trimmer's pet cat sitting contentedly on the stable door before I fell into instant sleep.

I don't know what time it happened, but I was awakened by a growl and a terrible screech. I grabbed my torch and shone it around, but could see nothing. Too tired to care much anyway, I was soon asleep again.

The Trimmers were early risers, and at six o'clock he woke me with a cup of tea. I washed, dressed and went in to breakfast, to find Mrs Trimmer very upset because her little cat had been taken by a leopard during the night. 'It's so difficult to keep a pet here,' she sighed. I was not surprised, and from then on kept the top half of my stable door closed.

That day I didn't work but went to watch the unit shooting scenes at the falls themselves. Murchison Falls Park was a huge area of bush, grass and scrub bisected by the River Nile, very wide and fast-flowing in the park, and absolutely alive with crocodiles and schools of hippopotami. In daytime the crocodiles lined both banks of the river, basking in the sun with their great jaws wide open as white tick-birds picked their teeth clean. There must have been thousands of them. The hippos wallowed in schools of several dozen by day, often fighting bloodily or pursuing their very active and gory love-lives, and went off into the savannah to graze at night. The hippos and the crocs seemed to have some sort of modus vivendi established between them, for while they shared the same stretches of water I never saw any conflict between them.

The crocodile is a fish- and flesh-eater and I once saw one rear up in the water, virtually balancing on its tail as it swallowed an enormous Nile perch, gradully getting it down whole in a series of gulps. Apparently it likes its meat rather high and drowns most of its prey by dragging it down before storing it away for a while in its 'larder', usually a cave in the river bank. There was one horrendous tale about a man from the native village near the Lodge who had been flipped into the river by a croc's tail, then dragged underwater and finally left to rot in the 'larder'. The man had eventually come to and made his escape, practically unscathed, only to be speared to death by the villagers who were convinced that he was a ghost – an evil spirit returned from the dead to haunt them.

They are horrid beasts, especially as they cruise around amongst the rushes in the shallows with only their horned eyes visible.

Even my short jeep drive to the falls was a bit nerve-racking, mainly because of my total ignorance of the conditions. I had an African driver and an Askari armed with a spear to accompany me. Very smart, willing and soldierly were these Askaris in their khaki shorts, boots, puttees and blue or khaki jerseys, and capped by a tasselled red fez, and we always had one or two with us when were were working. But I must admit to wondering just how effective their spears would be in the event of an attack by an elephant, and we only once or twice had a white Ranger with us armed with a rifle.

On this first trip we more than once had to stop or divert as a herd of elephants barred our way and stared at us, ears flapping. I had been told that an elephant is only likely to charge when it flaps its ears, but in my short experience they nearly always seemed to be flapping their ears when they looked at me. Certainly I knew that an African elephant is virtually untameable, unlike its Indian cousin. This was elephant country – thousands of them.

Finally we passed a large herd of perhaps a hundred jumbos, and on the other side of the hill came across our unit, happily filming at the head of the mighty gorge worn into the rock by the Nile at Murchison Falls. The sight and the sound were awe-inspiring and a cloud of spume and spray hung over the bush below, shrouding a group of buffalos which we could see moving about amongst the trees. They were probably the most dangerous animals in the region and I gathered would often attack a man on sight. Only when we were filming in a spot where they were known to lay up did we have an armed Ranger with us.

The fact that I had just passed a herd of elephants only a couple of hundred yards away round the hill did not worry Vince Sherman or the rest of the unit at all. They had been in the park for several days already, and had got used to that kind of thing.

I started work the next day, sailing in a small Arab dhow on the Nile. We had great difficulty with the fast current, but were under tow most of the time behind one of the motor launches so ran no risk from the hippos.

While we were eating our al fresco lunch near the riverside, we watched an amazing sight on the far bank which I managed to film with my Bell and Howell movie camera.

A small herd of buffalo was being chased by three lionesses. For perhaps half a mile we saw the little herd of three or four cows, three or four bulls and some calves racing along raising a cloud of dust, with the big cats about 100 yards behind. It seemed certain that the calves would soon falter in their dash when suddenly two of the bulls stopped, turned and charged back at the lionesses, who in turn wheeled about and fled. A while later the two bulls came back into sight cantering along quite calmly, obviously reassured that their protective duty had been done.

Once more I had a somewhat disturbed night at the Trimmers'. I was sleeping peacefully, all hatches battened down, when the whole building started to shake. I immediately thought it was an earth tremor and lay poised, ready to spring out of bed, put on my slippers (having first made sure there were no scorpions in them) and run. But then the rattling and shaking stopped and I slept again. In the morning Colonel Trimmer asked me if anything had wakened me during the night. When I told him about the earth tremor, he chuckled and said, 'It was just an old jumbo scratching its back on the overhang of our roof.' What next? I wondered.

The last three days of that location were the most alarming for me.

In the film I was an immigrant Irish peasant come to Africa to try his luck as a farmer on land where he had been told the soil could be paved with golden crops, like the streets of London. The last leg of his journey up the Nile is in a dhow belonging to an Arab trader. With the help of a friendly African labourer and a French girl (Juliette Greco) left stranded there by a previous hopeful immigrant, he clears a piece of land and plants his crop, only to see it ruined by drought. Penniless, he is persuaded to become a crocodile-hunter and to sell his skins to a couple of English traders. Having no idea how to go about this risky task, he is lucky not to lose his own skin before he learns the tricks of this dangerous trade.

Hence my presence here on a crocodile-infested stretch of the Nile, trying to manipulate a dug-out canoe with the aid of my trusty African henchman.

The latter was in fact the equally unskilled John Kitzmiller, a hefty, charming and cultured American black who had become resident in Rome for some reason. John was a great fellow with a lovely sense of humour, a good actor and a grand companion in any circumstances – except in a dug-out canoe on the Nile amongst crocs and hippos!

The canoe was the real thing: a tree-trunk hollowed out and rounded at both ends and terribly heavy and unwieldy – at least with us as crew. I had learned a bit of watermanship in my youth, but never with a paddle, and I don't think John had ever been in a boat in his life.

For three days we had an awful time trying to navigate that dreadful chunk of wood. John was a big fellow, and the more he tried to paddle the more the thing rocked alarmingly – and we were not on a peaceful reach of the Thames or the Serpentine in Hyde Park!

The rest of the unit were in powerful, sturdy launches, and Vince and the camera crew were on a flat-bottomed steel motor-barge. They did not seem to understand our problems. Time and again Vince, with his loud-hailer, would shout, 'Turn the thing the other way! No, not that way – this way! Not backwards – forwards! Steady now – hold it! Hold it! Oh, hell! Now you're out of shot! Paddle, for Chrissake! Now, just keep going straight – not too fast! Not too fast! Jesus, mind those hippos!'

Hour after hour this went on until our arms and shoulders and bums ached. If we paddled with the current we went too fast, yawing about wildly. If we went against the current, paddling like mad, we drifted backwards, nearly always towards a group of hippos any one of which might decide to surface and tip us into the water.

When we were supposed to be stalking a croc amongst the reeds in the shallows, I had to be crouching in the bow with my rifle at the ready, but poor John could never somehow steer a straight course single-handed. He was no boatman and I was no Crocodile Dundee.

The whole sequence was nightmarish for us, and we almost wept with relief when the last shot was printed.

I suppose there must be something humorous to remember about that week at Murchison Falls Park, but nothing struck me as being very funny at the time – except perhaps for one incident.

A member of the unit was having a bath in a room right next to the stockade, having left the window behind him wide open. As he happily scrubbed away he was startled to see the water level subside almost to nothing, and for no reason that he could see – until he turned round and saw an elephant happily showering himself with nice warm water. He had looked over the stockade and siphoned out the water with his trunk.

That particular jumbo was the Major, a very old outcast from the herd, with only one tusk left and that broken in half. He had become semi-tame and always hung around the Lodge. I was told that soon after our visit he had gone into 'must' – a very rampant, runny-eyed condition that all elephants experience periodically – had become dangerous and had to be shot. Moral: never share your bath with an elephant.

Our next month in Uganda was very much more enjoyable. We all stayed at the Lake Victoria Hotel, which was comfortable and efficient. Our location work was in a spot on the shore of Lake Victoria where a simple wooden farmhouse had been constructed and an irrigation water-wheel and aquaduct had been built for the later sequences where I and the French girl – later to be my bride – had at last succeeded in raising good crops from seed paid for by my crocodile-hunting.

I had hired a little Nash Metropolitan car for the month and spent the first day exploring the area with a sweet teenage English girl, Fiona Chard, as my guide. Her mother had agreed to assist with our wardrobe on the film, and was a great help to us. Fiona had decided to study nursing in England as soon as she had finished school, and I promised to keep an eye on her until her parents arrived home too. She did in fact become a very efficient sister at the Middlesex Hospital and was later awarded the George Medal for gallantry.

Fiona's brave exploit happened when she was a very young ward sister. One of the patients, somewhat deranged, had climbed out of a window and sat on a narrow ledge several storeys high, threatening to jump if anyone interfered. Fiona climbed out of an adjoining window and sat precariously on the same ledge beside the patient, quietly and patiently trying to soothe that disturbed mind as she talked and edged closer. After what must have seemed an interminable conversation, a young doctor also climbed on to the ledge and sat on the patient's other side. Between the two of them, despite threats that they too would be pulled hurtling to their deaths, the gallant pair eventually persuaded the patient to climb back into the building.

The young doctor's reward was not only the award of a George Medal along with Fiona's – he also won her heart in other ways and they were soon married. She was a charming, lovely young person.

After the first day's shooting by the lake I drove to Kampala as a guest of the Barbecue Ball at the Kampala Club, the very busy and pleasant social centre for all the Europeans in the area. Because I had the car, I was able to spend many good evenings in Kampala, which was quite a swinging place in those days and only about twenty miles from Entebbe. While they did their best at the Lake Vic Hotel, it was in fact pretty dreary there. Vince and I and some others had to go to Kampala a couple of times a week in any case to see our rushes in the local cinema.

Then Greco arrived . . .

I had seen her singing some years before in one of the many existentialist cellar clubs on the Left Bank in Paris during the early fifties, and had never forgotten her and the way she captivated her audience. Dark, pale, fragile, very simply dressed in plain black, she simply used her magnificent, challenging eyes and her voice to put across her songs, with none of the bouncing and jiggling that most pop singers rely on.

I was introduced to her in the Lake Vic Hotel on the evening of her arrival. We had all wondered what sort of person she would turn out to be, having heard of her fiercely independent ways and her sudden rise to fame as an actress rather than as a singer, partly due to her much-publicised relationship with Darryl Zanuck. I think we expected to encounter a fire-eater. Instead here was this shy, soft-spoken, demure, rather wan little thing, still slender, still pale, still without make-up, still with a long straight mane of shining dark hair. Only one feature had changed: the once long gypsyish nose had been trimmed and was almost *retroussée*.

I did not see her again that evening. She was obviously tired, and after supper with Vince she went straight to her room.

On the set next morning she maintained her air of reserve and still seemed unsure of herself. In the plain, tattered dress and minimum of make-up that she wore for her role she still looked lovely, a gamine, alluring little waif. But her part called for a deal of fire and grit and she soon showed that she had plenty of both. Though she spoke almost perfect English, I knew only too well how hard it was to work in a foreign language, and understood why at times this tended to slow down her delivery and to inhibit her performance. But as her confidence increased she was soon able to let fly in true Gallic fashion.

She was a joy to work with, and as the days went by we became great friends, laughing and enjoying ourselves even in the most difficult and taxing scenes. Because of our irreverent sense of fun, we reckoned that we were a couple of satyrs and even had a signal which we could transmit across a crowded room: running our middle fingers down our noses to denote the sign of a cloven hoof. Her end-of-picture present to me was a gold cloven-hoof charm that she had commissioned from Hermes in Paris.

Shooting of the film went on day by day with no hold-ups, and included scenes with old friends of mine: Finlay Currie (*St Joan*), Orlando Martins (*The Hasty Heart*) and Laurence Naismith (*The Dam Busters*). Most evenings I drove over to Kampala (the equator line was on that road) and often took Greco with me.

Then Zanuck arrived. His entrance was typically dramatic: an old B25 US bomber suddenly swooped over us one day and went on to land at Entebbe airport. Apparently Darryl was using it to scout locations for his latest independent film production. He was then no longer president of Fox, but planning an ambitious series of his own films. It was literally a flying visit because he flew off again the next day, so he was not able to join us at the little unit drinks party that I gave that evening.

A couple of days later we went to the Caledonian Ball at the Kampala Club where grand old Finlay Currie was the champion of the ball, resplendent in full Highland evening dress which I can only presume he always carried with him on his travels.

Darryl Zanuck returned for a couple of days and came to see our rushes at Kampala; he seemed to like what he saw. The next evening I was dining alone at the Lake Vic, utterly miserable because I had just had a cable telling me that dear old Sally bull terrier had suddenly collapsed and died. For some seven years she had been such a loved member of my family, and we would all miss her. Zanuck and Greco (we always called each other by our surnames) were at another table and must have noticed my depression, because he came over to me and asked if there was anything wrong. I told him my news and he was very sympathetic. A few minutes later he returned and thrust a large glass of brandy into my hand. 'Knock this back, Dick. It'll do you good.' I thought it was a kindly gesture.

Whenever he and Greco were together they always seemed to be arguing or squabbling and I think she was giving him a rough time, though she never mentioned him to me. He certainly looked glum during most of his stay in Entebbe.

King Freddie of Bugunda was ruler of the country in those days, and one evening a group of us was invited to join him after dinner in Kampala for a brief 'concert' in the Drum Hut in his palace grounds. Not knowing exactly what to expect, we filed in and joined about twenty of his entourage in the thatched and reed-walled building, not much bigger than a Nissen hut. At one end sat the drummers, about thirty of them, all in tribal dress and each with a bowl-shaped, skin-covered drum ranging in size from an enormous instrument behind which the drummer had to stand, down to a tiny little toylike affair no bigger than a pudding-bowl.

They started quite slowly and quietly, then gradually increased the rhythm and volume until the air pulsated with thunderous, rhythmic sound. It was impossible not to catch the excitement and join in the beat with hands and feet, heads and shoulders. The whole performance lasted perhaps no more than fifteen minutes, but was an unforgettable experience.

On our last evening in Entebbe the hotel gave a great party for us and our friends from round about. It was a very convivial affair and Dick Richards – the popular film writer for the *Daily Mirror* in London who had flown out to visit us – got very drunk, so my Good Samaritan act for the occasion was to put him to bed.

We flew back to England in a chartered Britannia aircraft and had a splendid flight, best remembered by me for the ministrations of the chief steward. He was apparently BOAC's top man. He had served Winston Churchill frequently, and was always called into service on special flights. I could understand why when I found my shoes being deftly removed when I dozed off and a pair of slippers being eased on; and, on waking, to feel my face being gently wiped with a warm, scented towel while a glass of ice-cold orange juice was pressed into my hand!

We stopped briefly at Khartoum where I bought gifts to take home, and arrived next evening, where Kitty and the children – and, of course, Baron – were at Heathrow to meet me.

The Naked Earth was completed in six weeks at Elstree Studios. I must say that I was greatly relieved to be working in the comparatively safe environment of Elstree after our experiences in Uganda, and both John Kitzmiller and I handled our dug-out canoe with consummate skill in the studio tank and on a nearby reservoir, where the hippos and crocodiles were all inanimate models. We even had the temerity to board one of the canvas and rubber hippos and paddle *it* around!

Greco was staying at the Savoy Hotel and we spent many evenings together, sometimes with John Kitzmiller.

The film was obviously turning out well and Vince Sherman was pleased with the results. However, an unpleasant schism was developing between him and the producer, who was also the screenwriter, and relations between them grew progressively worse. The atmosphere on the set became very strained, with Vince doing his best to be patient during some of their arguments but obviously resenting the interference with his plans for editing and cutting the picture.

Finally, Darryl Zanuck arrived in London at the beginning of October and decided to do most of the finished cutting himself. Poor Vince found most of the shaping of the end product taken out of his hands – not because of any failure on his part but because he had got thoroughly fed up with the bickering. Brilliant film-maker though he was, this was not one of Darryl's most inspired efforts, as the film became ponderous in places and in the end was not as good as it deserved to be.

On 17 October we finished filming on *The Naked Earth*; that same evening I joined Douglas Fairbanks, Michael Anderson and others at a preview theatre to see a running of *Chase a Crooked Shadow*. We were all thrilled with it. Here we knew we had a really good picture, and the reception for it was very enthusiastic from all who saw it. Celebrating afterwards at the Milroy Club, Doug, Mike and I joined Zanuck and Greco for a while.

During those weeks I had spent every spare moment preparing for our departure from Wayside House and our take-over of Haileywood – engaging staff, arranging for the foundation of our future milking herd to be bought at auctions, buying farm and garden equipment, deciding what improvements and alterations were to be made to Haileywood House and the cottages and planning farming policy with Paul Rosewarne, who proved to be a very wise and calm adviser.

It had been a pretty restless year for me, with trips to France, Spain and Africa, but now I was about to embark on perhaps the most exciting move of all: to Haileywood and my long-cherished entry into farming.

18

A-Farming I Did Go

My yearning to farm my own land was innate. Generations of my forebears had farmed in County Tyrone and I had spent much of my childhood at my step-grandfather's small estate in County Antrim, the ill-fated Brecart which I had been told would one day come to me. That it did not, owing to a family dispute following my mother's death, was probably the most fortunate thing that ever happened to me, considering the estate's luckless history and final disintegration. I was a countryman born and bred, yet I had somehow chosen to follow a profession far removed from any bucolic pursuits. I had always wanted to combine the two, and here at last was my chance.

Weeks before I took over Haileywood and its 100 acres from Christopher Mann I had engaged farm and garden staff, bought tractors and machinery and fourteen in-calf Jersey heifers which Christopher kindly allowed me to board at Haileywood.

From a surprisingly long list of applicants, Paul Rosewarne and I had chosen a farm foreman and a head gardener. The former was Mr Prevett, a pleasant, experienced farmer who had already held a management job for some years on a dairy farm. With him came his son Tom, a sturdy chap in his twenties who had worked for years with his father. There was also a teenage schoolboy son who would be helpful at harvest time and for odd jobs. So I had found my entire farm staff in one household! Furthermore, Mrs Prevett was prepared to help in our house.

The fairly large garden was already being run commercially as a market garden, so I needed at least three gardeners. As head man I engaged Mr Moreland, whose wife was also willing to help in the house – we would never be short of daily help!

Luckily I also inherited from Christopher Mann a lovely man who lived locally in a cottage which had once belonged to the estate. Joe Aggis was getting on in years and had worked on the estate for 50 of them, first as a carter and rick-builder and then as a vegetable gardener, but he did more work in a day than any of his younger colleagues. No matter what the weather, Joe – a tall, lean true man of the earth – just plodded on at his own methodical pace. When it rained he never paused except to drape a large heavy sack around his shoulders and don a battered old hat. He never got the hang of modern machinery, but stuck to the traditional tools of his trade. He used an old but beautifully made large wooden wheelbarrow with an iron-bound wheel; when, thinking to lighten his load, I gave him a light, strong galvanised metal barrow with a balloon tyre, he thanked me most politely – but never used it! Joe was nature's gentleman, surprisingly erudite and always courteous; an unerring weather-forecaster and an inveterate producer of prize vegetables at all the local shows.

A third gardener we would find in due course, but there was no hurry for this during the winter. Mr Moreland could easily handle the two greenhouses and keep the pleasure garden tidy.

We had also had changes in our domestic and office staff. Julia Stonor, daughter of my friends Sherman and Jeanne, came as assistant to Pat and would eventually concentrate on the farming business and records. Miss Murray-Hamilton had left after three years with us to take up a teaching post in the Domestic Science department of McGill University in Canada, and her place had been taken over by another young Scottish girl, Miss Henderson, who also had a Cordon Bleu diploma and had been found for us by Miss Hamilton.

White, the houseman, had gone – summarily sacked, in fact, after an unfortunate incident at one of our dinner parties. Fortunately all our guests that evening were close friends, so we were able to make light of it when White appeared tight, as drunk as a skunk. The pre-dinner drinks were airily wafted around from person to person on a silver tray which luckily had a raised edge to catch the spillage. As he bent over to serve the first course, I thought his face might end up in the plate and hoped that he would manage to stand erect again. It was one of the funniest performances I had ever seen, on a par with a famous theatre sketch which I had watched. However, before the second course I felt obliged to slip out and tell White to go to his room and keep away from the dining room. Marriott, one of George Reeve's colleagues who had come to help out, carried on by himself.

When the guests had gone I went to White's room to see if he was all right, but there was no sign of him. I searched around and eventually, guided by stentorian snores, I found him flat on his back in the grass. I fetched a jug of iced water and poured it over his head, which seemed to do the trick, and he tottered off indoors. He left the next day – taking one of my best suits with him. I was sorry for the poor chap in many ways. I had not realised that he had this problem – although I now understand why he occasionally took a day off and remained shut in his room, having explained beforehand that he felt a bout of malaria coming on.

Perhaps his departure was lucky for us, because we were blessed with the finest replacements as butler and head housemaid anyone could have had – Harold Dunant and his marvellous wife the sweet, irreplaceable Marcella. Dunant was a wiry, rather solemn little man who had an excellent wartime record as a senior NCO in the Royal Army Service Corps; after the war he had returned to Italy to find and marry Marcella, a young sempstress he had met there. They had since been in private service, were both in their forties, childless and utterly devoted to each other. Marcella, a neat, bustling little person from Padua, was never idle. She was a meticulous, cheerful houseworker and became self-appointed lady's maid to Kitty, taking care of all her clothes and the children's, and ironing, skilfully stitching and altering till late every evening.

This loyal couple were to be with us for ten happy years.

Such was the team that we took to Haileywood.

I took possession of Haileywood on 7 October, and the farm and garden staff moved into their houses which I had already had redecorated. At the same time a positive army of builders, painters and plasterers, plumbers and electricians moved into Haileywood House itself to start work on the renovations and alterations which had been planned for us by Ben Fick, who had done our drawing room at Wayside. On one day I counted 33 men working in the house!

Thank God I had a couple of lucrative years behind me . . .

The first priority was to get all the household staff quarters and kitchen facilities ready, so that at least the Dunants and Miss Henderson and the rest would be comfortable. Then the children's wing was to be done. After that the reception rooms and our bedrooms, bathrooms and dressing rooms would be tackled.

Wayside was sold now and there were only five weeks before we had to vacate it, so inevitably there would still be some chaos when we first moved in.

Meanwhile the farm staff were hard at work clearing out the farm buildings, painting them and checking all the milking equipment and the dairy. There was little to do for the as-yet tiny herd, since they were all dry prior to calving.

As my work at Elstree was now finished apart from a few stills sessions, I was able to spend a lot of time at the farm, walking it with Prevett and Paul Rosewarne and my old friend from my Welsh Players repertory days, Peter Trier, who had trained as an estate manager and was now manufacturing hen-battery and deep-litter equipment.

The farm was only small at present, just under 100 acres, so although I had every hope of adding to it for the moment it would only support a limited number of cattle.

It had originally been the home farm to Haileywood House, which by the 1930s had become the centre of an estate of some 2,000 acres. Much of the land had belonged to an old local family, the Baskervilles. Haileywood House, the home farm and some other farms had been bought or built by a wealthy retired Bristol businessman called Marden between 1908 and 1910. The story went that he had acquired much of the rest of the land and farms by judiciously presenting a case of vintage port at strategic moments to old Colonel Baskerville, the last of his line. Each time the two men had happily shared a bottle, the colonel had quite easily been persuaded to sell another farm.

The new owner obviously had a good eye not only for business but also for beautifying the estate; it had been splendidly planted with woods, spinneys and ornamental parkland trees, and around the big house were some lovely specimen trees. The views from the house were stunning: on the one side right across the Thames Valley and on the other across the farmland to Hailey Wood and Harpsden Wood. Most of the planting had been done some 50 years before I took over, so was in its leafy prime. The little home farm buildings were a model of Edwardian planning, while the house itself was excellent Edwardian mock-Tudor, on three floors and very well built. The entrance had originally been designed as a sitting-hall, panelled and with an imposing stone fireplace. We left it simply as an entrance hall and turned the billiards room into our sitting room.

The house was approached by a drive about a quarter of a mile long, winding and tree-lined, with a lodge, stables and garages at the road end.

Sadly the owner's son, Rex Marden, had been killed in the First World War, and eventually the estate had been broken up and sold, Reading University buying the biggest farm acreage and the rest being bought by tenants and others. The family had given Shiplake village a magnificent memorial hall and playing-field and a memorial wing to the local hospital in Henley-on-Thames in memory of Rex.

Some days after we took over, our first calf was born – a bull, which wasn't going to be much good on a dairy farm. However, we now had one cow in milk!

Then I went to my first dairy show in London, taking Mr and Mrs Prevett with me. It was an enthralling experience. If one enjoyed the atmosphere (or, rather, the ozone) of hordes of cattle, this was certainly the place to be! Under Peter Trier's guidance, I bought an electric butter churn.

I had to be in London a few times during this period, particularly for discussions about a film, *The Men from Moscow* – which was to be directed by Ken Hughes and distributed by British Lion – and for the Royal Film Performance of that year. But gradually our build-up for the move to Haileywood continued. Bob Armstrong brought over Damson and her foal, Courtier, from the stud farm to the Haileywood stables, and also found a pretty little pony for Peter called Jimminy Cricket, which could run out with Courtier.

One of my trickiest tasks was ferrying my small cellar of wine to its new location; this I did very gingerly in several trips. That same day I started up the central heating boiler and to my relief it worked perfectly – not like the old, clanking solid-fuel furnace which had given me so much trouble at Wayside. It was oil-fired, so no more coke-shovelling, thank God!

Finally the change-over took place. Nanny and Fiona were flown up to Scotland to stay with Kitty's parents, Peter went to stay at Cliveden with William Astor, Kitty and the staff went to Haileywood to see all the furniture in, and over that two-day removal period I camped out at Wayside. My last night on a camp-bed in the empty house was an eerie experience: so many memories of eight fortunate, happy years swept through my mind. The lovely old house had been kind to me and I felt deep sadness at leaving it, almost as if I had discarded a dear friend. I said a little prayer of thanks – and asked for more.

Then in the morning I loaded my new Land Rover with the last bits and pieces, handed over the keys to the new owner and went to spend my first night at Haileywood.

Kitty had got everything pretty well organised, but the dining-room and drawing-room stuff was still piled up in the hall and we had to use a spare bedroom, as our quarters were not finished.

A day later I met Milton Pickman at London Airport and we managed to put him up for a night before I left with him for meetings over a few days in London. After some discussion we decided that I should decline *The Men from Moscow*, as Fox were now ready for the last of my four-picture deal with them. Unfortunately, the screenplay they had lined up for me was, to my mind, a stinker. It was a melodramatic, unbelievable thriller called *Intent to Kill*, set in a hospital in Canada, and had all the merits of a run-of-the-mill TV drama. Pickman agreed with me and we did our best to persuade the head of Twentieth Century-Fox in London to get his masters in Hollywood to let me out of it. Sadly, Darryl Zanuck was no longer in charge there and his successor, Spyros Skouras, was adamant that I should do the film. I was sorry that my lengthy association with Fox looked like ending on a sour note.

Home again after a few days, I was just in time to start heaving all the dining-room and drawing-room furniture into place, with the help of the Prevetts, and to see the last of the builders and decorators. Bill Astor brought Peter back from Cliveden, Fiona and Nanny returned from Scotland and once more we were able to live as a family in our new abode.

All this activity had put quite a strain on Kitty. After dinner at the home of some friends she had fainted, and we left early. I then cancelled my appointments in London and called our new doctor from Henley, who diagnosed Asian 'flu.

Our bright spot at this time had been the arrival of our first heifer calf. We named it Peter's Special.

Nanny Northmoor had a couple of days off so I was left holding the baby, which meant that I potted the wailing Fiona and bundled her up very inexpertly in her nappies, watched on occasions by a giggling Peter who didn't seem to think any more of my efforts than she did.

All this restricted my time spent on the farm, but Prevett and I managed to walk every corner of it, checking on fencing and the general state of the land and planning the spring cultivations. I loved to realise that every blade of grass, every emerging seedling, every tree and every hedge belonged to me and depended on my resources for improvement and maintenance. It was worlds away from film studios and West End restaurants and clubs.

On the day when Kitty felt well enough to come downstairs, I drove to London to do some shopping for Christmas gifts and to see my dentist for the removal of a molar. It was while I was spitting out the blood that Pat phoned to say that Kitty had gone into hospital for an emergency operation after an examination that afternoon. I left for home right away and saw her in the hospital that evening, just before she was taken to the theatre. I went to see her again an hour or so after the op and she was much as one would have expected – muzzy and in pain. After that I visited her twice daily, except for a day spent in Brussels for *La Nuit Electrique*, an annual charity event based on a circus and variety performance during which a large group of European screen stars performed in the acts – one even going into the lions' cage alone and putting the animals through their paces. My act was much safer but somewhat claustrophobic. I was trussed up with rope and dumped in a padlocked box; then after a fanfare from the trumpets and orchestra, the box was opened and there I was – gone! How I did the disappearing act I truly cannot remember, so the Magic Circle need have no worries about the sanctity of their secret.

With Christmas and year's-end approaching Kitty came home but had to stay in bed, and Peter too was laid up with a bad cold and cough. So I did most of the Christmas shopping and fixed up the decorations and Christmas tree. Christmas Eve started with our second heifer calf (Fiona's Noël) being born, and ended with me creeping around the house doing my Father Christmas bit in the small hours. Before lunch all the farm and garden staff and their families joined us for a drink and to collect their presents. Joe Aggis was chosen as spokesman by his colleagues after a toast to our health (Fiona and I were the only fit members of the family at the time) and in his reedy, quavering voice announced that they had found their new boss to be 'very sociable, very sociable indeed'.

We all managed to get to the table for Christmas dinner, Kitty very groggy and Peter barking briskly – but at least we were all there! My gift from Kitty that morning had been a sweet gentle-eyed black great Dane bitch, who arrived with a large satin bow tied round her neck. Bess was only a puppy, all legs and feet, just as I remembered Baron when he first joined us, but she was much lighter in the bone and finer in the head.

Both children received gifts as usual from their Uncle Walt Disney.

On Boxing Day Prevett and I pottered around with guns and I shot my first Haileywood pheasants, much to my delight, while he got a hare. The rest of the day seems to have been spent mopping up after a very puddly Bess. We now had Baron, Wendy and Tinkerbell corgi and Trigger pointer, as well as Winnie the cat, so I was hopeful that Bess would soon learn from them and catch up on her house training.

Sadly, the next day Courtier, the young colt, died. An autopsy showed that he had eaten a bolt of mouldy hay, and thereafter we were very careful in the use of the hay we had taken over with the farm.

New Year's Eve of 1957 should have given cause for celebration, but none of us celebrated. Instead we were all abed early – a pretty gloomy end to a busy year.

19

Shooting a Mixed Bag

Our first month of 1958 at Haileywood did not exactly run smoothly for us. First of all, Kitty was not yet fit and had to rest every afternoon; then our nice young Miss Henderson fell sick and her parents drove her back to Scotland; I was trying to adjust to the demands of my two somewhat conflicting interests as an actor and a farm-owner; and our heifers kept on producing bull calves.

Fortunately Kitty's health gradually improved, though she tired easily; Mrs Prevett stepped into the kitchen breach and proved to be an excellent cook; I managed to shuttle back and forth to London for various meetings and still had time to walk the farm with the Area Agricultural Advisory Officer – who was very helpful and approved our stocking and cultivation plans – and to discuss with Paul Rosewarne and his architect plans for rebuilding the lodge and stables; and Peter started his first term at Friar Park School, then housed in the rather grotesque Victorian mansion which later became the home of a Beatle, George Harrison, and which had been built for a man called Crisp who must have been something of a humorist. Near the entrance was a statue of a monk carrying a frying-pan with a hole in it: the Holy Friar, from whom the house took its name. The grounds were very impressive and well-wooded, and contained a large grotto and a lake.

During January I took Anne Baxter to the première of *Chase a Crooked Shadow*, which received excellent reviews and was obviously going to be a successful movie; this was a relief to me, since I could not see my next assignment, *Intent to Kill*, being anything but mediocre. I had already started preparations for this Fox picture and had several sessions with the director, Jack Cardiff, and the production manager, Andy Worker. Jack, one of the greatest cinematographers in the world, had always been keen to direct and was a really sweet man; it was a pity that he had been landed with such a poor subject. However, he did his best with it and was a dear to work with.

At the end of the month I saw Kitty off by train to Brighton for a week's change of air, and then flew overnight to Montreal in Canada where we were to shoot a few days' location scenes in the snow-covered terrain. I was met at the airport by Andy Worker and my old friend Canadian Paul Sanguinet.

That evening I met my main 'consolations' for being involved in a film which I did not enjoy making: Warren and Lydia Stevens. Warren played the 'heavy' in the picture and was a nice chap, though rather morose and twitchy, and seemingly ill-matched with his stunning vivacious and witty wife Lydia, half-Russian and half-Irish, a very beautiful and successful American fashion model. The three of us became inseparable friends both in Canada and later in London.

My leading lady in *Intent to Kill* was Betsy Drake, ex-wife of Cary Grant, who was somewhat withdrawn and reserved. I don't think I ever saw her outside the studios.

Paul Sanguinet helped me to shop for gifts for Peter and Fiona, and I arrived home just in time for Fiona's second birthday.

Filming continued at Elstree for the next eight weeks, although I can't remember much about it. *Intent to Kill* was a totally forgettable picture, and I don't think I ever saw the finished product. I can't even recall the story, although I remember that it mostly took place in a hospital with all sorts of assassination attempts and skulduggery going on. However, my evenings with the Stevenses were always fun and we became Scrabble fanatics. I know that I put on a lot of weight with all the restaurant meals we consumed.

During February I managed to attend a meeting of my Lodge No. 21 and was passed as a Master Mason. I enjoyed those meetings and especially the dinners afterwards which were always enlivened by some very amusing and learned speeches, particularly from our distinguished legal brethren who at one time included five judges and a number of barristers.

One not-so-enjoyable meeting was with Roderick Mann, a film journalist who requested that I should meet him for drinks at Les Ambassadeurs as he wanted to do an article on me. I had met him at various times and never taken to him, but Leslie Frewin persuaded me that I should agree to join him.

Much to my surprise, he went out of his way to be utterly charming and almost sycophantic. 'I always thought you were rather pompous,' said he, 'but you're not at all. But you are enormously successful, aren't you? Look at the success your films have had in recent years.' I was embarrassed by his praise and muttered something deprecating like, 'Oh, do you think so? Oh, I don't know.'

Next Sunday his article appeared under the heading, ' "I'm not pompous; just successful," says Todd.' And I thought I had learned how to deal with press men!

My only regret when work finished on *Intent to Kill* was seeing Warren and Lydia Stevens leave London. They stayed on for a few days because Lydia was having her portrait painted by Sir William Russell Flint; then they left for France, where she owned a delightful mill-house at Méréville, near Paris, and Kitty and I joined them for a very relaxed week's holiday.

Much of my time during the stint at Elstree was spent in meetings with Associated British at which I tried to get the go-ahead from the Corporation to set up the making of a film based on *The Sleeping Mountain*, a book to which I had recently bought the screen rights. Other than a proposed film for Irving Allen, I had no definite subject lined up for the future and was anxious to get something going for my next job.

With more time to spend at home, I also had a chance to concentrate on the farm and gardens. I engaged Tony Cleaver as a third gardener and we began quite a flourishing market-garden business, selling fresh vegetables to local hotels and shops in Henley, with Joe Aggis excelling in producing bumper crops. I had also bought some new heifers to enlarge our herd, and arranged to rent a nearby 50-acre dairy farm to increase my acreage. We grazed our dry stock there but didn't need the dairy buildings, so started to convert them for use as pig-housing for the beginning of a porker enterprise. My intention was to build up to a really intensive small mixed farming unit to include milk production, pigs, poultry and garden produce.

Meanwhile Peter, whose pony Jimminy Cricket had turned out to be a vicious little brute and had to be sold, was loaned a beautiful little pony named Hinton Egrin; he did well in leading-rein classes at the Taplow and Windsor Horse Shows, and became quite a handy little horseman.

Sadly my dear friend Freddie Weil had died just before our move to Haileywood, so my own association with horses and Castleman's Stud Farm had come to an end. I greatly missed his wise advice on many things and those mornings at Knowl Hill watching horses at work. Bob Armstrong had established his own stable and took a couple of my horses with him, including Brimstone, a useful hurdler he had bought for me in Ireland, so I still had a slight interest in racing and continued to jog around on old Damson when I had time.

I found myself becoming more and more involved in local farming affairs and became a member of the Henley and District Agricultural Association Committee. I loved every moment of my new rural life. Apart from my daytime activities, there was nothing I enjoyed more than my evening walk down to the farmyard after dinner. Even my annual visit to the Cannes Film Festival in May seemed a needless interruption of a pleasantly rural way of life!

Bill Astor lunched with us one day and then drove me to Woking to visit the Ockenden Venture, a charitable foundation which had been started by Miss Joyce Pearce as a refuge and school for displaced children from German refugee camps. Bill was on the Ockenden Venture committee and I was invited to join it, which I did, and I remain a patron of this very active charity to this day.

I also joined Lord and Lady Douro in opening the Reading June Dairy Festival and later we dined with them at Stratfield Saye (they are now the present Duke and Duchess of Wellington).

My birthday that year was a memorable occasion, if only for my gifts: Kitty had given me a Jersey bull, while from Pat, Julia, the children, Ann Weil and others I received two cows, one heifer, two dozen ducklings, two dozen turkey chicks, a couple of piglets and two pigeon lures. When I arrived home from a birthday visit to Henley, I was greeted by a cacophony of squeaks, squeals and cheeps from the assembled company in the hall, only the cattle being deemed unfit to be entertained indoors.

Ann Weil gave us lunch at Castleman's Stud Farm and presented me with Freddie's lovely gold dress watch and one of his guns.

A few days later, Bette Davis and her sister and daughter spent a day with us at Haileywood and watched the afternoon milking session. I was glad to see that Bette's hair had completely recovered from its shaving in *The Virgin Queen*.

Around this time I also had a weekend visitor from America: Cornelius Ryan, an author who was in the midst of writing a mammoth tome about D-Day, 1944, which eventually was published as *The Longest Day*. He wanted to know in particular about my experiences during the capture and holding of Pegasus Bridge and the Orne River Bridge. He had obviously done his research and homework very thoroughly, because I could not fault a single sentence of what he had already written. I was merely able to add a few facts and anecdotes which he had not known about. Little did I think at the time that a few years later I would be appearing in the epic film based on his book.

At the end of June I also had my first experience of helping with my own hay harvest. The weather was good and my main contribution to the farm activity was in driving the tractor round the fields trailing the tedder and swathe-turner which helped the hay to dry out. Even through the tractor's diesel fumes the sweet smell of new-mown hay was a delight. Then I helped to stack the bales of hay on to the bale-skid after they had been ejected by the baler, which collected the nicely dried hay and formed it into neat, tied-up bundles ready for loading into the Dutch barn. By the end of the first week of July, our very good crop was stored and the surplus stacked.

Baron also did his best to add to our livestock numbers that month. He was mated to a very nice black bitch whose owner was willing to let me have the pick of the litter. She was brought over to Haileywood one afternoon, but did not appear to fancy her intended suitor and led him a hell of a dance around the garden, for which I could not exactly blame her. At seven years old, Baron was still a virgin, very inexperienced and somewhat over-eager in his approach. Worse than that, on the occasions when we thought the *moment critique* had arrived, he invariably caught sight of me, gave one of his embarrassed toothy grins and lumbered over to me as if to ask my pardon.

So I was banished from the scene and the two dogs were shut up in the tennis court. After a short time, the bitch's owner reported that all had gone well and promised to keep in touch.

Peter, too, distinguished himself at his birthday party. It was a wet day, but some fifteen children had a great time with an entertainer we had hired who led them in all sorts of party games, ending up with a request that each little one should come up on to the dais in the sitting room (former billiards room) and recite or sing some little piece of their own choice. Most of them obliged, to the benign approval of a dozen or so nannies, but these worthy ladies were not so amused when, after a series of 'Mary had a little lamb' and the like, Peter got up and lustily croaked, 'My old man's a dustman, he wears a dustman's 'at,' which was the current Lonnie Donegan skiffle song.

Meanwhile I was still beavering away trying to get some sort of a deal set up for a film based on *The Sleeping Mountain* before my year's option on the screen rights lapsed. Three months had gone by since my last picture, *Intent to Kill*, which I was sure would be a flop, and I was beginning to worry about the loss of good film time. I had to be careful not to get too absorbed in the business of farming instead of the business of filming.

Then in mid-July an offer arrived out of the blue, as they so often did when least expected. It came from Colin Lesslie, a charming and very experienced independent producer who was preparing a movie to be called *Danger Within*, a true story based on his own experiences of a mass escape from an officers' POW camp in Italy during the war. He wanted me to star in it and would send me a script as soon as it was ready. I told him that it sounded just the sort of thing I would like. I always thought that true war stories like *The Dam Busters* and *Yangtse Incident* had the edge on glorified tales of imaginary battle deeds. We arranged to meet again as soon as I had read a script.

The next day I saw Kitty and the children off to Scotland from Heathrow. After a lunch meeting in London, I was to fly up to Renfrew near Glasgow the same evening. Ian, the Duke of Argyll, and his wife Margaret had invited us to spend a few days at Inveraray Castle, their magnificent home in Scotland which I remembered so well from a visit years previously when filming *Rob Roy*. The high spot of our stay was to be a Highland Ball which the Argylls were holding the following week.

We arrived at Renfrew where Kitty was waiting and were driven on to Inveraray Castle. Ian was nothing if not a generous host, and I eventually crawled into bed about 1.30 am, practically comatose with a liberal supply of fine malt whisky.

Waking up in time for breakfast was no problem at Inveraray. The castle is a great square pile with a turret at each corner and a huge central inner hall which rises three storeys to a glass roof. The main bedroom suites are all ranged around a gallery on the first floor looking down into the hall, and at whatever time had been prearranged for reveille Ronnie, the Duke's personal piper, would march around the gallery skirling on his bagpipes, pausing for a while outside your door to give you the rousing benefit of your favourite piece. Whether you like the pipes or not, they are certainly hard to sleep through!

The four of us lunched at Lochgilphead and opened the Loch Fyne Festival, then spent a lovely quiet day looking around the castle gardens and grounds; after dinner we drove to a famous salmon-leap where, from an ornate little bower, we watched the great silver fish flash in the moonlight as they made their way up the river.

The following day we were joined by the other house-guests, General Sir Colin and Lady Vera Barber. He was then GOC Scottish Command, and I had met him in France and Germany when I was serving and he was commanding the 15th Scottish Division. At 6 feet 8 inches – the tallest general in the British Army – he was a foot taller than me and Vera was a foot taller than Kitty, so we must have made an ill-assorted foursome, but we became great friends. Years later, after Colin's death, Vera's home at Ripon in Yorkshire became my base for many a theatre tour.

We all dined that evening on board HMS *Barfleur*, anchored in Loch Fyne a few hundred yards from the castle walls, and the next evening the Highland Ball took place. This must have been one of the most glittering occasions seen in Scotland for many a day. The great stone castle was floodlit and so was HMS *Barfleur*, casting a shimmering gleam over the rippling waters of Loch Fyne. Most of the several hundred guests were in full Highland regalia, the men resplendent in dress kilts, velvet jackets and ruffled lacy cravats, and the ladies, including Kitty, girdled with tartan sashes. I felt positively dowdy in my evening tails and stiff shirt-front. A conventional orchestra played for part of the time, but a pipe band provided the music for the many reels, Gay Gordons and other Highland dances. Kitty's main partner was General Colin, and her only complaint was that the fur of his sporran tickled her nose.

It was an unforgettable event which finished with breakfast at 4 am. At 8.30 am Ronnie the piper aroused us and we left the castle at 10 am, were driven to Glasgow, had lunch with Kitty's parents, picked up Peter and Fiona, and by 3.30 pm were flying back to London none the worse for our exhilarating few days.

The following day I agreed to do *Danger Within* for Colin Lesslie, and celebrated later at the International Horse Show.

My next film assured, I now felt in a position to add some more land to the farm, and with Paul Rosewarne's advice I purchased exactly 50 adjoining acres from a Mr Keene, so I was now farming some 200 acres.

We had taken a very nice house in Jersey for the month of August, and flew there with the children and Nanny. It was a charming place in a lovely position opposite the official residence of the Constable of Jersey, it had a beautiful garden and was complete with gardener, cook and housemaid. There were only two problems: the cook was a rather formidable woman who talked in a strange French-English local patois and served everything soaked in a gravy seemingly made from Oxo cubes; and it rained and rained and *rained*. We had a few chilly days on quiet little beaches, and for the rest of the time tried to amuse the children by exploring the attractive island in our hired car. I visited several farms and managed to buy a couple of good but very expensive heifers.

I had to fly back to London a couple of times for meetings with Colin Lesslie, and also to do a broadcast appeal for the Ockenden Venture. The film script was excellent, and with Colin I visited a sandy, heathy area near Chobham in Surrey where the prisoner-of-war camp for the film was being constructed. Laurence Harbottle had drawn up my contract, and all was well. The film was to have a very strong cast, including Richard Attenborough, Michael Wilding, Bernard Lee, Peter Arne, Terence Alexander, William Franklyn and a young man called Michael Caine who had a tiny part as one of the prisoners.

I also had meetings at ABPC and with the Film Finance Corporation about the future financing of *The Sleeping Mountain;* and I met Frank Godwin, an independent producer whom ABPC suggested should be my executive producer if we got the project set up.

Within a few days of my final return from Jersey, I had wardrobe fittings at Bermans for my uniform. I was to play a major in the Parachute Regiment, one of the POWs, and decided to wear my own cherished red beret which I had worn from D-Day to the end of my service in Palestine and which was now bleached to a mottled pink. Sadly, at some point during filming I left it lying around somewhere and it disappeared, despite the fact that our security guard was the great old British heavyweight champion, 'Bombardier' Billy Wells – he also happened to be father-in-law to my stand-in, Harold Coyne, who had worked with me since *Robin Hood* years before. I never recovered the shrunken little red keepsake, and was very sad about it.

That was not the only memento I was to lose. When HMS *Amethyst* was eventually scrapped, the Admiralty presented me with the teak and brass-lettered nameplate from her quarterdeck. This hung on the walls of my studies in various houses over a number of years and was a prize exhibit. Then during the 1970s I lent it to an acquaintance, Alex Sterling, to decorate a wall of his club, the Sterling Area, but when this establishment was eventually sold, my *Amethyst* nameplate went with it, obviously forgotten by Alex in the list of fixtures and fittings. So somewhere somebody has this historic object and perhaps it will return one day to its rightful owner.

I really enjoyed working on *Danger Within*. A splendid true story of Colin Lesslie's own experiences in a POW camp in Italy, the whole film had the ring of truth about it. We spent the whole of September on location on the Surrey heathland – ideal for rambling around with Baron – and with such a cast it was very relaxed and smooth-running.

There were about 100 extras, and most of the lunch-breaks were spent playing 50-a-side football in the sandy confines of the camp. I had a caravan to change, rest and eat in, and nobody entered there while Baron was in charge!

The story showed how the entire camp of British officers escaped along a tunnel connecting the recreation hall to the heath outside, painstakingly dug over months under the direction of the Escape Committee of which I was head. All the sandy spoil from the tunnel was distributed about the camp from bags slung inside the prisoners' trousers. Our *bête noir* was an exceedingly unpleasant young Italian officer played by Peter Arne, and our other problem was an informer played by William Franklyn.

The actual break-out was during a concert performed by the prisoners in the recreation hut, with only POWs present. The entrance to the tunnel was under the stage, and as the show went on rows of prisoners filed along the tunnel and disappeared into the darkness, each to make his own way to safety in other areas as best he could, dressed in all sorts of craftily prepared civilian clothing.

Colin Lesslie himself had caught a train to Rome, wisely occupying a compartment full of German soldiers who spoke no Italian and who left him to himself. In Rome he had all sorts of adventures, hidden by various sympathisers including a network of prostitutes who hid him in their quarters while they plied their trade, mostly with Germans. At one point he was hidden by a Vatican gardener in a shed in the grounds of the Pope's home. He roamed relatively freely about the city and his most cherished souvenir was the autograph of Field Marshal Kesselring, the German C-in-C, which he had sought and obtained at the opera one night. Cheeky!

As the last prisoners hurried along the tunnel, the few remaining ones set up loud applause and the final man spent a hectic few moments operating the revolving clapping-machine (strips of leather attached to a drum and cranked furiously), completely fooling the guards outside, until he too popped into the hole, put the lid back in place and scurried away.

The film was very well directed by Don Chaffey, and had one of the best openings I had ever seen: the credits and titles rolled to a background of a mighty North African desert battle; guns roaring, tanks rolling, infantry advancing, machine guns rattling and shells exploding in great gouts of sand. Suddenly all was quiet, and the camera came in close on the khaki-clad body of a British soldier lying face down in the sand, evidently one of the casualties. Then, as the camera was craned back, one of the 'dead' man's hands came round and lazily scratched his behind, and as the camera pulled further back he was seen merely to be a prisoner taking a nap in the prison compound.

A fair number of visitors came to watch the proceedings from outside the barbed wire, and two of them were particularly welcome: a couple of good-looking teenagers, brother and sister, who volunteered to look after Baron while I was working. The girl was particularly enchanting, and no wonder: she was Arlette Dobson, who later won the Miss England title.

My weekends had now settled down to a routine of walking the farm with Prevett every Sunday; I had missed the Henley and District Agricultural Show, which was on a Saturday. We entered six of our Jerseys in a couple of classes and won a first, two seconds and a third prize. As always Joe Aggis won all sorts of awards with his vegetables and fruit, so Haileywood got off to a good start with its exhibits. Later I was able to see Peter win third prize on his pony Hinton Egrin at the Royal East Berks Show at Windsor, while our bull Southpark Golden Sovereign ('Willy' to us) got a third at the same show.

I was also now seeking a secretary to take over from Pat, who was going to join her sister in Bermuda and had landed a very high-powered job there with the Bermuda Development Corporation. A Reading newspaper had run an article on my search and we had shoals of applicants. In the end we chose Ann Waugh, a charming girl, a fine horsewoman – she had won the Newmarket Town Plate, then the only ladies' race, three times – and the daughter of Jack Waugh, the trainer. She moved in to work alongside Pat for a few weeks.

Soon after we started studio shooting at Shepperton, we had a tragedy at home. Poor gentle Bess, my Christmas present great Dane, had to be put to sleep. She had begun to show signs of uncoordination, and could not seem to control her legs which simply buckled under her. Various treatments were tried by the vet, but the symptoms grew steadily worse. Myasthenia gravis was diagnosed. It was harrowing to see her great amber-brown eyes look so beseechingly when she tried to run to greet me and could only collapse spread-eagled half-way across the floor. Our vet, one of a pair who had taken such good care of all our animals for years, came to the house one day to make a final decision. Neither of us could bear to be the judge of her fate. We talked of all the possibilities for a few minutes while Bess lay at one end of the hall on the carpet runner that led from the front door. Finally he said, 'Call her to you, Mr Todd.' 'Come on, Bess. There's a good girl,' I choked, hoping against hope.

She clambered to her feet, took a few uncertain steps and fell in a heap, still yards away. Her eyes seemed to brim with tears, as ours had done. She had tried so hard right up to the end, and was finally quickly put to sleep where she lay. I wrapped her in an old coat of mine, and buried her by the side of the tennis court, where there was already a stone to the memory of old fat Sal, the bull terrier.

A few days later Colin Hunter, who was secretary to a small local shooting syndicate, came to discuss my putting my land into the syndicate. It made good sense, as I had very little woodland other than spinneys, and my land now surrounded Hailey Wood which Colin's group rented from the Forestry Commission for the shooting rights. Most of my birds were held in patches of kale and a field of mangolds which we grew for winter feed for the cattle. I agreed to the merger and took two guns in the syndicate, whose land was largely farmed by my neighbour Fred Doble, a leading local producer of barley and dairy cattle. So we now formed a small but sporting shoot of about 1,100 acres which included nearly 100 acres of young, well-managed woodland and over 100 acres of water meadows by the Thames which yielded some excellent duck-shooting when they were partially flooded. I retained the right to walk up and shoot birds on my own land when I wished, but not to enter the woods.

By the end of October we had finished work on *Danger Within*. I enjoyed the studio filming as much as the exteriors, and particularly remember an intimate little scene with Richard Attenborough while we discussed the possible identity of the informer in our midst. What a good actor! Just once in a while one knows for sure that a scene is going to grip the audience and keep it enthralled without any heroics or massive effects. This was one of those moments: quiet, pensive and studiously underplayed. Dickie and I had talked a lot together during our two months on the film; he had told me something of his plans and aspirations and I had realised that here was a very determined character. His record since has proved my original assessment of his abilities. He was then planning an independent production with Bryan Forbes, *The Angry Silence*, which was a great film though not a money-spinner.

When I saw a rough-cut of *Danger Within* a week or two after we had finished, this scene still stood out in my mind. I watched it with Colin Lesslie and we later discussed the possibility of making a sequel showing his later adventures in Rome. Unfortunately, that story never came to the screen.

Work on the film finished in November, and for the rest of the year I returned to a more domestic routine, mixed in with plans for the farming enterprise and meetings to discuss various film projects, especially for *The Sleeping Mountain*.

Robert and May Clark visited us at Haileywood and were suitably impressed with the farm. I remember we had a business chat together after tea, and I asked him if he had any idea of the extent of his wealth, now that he was heavily engaged in London property deals. In his dour, laconic Scottish way he replied, 'No, I've no idea. Probably about seven million.' That figure was multiplied several times over in later years.

A few days later I took Baron to the Royal Veterinary College in London. His mating had not been a success, and I wondered whether he was infertile. A vet took a seminal sample from him, looked at it in a test-tube and pronounced it useless. He felt his abdomen and said it was full of lumps, probably cancerous. Then he took us to consult with the head man, who agreed with him. Now thoroughly alarmed, I said I had children and other dogs. Should Baron be put down? Was there any danger of infection? He gave it as his opinion that I should have the dog put down at once, as any discharge would indeed be dangerous. Miserable, I decided to defer any decision at least for a few days – the old boy seemed so fit in every other way. Fortunately, on our way out of the main hall of the building the first vet pointed to a very natty gentleman, complete with black coat and striped trousers, who was descending the stairs. 'He's a specialist in cancer research; he keeps some of his experimental animals here. I'll ask him.'

When he had listened to the story, the specialist laughed. 'My dear chap,' he said. 'If cancer could be caught, or passed on from one to another, we'd know what it was and could cure it or prevent it. All old creatures have a few lumps around. He's probably perfectly well. If he ever starts to waste away, *then* think about putting him down because he'd probably be in pain.'

Baron lived for another active four years.

One new canine addition to our family was Dash, a lovely springer spaniel. We had driven north to shoot with Peter Jackson's father, Hal, a very famous spaniel breeder and trainer, in Lancashire. He had no dogs for sale at the time but suggested that, as we were going on up to Glasgow, we should visit John Windle, a keeper, breeder and trainer at Dalswinton near Dumfries.

A couple of days later we reached Dalswinton and found Windle, a sturdy, tweedy Geordie, as he emerged from a belt of forest with a group of lively, but beautifully controlled young spaniels. I was particularly charmed with a lovely bitch, then called Geordieland Dazzle, and bought her on the spot, arranging for her to be sent down to us as soon as her training was completed.

On our way back from Glasgow, with Kitty's mother as passenger, we stopped the night at the Devonshire Arms Hotel at Bolton Abbey in the midst of the Yorkshire Dales. It was a charming old Georgian country hotel, beautifully furnished, and we had a memorable dinner which included a pheasant magnificently presented in a basket of woven potato chips – the bird, complete with tail feathers for decoration, sitting on small potatoes to represent eggs and nested on a bed of cress. Not the sort of dish to be found today in the average country hotel!

Next day we lunched at the ancient Angel and Royal Hotel in Grantham, where we had another splendid meal in this old inn which had once housed King John on his way from Newark Castle to sign the Magna Carta. I noted in my diary that we enjoyed a magnificent bottle of Rauzan-Gassies 1937.

A week or two later Dazzle – whom I immediately renamed Dash – arrived and soon settled in. Within days she was my second shadow, rather to Baron's disgust, but they soon became the best of friends. I shot over her a few times on the farm and she was brilliant – very fast and bold, but very biddable.

Our second very happy Christmas at Haileywood was again marred by a tragedy. On Boxing Day Wendy corgi was obviously sick. She died on 27 December, and Kitty lost her constant companion and loving pet. She was just over ten years old and had seen us through all our ups and downs since our first holiday together in 1949, when we found her on a Yorkshire farm. She was in her basket in our bedroom when we heard a long, shuddering sigh – and that was that. She was buried close to Bess by the side of the tennis court.

So 1958 ended on a saddened note.

20

A Blank Check

As far as my film career was concerned, 1959 was a bleak year for me. Although I made plenty of efforts to get things going and there were all sorts of possibilities, promises and plans, with countless meetings and discussions in London, I did not make a single film that year. Postponements, cancellations, disappointments and poor scripts wrought havoc with nearly everything I touched.

The movie industry itself had moved into a rather sluggish period, and finance was hard to come by. The tempo of production planning had slowed down quite considerably since the middle 1950s.

To begin with I was not too worried, since I had completed a good film only recently. And anyway, apart from my career projects I had plenty to occupy me and became more and more involved with farming matters as well as family affairs.

There were innumerable meetings with Jimmy Wallis at Associated British concerning the setting-up of *The Sleeping Mountain* as a film, and it was eventually agreed that ABPC would fund the purchase of the film rights and scripting while I retained the copyright. So at least some headway was made there. A draft screenplay was commissioned from the TV writer Ted Willis, but it did not turn out too well. Meanwhile, my agreement with ABPC had been drawn up by Laurence Harbottle.

One of my other interests got off to a good start when we went to Woodstock for the English Spaniel championship field trial where my friend, Hal Jackson, won the championship with his dog Willy of Barnacre, whose dam had won the award previously. Quite a record. The Jacksons spent the weekend with us at Haileywood and we all celebrated suitably.

Soon after that we flew to Scotland with Dash for a few days' shooting with Lady Jean Fforde on the Isle of Arran. We stayed at Jean's house, Strabane, just below her old family home, the massive and ancient Brodick Castle. On my first day there, before the rest of the party arrived I walked some rough ground with McAlpine, the head stalker, and shot some hares which Dash put up and retrieved. Then we noticed that a stag had got into some young forestry and was doing a lot of damage. I was given permission to stalk it, and eventually shot it cleanly with a borrowed rifle – my first stag!

Then followed two days of exciting mixed shooting of hares, pheasants, grouse and woodcock. After each day's shooting guns sat out by ponds waiting for the evening flight of wild duck and geese, a pretty chilly experience. The weather was wretched, with squalls of snow and sleet, but ideal for wildfowling. However, I had a small hip-flask of brandy to cheer my spirits!

There is nothing more exciting than the moments spent crouching by a sheet of water in the darkening evening waiting for the honking and quacking of birds coming in to land, then hearing the whirring of wings while one's eyes strain to catch a glimpse of something against a light patch of stormy sky, and firing more by instinct than aim.

On the second night there was some muddle about where I was to be picked up on the road back to Strabane, and I finished up by slithering the several miles over hard-packed snow back to the house, lugging my quite heavy bag with me. I got back just in time for dinner, but found that the others had already used up all the hot water so I had to content myself with a quick splash in a tepid bath.

On the fourth day Jean took us around the Castle and for a tour of that marvellously scenic island which had mostly belonged to her mother, the late Duchess of Montrose. That evening we had a very jolly supper party which included Dorothy Tutin, who was a frequent visitor to Arran, and next day flew back to London.

My next shooting experience was even more memorable.

I had been invited to shoot on the last Saturday of the season, 31 January, at Stratfield Saye with the Duke of Wellington. The night before was the Garth Hunt Ball, and we were dining first with Lord and Lady Forres. Kitty had just had a wisdom tooth removed and was not well enough to go, so I set out alone. After a splendid dinner we all went on to the Hunt Ball at the Guards Club in Maidenhead, where I enjoyed myself well but not too wisely, lacking Kitty's restraining influence. I had completely forgotten my shooting date the next morning until I suddenly thought, 'Gawd! I'd better get home,' which I did in the middle of the night, rather the worse for wear.

Now I had been given as a Christmas present a very rare Methuselah of Drambuie (export only, I think), which I kept of course in the bar I had created out of the cue room off the sitting room (formerly the billiards room), converting the cue cupboard with shelves for bottles and glasses. This long, narrow little room had a men's loo at one end and a stone-tiled floor, so I kept Dash in there with her basket in one corner. The Drambuie bottle was too big to fit on the shelves, so I had put it on the floor in the corner.

Dunant had a heck of a job waking me that morning at 7 o'clock, which was only some three hours after I had got to bed. As he handed me my cup of tea, he said, 'Sir, can you stand a shock? It's Dash, sir, and the Drambuie.' The import of his words finally got through into my splitting head, and I tottered hastily downstairs.

My worst fears were soon confirmed: the shattered bottle of Drambuie lay on the floor in a glutinous puddle, and the most pie-eyed little dog you ever saw sat woefully on her bed, her eyes blinking sleepily, her whiskers and leg-feathers a sticky mess. She was as tight as a tick and God knows how she had survived her carousal.

There was no time to waste. I asked Dunant to clean her up as best he could and to take her for a quick walk while I dashed upstairs and shaved, bathed and dressed as fast as my shaking hands allowed. Meanwhile, Dunant had brought the Land Rover round to the front door and piled into it my shooting gear, which I had left ready the previous evening.

After a hasty breakfast and a glass of Alka-Seltzer I then loaded Dash into the back of the Land Rover. Normally ecstatic at seeing me in my shooting-suit, she would hop in with one bound, but this time after a few ineffectual attempts – rocking back and forth and trying to scrabble up the back flap – I had to heave her in bodily and set off with the drunken little dog snoring in the back.

Arriving at Stratfield Saye, I met the other guns – who included the Duke, Lord Douro, the Earl of Westmorland, Sir Edmund Stockdale (later Lord Mayor of London) and a one-armed retired Brigadier Pepys who shot brilliantly – and drew for my number in the line, which was next to the Duke. In such august company, and especially as my host was in a good position to see my shooting prowess (or lack of it), I naturally hoped to acquit myself well and so be invited there again.

It was a cocks-only day, which meant that none of the breeding stock of pheasant hens were to be shot. Unfortunately, to my bleary vision everything looked dark-coloured on that cloudy day and I tended to delay my shots so as to be absolutely sure I would not commit the unpardonable sin of hitting a hen. The first drive was over a narrow ride in a wood with very little time to do anything but take snap shots overhead. Even so I managed to bring down a couple of good birds, while Dash huddled shivering and somnolent under my feet, making footwork difficult.

The second drive was out of another wood, with guns standing mud-balled in heavy plough, which again made footwork hard especially as Dash continued to doze underfoot. It was then that I made the dreadful mistake of downing a hen; it was a very high bird, going like the clappers over me, and I could have sworn it was dark brown and long-tailed. Fortunately the Duke was busy on his own account as scores of birds exploded out of the wood near the end of the drive. But Valerian Douro, who had seen my gaffe, was nice enough at lunch to congratulate me on a good shot, not mentioning that it was a hen!

After lunch Dash seemed to have made a complete recovery and was over-keen to make amends, dashing about all over the place to pick up birds and bring them to me even if I had not shot them, until I had a pile of pheasants by my stand and other irate shooters had none. Sitting with me on the last drive, Diana Douro commented on Dash's speed and keenness. Little did she know!

Despite our errors, happily we were invited to Stratfield Saye the next season . . .

Next day I changed hats and attended a rehearsal for the annual Royal Film Performance. I was glad to meet Juliette Greco again and had tea with her at the Savoy. The film that evening was *The Horse's Mouth* with Alec Guinness, and after the show a line of us were presented to the Queen Mother, who was her usual charming self. Alec played an extrovert painter in the picture and all the paintings shown were by John Bratby whose characteristic dauby style impressed me – so much so that I bought one of his works a few days later at an exhibition.

That week I discussed with Colin Lesslie the possibility of making a sequel to *Danger Within*. Before going out to dinner I went to collect a young South African girl called Aldine Honey, whom friends had suggested I might be able to help with her modelling career. As I arrived at the little hotel in Earls Court there she was waiting, a stunning sight. Tall, shapely and really beautiful – I could not have wished for a more attractive companion at the River Club, where we all dined. Later I was able to introduce her to Michael Whittaker, a leading designer and presenter of fashion shows, and her very successful career was launched.

Also that week Queenie Pampel started part-time work in my office, keeping my private and farm books in order and doing the wages and tax returns. Julia Stonor had left for a London job, and Annie Waugh's strong point was not book-keeping. We had chosen Queenie from several applicants for the job but were in fact quite surprised when she accepted the post. We thought her much too high-powered, as she already had a managerial post with part of the Isaac Woolfson empire. Nevertheless she agreed to join us, and it says much for her attitude to her work that she even took a night-school course in farm management. She lived with her parents in Reading a few miles away, and it was one of my lucky days when Queenie became part of the household. When Anne eventually left to get married, Queenie took her place as my full-time secretary and now, some thirty years later, is still my assistant and, more, one of the firmest friends of my family.

A few days later Kitty and I went to Estoril, in Portugal, for a short stay as guests of the Portuguese government at a series of star-studded receptions, culminating in the Rose Ball at our hotel, the Palacio. Kitty had a rose-coloured gown for the occasion, but I jibbed at wearing a pink dinner jacket that I could never use again, and instead wore a rose-tinted tie and handkerchief. It was nice to meet my old friend from Washington, Mario Ferreira, and we dined with him on our last night there. Later he sent me a case of Ferreira's port!

On our return to London, we moved into a new, larger flat in Nell Gwyn House and started to collect a few more bits of furniture as soon as the redecoration was complete. Also our new head herdsman, Peter Webb, moved into the gate lodge at Haileywood. He was a marvellous cowman and an aggressive worker whom I had filched from the Grass-land Research Station at Hurley. His wife had been a schoolmistress and soon started a successful and exclusive little school for toddlers, so Haileywood became quite a thriving community.

Towards the end of February *Danger Within* was premièred, and got a splendid reception and good press reviews. But I still had no follow-up film arranged. Then a week or two later, I saw an excellent play at the Royal Court Theatre, *The Long and the Short and the Tall*, by Willis Hall and Keith Waterhouse. This was about a jungle patrol in Burma gradually being eliminated by Japanese forces, and in it a new young actor, Peter O'Toole, was quite brilliant as the facetious Cockney. Looking as he did then, with dark hair and a long, beaky nose, his drollery was a tremendous foil to the more disciplined, serious leader of the group, a sergeant well played by Robert Shaw.

I could see the film potential of the piece, and soon afterwards Associated British bought the screen rights for a film to be made that year with me playing the sergeant. I was delighted at the prospect.

Typical of my topsy-turvy existence in those days was a seven-day period when I managed to fit in the opening of a new ABC Cinema in Preston on the Saturday, followed by a mayoral reception in Blackpool;

attended an Ockenden Venture meeting on the Sunday; was present at a masonic meeting and dinner on the Monday; went to Newcastle for a press reception for the opening of *Danger Within* on the Tuesday; was guest of honour of the Ayrshire Breeders Association Dinner in Reading on Wednesday, and replied to the toast to the guests; was part of a film industry delegation to the House of Commons on Thursday appealing for tax relief for British films; had lunch at Abingdon airfield with Brigitte Bardot who was filming there on Friday, then went up to meetings with Wallis and Harbottle in London to discuss *The Sleeping Mountain* agreement and *The Long and the Short and the Tall*; and finally, on the Saturday watched the last of the spring corn being drilled at Holmwood Farm, finishing up that evening in London at a Parachute Regimental Officers dinner.

Further press receptions and openings for *Danger Within* followed at Cardiff and Middlesbrough, where the film went down very well.

In May the Queen Mother attended a garden party held in Wokingham by the Ockenden Venture, and the same day Peter won his first cup on Hinton Egrin at the Wokingham Show. Being now seven, he was allowed to display his cup at a dinner party we gave that night, and serve the cocktail savouries.

That month I also flew to Cannes for the annual Film Festival. I was accompanied by Arthur Watkins, Chairman of the British Film Producers Association, and during my three days there did all the usual press and TV interviews. It was not the most exciting festival and no British film gained any honours.

The day I returned home, we spent the afternoon at the Windsor Horse Show where Peter came only seventh in his pony class – poor judging, I reckoned! That evening we drove to London for the première of a film called *Serious Charge* and at a reception afterwards I met Lady Churchill. She told me that *The Dam Busters* was her husband's favourite film, and that he had seen it privately a number of times.

I also went to Dublin for a few days for the opening of *Shake Hands with the Devil*, a Michael Anderson film starring Dana Wynter, whom I was delighted to meet again. After a reception at the President's residence, she joined me and my cousins, Maureen and Ivan Vaughan, for dinner at our hotel. The Vaughans and my aunt and uncle FitzPatrick lunched with me next day and took me to the airport.

All this rushing around, mixed with a busy social life – plus innumerable meetings with Jimmy Wallis, now managing director of Associated British Films, and other people – still had not produced a firm commitment for a film for me in the near future, and I was getting pretty depressed about my professional stagnation. *The Sleeping Mountain* still had no workable script, *The Long and the Short and the Tall* had been postponed, and none of the other offers I had had, including a Carl Foreman subject, seemed right for me. I had also bought the screen rights to *Love From Everybody*, a very funny book I had read, but it would be some time before I could get that set up.

Still I pressed on, hoping for the best, hay-making one day and having London meetings the next.

We had added to our domestic stock as well. I had bought a sweet little pug whom we called Biscuit to replace Wendy on Kitty's lap, so we now had a great Dane, a corgi, a pointer, a spaniel and a pug – quite a mixed bag! I had also bought Peter a hamster for his birthday, but she did not last long. She was apparently pregnant, although we did not realise it, and the peace of the house was shattered one day when Fiona came downstairs yelling, 'Mummy! Mummy! The hamster's having babies and she's eating them all!' It was only too true, so the hamster became *persona non grata* with us and was promptly given away.

I had also rather less than distinguished myself by tripping up and falling flat on my face in the fathers' race at Peter's school sports, when the betting was heavily on a win for the doughty Robin Hood and Rob Roy!

I was by now, at the request of the president of the Federation of British Film Makers, a member of that organisation which represented independent film producers, and had been co-opted on to the co-production committee whose purpose was to encourage Anglo-European projects. This activity occupied me with a lot of discussions and travel.

June brought two widely differing occasions for us. First Lord and Lady Ronaldshay were lent Cliveden by Bill Astor for a coming-out ball for their daughter; we had a dinner party for some of the guests beforehand and then went on to the glittering occasion which was attended by Princess Margaret. Then at the end of the month we held our first public open day at the farm organised by George Speakman, head of the June Dairy Festival and instigator of the 'Drinka Pinta Milka Day' promotion. It was a showery day, but we were delighted with the turn-out, with people coming by car and coach from a wide area. The Milk Marketing Board helped greatly with the organisation and supplied a marquee with a milk bar and dairy produce stall. I believe we were one of only four farms to do this in Britain, and we continued it year after year with ever-increasing success. It was great for the pride of my farm staff, and a lot of painting and whitewashing and general sprucing-up had gone on. Joe Aggis had a field day with his vegetable sales. We also had several visits from school groups during the summer.

After a few days with Kitty and the children on the Isle of Bute at her parents' house, I returned to London alone, had a day at home in the office, did my packing and then set out on one of the most fascinating trips I had ever made:

I flew to Moscow as part of the British delegation for the Moscow Film Festival. With me on the flight were, among others, Tommy Steele, Carole Lesley, C. J. Latta (managing director of Associated British Pictures), Jack Goodlatte (MD of Associated British Cinemas) and Eric Fletcher, MP (a director of ABPC). We flew in a specially-provided Russian TU104 aircraft, a beautiful, sleek machine whose exterior lines matched the grace of our own Comet. But there the likeness ended: the interior was more like that of an old-fashioned railway coach and just as dingy. It was typical of what we were later to find in Moscow: a curious juxtaposition of up-to-date technology side-by-side with shabbiness and inefficiency.

Even the oxygen masks were not stowed away but dangled gruesomely above the passangers, and the luggage racks were cane-bottomed shelves held by heavy metal brackets. The galley was like grandma's kitchen, with lots of grainy woodwork and brass fittings. However, the thing flew very sweetly and the cabin staff, beefy ladies in plain overalls, could not have been more friendly and anxious to please, and plied us with caviar and vodka. I would have loved a gin and tonic, but that was expecting too much.

We stopped at Copenhagen for an hour, and arrived in Moscow after dark. The airport was a scene of utter confusion as crowds of people jostled about trying to locate their baggage which was being trundled in on hand-carts. However, our four interpreters were there to meet us and restored some sort of order. They were Inga, Nina, Arthur and Juri, and there was no doubt as to who I wanted to assist me: Inga was obviously the most competent one and was also the most attractive and chic girl I saw in Russia, slim and dressed – I later found out – in smart Western clothes which had mostly come from Switzerland somehow. She was in her twenties, divorced and a university lecturer in English.

There was a line of black limousines waiting outside for our party and, certain that Inga would be the last to leave having made sure that all our baggage was safely recovered and stowed aboard, I bundled myself alone into the car at the end. I was right – the others moved off and finally Inga came out and joined me. I wasted no time in extracting her promise that she would attach herself to me for the duration of our stay.

As we passed grim, bare-faced blocks of flats on our way into the city, I was slightly surprised when the cosmopolitan Inga pointed them out with pride as an example of how the workers were housed: 'and every family has two rooms to itself', she said. But her English was perfect and her looks even more so.

We were to stay in the Hotel Moscow, an enormous barrack-like building in the centre of the city with a hall that we all dubbed the 'Great Western Station', and lifts operated by stern-faced attendants.

The room keys were not kept at a central desk, but by grim old ladies who sat at tables opposite the stairs and the lift entrance. Once arrived at this table you contrived to indicate your room number and waited, quailing, while this jailer-like creature eyed you suspiciously, checked a list before her and finally handed you the key. There was to be no hanky-panky in this establishment.

I started off in a dull little cell with a bathroom that reeked vilely. I protested that the drain had become blocked, and was moved up from the fourth floor to a very similar habitat on the fifth, much to the disdain of my key-lady.

We had all arranged to meet at 'Platform One' (our name for the dining room) but then we had to wait ages for our food to arrive. This was the malaise of Moscow: everything and everybody was invariably late. A meal took about two hours to be served and cars never arrived on time.

Moscow then was a city of anachronisms: wide tree-lined boulevards, scrupulously clean, but with almost no traffic and that composed mostly of black, stodgy cars and taxis; great churches with no services and few attenders; impressive modernistic buildings side by side with rickety shacks; enormous stores like Gum, with little stock for sale; drab civilian clothing outclassed by hordes of smart official uniforms; marvellous subway stations, marbled, chandeliered and muralled but with ancient and outdated rolling-stock; the great Red Square walled on one side by the Kremlin fortress and always with a huge queue shuffling along patiently to visit the Stalin/Lenin tomb; queues, too, outside food shops.

We had all been given badges to wear to denote our official position as visitors to the festival, and were quite free to wander about but always with our interpreters. Everywhere we went people were very friendly, though we had been warned not to get into any political discussions, even amongst ourselves. We had also been advised that our rooms might have been bugged and that we should avoid any sort of 'compromising situation', whatever that meant.

On my first morning I went to the Gum store to see if I could find anything typically Russian to take home. In the end I bought two small goblets of brass or some such metal, each of them with lovely colourful designs on the outside done in lacquer in the manner of some of the Fabergé pieces I had seen. Evidently this was still a craft practised in Russia.

We were given special passes to the Stalin/Lenin tomb, so we did not have to join the queue. It was almost eerie filing past the two recumbent figures in their glass cases, dressed and bemedalled, the ashen skin of their faces showing a slight stubble that had grown after death.

We also had to attend a few evening receptions, one given by the British chargé d'affaires, one by ABPC and one by the German delegation. We invariably arrived late as our cars were not on time – but, then, so did everybody else!

On our last day, some of us visited the Yusipov estate not far from Moscow. Prince Yusipov had apparently been the richest aristocrat in Russia and his mansion was a great French château-type building surrounded by parkland and lakes, now taken over by the state and opened to the public. The interior was very French in style, with copious gilding, and full of magnificent Louis XV furniture and works of art. I was interested to see the reverence and admiration with which parties of Soviet visitors gazed upon all this splendour. I should have thought they would have considered it to be worthy only of contempt as an example of capitalist decadence.

One thing there could well be copied by our own stately homes: in the hall was a huge mound of flannel squares, taped at the corners. These you tied over your shoes (or your feet if you were a woman with high heels) so not only did you not damage the floors but you actually helped to polish them as you shuffled around.

We all had a swim in the lake and the whole day was reminiscent of a family outing at some National Trust property.

That evening I had further experience of Russian friendliness.

Inga and I had gone for a supper-dance at what was considered to be the most fashionable restaurant in Moscow. Also there was our PR lady, Lee Langley, and her husband who was our official photographer.

It was a large room, with a central square dance-floor, and must have held a couple of hundred people. The atmosphere was almost that of an Edwardian palm court, very staid and rather gloomy, with a string orchestra which played nothing more *avant-garde* than foxtrots and waltzes to which the guests lumbered round ponderously. This was too much for Lee and her husband, and it was not long before they were jiving and jitterbugging. At first the other dancers stared incredulously, but soon they were all trying to join in. A stop was temporarily put to this by a scandalised head waiter, who tapped the Langleys on the shoulder and indicated that they should leave the floor. But as they left they were clapped and cheered vociferously by the others, who then spent the rest of the evening doing their clumsy best to emulate them. The whole place had brightened up considerably.

Towards the end Inga and I had our own spot of bother. We had danced a few times and were having coffee when a tousle-headed young man lurched over to our table and said something to her to which her answer was a decided '*Niet*'. He then harangued her for a few moments before tottering away. I asked her what it was all about. She said, 'Oh, he's with a party of Georgians who are all drunk. He asked me to dance, and when I refused he said I should be ashamed to be dancing half-naked with a foreigner.' She was wearing a chic and perfectly decent off-the-shoulder dinner dress, part of her Swiss collection, no doubt. She explained that Georgians were the wild ones of Russia and were great roisterers, frequently getting truculent.

As we were having our final dance together we suddenly became aware of this Georgian group, five or six of them, getting up and heading towards us. Inga took my arm and began to walk back to our table, but we had scarcely left the floor when some people sitting at a nearby large table insisted that we join them. They had noticed the little incident and were obviously anxious to protect us from any further embarrassment. It was a charming and very welcome gesture. We had drinks with them, everything settled down, and soon we were able to leave.

As we left the door to get into our car, however, a group of the same troublemakers – who had evidently been ejected – lunged at us but were fought off by doormen and others. We were safely bundled into the car and drove off. It was about as near as I had ever been to an international incident, but the friendliness which we had otherwise been shown left a good memory.

Inga gave a little party for us on our last evening and had invited several Russian actors and dancers to meet us. Her flat was surprisingly large and well-furnished and she was a charming hostess, obviously one of the favoured few. As a parting gift she gave me a beautiful crystal goblet etched with wild duck. When I asked her if there was anything

I could send her, she staggered me by asking for an anthology of Rudyard Kipling. I never knew whether it was her literary taste or her sense of humour that prompted her . . .

When we left the airport it was quite an emotional farewell: all four of our interpreters were in tears. It seems that Russians are like that: very warm-hearted and expressive.

I and the rest of the ABPC party spent a couple of days in Copenhagen on our way back. I was very taken by the charm of that city and its inhabitants, and most impressed by the agriculture that I saw when we were driven around the countryside, and I determined to spend more time there sometime in the future.

The family were still on holiday on the Isle of Bute when I got home, so after a lot of time in the office with Anne and Queenie and some meetings in London (the most important of which being with Dennis Cannon, who agreed to do a script of *Love From Everybody* for me), I flew up to Scotland and had a lovely week on the island, staying with Kitty's parents. The weather was beautiful, the beaches perfect and we fished and swam, boated and picnicked daily.

Meanwhile I had taken on the responsibility of engaging a new cook, Miss Cripps, and for once my choice could not be faulted. A middle-aged woman, she had spent all her working life in country-house kitchens, first as a scullery-maid, then an assistant cook and finally as a cook in her own right. Her last post had been for some years with a family who lived on a large estate in England and also had a place in Scotland which they visited every year for fishing and shooting, so there was nothing that she did not know about the preparation and cooking of game and fish. I was conscious of the fact that my household was much humbler than those that she had been used to, and also that she would have to do all the food preparation herself. Rather nervously, I said that all our vegetables were fresh from the garden and would need to be cleaned and prepared. 'But, sir, I wouldn't use anything else,' said she, much to my relief. So, every morning Joe Aggis came to the kitchen to get his order for the day, and Miss Cripps did the rest.

So when we arrived home from Bute, Miss Cripps was already *in situ* and seemingly quite content – certainly very efficient.

Up to now this had not been a good year for me as far as films were concerned, and Jimmy Wallis added a further load to my depression by announcing, soon after my return from Scotland, that for various reasons *The Long and the Short and the Tall* was to be postponed until later in 1960. So I redoubled my efforts to get something moving with *Love From Everybody* and *The Sleeping Mountain*.

I began to get some movement with the former subject. Soon ABPC agreed to finance and distribute the picture, the National Film Finance Corporation agreed to come in for some 40 per cent of the cost, and Frank Godwin and Dennis Cannon agreed to work with me as executive producer and screenwriter respectively. The film would be a Haileywood Films production, made by a company which I set up for the purpose. But it would be months before it was ready to start shooting.

In other ways September and October were very active months for me. To begin with, I had lunch in London with Gina Lollobrigida and the following weekend she and her husband, Milko Skofic, came to spend a couple of days with us at Haileywood.

A few days later I drove to Portsmouth for the annual Royal Naval Film Corporation dinner aboard HMS *Victorious*, the flagship of Admiral Sir Charles Evans who was then C-in-C of our carrier forces. Admiral of the Fleet Earl Mountbatten of Burma was present, as was a host of other naval dignitaries and representatives of the film industry. It was a very jolly evening altogether, and I was one of the last to leave (true to form, as always) and finished up having a few hefty nightcaps with a handful of others in the Admiral's large cabin in the rear of the ship. Since I had not arranged to stay locally Sir Charles offered to put me up in his spare cabin, but I decided to take the risk of driving home – something I would not dream of doing today! The next morning was the start of the Henley and District Agricultural Association Show, and I did not want to be late for that. Just as well, too – Peter got second place on his pony, Joe Aggis won all sorts of awards for his vegetables and Haileywood Home Farm received second prize for a field of standing oats.

I also flew up to Glasgow for the Scottish Industries Exhibition, which I was to officially open in the Kelvin Hall. Met at Renfrew Airport by Sir Alexander King, a leading Scottish cinema-owner and exhibitor, I did a private tour of the show, lunched at my old *Rob Roy* base – the Buchanan Arms at Drymen – and performed the opening ceremony at 2.30. It was a lucky day for me: as I've already mentioned, I was given by John Rollo (the industrialist whom I had met before) one of his Croftmaster miniature tractors, a tough little machine which was the forerunner of modern garden tractors. It would come in very handy in my garden and orchard at Haileywood. Not only that, but my suite at the Central Hotel had been occupied the previous day by the Queen Mother and I have never sat and slept amidst such an abundance of floral decoration.

Since my brief visit to Moscow I seemed to have been in the Russians' good books, perhaps because I had played Robin Hood – who was almost a hero of the Soviet Union, robbing the rich and giving to the poor – and the film had been popular there. We were asked by the British Council to give lunch and a day in the country to two members of a Russian film delegation: Kazentov, a director, and Strichenova, a leading actress. We agreed, and they duly arrived with two Russian-speaking members of the British Council and a Russian interpreter whom the Soviet Embassy had insisted should also be present.

After lunch, we all attended the Haileywood Gymkhana which had been organised in one of my fields by our local Woodland Pony Club. It was a jolly little show and the Russians were most impressed by the horsemanship of the children, seeming quite surprised that we could let such little youngsters take such dare-devil risks in some of the events. Great child-lovers, the Russians . . .

Peter won first place in his class – no favouritism there, of course!

There was a week's festival of Russian films at the Curzon Cinema and Kitty and I felt duty-bound to attend the opening night, where we sat through a very heavy so-called comedy movie whose sub-titles must have been gleaned from a turn-of-the-century dictionary. Finally, we were invited to a reception at the Russian Ambassador's house, sited despite his political beliefs in 'Millionaires' Row', Kensington Palace Gardens.

Willy, our Jersey bull, had meantime been active, and the herd now numbered some 40 milking cows and heifers. Nearly every evening after dinner I would wander down to the farm buildings to look at the enchanting little calves, who would enthusiastically suckle one's fingers in greeting. Before Willy's arrival we had used artificial insemination designed to bring various new strains into the herd. One day a car arrived at the house just as I was leaving, and two men got out. One of them asked me where they could find Julia; as Julia Stonor was then working for us, I said, 'She's in the office. I'll show you the way.' Both men looked a bit puzzled but obediently followed me through the house to my office. When we arrived there and I introduced Julia Stonor, they burst into gales of laughter. One of them then explained that they had come to artificially inseminate Julia, one of my cows.

At last a film was offered to me. Peter de Sarigny, a leading independent producer, was preparing a film to start shooting in January. Tentatively called *Moment of Truth*, he wanted the subject to star me with

Peter Sellers, who had recently had an enormous success in Britain with *I'm All Right, Jack*, but who was already a popular celebrity for his comedy work with the Goons. This film was to be something of a departure from his usual roles for him, as he was to play the heavy, a real villain. De Sarigny gave me the script; I read it, thought it terrific and soon contracted to do the picture.

Before meeting de Sarigny I had decided to do a TV documentary for the BBC. Alan Sleath, a leading BBC producer of drama and adult education programmes, had asked me if I would go to Bavaria for a week to make a film about the Oberammergau Passion Play preparations. This sounded fascinating and I readily agreed. The offer also came at a time when I was itching to get to work on my profession again after a barren year.

It had been a depressing period for me professionally, with postponements, frustrations and not a few disappointments. Even a film script based on *The World of Suzy Wong* which Pickman sent me from New York and which I read in the plane to Munich, seemed pretty poor and not right for me anyway.

So I was delighted to start on something definite and interesting.

Kitty and I flew to Munich in mid-November, and Alan Sleath drove us through the marvellous, snow-covered countryside to Oberammergau, a totally enchanting and unique village, mountain-girt, its chalet-type wooden houses with their gaily-painted exteriors and shutters a bright splash of colour in the white wilderness of snow and forest.

We were staying at the Alte Post Hotel, a charming, snug old building owned by Anton Preisinger, who was to play Christ in the Passion Play. When we arrived it was something of a surprise to see Christ and a group of his disciples, all heavily bearded and long-haired, happily playing some card game with their huge steins of beer beside them. Not exactly reminiscent of the Last Supper!

The play takes place every ten years, preparations and rehearsals go on for months and the whole village is involved, from the youngest children up to arthritic ancients. From the beginning of the preparations none of the men of the village shave or have their hair cut. Since the days of flower-power, hippies and long-haired pop groups, perhaps their appearance might not come as much as a surprise to visitors now as it did to us then.

The main industry of the area all revolved around wood: furniture-making, carving and so on. The only trade which came to a complete halt for the best part of a year was that of the village barber. He, poor chap, sat idly in his shop with no customers, but he did eke out an income from the only other craft he knew – carving. It seemed that he had only learned to fashion hands, and his establishment was crowded with shelves covered with wooden hands, beautifully carved. I bought a pair from him and they still occupy a prominent place on my sitting-room mantelshelf.

We filmed interviews with many of the leading players, the producer, the burgomaster, and many others, and did set-ups in the surrounding hills, the auditorium and the Rathaus. Our mountain viewpoints were reached by cable car.

It had been an enthralling week and I was only sorry that I might not be able to return to see the actual performance the following year. Our flight home was delayed for a day by fog so we stayed the night in Munich, lunching the next day at the famous Humplmayrs Restaurant.

I then had a few days at home, during which I lectured to the Nettlebed Young Farmers Club (I'm sure they could have taught me a bit about farming), arranged with the local Henley Regal Cinema for a charity film performance for the following March (an idea I had discussed with Tom Caden-Prescott, a Henley hotelier and indefatigable charity-worker), and went to Elstree for a meeting with my Fan Club organiser and the ABPC Publicity and PR chief, Alan Thompson, where it was decided that we should improve the quarterly Fan Club magazine which ABPC would print and publish. We now had several thousand members worldwide.

It seemed that the gap in my working life was now being filled in by TV activity. I had not done a TV drama since *Wuthering Heights* years before, and had had no particular desire to be involved with television, which we in the cinema industry still regarded as being the poor relation of films. However, TV drama had greatly improved since my first experience of it, was recorded now instead of being broadcast live, and I was glad to accept the leading role in an Anglia TV production of *Carrington VC*. Anglia had gained a splendid reputation for the quality of its drama productions under the guidance of John Woolf, the very successful film producer who had become Anglia's executive director. The screenplay was a fine adaptation of the play, and George More O'Ferrall was to direct. Above all, my two co-stars were to be Dorothy Tutin and Ann Todd, while Allan Cuthbertson and Hugh Manning would be in the cast too. What a company! I knew this had to be good.

I drove to my first rehearsal for *Carrington VC* in my new car that had just been delivered. At the Earls Court Motor Show in October I had fallen totally in love with the centrepiece of the show, a gorgeous ivory-coloured Armstrong-Siddeley Star Sapphire, the latest model from that famous marque. I bought it on the spot, and arranged to have it serviced and brought to me as soon as it had finished being exhibited at Earls Court and Glasgow. I also bought Kitty a small estate car as a replacement for her Austin Metropolitan.

I was sorry to see Belinda Bentley leave us and to end a ten-year run of two Bentleys and one Rolls-Royce, but the Sapphire was a beautiful car to drive and had every modern improvement and gadget.

Rehearsals for *Carrington VC* were a real pleasure. We all got on splendidly together and George More O'Ferrall was a dear to work with. After the usual traumatic day of final camera rehearsals at Wembley Studios, we filmed a very successful production on 18 December and finished up exhausted at about midnight at the end of nearly three weeks' hard work.

Before I had even finished rehearsals on *Carrington* I had agreed to do another TV play, this time a thriller called *The Man Who Could Find Things* with Renée Asherson. This was to start rehearsals the day after I finished on *Carrington*, so 1959 was ending in a spate of television work after nearly a year without seeing a camera.

My weekends had been fairly busy, too. I shot a few times with our small syndicate, and had two good days with the Phillimores at nearby Coppice Hall and with Valerian Douro at Stratfield Saye, though I was without Dash for some weeks as I had sent her up to John Windle in Scotland to run in field trials. There was also the usual round of dinner parties locally, including one at Cliveden where I was seated next to the redoubtable Nancy, Lady Astor, Bill's remarkable mother. For some reason she and I always got on well together, and I was always her table companion whenever she was at Cliveden – perhaps because her wit found an appreciative sounding-board in me. She was also very fond of Peter. Her opinions of other people were not often repeatable.

I had also had several meetings with Peter de Sarigny about *Moment of Truth* and had been given a new script developed by him, the screen-writer and John Guillermin, who was to direct the picture. It was excellent, and I looked forward to a good start to the New Year.

Christmas Day saw us sitting down to a wonderful lunch all provided by our own Haileywood produce, including the turkey, an enormous 30-pounder. We had our usual Christmas tree ceremony in the morning, and that evening we dined with the Palmers. I must have put on pounds in weight that day!

21

A Trilogy of Films

Just as the previous year had seen a dearth of cinema films for me, so 1960 was to produce almost a glut of screen work. I was to make three pictures over the next twelve months, to be individually categorised in my estimation as good, bad and indifferent. And at least the third was my own independent production, based on a book that I had liked and bought, and the result of months of grafting, arguing and hard dealing on my part – greatly helped by my favoured association with Associated British and the sympathetic aid of Robert Clark and Jimmy Wallis.

The first of the three films was *Moment of Truth*, Peter de Sarigny's production later to be marketed under the title *Never Let Go*. Rather offbeat in style for a British picture, with a splendid cast of skilled old-timers and some interesting newcomers, and a very definite change of character casting for me, it was to be one of my favourite movies and, to my mind and according to the critics, a damn good one. A first-class script, de Sarigny's expertise as a producer and John Guillermin's sure and excellent directing came together to make a slick and absorbing movie.

The central character (mine) is a very insecure travelling salesman eking out a penurious existence from commissions barely enough to keep him and his wife (Elizabeth Sellars) in food and lodging, always with dreams of better things to come, moving around to his customers in a rickety little car that he cannot afford to insure adequately.

Disaster strikes when the car is stolen. The police are not helpful, and tell him that it might turn up somewhere some time, having just been taken by joy-riders or by somebody wanting to get a free ride home. At worst, it may have been nicked by professional car-thieves, either to be used for spare parts for another similar car or to be transformed, resprayed and resold. Meantime, it may be weeks before the insurers are satisfied about its fate and prepared to pay for replacement.

Desperate, the little salesman tries to keep his job going by taking buses, tubes and taxis which he can ill afford, frequently arriving late for appointments and gradually losing customers, including a hard-nosed John le Mesurier playing the head of a department store. The outcome seems inevitable: he will lose his job.

Driven by anxiety, anger and frustration, he decides to take the law into his own hands and try to track down his car, armed with a few clues that he unearths. His sleuthing leads him into all manner of risky and violent situations when he is confronted by a gang of young thugs, led by Adam Faith; they are the suppliers of stolen cars to a bent garage proprietor (Peter Sellers) who specialises in disposing of hot vehicles through an ostensibly legitimate motor dealership.

Finally, his part-time detective work brings him face to face with a very violent Peter Sellers, who does his best to dispose of him in a gory fight in the garage, with shunting cars, swinging hoist chains and all manner of dirty tricks. Eventually I triumph, call the police and get my car back, before painfully staggering home to my wife, bloody but unbowed and with a new confidence in myself.

We started work at Beaconsfield Studios soon after I had finished the TV play *The Man Who Could Find Things*. During our three weeks shooting interiors there I worked with Peter Sellers, Elizabeth Sellars and Mervyn Johns; the latter gave a very touching performance as a lonely old pensioner who is roughed up by Adam Faith and his gang and who is devastated by the loss of his only companion, a terrapin which is squashed underfoot by one of the young thugs.

Peter and I worked happily together, though I think John Guillermin found him rather argumentative at times. Peter's role as the heavy was the complete antithesis of his usual light comedy work, and perhaps he felt a little insecure about it. I noticed that he arrived each day with one or two companions, and they seemed to be having little conferences before each scene. He was quite withdrawn and rarely came from his dressing room except when actually filming, yet he was always charming and friendly towards me when we were together. He took his work very seriously, and had even had a gold cap made for one of his front teeth as a bit of character make-up: a nice little touch, I thought. But there was something almost morose about him at times. I believe he was a great worrier. I also feel that he started the picture on such a hard, villainous note that there was nowhere for him to go at the end except over the top, but who am I to find some tiny fault in one who was to have such a brilliant career!

A lot of interior shooting was in my little flat with Elizabeth, who was a delightful, quiet person. The make-up artist had a great time working on my battered, swollen and bloody face for the final sequence, possibly simplified by the fact that I had a streaming cold. Feeling dreadful, it was not hard for me to take on a thoroughly crumpled, bleary-eyed look.

While we were at Beaconsfield I had been invited to present the annual Variety Club of Great Britain Awards at a Savoy Hotel luncheon. This is quite a big event every year, covered by TV, radio and the press. As there were to be ten awards to ten different recipients, I spent quite a deal of time preparing and writing out my ten speeches. The day before the ceremony it was suggested by Monty Berman, then Chief Barker, and David Jones, the Variety Club publicity chief, that I should see the film of the previous year's awards which would be run for me at Lime Grove Studios after my day's filming. I thought this a helpful idea and agreed.

That afternoon Bob Webb, from the Elstree publicity department, called at Beaconsfield to ask if I had any snippets of news about the film that he could place in the newspapers; this was quite a usual practice. At the end of the day he asked if I would give him a lift to London, as he had used a hired car to come to the studio. When I explained that I was only going as far as Lime Grove at Shepherd's Bush, he said that was fine for him: he could get a taxi from there. As we arrived I was surprised to see a line of Airborne Army trucks parked nearby, but thought nothing of it.

At the Lime Grove Studios I was met by Alan Sleath of the BBC, Monty Berman, David Jones and some others, and given a quick drink in the hospitality room before we all moved off to the viewing theatre to see the awards film. Anyone familiar with Lime Grove will know that it is a honeycomb of corridors, but eventually we found the theatre.

The film started, but in a few moments the projector apparently broke down, so Alan Sleath suggested that we should all go back to the hospitality room until it was fixed. 'No need to use the corridors,' he said. 'The "Today" programme on Stage 1 has just finished and we can cut across there.' As we entered Stage 1 there were all the signs of a wrap-up, with cameras and scenery being moved away and a small group chattering in the centre of the floor; this included Cliff Michelmore, the presenter of 'Today', and Eamonn Andrews, both of whom I knew quite well. I stopped for a moment to talk with them and suddenly a thought struck me. Turning to Eamonn, I asked if he was not doing 'This Is Your Life' that evening. His reply was devastating: 'Yes, I am. And, Richard Todd, This Is Your Life.'

It was all done live in those days, and they had trapped me beautifully. Bob Webb had been sent to Beaconsfield to make sure that I got to the studios on time, 'Today' had lent the last five minutes of its programme time to 'This Is Your Life', and my companions were all there forming a phalanx to make sure I did not duck away. Apparently they were nervous that I might refuse to take part. I was rushed to an exit door, bundled into a car with Eamonn, and sped with a police car the wrong way down a one-way street to the theatre on Shepherd's Bush Green where the programme was always done. Hurriedly Eamonn explained that we had just four minutes to make it on stage, during which time viewers would be watching a clip of the car dash from *Chase a Crooked Shadow*.

Everything went like clockwork. Completely flustered, I wished I could phone Kitty to tell her to watch the show. It never occurred to me to wonder why she had insisted that morning that I wear a decent suit to Beaconsfield instead of my usual baggy cords and old tweed jacket. We had quite a spat about this, I remember.

But I need not have worried – she was one of the first people to greet me on the show.

The BBC had mustered an imposing array of my old friends and colleagues for the programme. Walt Disney had recorded a special message from Hollywood; General Sir Richard Gale, my old 6th Airborne Division commander, then 2 i/c of all NATO forces, spoke face to face with me on the Eurovision link; Sergeant Grinsell, my old platoon sergeant from Iceland service days, had been brought down from Yorkshire, as had Kate Hancock, a cleaner from the old Dundee Repertory Theatre; Colonel Pine-Coffin, my former CO in 7 Para Battalion, was there; so was Joyce Pearce, the founder of the Ockenden Venture; and Bob Lennard, Jimmy Wallis and Michael Anderson, my film associates. Towards the end I heard the clip-clop of pony hooves on the stage behind the curtain, and I thought, 'My God – they've got Peter on the show!'

But the spectacular ending, when the curtain was raised, turned out to be the massed bands of the Parachute Regiment giving a thrilling rendering of 'The Ride of the Valkyrie,' their own regimental march, and 'The Dam Busters March', complete with their pony mascot smartly accoutred and steady as a rock. Hence the parked line of Airborne trucks!

The research had taken months. Kitty had been let into the secret long before, and received numerous phone calls usually prefaced by an anxious, 'Is your husband there?'

The Saturday before the show we had given a dinner party; conversation had somehow got around to 'This Is Your Life', and I'd been asked whether, if I found myself as the subject one night, I would go through with it. I said, 'Good God, no! And, anyway, Kitty would never allow it.' The guilt-ridden Kitty, harbouring her dreadful secret, nearly died of embarrassment.

However, once trapped, it had been a memorable and emotional occasion for me. We all met and chatted nostalgically at a BBC reception afterwards.

Next day the Variety Awards luncheon went well and afterwards I went with Alan Sleath to a showing of *The Vow*, the Oberammergau story, at Lime Grove. It was pretty good.

Now that all the studio work on *Never Let Go* had finished, we began on location scenes. These were mostly in a seedy area of Paddington which was due for demolition, and included a number of miserably cold and foggy all-night scenes involving John Cummings' confrontation with a bunch of Hell's Angels led by Adam Faith and including his girl-friend, played by Carol White. These two were excellent and a credit to Peter de Sarigny's casting. Adam was already a popular pop singer, but he and Carol both went on to carve out successful acting careers.

During the daylight locations, Peter Sellers clicked happily with his camera. He must have taken hundreds of shots, and seemed quite obsessed with his hobby. One he had taken of me he had printed and gave me with a very charming message.

During my filming on *Never Let Go* Dash was twice mated to Willy of Barnacre (the Field Trial Champion) but sadly proved to be barren, so our canine population remained unchanged. Gemini, the filly, was sold to a good home, and old Damson was retired to a home of rest. Farm workers don't particularly like looking after horses.

I had a number of meetings locally, planning our Henley Midnight Matinee, and started to write dozens of letters to various celebrities inviting them to join us in March for the occasion. I had a number of acceptances including one from Richard and Sheila Attenborough to be our house-guests for the weekend. When the day arrived we enjoyed a splendid evening and everything was arranged like a charity première in London. First of all we had a supper party at Haileywood for about 60 special people – including the film and TV personalities from London and an impressive list of local big-wigs to join with them – and then on the stroke of 10 o'clock we set off to Henley in a convoy of cars, with a police escort in radio contact with the cinema. There we were greeted by a guard of honour from an RAF base, complete with band and buglers, and then met by a group of girls from the Ockenden Venture, all prettily dressed in their national costumes, before settling down to enjoy the film – a pre-release picture loaned for the occasion by Associated British. Afterwards there were drinks, coffee and snacks at Haileywood. We were able to hand over nearly £1,500 from the event to the Ockenden Venture – quite a lot of money in those days. I was very grateful to the 30 or so celebrities who had made the trip down from London for the occasion.

There were also a couple of rather disappointing meetings with Leslie Norman, who had been assigned to direct *The Long and the Short and the Tall*. First of all, I didn't particularly care for his screen adaptation of the play, and I was amazed that he had meekly agreed that the entire picture should be shot in the studios. I felt that it would merely come out as a photographed stage play, with no real feel of a jungle setting. Leslie was a nice chap, but seemed rather indecisive and insecure. What really upset me, though, was that ABPC were not going to use Peter O'Toole as Bamforth, the part he created so magnificently in the original Royal Court Theatre production. I argued this over and over with Norman and Jimmy Wallis, but got nowhere. They did not feel that Peter was sufficiently well known to be starred in the film. Typical film thinking: never mind the quality – feel the width. In the end, they cast Laurence Harvey in the role. I was delighted when very soon after it was announced that O'Toole was going to play Lawrence of Arabia and become a major international star.

In addition I had endless meetings with Wallis, Frank Godwin, Fritz Gotfurt (head of the scenario department) and Dennis Cannon (the writer) about preparations for *Love From Everybody*, which was now being scripted. We had budget discussions, talks with John Terry at the National Film Finance Corporation and began to think about casting. All seemed to be coming along nicely, and everyone agreed that it was a very funny story.

As soon as *Never Let Go* was finished – except for some later post-synching – I took Kitty for the short holiday I had promised myself in Denmark.

We sailed from Harwich complete with the Star Sapphire in a very comfortable Danish ship, the *Kronprins Frederik*, and were allotted the royal suite for our overnight trip – very grand and comfortable, and something of an honour! Arriving at Ejsberg, we drove and ferried across the three islands of Denmark and got to Copenhagen in the early afternoon. It was a lovely drive, through wonderfully-farmed areas of tidy, neat countryside. We used Copenhagen as our base, and explored every day – visiting Elsinore of course! We found the Danes marvellously friendly and jolly, and gorged ourselves in various restaurants. Our pleasantest day was probably when we drove round the middle island, Funen, which is the flower of the country. At one point we espied a real fairy-tale castle built in the middle of a lake and approached by a narrow causeway complete with drawbridge. I couldn't resist the temptation to get out and trespass in order to have a closer look. We were presently confronted by a tall, tweedy man who politely asked what we were doing there. I explained that we were so fascinated by the beauty of the place that we just had to stop and look. I apologised and prepared to return to the car. 'That's all right,' he said. 'You're welcome. Come and have tea – and would you like to look around the home farm?' It turned out that this was the owner of one of the greatest estates in Denmark, Count Bille-Brahe. It was our lucky day.

On our return to Ejsberg we drove around Jutland for a few hours, and at one point I was fascinated by a tiny, isolated and very ancient church. Inside I was amazed to find the tomb of Bothwell, one of Mary Queen of Scots' unfortunate husbands, whom I later discovered had lived in exile in Jutland. Judging by the size of his tomb and his effigy on the top, he was a tiny little man – no match for Vanessa Redgrave!

I had over two months to wait before starting work on *The Long and the Short and the Tall*, and during that time I had very little to do with the forthcoming production apart from a couple of lunch meetings with Leslie Norman. It was a job I had to do, since it was a contract film for ABPC, but I was not particularly looking forward to it. There had already been so many postponements and arguments that I would not have been all that surprised if the whole project were cancelled.

Meanwhile progress was being made with our *Love From Everybody* preparations. Frank Godwin and I settled on Cyril Frankel to direct the picture, and we reckoned we were lucky to get such an experienced and sophisticated film-maker, exactly right for the glossy type of comedy we hoped to make. Also, although he could give us only about six weeks' work, as he was already contracted to another production, I had persuaded Geoff Unsworth to start the cinematography. I knew he would set his stamp of excellence on the lighting and camerawork. Between us, we had also cast June Thorburn to play one of the leads, my fiancée in the story, and had decided on most of the supporting actresses and actors. There were only two main parts yet to be filled:

that of a Rhine-maiden type of athletic German blonde, and a beautiful chic French girl.

During this period I also spent quite a lot of time with the co-production committee of the FBFM, including a two-day visit to Paris to talk with our French counterparts. So I was by no means idle.

My private life was fairly busy, too.

A new boys' public school had been founded at nearby Shiplake Court and I took some interest in its development, giving a couple of lectures there and arranging for the school to run weekend activity camps for less privileged boys from the South Islington Boys' Club with which I was connected.

We also took Peter to see his future prep school, Wellesley House, in Broadstairs, and he was delighted with what he saw. At the Friar Park School Sports he became *victor ludorum* that summer.

That was the year when Shrewsbury School crew won the Princess Elizabeth Cup at Henley Regatta in record time. They had spent all their spare time with us at Haileywood and on the Saturday of the final race we hurriedly got together a party for them that evening, gathering all the young people we knew in the area, including Prince Birendra (now King) of Nepal who was staying with the Stonors. Boys, parents, Peter Gladstone and our friends made a very jolly evening of it, ending up at the fun-fair in the regatta grounds.

I also contrived to make my annual scoreless appearance leading my President's Cricket XI at the Shiplake Memorial Hall!

Early in June *Never Let Go* was premièred at the Odeon, Leicester Square. The film was well received by a packed audience, but got mixed reviews – ranging from 'brilliant' to 'overdone'. I believe that those who criticised it were not able to adjust to Peter Sellers playing a straight dramatic part – or, for that matter, to me playing anything but a stiff-upper-lip, true blue type. Nevertheless, the film subsequently did well.

My birthday that year was a memorable one. At the time, we had an Area Scout Camp in the park at Haileywood; over 100 young lads were under canvas there and the evenings were enlivened with their camp-fire and songs. On 11 June we had a dinner party at the house and had been invited by the head scoutmaster to join them by the bonfire afterwards. As I and my guests filed through the little kissing-gate from the garden into the park, a double row of Scouts held sparkling torches aloft and sang 'Happy Birthday'. We sat on logs around the camp-fire and joined in the singing. I found it very moving to see that circle of fresh, happy young faces in the flickering light and could not have wished for a more touching benediction.

When *The Long and the Short and the Tall* started filming at Elstree in mid-June, I almost wished it hadn't, since it turned out to be the most unpleasant film I had ever worked on. Apart from the staginess of its treatment and setting, other problems soon arose. *The Hasty Heart* – which I had made twelve years before – had also been a jungle story entirely shot indoors, and had been adapted from a stage play, but its action had taken place almost totally inside a large hospital hut so that outside effects were not needed. But films had progressed since then and were often photographed in actual exterior locations, thus gaining a verisimilitude that made all the difference between cinema films and their more restricted TV counterparts.

Admittedly the jungle set for *The Long and the Short and the Tall* was cleverly designed, with streams, steamy heat and lots of palms and thick greenery, but it was nevertheless nothing like the real thing. Even the sound effects had an indoor reverberation about them.

The cast was excellent, and the members of the little patrol included Laurence Harvey, Richard Harris, Ronald Fraser and David McCallum, all well-known and experienced screen actors. The patrol involved was an audio-warfare unit in Burma equipped with loudspeakers broadcasting demoralising messages to the Japanese who infested the area. With its one terrified Japanese prisoner, the patrol is surrounded and picked off one by one by snipers until it is finally exterminated. Despite its rather gruesome and hopeless situation, the group manages to come up with a fair amount of earthy humour, mostly provided by the irrepressible and vicious Cockney wide-boy, Bamforth, Peter O'Toole's part now played by Harvey.

The real irritant we had was Laurence Harvey himself. A good and extremely successful actor, there was much to be admired about his courage and determination to succeed. Born Larushka Mischa Skikne, a Lithuanian refugee of humble origin, he and his family had emigrated to South Africa. From there his talent and ambitious single-mindedness had eventually secured him a place in the Royal Academy of Dramatic Art in London. At the start of his acting career, beautifully-spoken, suave, good-looking, he showed no trace of his impoverished start in life.

Ambition for the good life and an abundant ego were his driving force. Other and more gentle qualities he may have had too, but we didn't see much of them at Elstree. With his consuming desire always to be the centre of attention, he became a mischievous and disruptive influence on our working days. A lot of time was wasted while he clowned around, and his influence started to affect some of the others

– in particular Richard Harris, not the most difficult subject to be led astray in those days. The pair of them took to lunching outside the studios and returning for the afternoon schedule more than a little over-indulged. The hapless Leslie Norman finally gave up trying to curb them, and seemed to lose control of things altogether.

Finally one day Vaughan Dean, the head of the studio – having looked at some of the time-sheets and visited the set once or twice – asked me if there was anything I could do as the senior actor on the production.

I decided to have a word with Richard Harris. He came to my dressing room that evening, and I told him what an ass he was making of himself, and how he was letting himself be led into being a nuisance to all concerned. To my amazement he actually shed tears, said he was sorry and was as good as gold from then on. Despite any reputation he may have gained as a hell-raiser, Richard is a hell of a nice chap, and very sensitive: unruly perhaps, but really good-hearted.

We finished the picture in mid-August, almost on schedule.

As soon as *The Long and the Short and the Tall* was out of the way, I had a few days with the family on the Isle of Bute. We all had a lot of fun water-skiing daily with Lady Bute and her children and Charlie Crichton-Stuart (a relation of the Butes) on a loch belonging to the Marquess – that is until Lord Bute himself turned up one day, furious because we were disturbing his trout, and ordered us off. All of us, including his family, turned tail and slunk away.

When I returned to London we were in the final stages of preparing *Love From Everybody*. A new title for the film *Don't Bother to Knock* – taken from an old Marilyn Monroe picture – had been secured, and that was the name of our production from then on. We soon had the cast under contract, but still with the exception of two important parts, a chic French beauty and our German athletic blonde. We had gone through numerous lists of suitable actresses, but those we wanted all seemed to be already engaged. Frank Godwin, Cyril Frankel and I spent many worrying sessions trying to sort the matter out.

In the end I solved one of the problems by a sheer stroke of luck and opportunism. Sitting lunching one day alone in the Elstree dining room, I was riveted by a gorgeous auburn-haired beauty deeply engaged in conversation with Mario Zampi, the prolific producer of a series of run-of-the-mill comedies who had a film just starting at the studio. I asked Eileen, the waitress, if she knew who she was, and she replied, 'Oh, that's the French actress, Nicole Maurey. She has just finished a film in America with Bing Crosby, and I suppose Mr Zampi wants her for his picture.'

Here, right across the room from me, was the girl for whom we had been searching for weeks!

Guessing that she would probably visit the Zampi set after lunch, I strolled on to the stage myself and found Miss Maurey sitting alone with a script in her lap, watching the shooting. I introduced myself and sat with her for a while. I gathered that she was waiting for a studio car to take her back to London. I said that I knew the studio cars were very busy at that moment because of an Associated British executive conference being held that afternoon in London. (Absolute lie, of course! I had already phoned the studio hire-car company to cancel Miss Maurey's car.) But I told her she need not worry because I was leaving for London that very moment and would happily give her a lift. Apparently quite relieved, she accepted.

As we drove along, I asked her if she contemplated making a film for Mario Zampi. She replied that she had just been given the script to read. 'For Mario Zampi?' I said, seeming astonished. 'Good Lord . . . He's an awfully nice man, of course. Makes lots of little comedies quite successfully. But I wouldn't have thought that they'd be up to your standard.' A silence ensued, as she obviously mulled this over in her mind.

As we neared the Mayfair Hotel I decided that now was a propitious moment to play my opening gambit. 'Pity about the Zampi picture. I have a production due to start in a couple of weeks with a leading part absolutely perfect for you. I do wish you had been free. As a matter of fact, I happen to have a copy of the script in the car. Perhaps you'd like to read it, just out of interest?' I knew she was leaving London the next day, but I had a feeling she would read both screenplays that evening. She took my copy of *Don't Bother to Knock*, thanked me for the lift, and I arranged to phone her next morning and collect my script from her.

Sure enough, when I called her she said she loved my script and would like to make the picture.

I hurriedly arranged to take her to lunch at the Mirabelle restaurant to discuss things with Frank Godwin and Cyril Frankel. By 2.30 that afternoon we had our French star, subject to contract which we had drawn up without delay, even though it strained our budget a bit.

So now things were improving. We already had June Thorburn, Nicole Maurey, Judith Anderson, Rik Battaglia (from Italy) and Ronald

Fraser (very funny as a travel courier) and an amazing list of notable actors and actresses playing quite tiny roles, including Colin Gordon, Eleanor Summerfield, John le Mesurier, John Laurie, Liz Fraser, Kynaston Reeves, Fulton Mackay and Warren Mitchell. Our group of American students in the film was headed by Jane Merrow, Angela Douglas and Amanda Barrie.

Our studio space had been booked, the sets designed and being built, the locations scouted and prepared, the budget agreed and everything ready to go – but for one thing: right up to a few days before shooting was due to begin we still had no German Amazon booked. Then Cyril, who had recently made a picture in Germany, suddenly remembered a girl who might fit the bill: Elke Sommer. He had thought her a bit inexperienced and was not sure if her English was good enough, but. . . .

'At least let's test her,' I said. Her agent was contacted in Germany and the very next day I met her at London Airport. I was slightly taken aback by her straggly hair and scruffy appearance, but she had an infectious naturalness about her that was very engaging, and certainly all the physical attributes the part would need. I rushed her to the Mayfair Hotel, called our wardrobe mistress, Mrs Jackson, to come and take her out to find a wig and some clothes for the screen test the next morning, then later took her to dinner and gave her her test scene to read. She was really likeable and fun, full of good humour and seemingly not in the least worried about her ordeal the following day.

She did an excellent test, seen and liked by Jimmy Wallis and the rest of the ABPC executives concerned, and was engaged for the film. Her salary was pretty low, I'm afraid, but at least I had managed to give Elke Sommer her first English-speaking role and very soon she was making headway in Hollywood. I also found a cheap flat for her to share with her mother, who came over to join her.

While all this was going on – and even when I was still working on *The Long and the Short and the Tall* – my evenings and weekends at home were well filled. I usually walked the farm with Prevett on Sunday mornings and went through the milking records with him, and more often than not found myself opening some charity fête. A South Islington Boys' Club party came down for their first weekend camp at Shiplake School, and I watched them having a great time boating, playing cricket and generally enjoying a couple of days in the country.

Peter had been given a go-kart for his birthday and we all took turns racing around the garden on this. One Sunday Dick and Catherine Brandram came to tea bringing with them ex-Queen Helen of Rumania, Catherine's sister, and the pretty young Princess Elizabeth of Yugoslavia, a niece. The rather severe ex-Queen watched disapprovingly as Kitty, Catherine and the princess careered around the big lawn on the go-kart, their skirts flying around their heads.

On the last day of August, work started on *Don't Bother to Knock* on location in Edinburgh.

Edinburgh was the focal base of our story, which concerned a successful and philandering travel agent, whose business took him all over Europe from his office in the Scottish capital. His romantic encounters during his trips had been numerous until his recent engagement to a local girl (June Thorburn), as a result of which he was trying hard to reform his ways. However, he still continued to carry with him a supply of his special talisman: a golden key to his flat in Edinburgh. These he would present to whatever attractive subject caught his eye as an earnest of his sincere intentions. 'This is the key to my home,' he would say. 'Use it whenever you wish. Don't bother to knock – just walk in and you'll always be welcome.' On one such trip he distributed a few of these gifts, quite forgetting the forthcoming Edinburgh Festival, a magnet for overseas visitors. To his horrified embarrassment and his fiancée's fury, his flat was suddenly besieged by a trio of attractive females who had been recipients of his keys, and who had decided to take up residence there while they visit the Festival. They include Nicole Maurey and Elke Sommer, of course, and a teenager, Dawn Beret, who has had a key slipped to her by a waiter in a Venice hotel when it should have been given to her attractive mother, Eleanor Summerfield.

The resultant chaos in the travel agent's situation during Festival-time leads to a light-hearted comedy of errors, lame explanations, attempts at concealment and utter confusion.

After a few days in Edinburgh we all moved down to West Wittering, an area of lovely sand and dunes on the Sussex coast. Our production manager, Leigh Aman, also happened to be Lord Marley, and I think his title so impressed the local authority that we were allowed to use an area of private beach which was wonderfully quiet during the weekdays. After a dull first day the weather became beautiful and we got some splendid screen footage, especially round a moored raft surrounded by the gaily-coloured sails of the local yacht club, whose members were only too glad to co-operate.

From the very beginning *Don't Bother to Knock* was an enjoyable picture to make, partly because of its amusing story line, partly because we were a very happy company, and not least because we were always surrounded by a carefully selected bevy of beautiful women – a factor that brought some light and sparkle to the otherwise rather gloomy studio complex. Frank, Cyril and I were the envy of the other film-makers, especially at our large table in the dining room at lunch-time. Gary Cooper, who was filming at Elstree at the time, eventually asked if he could join us each day and brought his own special charm to our group. We never lacked for visitors on our sets.

Since this was a story essentially about foreign travel, the variety of our locations and sets also helped to brighten the usually rather turgid grind of studio work. We had scenes ranging from concerts at the Edinburgh Festival to night-clubs and restaurants in Italy, Spain and Bavaria, the latter complete with a troupe of *schüplatte* dancers whacking out their routines, and a group of flamenco dancers and musicians in the Spanish sequence. These I had frequently watched at a Spanish club-restaurant which I quite often visited as it was just round the corner from my flat in Nell Gwynn House, and we were able to hire them for a couple of days without any searching or auditioning.

When Geoffrey Unsworth had to leave us in October, Ted Scaife took over as director of photography and did a splendid job, indistinguishable from Geoff's work.

Elke Sommer celebrated her twentieth birthday with us at Hailey-wood. The Saturday happened to be Guy Fawkes Day and she and her mother were treated to a fireworks display that evening. I managed to convince them that our pyrotechnics and those all around the neighbourhood were in honour of Elke's anniversary. On the Sunday Frank, Cyril and some of the cast came down to join us for a buffet lunch, and that evening we were all invited to drinks at Sherman and Jeanne Stonor's beautiful and ancient house at Stonor Park. Just another example of the happy family atmosphere in our *Don't Bother to Knock* company . . .

By now much of the film had been put together in a rough-cut and all the ABPC hierarchy were delighted by it; so much so that I was able to convince them it would be worth splurging a little extra budget to shoot our Bavarian scenes in Oberammergau instead of in the Welsh mountains as originally planned.

We managed to do all our location work in Oberammergau without any difficulty in just two days, since I used exactly the same mountain set-ups which we had had the previous year for the BBC film, so we had no need to do any scouting or to send out an advance party, and required only a minimum unit. Frau Lang, who had arranged all the facilities for the BBC unit, did the same for us, and we had no problems.

In fact, our shooting in Bavaria probably cost less than the Welsh visit would have done, and certainly took less time.

So that was the end of our shooting on *Don't Bother to Knock*. We bade farewell to Elke Sommer, whose cheerfulness and zest for work had been a tonic for us all. Altogether it had been a very happy ten weeks, and in stark contrast to the gloom and acrimony of *The Long and the Short and the Tall*. Perhaps some of my enjoyment of that period had stemmed from the fact that the picture had been made by my own company, and was based on a story which I had bought off my own bat.

The next three or four weeks were mostly spent at Elstree, post-synching, doing stills photographs with Frank Buckingham, the brilliant resident portrait photographer, and adding a few pick-up shots – and, of course, spending hours watching the final cut version being put together and 'musicked'. Everybody, including C. J. Latta, Robert Clark and Jimmy Wallis, seemed very pleased with the results.

My weekends were mostly spent shooting, either with our own syndicate, which was now functioning well with two part-time keepers, or at Cliveden and once, memorably, with Aubrey Buxton at his famed wildfowl shoot on Hickling Broad in Norfolk.

One little hiccup occurred when Kitty had a slight accident in the brand new Austin Countryman estate car that I had just bought for her. Nothing serious, it nevertheless left her very upset and nervy for a while and caused quite a strained few days. However all was well for Christmas Day, when we had a nice family lunch after the Christmas tree gift-opening ceremony, followed that evening by our annual dinner with Tory and Raymond Palmer at Pinkney's Green. On Boxing Day I shot at Harleyford Manor, near Marlow, and later we dined at Cliveden with the Astors.

Peter, who had now left Friar Park School, had his first day's hunting with the South Berks Hunt who met at Haileywood. It was a pouring wet day, but his spirits were by no means dampened as he set off on his pony under the watchful eye of Ann Waugh, who was also riding.

And then, with only two days to go before the end of 1960, Robert Lennard asked me to his office to discuss a script that he had just been given for me to read by Irving Allen and 'Cubby' Broccoli of Warwick Films, a major independent production company with some pretty hefty screen credits to its name, including years later the Bond 007 films. Out of the blue, my next picture for 1961 had fallen into my lap. *The Hellions*, set in South Africa.

You never know your luck ...

22

Flying Visits

Over the next few months I was to spend a good deal more time in aeroplanes than ever I had done as an Airborne soldier during the war.

I was due to leave for South Africa in February 1961, but before then there was plenty to be done both at home and abroad. To begin with, Cyril Frankel had contracted a mild bout of pneumonia, so Frank Godwin and I worked at Elstree overseeing the dubbing of our film. Most evenings I spent at Irving Allen's sumptuous London office, with its fine display of Alfred Munnings' horse paintings, going through the script of *The Hellions*, the South African subject, with Harold Huth, the producer, and Ken Annakin, the director, who had guided me through *Robin Hood* and *The Sword and the Rose* for Walt Disney.

In mid-January I flew to Argentina for the Mar del Plata Film Festival, a long and tiring flight which included stops at Paris, Madrid, Recife, Rio and Buenos Aires, and then a short, bumpy hop to Mar del Plata.

This South American festival was nothing like as lavish as the Cannes affair, but was a good shop-window for our films in the South American circuit. We showed *The Long and the Short and the Tall* and were greatly supported by the British Ambassador who came specially from Buenos Aires and made sure that all our cars were equipped with Union Jacks. The Argentinians themselves were most welcoming and kindly and seemed very pro-British in their attitudes. One local and very rich family, Martinez de Hos, invited us to their imposing mansion and stud-farm, with its polo grounds, for a typical English afternoon tea. Their children all spoke English as a first language, ably supervised by their Scottish governess.

One of our British delegation, Shirley Ann Field, had an appendix operation in Mar del Plata, and we all spent as much time as possible visiting her to cheer her up, although she was in good hands and would soon follow the rest of us home.

My flight home was delayed by a heavy storm, but I got away the next morning at dawn, arriving in the middle of the night at Heathrow feeling somewhat weary.

A few days later, we saw Peter off from Victoria Station, where he joined a party of boys going to his new prep school, Wellesley House, in charge of a couple of masters. We had just previously taken him to lunch at the Caprice, but the poor chap hardly touched a morsel of food as he sat there very white-faced and red-eyed. Anybody who has seen a little boy depart for his first term at boarding-school will know what it feels like for parents and child. On the station platform the tears began to flow and an understanding master gently led him into a compartment with the other new boys. We waved at the woebegone little face at the window as the train began to move, our own eyes brimming. For years it was never easy for any of us.

Our next farewell that month was to the Prevett family, who left to run a farm in Hampshire. Prevett was a good, experienced farmer, but not really suited to be a farm manager with all the documentation and paperwork that the job entailed. His replacements – Mr Wade with his son Michael – were excellent and very efficient. Wade and the herdsman, Webb, made a splendid team, while Michael took over the pig-rearing side enthusiastically and successfully.

In mid-February I flew out to Johannesburg for work on *The Hellions*, the Irving Allen Warwick Films picture that was to be distributed by Columbia Pictures of America.

I must have contracted Asian 'flu just prior to leaving, and was feeling ghastly and frequently being sick during the last hours of the long flight. As I tottered off the plane, pea-green and queasy-weak, I was aghast at what I faced.

The Jan Smuts Airport was simply crammed with people, all waving and cheering, and it gradually dawned on me that this noisy, good-humoured reception was for me! In those days South Africa had no television and little theatre, and pop stars had not yet been invented. The 'fillums' were the sole source of entertainment, so that film stars were accorded the kind of excited welcome now reserved for pop stars. Only out there the enthusiasm was not confined to youngsters, but included film fans of all ages.

So there I was, being cheerfully jostled and back-slapped all the way to where my car was waiting, doing my best to respond to the friendly crowd when all I wanted to do was to crawl into my feverish bed and pass out. I was met by Willi Herbst, a beefy and none-too-bright member of the film company, and he and a group of policemen finally bundled me into the car; then Willi really excelled himself: try as he might, he simply could not get the engine to start. Sweating and swearing in what I took to be Afrikaans, he finally turned to me and sheepishly admitted that he had never driven this car before. By now a large group of people helpfully decided that we needed a push-start and began to shove us ignominiously out on to the main road. It was then I noticed that he had left his gear-lever in 'Drive', so naturally the ignition wouldn't work. He had never driven an automatic-drive car before either, and all the excitement had been too much for him. Once in 'Start' we started up and were away, leading a procession of cars all the way to the hotel in Pretoria which was to be our base.

I went straight to bed without even unpacking, was visited by a doctor and slept, miraculously waking up the next day little the worse for my brief bout of 'flu. My recovery was no doubt speeded up when breakfast was brought to me by none other than Willi, but backed up by his PR assistant Norma Vorster, whom I had met years before in London when she was Miss South Africa in the Miss World contest.

None of us was quite sure what to expect of South Africa. When we arrived there the country was still part of the British Commonwealth of Nations, the Springboks still toured the British Isles and the rest of the rugger-playing world, the word apartheid was not yet in common parlance and we knew little of the politics of the nation. All we did know was that everybody at home bought and ate large quantities of South African fruit and drank a lot of South African wines; that the scenery was varied and spectacular and the climate superb; that a high proportion of British expatriates had settled there and that South Africa had played a large part in the history of the British Empire; and that many South Africans had voluntarily come to our aid in two World Wars. We were there to work and hopefully to see some of the country and visit the Wildlife Game Parks. We were not there on a fact-finding mission, and when you don't search you don't see much.

Of course there had been a little dust-up called the Boer War, but that was before our time and, we hoped, no longer rankled with the Afrikaners. We did have a vague unease about this and wondered what sort of attitude the Afrikaners would adopt towards us Brits, especially as we were to be living and working in the Transvaal State where the Boer tradition was particularly strong – typified by the Voertrekker Monument near Pretoria, the shrine to the early Boer settlers.

We need not have worried: everywhere and by everyone, we were shown great friendliness and hospitality. In a sentence, we enjoyed our weeks out there and saw nothing to disturb us. But then, as I said, we didn't go looking for it. We could understand why South Africa was a holiday and tourist centre for those who could afford it.

The Hellions was set in one of the early gold-mining areas towards the end of the last century and was a kind of Western, with me as the local police sergeant trying to keep some form of law and order in a pretty lawless and tough community – a kind of mini-John Wayne, except that I wore a uniform instead of just a sheriff's star. My main antagonists were a wild family of desperados led by the father, a ruthless criminal played by that marvellous actor Lionel Jeffries, who like me was an old Wimburnian. His unruly and uncouth sons were Colin Blakeley (a Northern Irishman, also like me), James Booth, a rather moody product of the Theatre Workshop, and Marty Wilde, a charming, quiet ex-pop-star and surprisingly good actor. Altogether we had a very strong male cast, which also included a popular local actor named Jamie Uys. Not the least important member of our company was that master stunt expert, Bob Simmons, who had worked with me several times before and who later devised and performed many of the stunts for the Bond films. Bob trained my horse for me and did all the really tricky stunts, doubling for Lionel Jeffries in a fall from a roof and for me in a dive through a glass window. Finally, we also had with us in a leading part Ronald Fraser; he had worked with me on my last two films and I was delighted to work with him again.

The film was shot almost entirely out of doors and nearly all in a nearby town called Brits. The place was like a time-capsule, a typical late-nineteenth-century dorp with colonial wooden houses and shops straggling along one dusty earth-floored main street. No Hollywood Western set could have been more suitable for our purposes. The populace were mostly Asians, and they were thrilled by the sudden notoriety we brought to their shabby backwater, with our motorcade of camera vehicles, trucks, caravans and press cars.

We did spend a few days filming interiors in a dreadful little studio near Pretoria, which was no more than a large barn with a galvanised iron roof and almost no facilities. It was an unpleasant experience as we sweltered in temperatures that reached 110°F. We were issued with salt pills, but they made me sick, so I kept going by drinking lots of fluid.

We kept well within schedule and the film was taking good shape until, just after the half-way stage, our director Ken Annakin was smitten by a serious and mysterious illness. He was taken to a nearby

Roman Catholic hospital staffed most efficiently by nuns. We never knew what bug had hit him and were all very worried for him – even polio was rumoured, as a form of paralysis had developed. His wife Pauline was constantly with him, and the rest of us visited as often as we were allowed.

Harold Huth, who had directed films in the past, bravely took on Ken's job, but he was quite elderly and inevitably the pace slackened. James Booth, never the most disciplined of actors, gave him a particularly difficult time. However, we ploughed on fairly successfully.

Kitty had joined me after a couple of weeks and stayed for a month. Much of her time was spent with Oscar Hurwitz and his wife in their lovely house and garden. Oscar was one of South Africa's leading architects and much involved in the designing and ownership of hotels, apartment blocks and office complexes all over the country. He and his family were absolutely charming to all of us, and much of our time was spent with them, especially at weekends when the whole unit was made welcome around the pool. Their hospitality was boundless, and they never seemed to mind how many of us turned up for cold drinks and barbecues. Other people made us welcome too, and there was not a single member of the unit left with nowhere to go. Our stay in South Africa was almost totally happy.

At one stage I had a long weekend free and decided to drive my hired car down to Durban, with Norma Vorster as my guide since she was going there to visit her family. The trip was about 500 miles, but on a good road and through marvellously varied scenery, and easily accomplished in one day. I was greatly taken with Durban, its seafront splendour of Edwardian elegance mixed with modernistic apartment buildings and its miles of marvellous beaches, and everywhere colourful displays of exotic flowers.

During my stay in South Africa I had been struck by the enormous potential there for an important film industry. It has everything: scenery varying from mountain to English parkland, from bush to jungle and from green and pleasant pastures to arid desert; a wonderful climate bringing snow on the high places and sweltering heat in low areas; plenty of potential investment money looking for overseas outlets; and in those days a large pool of English-speaking actors and actresses already active in theatre and radio work. All it lacked was entrepreneurial and technical know-how.

As this was long before South Africa had become ostracised by the rest of the world politically and ideologically, I gave the matter quite a lot of thought while I was there, and eventually had a chance to discuss it with Professor Barry Wiehahn, an economist living in Pretoria who had masterminded the decimalisation of South African currency. He suggested that I should go for talks with some of the government ministers, who were then sitting in Cape Town, and arranged meetings for me.

So a couple of days before I left for England I flew to Cape Town early one morning. I had discussions with the Ministers of Economic Affairs, Finance and Defence, and they all assured me that any effort to start an international film industry in South Africa would be assured of the cooperation of their departments. I had lunch in the House of Parliament, briefly watched a debate at which Sir de Villiers Graff, the leader of the Opposition, was the main speaker, and flew back to Johannesburg.

At a short and steamy stop in Dakar, I went to get a cup of coffee and noticed a bottle of orange juice labelled 'Pssschitt'. I bought it for its intriguing name, put it in my holdall and when asked by customs at Heathrow if I had anything to declare, I said, 'Only this.' The officer was not amused.

Three days later I was back at Haileywood.

Home again after such a long overseas absence, I faced quite a pile of work and was office-bound for days. Everything on the farm was flourishing in the capable hands of Mr Wade, the manager, so I had no worries there; he even had a projected budget for the next two months prepared for me. The herd was by now considerably enlarged, but I was still subsidising a lot of farm improvements out of my professional earnings and repaying bank loans for the extra land I had bought.

I did take an evening off to go to the première in London of *The Guns of Navarone*. The previous year I had refused the offer of a leading part made to me by Carl Foreman, the producer, and now I realised that I had made a crass mistake. It turned out to be a fine and successful movie, but I had thought the story a bit far-fetched – and, besides, I was trying to avoid being typecast in army roles. I had turned down *Ice Cold in Alex* years before for the same reasons, and should have learned from that mistake.

I had been having a bit of trouble from the shoulder and neck injuries I had incurred during the war and, at Bill Astor's suggestion, I went for treatment to Stephen Ward, a brilliant osteopath who numbered Bill and Sir Winston Churchill amongst his patients. I found Stephen

– whom I had met once or twice previously at Cliveden – a most engaging and amusing man as well as being expert at his profession. He was also a gifted artist, and examples of his portraits were hanging in his consulting room. I was flattered when he asked if he could do a charcoal sketch of me, and I readily agreed. In about half an hour he produced an excellent likeness. Little did I realise that he was soon to figure in a most tragic scandal, and that somewhere among his effects when he died would be that drawing of me.

I also had to collect from Harrods' warehouse the crates of hired china and glasses which we needed for our annual Henley Midnight Matinée on 5 May. We had eighty people to a buffet supper that night, and the charity evening was once more a great success.

There were a few days of post-synching for *The Hellions* to be done with Ken Annakin, now completely recovered from his mysterious illness, and I ran some of the 16mm film I had shot in South Africa, which I had roughly spliced together at the Warwick Films little preview cinema. Quite pleased with my home-movie efforts, I decided to order a 16mm projector.

In mid-May I flew to Cannes for a few days at the Film Festival, where I was by now almost an annual fixture. We showed *Don't Bother to Knock* to an invited audience and it went down very well, its light-hearted comedy content being something of a relief to film people normally subjected to some pretty heavy cinema fare at these gatherings.

We also opened a new ABC Cinema in Sheffield with the picture, and it was heartening to see and hear a large audience revelling in it.

At the end of May the June Dairy Festival was officially opened at the Mansion House in the City, with the Prime Minister as chief guest and speaker. I had lent one of my Jerseys for the occasion and a proud Peter Webb showed her off to an admiring crowd outside. Next day my farms opened to the public for the whole of June, and we had several thousand visitors during the month; some came by coach from as far as the Midlands, and all were led around by Mr Wade who was something of a showman. George Speakman's Dairy Council gave us a lot of help, providing a marquee and ladies who did a brisk trade in teas and the sale of farm and garden produce. Only dear old Joe Aggis seemed unaware of the throngs of people and just plodded on with his work.

Finally came the press showing of *Don't Bother to Knock*, followed by the première on 1 June at the Plaza Cinema near Piccadilly Circus. We had previously run a sneak preview of the film at the Hammersmith ABC Cinema, attended by some of the ABPC hierarchy. They were all delighted by the audience reaction, and after that and the Sheffield opening, we were very hopeful of a good press and a money-making movie.

How wrong we were!

The film was hammered by most of the press and the première was a nervy evening – for me, especially – even though the audience again gave it an enthusiastic reception. Why the press and the public were at such variance about the picture I shall never know. Perhaps it was my fault because the critics refused to accept me in a light comedy role. Certainly it was no fault of the director or the other artistes.

It was all very depressing, and my feeling of dejection was not improved when a few days later Baron collapsed. My beloved old Dane was now eleven years old, a considerable age for such a big dog, and had become pretty stiff and feeble, unable to travel around with me as he had done for years. I sat up with him all night as he gasped and shuddered, and for several days Kitty and I took it in turns to sleep downstairs so as to be near him. Gradually he recovered and was able to walk unaided, but had to be led out very slowly for his necessary visits to the orchard. There was obviously not much time left to him.

It was a thoroughly upsetting time for me altogether.

And I began to realise that I had made another serious mistake: offered the choice of two release dates for *Don't Bother to Knock*, either an Easter or a summer release, I had picked the latter. Easter-time was always a fairly good period for cinema business, but the summer release was frequently a bonanza for films in Britain when the seaside resorts were crowded and the weather usually filthy. This was long before the days of cheap overseas holiday package travel, and at a time when films were the main indoor attraction at coastal resorts. It was just my luck that this was a brilliant summer, and as I travelled round the country doing personal appearances with the picture it was not at all encouraging to see the beaches packed with people cooling off almost until after dark, while the cinemas were drawing very skimpy audiences. We were doing good business in the inland cities, but this did not exactly balance our books.

Two things did happen to cheer me up: one completely unimportant but very enjoyable, and the other important to me professionally and later to lead to an intriguing couple of weeks.

First, we were invited to spend Gold Cup day at Ascot races in the private box of my friend Boyd Gibbens and I backed five winners – including, of course, Lester Piggott's horse in the Gold Cup itself.

Then I had a phone call from Paris. A well-remembered nasal twang rasped down the line.

'Hi, Dick! It's Darryl.' After a brief exchange of pleasantries, the great Zanuck came to the point:

'I'm going to film *The Longest Day*.'

'My God! That'll be some epic.'

'Yeah. And I want you to play yourself.'

Taken aback, I demurred at this.

'I was there, but I didn't do anything special that'd make a good sequence for you.'

'OK. Well, will you play John Howard, who led the glider attack on Pegasus Bridge?'

That was different. I had talked myself out of so many pictures, but this time I had been offered a great alternative.

'Yes, I'd love to!'

'Fine. See you in Normandy in September.'

So there was another picture in the bag for 1961.

As I've already mentioned, a year before Cornelius Ryan – the author of *The Longest Day* – had spent a weekend at Haileywood with me checking my memory of D-Day and especially the capture and holding of the crucial Pegasus Bridges over the Canal de Caen and the River Orne, some three miles inland from the Normandy coast on the extreme left flank of the invasion. Corny Ryan had obviously done his homework and I found no fault in his version of the British airborne assault (which I myself have now dealt with at some length in the first volume of my memoirs, *Caught in the Act*). Perhaps I was able to add a few reminiscences which he could include in his monumental work.

Little had I thought at that time that this huge epic story would one day a year later find a man with the courage to transpose it on to the cinema screen.

Family and farm affairs were occupying me during my efforts to promote *Don't Bother to Knock*. Queenie Pampel had taken over from Anne Waugh and had already become very much a cheerful part of the family. Less happily, Fiona's progress at Rupert House – a small private school in Henley – had been worrying us. Her reports were bad, mainly based on her inattention during classes, and we had discovered now the reason: her hearing was well below normal, so that she scarcely heard what her teachers were saying. A child of her age has no means of knowing just why she is not keeping up with the others, and I'm sure this situation applies to many other young children who are slow starters at school. As soon as the cause was identified she had an operation at a Reading hospital on her ears and sinuses, and her hearing improved enormously, but for a while she still had to go every so often to a specialist for fluid to be drawn off, and was on antibiotics for a long time.

During that beautiful spell of sunny weather we had one day of rain right in the middle of our hay-making period. Although the downpour did our hay no good, it was excellent for the grass. We now had a small flock of sheep and a couple of rams which were folded around the grassland when parts of it were rested after grazing by the Jersey herd, which was building up almost to capacity for our acreage and buildings. The sheep 'hoovered' the fields, keeping the sward very clean and level, and were fine for our grassland management. Mr Wade decided that one of the rams was rather idle and not paying enough attention to his harem, so he took him to be sold at a Reading market while he chose a replacement. Peter went with him, and that evening excitedly told me that they had bought a new Suffolk ram. 'He's rather small but very active,' he informed me with a knowing air.

We were invited to spend a few days in Belfast at various functions organised by the Milk Marketing Board, accompanied by George Speakman, head of the Dairy Council. They kept us very busy at a string of official occasions, Ulster TV interviews and the final showpiece, which was the election of the Ulster Dairy Queen at a ball in Belfast Castle. However, I did manage to make a personal appearance at the opening of *Don't Bother to Knock*.

Then came the annual Henley Regatta, where Shrewsbury School again won the Princess Elizabeth Cup. Their coach, Peter Gladstone, arranged for me to travel in the umpire's launch, so I had a view of every stroke during the final race. On the Saturday evening we gave a celebration party for the boys, their parents and friends.

We also decided that summer on Fiona's future school. Out of several that we visited we chose St Mary's, Wantage, which was run by Anglican nuns in those days. It was a decision that we would never regret and one that was to prove ideal for Fiona.

I was still flitting around the country promoting *Don't Bother to Knock*, and even managed to be in Brussels for the première there, accompanied always by Cliff Elson, one of the Elstree PR team.

About this time we received the sad news that Kitty's father had suffered a stroke. He had to retire from business, and it was decided that he and Mrs Grant-Bogle would come south for a while to be near us, and allow him to rest and get a change of atmosphere; so I rented a pretty little house in Henley-on-Thames for them to move in to during September.

We had a marvellous two-week holiday that year at Cavalaire, near St Tropez. I had rented a beach-front flat complete with Fabresse, who was a super cook and made life very easy for us.

I drove down to Cavalaire in Kitty's estate car, and met the family at Nice airport when they arrived a couple of days later. The beach was kept immaculate by Monsieur and Madame Paris, who had a concession on a large stretch of the sands. They were both physical training instructors at schools in Paris, and organised games every morning and afternoon for all the children besides giving swimming lessons. I wish more seaside areas had similar facilities so that parents could relax and not worry about their children.

During the weeks since Darryl Zanuck's phone call I had been kept informed of the progress of *The Longest Day* and was given the script by Elmo Williams, Zanuck's associate producer, based in London. Three days after my return from our holiday in France I was once again on the ferry back to that country, for location work in Caen.

23

D-Day Plus Seventeen Years

My drive along the coastal route to Caen evoked many memories for me, even though most of the places that I passed through were scarcely recognisable as the shattered, war-torn villages and towns of 1944. The scars had been almost totally obliterated and the reconstruction work showed the phenomenal resilience of the French people. Normandy was once again an area of great charm and beauty, of orchards and lush meadows, lovely old farmhouses and *manoirs*, ancient churches and pretty cottages.

I was amazed most of all by the rehabilitation of Caen, the great old city which I had once seen as a scene of utter devastation, just piles of rubble pervaded by the stench of death. Some of the important historic buildings had been restored, and the rest new-built into a modern, thriving and busy centre. One such new edifice was the Hotel Malherbe, where most of us were quartered. I arrived in the evening and was met by Zanuck, Ken and Pauline Annakin and John and Joy Howard.

We all had dinner together in the hotel and Zanuck was in an ebullient mood, well pleased with the filming that had been done so far. He was particularly proud of his temporary command, which comprised a huge body of American, British and French troops. Indeed, he had a little medal struck to be presented to all those who took part and called it the DFZ, after his own initials.

Work started the following day and began with a script meeting between Ken Annakin, John Howard, Lord Lovat (who had commanded the Commando Brigade on D-Day) and myself, then moving to an inspection of the Orne and Bénouville Bridges area which was to be the centre-piece of our British airborne attack sequence. An emotional reunion with the Gondrée family at Pegasus Café took place, amidst much hugging and kissing for John and myself. Since John was our official adviser and I had been present during the capture and holding of the bridges on D-Day, Ken was determined that this sequence in the film should be as factual and accurate as possible. Certainly, he would not lack for first-hand advice and detailed description!

That evening Kitty phoned to tell me that dear old Baron would have to be put to sleep the next day. I had realised that this was inevitable sooner or later as he had become almost helpless, but still the news came as a shock to me. So it happened that my first day's work on *The Longest Day* coincided with Baron joining Wendy and Bess beside the tennis court at Haileywood. I would miss him sorely; he had given me years of utter devotion and loyalty.

As the film unit gathered for the first shots around Pegasus Bridge I had a distinct feeling of *déjà vu*. Here was I, dressed and equipped exactly as I had been seventeen years before, on ground that would for ever be stamped on my memory, and surrounded by young British soldiers indistinguishable from those who had been with me on D-Day. They were, in fact, a company from the Oxfordshire and Buckinghamshire Light Infantry which the War Office had allotted to the film, and were similar to the unit of that regiment which John Howard had so gallantly led in the glider-borne attack on the bridges.

It was a strange feeling for me to be re-enacting an exploit which I had once seen and participated in. I think I must have shed years at that moment, and felt once more some of the tingle of excitement and fitness as we went into action. The main differences were that I was portraying not myself but John Howard, and that this time there was no ironmongery flying about and explosions were all carefully controlled. At one point in the film I (as John) was seen in brief conversation with an officer of the Parachute Regiment who was meant to be me, so I was in effect standing beside myself talking to myself.

Replicas of the Horsa gliders had been constructed for us, the German defensive positions had been re-excavated and wired round and the whole sequence was as true to life – and death – as it was possible to make it.

Our filming went apace for just over two weeks and I enjoyed every moment, both on location work and during our free time. The Annakins and the Howards and I discovered a number of great little restaurants where the cuisine was in the Normandy style, based on cream and followed by exquisite cheeses. I put on a hell of a lot of weight during that period.

The food in the Hotel Malherbe was excellent too, and I was very impressed with the young wine waiter, who had that year been the winner of the Concours des Sommeliers de France – an annual professional wine-tasting competition. Once when I mentioned that he must be a keen wine drinker himself, he replied, 'No, sir. I am a Norman. I only drink cider.' He must have had a very pure palate!

Towards the end of my stay in Caen a new arrival joined us; it was Sean Connery, who had a small part in the picture. Not yet world-famous, he was a nice chap who seemed rather shy and kept very much to himself.

When I eventually saw the finished film I thought it a pretty fair record of the build-up to the invasion and the landings themselves, though perhaps it did tend to show the American efforts as somewhat overshadowing the British achievements on the beaches and especially on the airborne fronts. The 6th British Airborne Division on the left flank scarcely entered the picture, apart from the capture of the bridges.

The Germans took all the acting honours, except perhaps for a fine performance from Henry Fonda.

I arrived home just in time to see Peter off to school at the end of his holidays. This time we gave him lunch at Fortnum and Mason. Garfield Weston, who owned that famous emporium, asked us to join him at his table and seemed to be particularly taken with Peter; so much so that a box full of Fortnum's goodies arrived at Wellesley House School a few days later.

We still had the same tearful parting on a Victoria Station platform.

For some weeks after my return from Normandy my routine dropped back into the old familiar pattern of office work, London meetings, farm walks and shooting at weekends – and wondering what my next film job would be. The shadow of insecurity always hung over me. My income was admittedly pretty hefty in those days, but then so were my outgoings. And taxes took a fair chunk of my earnings.

I had recently bought an option on the screen rights to one of Hammond Innes's books, *The Land God Gave to Cain*, which I thought would make good film material. I started discussions with Robert Clark and others about getting a screen treatment written, but sadly I never managed to promote this subject and eventually lost my option.

I was missing my old black shadow Baron greatly, and as an advance Christmas present Kitty bought me Baron II, a fawn Dane puppy by Sabre, a dog whom I thought was one of the finest I had ever seen. Baron II grew to look very like his sire, with a magnificent body and smoky-black muzzle. Like his predecessor, he too became quite devoted to me, but was a very different character from old black Baron. He was quite hard to train, mainly because he had an evil sense of humour and seemed to enjoy provoking me, especially at night when I took the dogs on their final walk. Time and again, when he refused to come in, I would slam the door and leave him out there. But invariably I was outside calling him within an hour. I could never settle in bed until he was safely in his place in my dressing room.

He was the only dog I had ever been unable to control and eventually I sent him off to spend six weeks with a professional dog-trainer in Surrey. He came back slightly improved, but with a report which ended with, 'P.S. Have you ever considered that this dog may be daft?' A couple of years later Baron II started sheep-chasing; he didn't savage them at all, but seemed to derive a wayward glee from seeing them scatter and run. Even so, this obviously could not be allowed to go on, especially when it came near to lambing time and some very pregnant ewes were put to flight. Something had to go – so as a last resort I eventually had him gelded and he became a reformed character.

A pleasant break from routine occurred when I was invited once again to join a panel of judges for the Miss World contest at the Lyceum Theatre. In the final order of placing Miss UK came first, Miss China second and Miss Spain third. My own highest mark had in fact gone to Miss Spain, partly because I thought she was absolutely stunning and partly because I thought she had more dignity and style about her than any of the others. Also, I must admit, I liked the flashing smile she gave me whenever I caught her eye.

After the coronation ceremony for the newly-elected Miss World, the judges and all the contestants and their chaperones, with the various guests involved, were due to gather at the Café de Paris for dinner and dancing, but I decided to avoid this and make my way straight home to the flat. As I reached the stage-door exit from the Lyceum I heard the patter of high heels on the concrete floor behind me and a voice calling my name. I turned around, and there was Miss Spain.

'You are not coming to the dinner? Oh, please come, please! I have always wanted to meet you.' I was not proof against this kind of blandishment, especially from somebody so gorgeous who actually stood there with tears in her eyes as she pleaded.

Half an hour later I was seated at the Café de Paris with Carmen Cervera and revelling in her company. She was totally charming, bubbled with humour and had a spontaneous enthusiasm for life. When the party at the Café de Paris began to get rather noisy, Carmen got permission to return to her hotel, saying she did not feel too well. I slipped away too and took her for another hour or so to my favourite club in Hamilton Place. It had been a surprising evening, and one that did my ego no harm at all.

I subsequently met Carmen several times, especially when she was married to Lex Barker, a former Tarzan. After his sudden collapse and death she later became Baroness von Thyssen, wife of one of the world's richest and most powerful men; reputed to have the greatest art collection in private possession, I'm sure he must regard her as one of his most coveted treasures.

In complete contrast to the intriguing encounter, I later spent a day at the School of Infantry at Warminster. I had gone as the guest of Lt-Colonel Harbottle who commanded the 1st Green Jacket Battalion stationed there, and whom I had met recently in Normandy. He obtained clearance for my visit from the War Office, and I was able to see fired some of the latest weapons used by the infantry, including the anti-tank Wombat. At the end of an interesting day I dined in Mess and spent the night once more in army quarters.

As so often happened in my career, my next film came from a totally unexpected source. My agent in Paris suddenly phoned me to say she was sending me the script of a film in which I would co-star with Danielle Darrieux and Michèle Morgan – to be directed by Gérard Oury, who had played the French Dauphin some years before in *The Sword and the Rose*. The screenplay arrived, I liked it, so my next film was organised. It was to be an episodic picture and my episode, with Danielle Darrieux, would only take about three weeks so that I would be home for Christmas. The title, originally *Crime Does Not Pay*, later became *The Gentle Art of Murder*.

I had also been approached by Sidney Furie, a Canadian director, about a subject he was hoping to make in England in the near future, provisionally titled *The Boys*. I suggested that he should talk to me again when his project was more advanced.

The day before I left to work in Paris our new head gardener, Dykes, arrived to take over from Moreland who had reached retirement age. Dykes had recently been working for the Earl of Avon (formerly Anthony Eden, Prime Minister) and had a good record, so I hoped he would settle down well with us.

Once more I was on the car ferry from Dover to Boulogne and heading for the Prince de Galles Hotel in Paris.

We filmed entirely on interiors at Billancourt Studios less than thirty minutes from my hotel. It was an intriguing little story and I particularly enjoyed working with Danielle Darrieux, still very beautiful and always charming. Working in Paris had its consolations, particularly culinary ones, and I spent many evenings with my old friend Mario Ferreira who knew his way around the restaurants particularly well.

At one point Sid Furie and his wife arrived to spend a night in Paris at my expense for further talks about his film. I felt rather sorry for them, as they were obviously having an uphill struggle and could not afford to wait much longer. The script seemed quite good, so I told him to discuss things with Robert Lennard.

After a fairly uneventful three weeks I drove home via Boulogne, arriving just in time to change 'and go to dinner at Cliveden. Then followed our usual Christmas routine of a staff gathering on Christmas Eve morning, presents round the tree on Christmas morning, lunch at home, supper with the Palmers, the children's party at Cliveden on Boxing Day and a visit to the Olympia Circus.

New Year's Eve was marked by a very heavy snowfall, which had us all out digging paths and wiring up tree branches. I collected Kitty's parents from their house in Henley for a little Hogmanay celebration, using the Land Rover.

24

Here, There and Everywhere

There were times during that period in my life when I wondered if I was perhaps taking on too much. During the first ten years or so of my film career I seemed to go smoothly from one film to the next, enjoying the breaks at home between pictures, cosseted by my full-term contract with ABPC and never having much to worry about either financially or professionally. Each year turned out to be almost invariably better than the previous one, with frequent visits to America and a steady run of prestigious pictures.

Then, after my move to Haileywood in 1957, not only had the going got much tougher in the film industry but I had become more deeply involved in all manner of private activities. Film production, which had so far only succeeded in setting up one independent movie, *Don't Bother to Knock*, entailed a lot of spade-work, wheeling and dealing, and endless meetings and discussions with writers, other producers and directors and various sources of finance; subjects had to be read and options bought; and my limited business acumen was stretched to the limit when dealing with the shrewd and experienced movie-makers whom I had to contend with in the independent production field.

Farming, which I loved, had not been without its problems and risks too, even though with Mr Wade's able management we were now building up a viable enterprise. Perhaps I gave too much time and thought to this side of my life, but it did after all represent my main capital asset.

Even my family life was becoming more complicated. Two growing youngsters had to be cared for and their schooling planned and provided for, while Kitty's uncertain health was always a worry. Perhaps our house and garden staff was something of an unnecessarily expensive luxury, but I could not visualise Haileywood House being run without the splendid Dunant and Marcella and Miss Cripps. At least Queenie managed now without any assistance, unlike her predecessors.

I had also become more and more involved in charitable work, both locally and in London. That and my Masonic connection, now that I was an officer of my Lodge, all took time and thought. Each year I opened numerous charity fêtes and spoke at many fund-raising dinners and luncheons. I reckoned I was lucky to be invited and to be in a position to help, but there had to be some limit to the ubiquitous scramble of my activities.

The alarm bells really rang for me when Victor Ratner, my London doctor, told me that the recurrence of trouble from old neck and shoulder injuries was stemming from stress, and that I should try to slow down.

But how? I still had to keep gainfully employed, and my other interests were genuinely part of my way of life and my nature . . . I rarely sat for a moment in the garden without seeing something to be done: a bed to be weeded or a lawn needing mowing. I should count myself lucky, I repeatedly told myself; I was a lot better off than most actors, lived a good life, took holidays and was rarely without some film offers.

But the nagging worries about the direction my film career was taking bore down on me. With the exception of *The Longest Day*, I had not made a major international movie for some years. True, *The Hellions* was Columbia-financed and due for American release, but for some years the others had been purely domestic British or French pictures.

Never mind, I persuaded myself, something will turn up. Just keep on beavering away. Surely either Associated British/Warner Brothers or Twentieth Century-Fox will come up with something.

Meanwhile, final preparations were being made to start filming Sid Furie's *The Boys*, and I met him several times weekly for script talks. Robert Morley and I were to play defence and prosecution counsel respectively, in a case dealing with a group of juvenile law-breakers. Robert would be splendid in his role, full of righteous indignation and quivering jowls, and the youngsters were marvellously cast by Sid. It promised to be an engrossing story.

January was a busy month, with script meetings, talks about other films, a quick trip to Paris to do some post-synching on *The Gentle Art of Murder*, several good days of pheasant-shooting – including one at Cliveden where Peter kept me company and handled Dash for me – and even a few days with the family. We gave a party for the children; the film *Rob Roy* was a great success when I projected it on my new 16mm machine, and Fiona looked lovely in a red velvet dress I had brought her from Paris.

We now had Kitty's parents virtually living with us. Poor Mr Grant-Bogle had never quite recovered from his enforced retirement and his heart attack, and was pretty tetchy and not easy to deal with. He had taken a dislike to the house I had rented for them, so just beside Haileywood House I had built a large six-car garage with a pleasant two-bedroom flat above, which they now occupied. They spent little time with us however, as Kitty did not exactly overwhelm them with hospitality. Nevertheless they were safe and snug, and could decide what they wanted to do eventually.

Just before the end of the month we started shooting *The Boys* at Elstree. My part was almost entirely confined to court-room scenes and would take up only three weeks, but needed a lot of hard work, learning and concentration, as wordy legal battles often do. I was up against an impressive adversary in Robert Morley, whose sheer girth added weight to his natural authority. Beside him I felt quite a lightweight, both physically and dramatically, but did my best to wield the rapier against his broadsword.

Robert was a pleasure to work with, a tremendous professional and a fine actor who kept me fine-tuned in all my scenes with him. But his bonhomie and clearly-spoken wit and humour shielded a surprisingly emotional soft centre and some profoundly radical political beliefs. In some ways, he was the most anti-Tory liver of the good life that I had ever come across. One day at lunch in the private dining room at Elstree I had mentioned something quite innocuous about South Africa. Robert – who so far as I know had never been there – exploded into a tirade against the administration and policies of the South African government, his jowls a-quiver and his eyes flashing. Whether or not I totally agreed with him, I quickly realised that one had to pick one's subjects carefully in conversation with him.

Our filming went smoothly, thanks to Robert's expertise and the excellent young actors including Carol White, who had been so good in *Never Let Go*. It was very concentrated work and I did little else during my three-week stint. I did attend a charity function one evening, the Docklands Settlements Dinner held at Grocers' Hall in the City. I had the honour of being invited to speak after the Attorney-General (Sir Reginald Manningham-Buller), Viscount Simon (Chairman of the Port of London Authority) and Lord Douro. I missed Fiona's sixth birthday at home, but managed to phone her.

During the last few days of work on *The Boys* I was joined by Faith Brook, who played my wife in the story. I had worked with this charming and skilled actress on *Chase a Crooked Shadow* in which she had so effectively played the heavy member of a gang of crooks. Incidentally, throughout the film I was full of admiration for the natural talents of the youngsters, all cast as delinquents. They were so natural and had obviously learned most of their craft on television. Maybe they would not have qualified as all-round actors, but within their limits they were excellent.

I finished my main work on the picture by the end of February, just in time for the trek down to Kent for Peter's half-term. During his first years at Wellesley House the boys were not allowed to leave Broadstairs and come home, which meant an expensive and perplexing long week-end for the parents who had to stay at nearby hotels. What to do with the boys during those days was always a problem. I solved this partly by taking him one afternoon to explore one of the Dover car ferries, where an officer kindly showed him round the engine-room and the workings of the bridge controls; then the next day I took him to look around the Dymchurch Redoubt, the large Napoleonic fort where I had commanded the infantry unit for a time in 1941 while we expected a German invasion. My depressing brief then had been that we were to be abandoned by the coastal forces, who would retire to the high ground some twelve miles inland, while we were to remain fighting to the last man and last round of ammunition. Happily for me, the enemy did not invade – perhaps they had got wind of the formidable barrier that my platoon would present with its thirty rifles, three Bren guns, one old Lewis gun and an assortment of anti-tank obstacles!

Soon after that we had an American film unit shooting around the house, farm and garden for a programme to be screened in California called 'Here's Hollywood', though where the connection between Hollywood and Haileywood came in I failed to see.

I had also started meetings for that year's Henley Midnight Matinée, and began writing invitation letters to all the theatrical celebrities I could think of. This year's proceeds were to go to Turner's Court, a local farm school run to train young civil court offenders and other boys in need of attention and help who might otherwise have become complete delinquents. The school was run by a kindly and firm ex-Commando officer, Colonel Ron Menday.

I also took a Saturday off to watch Brimstone, my sole remaining horse in training, run in a hurdle race at Stratford-on-Avon. Sadly, while well in the lead he struck a broken hurdle which pierced a foreleg, and he never ran again.

In mid-March, I flew to Israel accompanied by Ken Allen, an ABPC PRO, to attend the opening there of *The Long and the Short and the Tall* at the invitation of the press and cinema group. We had a fascinating few days staying in Tel Aviv, unrecognisable from the sprawling, strife-torn city which I remembered from my Army service there in 1945/46. After the première we were taken for a day in Jerusalem, where I had lunch with Teddy Kolek, the mayor and head of the Prime Minister's office, who took me to meet David Ben-Gurion, the Prime Minister, and other members of the government. They were all very friendly and hospitable much to my relief, despite my having been a member of the hated 6th Airborne Division during the difficult days of the foundation of the state and the problems of illegal immigration. I spent a couple of hours that evening with General Moshe Dayan, then Minister of Agriculture, talking about the development of Israel's farming and fruit industries. Next day we were taken on a most interesting tour of Acre, Tiberias and Nazareth before our flight home.

Days later I was again in Paris, post-synching for *The Longest Day* with Darryl Zanuck. When we lunched together he was cock-a-hoop about the way his epic film was turning out.

Soon after, the Henley Midnight Matinée was a great success. We had some fifty people to supper at Haileywood; many of them returned there for snacks and coffee after the show, the last guests leaving at 3.30 am. It was worth the effort and we were able to hand over £1,450 to Turner's Court, a tidy sum not comparable with a big London charity do, but a lot for a small country town.

Then came a real blow for me: on 3 April Robert Lennard told me that he had been instructed to inform me that my one-film-a-year contract with ABPC would not be renewed the following year. The news was not totally unexpected, since this was the pattern throughout the film industry. The major movie production companies had all pared down their work-forces, and long-term contracts were a thing of the past. For some time I had been ABPC's sole contract artiste, and it had obviously been only a matter of time before I too would become an expensive burden when future production plans were in limbo and the corporation was becoming more and more dependent on independent productions being made under its banner. The scenario department had already gone, the publicity department was down to a few publicists hired on a film-to-film basis, and Elstree no longer had a forward-schedule of pictures planned or in the pipeline.

Nevertheless, it was a sad moment for me. For fourteen years I had been a part of the ABPC family, even though most of my films in recent years had been made for other companies. Now I was to be on my own, except for certain facilities that I would be granted for at least another year such as the Fan Mail department which would continue to produce the Fan Club magazine, and the support of PR companions for all major personal appearances.

In a subsequent meeting with Jimmy Wallis, it was agreed that I should also have a compensatory payment after the next year, in return for which ABPC could continue to advertise me as an ABPC contract artist in all my screen and TV credits.

So an era ended on a friendly note.

I had at this time become a close friend and associate of George Willoughby, an experienced and respected independent film producer. Norwegian by birth, George and his delightful wife Stanie (also Norwegian) had lived in London for many years and he had not only produced a number of successful films, but was a film-budget expert frequently consulted by Film Finance, the completion guarantors. George had secured an option on the screen rights of an Ian Fleming book, *The Diamond Story*, an intriguing exposé of illicit diamond-buying in Africa and of the undercover activities of agents who worked to counteract it.

Partly because of my contacts then in South Africa, George and I decided to become partners in this project and set about securing a screen treatment of the book, an operation which was to lead to a great deal of to-ing and fro-ing over the next few months.

I had not been inactive on the farming front either. I had felt for a long time that the premium paid for Channel Island high-quality milk did not match the costs of production from the relatively low-yielding Jersey cattle. At that time we were paid a premium of only 2d (1p) per gallon for Channel Island milk by the Milk Marketing Board, through which all milk was sold under contract to the various dairy companies. The Board controlled all milk sales from the farm, which was basically an excellent arrangement since it monitored quality, hygiene and nation-wide prices. But in order to earn a fairer profit by selling direct to the customer, one needed a special licence.

Now the cream which we produced for our own domestic use was absolutely splendid, beautifully flavoured, creamy-coloured and thick – or rather viscous, as it was termed. So I began to consider finding a commercial outlet for it, and discussing this possibility with Derek Baylis, who owned a group of supermarkets in the Reading area. I took him round the farm and showed him our dairy and milking procedures and our hygiene test records, also letting him sample some of our cream. He was very impressed, and agreed to take all our product provided I could obtain a licence as a dairy manufacturer.

I then approached the Milk Marketing Board, who agreed to grant me a licence. This was lucky for me, as these were hard to come by and usually involved the purchase of an existing dairy company.

My next step was to buy a little van for our deliveries, and to purchase the necessary equipment, including a large separating vat.

None of this would have been possible without the support and capable management of Mr Wade and the skill and enthusiasm of Peter Webb, our head herdsman – and, of course, the rich cooperation of our expanding Jersey herd.

In April 1962 the Shiplake Dairy Company was formed and we were in business. I had added 'Dairyman' to my list of credits, and prayed that my first business venture would prosper.

25

How Not To Get On When Really Trying

I used to have a recurring dream in which I was running as hard as I could either away from something or towards some point, and the faster I tried to run the more static I remained, sometimes even moving backwards. Often I was naked, for some reason or other, and was scurrying along trying to find some cover, with amazed or jeering onlookers pointing at me as I desperately strove to get out of sight but still only succeeded in marking time at the double.

Perhaps this is not a unique experience. Nevertheless, it was disquieting, and something which I could easily translate into reality at that stage of my professional life.

Frustration there was in plenty, and for a time it seemed that the more effort I put into advancement, the more I appeared to be grabbing at thin air.

1962 had started with quite a flurry of activity, and the pace was to keep up until late in the year. First there was the film *The Boys*, then the formation of the Shiplake Dairy Company, and in April I was approached by a leading BBC TV producer, John Warrington, with the offer of a TV play with Eartha Kitt. She had already agreed to take part and if I also agreed then the author Peter Voisey would adapt his story specially for us. The story that John outlined for me – about the schism caused between two brothers, partners in a family firm, by the marriage of one of them to Miss Kitt – seemed interesting, topical and to some extent controversial, and I accepted his offer. To work with Eartha Kitt was an intriguing prospect, especially as I remembered how fascinated I had been years before by her talents in cabaret in Paris, when Michael Wilding and I had watched her.

I met her at dinner one evening with John Warrington and found her just as alluring as I had imagined, though not particularly easy to talk to. There seemed to be a defensiveness about her which made her rather hard to communicate with at our first meeting.

Our three-week rehearsal period got off to a slow start, with Peter Voisey busily rewriting parts of the script, but we soon settled into a smooth daily routine. We used one of the many rehearsal halls rented by the BBC, and the cast was extremely good and worked happily together – with the occasional exception of Eartha, who for whatever reason was frequently touchy. She seemed to crave attention, and did not blend in easily with the rest of us. One morning she failed to turn up at all, and arrived later in the day without having contacted anyone to explain her absence; she had apparently been to Paris for the night and eventually wandered in, garlanded in a massive and very un-summery mink coat. We had all agreed to carry on as if nothing untoward had happened and we had not noticed her absence, hence a somewhat deflated Eartha took her place on the floor and got on with the job.

On the first Thursday of the rehearsals I was a guest at the Screen-writers Guild dinner, and presented one of the annual awards. The following week I put on one of my other hats for a couple of hours and attended the National Pig Breeders Association luncheon at the Hyde Park Hotel, returning to rehearsal no doubt full of good pork.

Two days later it was my turn to disrupt the rehearsal routine. The previous evening Kitty had seen her doctor, and she was ordered to the London Clinic for an emergency internal operation. I was rehearsing while the operation took place the next morning, then rushed to meet Peter for lunch with his grandmother. We all visited Kitty in the clinic that afternoon, then I took Peter to Victoria Station for the start of his new school term, getting back to the rehearsal room in time to do a couple of hours work.

That evening I had dinner with Yael Dayan, daughter of the famous General Dayan whom I had met in Israel. She was in London for a few days and at her father's suggestion had contacted me. A delightful and gifted girl who had already written a couple of books and was active in film production in Israel and Greece, she was in London to discuss a film she had scripted which was shortly to go into production in Israel.

I managed to spend a couple of hours with Kitty at the clinic each evening during her week there. She had made a good recovery.

One Sunday, after a hurried visit to Haileywood and some office work, I drove back to London, visited the clinic for an hour or so and then went to a meeting with Raymond Stross, an independent film producer, and Cyril Frankel, who had directed *Don't Bother to Knock* for me. They had a picture set up and ready to shoot at the end of June, and wanted me to star opposite the very pretty Anne Heywood, Raymond's wife. The film was mostly to be shot at the Ardmore Studios near Dublin, with locations first in London. I collected the script from them and read it that night; it was good, a taut story about a couple whose life was shadowed by the menace of a semi-maniac who had become sickly attracted to the wife. I liked it and phoned Raymond to ask him to join me with Anne and Cyril the next evening for supper. I also asked Yael Dayan to join us, as I knew that Raymond and Cyril had Israeli connections. That evening I agreed to do the film, and especially looked forward to working with Cyril again.

We finally reached the last stages of rehearsals for *Member of the Family*, the TV play, and moved into the TV Centre to work on the actual set and with the cameras and technicians who would be photographing it. As with all TV plays, and most live theatre productions, up to then we had spent weeks in the rehearsal hall with the set merely marked out with taped lines on the floor and a rough assemblage of objects to use as props and furniture – such as a row of chairs to represent a sofa, or an old tea-chest as a table. Towards the end of that period, the cameramen and the lighting man would sit in and watch, preparing a rough idea of what would eventually be required of them.

Now we had to get used to the real set and to cameras gliding about, their cables snaking around all over the floor. It was always a muddled, confusing business and nerve-racking for all concerned. We had a very long day, from 10 am until 11.30 pm.

The next day, a Sunday, we recorded the show. Having rehearsed again all day, we started recording at 9 pm. Due to the tight schedule for the recording period, stops for any reason were not encouraged and one floundered on hoping not to make any bad errors. There was a popular belief that the only real justification for a scene to be halted was if one of the actors uttered a loud four-letter expletive – a ploy which had apparently been used more than once!

This 'carry-on-regardless' necessity was one of the weaknesses of TV drama in those days: it was the glaring difference between TV and cinema filming, until later when the cinema methods and techniques became the norm.

In the event we did have a number of stoppages and ran well over our allotted time, partly due to technical problems and partly because of actors' mistakes. Everybody was weary and nerves were frayed by the time we finished. I don't think the show was as good as it might have been.

Within days I was off on my annual visit to the Cannes Film Festival, this time to promote the presentation of my French film, *The Gentle Art of Murder*. There was the usual series of TV, radio and press interviews, culminating after three days in the opening of our picture which was enthusiastically received by the predominantly French audience.

Until I started filming on the Stross picture, *The Very Edge*, most of my time during the intervening weeks was spent with George Willoughby in numerous meetings in our effort to set up a production of his subject *The Diamond Story*, by Ian Fleming. First of all we arranged for Derry Quinn, a screenwriter with a good record for imaginative episodes in TV crime and thriller series, to start work on a screen treatment of the book, not an easy task with the complex nature of illicit diamond buying in Africa and the counter-measures employed by various agents of government and the big diamond mine owners. We spent many hours together chewing over possible story lines.

Then there was the question of finance. In this we were very encouraged by a visit from Ernesto Bisogno, whom I had previously met in South Africa, a businessman and entrepreneur who had dabbled in small-scale film production there and who had now formed a new production group in Johannesburg. He brought with him a Mr Marais, an official of the South African Industrial Development Corporation with whom I had had discussions in Cape Town the previous year. Their reactions to our proposals for *The Diamond Story* were very favourable, and they seemed in little doubt that all the financing could be arranged in South Africa, where there were many corporations and individuals looking for overseas-earning investments.

I was also dashing around touting for outlets for my Shiplake Dairy Company cream and met with some success, adding more shops and hotels such as the French Horn at Sonning to our list of customers. We were building up our Jersey herd as fast as our heifers and artificial insemination would allow, and had added a couple of ladies to our part-time dairy staff as cream-makers.

The farm was now once more open to the public for the June Dairy Festival month, and our cream teas were immensely popular with the ever-increasing crowds who had hiked around the farms. Surprisingly, perhaps, the pig unit at Holmwood was a particular attraction, especially the farrowing crates where tiny new-born piglets suckled busily at their dams. Michael Wade had done a splendid job in converting the dairy buildings there to pork and bacon production, with lovely clean weaner pens and fattening houses. Most people expressed themselves surprised by the cleanliness of the pigs and their housing. We were great believers in free-ranging for conditioning and good health: the baconers and the sows who had weaned their litters were all running free in wired-in enclosures in the fields.

Other bright spots that month came when we spent Ladies' Day at Ascot in Boyd Gibbins' box, followed by a visit to Smith's Lawn where Boyd's own polo team was playing, and a party later at the glamorous Marlow house of Jack Cotton, the financier and property tycoon; then there was Peter's tenth birthday, which that year coincided with his half-term holiday. Thank goodness it had been decided that boys at Wellesley House could now come home for half-term, saving us the awful trail down to Kent. He had been given a tent as his main present and of course insisted on spending his weekend under canvas, as any boy would, with Baron II for company.

I even managed to break my duck when batting in the annual President's Match against the Shiplake team. I played a forward defensive stroke, snicked through the slips for a boundary, and was out next ball. But at least I *had* scored.

On 2 July I started work on the London locations for *The Very Edge*. At the end of a successful week only slightly hampered by poor weather, I handed over my car – for shipment to Ireland ready for my filming there – and went home in a hired vehicle. On the Saturday Kitty and Fiona saw me off from Heathrow on my flight to Dublin, where I arrived at the Gresham Hotel in the early afternoon, then went to the docks to collect the car again.

It was the first occasion I had spent any time in the city of my birth since the wartime leaves at Dundrum with my FitzPatrick aunt and uncle, and I was looking forward to the chance to explore during my days off. The Ardmore Studios near Bray was an excellent little unit, not unlike the Teddington Studios near London where I had once worked. A charming country house hotel, the Old Conna, was nearby, and I took the chance to nip up there for lunch once or twice. I found that Alec Guinness was staying there while he was also filming locally and we lunched together several times. I had never worked with him, but found him utterly charming, quiet and reserved but with lots of humour. The only time we had ever vied with each other was way back in 1950 when we shared the *Daily Express* Tribunal Award, he for *Kind Hearts and Coronets* and me for *The Hasty Heart*.

I was so enchanted with the Old Conna Hotel and its suites – all named after great Irish writers and poets, such as Sheridan and W. B.

Yeats – that I booked rooms there for a long weekend which Kitty was due to spend with me, though I kept my studio-suite at the Gresham.

Raymond Stross and Cyril Frankel had brought together a very strong cast for *The Very Edge* and we were a happy unit. I had already done my London location shooting with Patrick Magee, who played a sinister janitor in his own rasping way. Now I found Anne Heywood absolutely sweet, very competent and hard-working in her part as my wife. She had been a beauty queen – Violet Pretty was her most appropriate real name, I believe – and was one of the few who had successfully made the transition from the catwalk to the big screen. Jack Hedley was a convincing CID detective and Jeremy Brett was chillingly good as the lurking maniac.

I only had one problem during filming: a sequence in which I was in bed with my screen wife. Although there was nothing torrid about the scene, I did find it a bit embarrassing cuddling up to Anne when her husband Raymond was watching by the bedside. This had happened to me years before when playing a love scene with Valerie Hobson while her then husband, producer Anthony Havelock-Allan, looked on. I do feel that the presence of spouses can be somewhat inhibiting at times!

Most days when I had been up very early and spent long hours at the studio I was glad to get back to the Gresham, have supper, learn my lines for the next day and get to bed. However, I did have dinner with Uncle Fintan and Aunt Eileen FitzPatrick, with my godfather Major Brett, and with my Vaughan cousins at Ticknock Lodge, their pretty house in the Dublin Hills.

When Kitty arrived for a long weekend I managed to take her to the beautiful Glendalough area, and we also followed part of the Irish Open Golf Championship at nearby Woodbrook, fittingly won that year by Christie O'Connor, the great Irish master.

After a month at Ardmore I suddenly found I had several days free, so on impulse I took a late evening plane to London and was home at Haileywood by midnight. The family were due to leave for their summer holiday in Cavalaire, where we had rented the same flat as in the previous year, and I wanted to see that all was well for their departure. We had a pleasant relaxed day together, then I saw them off the following morning at Heathrow and caught my own plane back to Dublin.

Next morning I set off for a weekend in Kerry. I had always wanted to see the remains of my mother's ancient family home there, Ballymalis Castle, and now was my chance.

I stayed at the excellent Great Southern Hotel in Killarney, and the following morning had no trouble finding the lane leading to the castle. There was little left of it, mainly the keep which still had stone stairs up to the parapet and a few ruined fragments strewn about the field in which it stood, giving little idea of the size or shape of the building as it had been. There was a metal plaque on one wall mentioning Alexander Agar, my progenitor, who had come into possession of it in 1660.

While there is always something romantic about an ancient ruin, it was the setting of Ballymalis that was breathtakingly beautiful. The castle had been sited right beside the River Laune, one of the great salmon rivers of Ireland. The green fields round about and the woodlands were all so peaceful, and there were marvellous views from the keep and the parapet running along the wall which was still standing on the river side. Across the river was the estate of the McGillycuddy of the Reeks, head of one of Ireland's oldest families, and the scenery – with their wooded demesne in the foreground just beyond the far bank of the river – carried right to the mountains beyond.

It was magical and I loitered there for a couple of hours, my imagination and my memories of my mother stirred.

On the road once more, I soon found the Tower Hotel at Glenbaigh, famous as a hostelry for fishing men. I went into its luxurious hall entrance and found my way to the bar, where I told the lady in charge that I had a booking for lunch. When the waiter arrived with a menu, there was no doubt what my choice must be: the grilled salmon.

At my table there was a bottle of champagne already waiting in its ice-bucket. I turned to the waiter and said there must be some mistake, but he told me, 'The manager says please will you have it with him, sir.'

Then my salmon arrived, garnished with the most lovely little new potatoes and fresh peas. Never had I eaten a salmon steak so juicy, so sweet and so perfectly cooked. Just when I was relishing the last tasty mouthful, the chef himself appeared by my side, complete in white coat and tall white chef's hat.

'How was the salmon, sir?'

Lost for words, I could only say that I had never eaten a piece to better it.

'Sure we took it out of the waters of Ballymalis for you this morning, Mr Todd.'

It was almost poetic, this piece of Irish blarney, whether true or not.

'Would you like another one?'

Would I not!

The second helping was every bit as delicious as the first. Then I discovered from the waiter that the chef was also the owner of the hotel, so I asked him to join me in finishing the champagne, which he did.

When I asked for the bill I would not have minded if all this hospitality had been reflected in the charges. But my account was surprisingly modest, and showed no drinks at all. Such kindness is of a sort that one rarely encounters.

I left Killarney the next morning and was on the set at Ardmore Studios after the lunch-break.

This was now the start of one of the maddest, noisiest periods in the Dublin calendar: Horse Show Week. Suddenly the Gresham was full of horsey types, many of whom I knew. On my first night there I had supper with the Chapmans (former near neighbours of ours in Berkshire) and Robert Hanson, the great Yorkshire breeder and transport tycoon and founder of the Hanson empire now headed by his son, Lord Hanson. I took them on to a party and reception given by John Byrne at Simmonscourt Castle, in Ballsbridge.

Almost every night there was a hunt ball at the Gresham and only a deaf pneumatic-drill operator could have slept through the din of revelry, hunting horns and loud 'yoicks' which rent the peace of the hotel.

If you can't beat them – join them. So I did!

I was still leaving the hotel each morning at 7 am and doing a full day's work at Ardmore, but mercifully by the Saturday everything was quiet when I returned from the studio, and I had the Sunday to recover.

I was thrilled to be phoned one day by Tony O'Reilly, the great Irish Rugby winger and darling of the Twickenham crowds, asking me to join him and his wife for dinner. He was then general manager of the Irish Dairy Board, a very important post in that milky country. They were a striking couple: he huge and very handsome and she a real Irish beauty, dark-haired, peachy-skinned and blue-eyed. We had a lot to chat about and much in common. He later became head of the Heinz empire in Europe and then, I believe, went to America to be head of all the '57 Varieties' in the world.

Queenie came over to do a couple of days' work with me and to bring me up to date on the state of things at home. Fortunately I was on stand-by at the studio for those days and we were able to get a lot done.

Towards the end of August my very pleasant weeks in Ireland came to an end. I had enjoyed doing *The Very Edge*, which I knew would be no block-buster but I reckoned would be a well-made, gripping thriller.

Raymond, Cyril and Anne had all been sweet to work with and it had been a harmonious unit.

I had a brief weekend at Haileywood, mostly spent with Queenie and Mr Wade in the office, then took off for Nice in the South of France to join the family at Cavalaire for a fortnight. Thank God I had such reliable stalwarts as Queenie, Mr Wade and the Dunants to hold the fort during my absences!

The day I arrived home from France coincided with one of Milton Pickman's flying visits to London, so I went straight up there to spend the evening with him. We had a lot to talk about. There had been great changes lately in Hollywood, as in London, and a whole new breed of studio heads had moved in. My contacts out there had dwindled therefore and unfortunately none of the films I had made in recent years was going to be big in America – with the exception of *The Longest Day*, and in that I was only one of the cast of thousands. British films still had a limited appeal and distribution in the United States.

Unless something totally unexpected turned up, I would have to try to create my own cinematic opportunities. I was already doing my best, but I was surely heading for a difficult period.

From September onwards that year, I seemed to be living out my recurring running-on-the-spot nightmare. Very few things appeared to go right and there was a sense of so-near-and-yet-so-far pervading nearly everything I was trying to do.

George Willoughby, Derry Quinn and I had incessant talks and arguments about the story line for *The Diamond Story*. We had had the carrot of adequate finance dangled before our noses by Bisogno and Marais from South Africa, and I was sure that we would eventually get a distribution deal from Associated British when everything else had taken shape. But always the problem was 'Where's the script?' My flat at Nell Gwynn House became a charnel-house of abandoned drafts and screen treatments.

Our problems had been compounded by another venture. George had read a fascinating book by Colonel O'Brien-Tuonig, former head of the Queen's Messenger Service; it was an anthology of true stories about the adventures and dangerous experiences of this august body of men, nearly all ex-Service officers, who are entrusted with the safety and delivery all round the world of highly secret government, service and state documents and papers, mostly to and from our embassies, and we both believed it was tailor-made for a TV series.

So evidently did Jimmy Wallis, since he readily agreed that ABPC would advance the cash required to buy the rights in my name provided we offered first refusal of the series to ABC TV. After much to-ing and fro-ing between ABC, author's agents and solicitors – including ABPC's Cross and my Laurence Harbottle – the deal went through.

Our next move was to see Brian Tesler, the programme controller of ABC TV (now Thames TV) to find out if he would be interested in the project and in financing it 100 per cent. He seemed quite taken with the idea of the Queen's Messenger stories and their potential as TV series material, but then said, in effect, 'Fine. Let's talk about it again when you have a presentation format.'

Now not even George, with all his experience as an independent film producer, had ever prepared a TV presentation format. It had to be quite a complicated technical brochure laid out as glossily as possible to include projected budget, studio space requirements, length of episodes and all manner of technical data which, with our limited knowledge of television production, we were not equipped to provide.

So once again George and I set about coming up with some answers and it was then that he introduced Archie Ogden to be our associate. Archie had some experience of setting up presentation formats, and was enthusiastic about the potential of our Queen's Messenger stories. However, the format would also require at least two fully-written episodes as examples of how the series would look; that in turn would mean a writer to script them, and how would we do all this with our limited resources? Already we had both begun to feel the pinch with our outlay on various facets of *The Diamond Story* project.

So another associate entered our arena: Dick Brand, a writer.

Day after day we worked away on our two projects, and my flat became even more like a mad-house. Usually George, Derry and I would work all morning on *The Diamond Story*, have a cold snack lunch, then George, Archie, Dick and I would try to come up with a suitable presentation for the *Queen's Messenger* series.

By the end of the year we had still made little progress.

At one point I decided to fly to Johannesburg in an effort to ensure that at least the financial position was sound for *The Diamond Story*. I was met there by Ernie Bisogno and some of his associates, who had formed a production company of their own; they were full of airy plans for future projects, including the erection of a complete new studio complex in a Jo'burg suburb. That first afternoon I spent three hours with them at the Standard Bank Headquarters. It appeared that they did have substantial backing but I was uneasy about how they intended to use it. From the way they boasted of their plans, I was afraid that there would not be much finance left by the time *The Diamond Story* came to be made. It was a disquieting visit altogether, the one good aspect being when I spent the last evening with my old friend Oscar Hurwitz in Pretoria. Kind and as good-humoured as ever, Oscar advised me to tread warily.

The growing success of my dairy company was now beginning to present me with new and unexpected problems. Such was the demand for our product that we simply could not produce enough of it. I needed more land and larger and improved buildings for the herd – and for this I would need more money. Paul Rosewarne, Basil Stebbings and I had lengthy discussions about this. I already had some not-too-heavy bank borrowings from my recent land and equipment purchases, but nevertheless I felt that my dairy business would have to expand if it was to be a real money-maker. Through Basil's good offices I moved my account, overdraft and all, to the Midland Bank, who were most welcoming and supportive. After all, as my new manager pointed out, I had bags of collateral. Just the same, I was always scared of owing money and hoped that a nice juicy film contract would soon come my way.

Another source of worry was Kitty's health. In mid-October she again entered a London nursing home for two weeks to have treatment for a nervous disorder. During that fortnight I went to visit her every day, whether I was in London or not, and a couple of times Fiona came with me and we lunched at the home with her. She was very depressed and needed all the cheer we could give her.

Dr Victor Ratner, who was treating Kitty, had meantime discovered the cause of Fiona's hearing problem. She had already had a couple of minor operations to draw off fluid, and the Reading ENT specialist had her on long periods of penicillin tablets. When Victor took a swab from her he found that the bacteria affecting her was resistant to penicillin; therefore he prescribed a different drug which completely cleared up her condition and left her with only the minimal damage which had already been caused. I had much to thank him for.

Not all was gloom that autumn, however. We had some exciting evenings at the Horse of the Year Show at Harringay. The first of them had been in aid of the Variety Club, and I and Lord Mountbatten, who was a great supporter of Variety, presented some of the winning rosettes.

In September, our cook Miss Cripps decided to retire, and we knew a replacement for her was not going to be easy to find. One day, after a particularly harassing time in London, I got home in the evening to find Joyce Pearce (founder of the Ockenden Venture) already there with Halucia, a comely nineteen-year-old. She had been one of the first group of five little girls that Miss Pearce and her sister had brought home to England, to give them schooling and a new start in life, having found them living in dreadful conditions in a displaced persons' camp in Germany. This the Pearce sisters did at their own expense, returning with their charges each year to Germany, where more and more despondent parents begged them to help with their children, boys as well as girls, until when they had fourteen youngsters living with them, they sought and were granted charitable status. Thus was the Ockenden Venture founded and patrons, who included Lord Astor, aided the committee that was formed to help distressed children all over the world.

Halucia had been born in a notorious German concentration camp during the war, where her mother – a refugee from one of the Baltic states – had died. A bright, witty girl who had done very well with her schooling and resettlement, she had lately taken a Cordon Bleu cookery course with honours. She had seen me many times at Ockenden meetings and functions, and was one of the group of Ockenden youngsters who had attended our first Henley Midnight Matinée in their national costumes, selling programmes and bringing a splash of colour to the proceedings.

Miss Pearce had heard of our staff problem at Haileywood and mentioned it to Halucia, who immediately said she would like to help us out and take over our cooking. Within days she had moved in with us, and proved not only a brilliant cook but a most cheerful addition to our household. The enigmatic Dunant was frequently the butt of her sallies. 'Oh, Harold – don't be so stuffy!' she'd tell him. Her childhood experiences had certainly not left any scars on Halucia, and we were all charmed by her – even stuffy Harold.

One weekend saw the unexpected arrival of my two slightly dotty but indomitable aunts, Amy and Dolly Hunter, half-sisters of my mother. After the sale of their family home in Northern Ireland, they had decided to go to Australia for a while to visit their only surviving brother, Bertie, and had settled there for some years, living in the Blue Mountains outside Sydney. Now they had decided to see out the rest of their lives back home in Ulster.

I went to meet them at Southampton docks and we had a very chatty weekend at Haileywood while they filled us in with some hilarious details of their experiences down under.

Not so funny was news of the fate of their youngest brother, James, who had disappeared without trace before the war when sent on a round-the-world trip by my grandfather. The curse on Brecart, which had decreed that the family living there would end in degradation and ruin, had come true. Ruin there certainly had been on my grandfather's death, when my two aunts were forced to sell up piecemeal. The degradation was also complete. James – who had been heir to the place, and who would have been the last male Hunter to live there had he not disappeared – had apparently died of syphilis in some obscure Australian lunatic asylum.

A brighter moment, just before Kitty went into the nursing home, had been the opening of *The Longest Day*. That day I had done a couple of TV and press interviews with Darryl Zanuck before we went on to the Royal premiere, and he was brimming with confidence. Rightly so, as it turned out, because the film was a huge success. I was delighted for Darryl, because his courage and determination had not only vindicated his herculean task but had saved the ailing Twentieth Century-Fox. Our dinner afterwards at Claridges was a true celebration party.

My hopes had been temporarily raised by a call from Mike Frankovitch, the head of Columbia Pictures in London. He wanted me to meet Peter Kortner, a producer with Screen Gems – the Columbia TV offshoot in America – to discuss a forthcoming major TV series which they wanted me for. I phoned Pickman in Hollywood to get his confirmation that this was a *bona fide* probability, and he agreed that it was. I also alerted Robert Lennard to the possibility. Subsequently I had a long meeting with Kortner on my return from South Africa, and all seemed to be set . . .

I never heard anything further.

I was again invited to join the panel of judges for the Miss World Contest. Miss Holland was our choice this time.

My old CO when I was first commissioned at Strensall in the KOYLI was Brigadier Leslie Wieler. He had been Major and Resident Governor of the Tower of London for some years, and he invited me there one day for lunch to discuss a *son et lumière* project for the next summer, featuring the Tower seen from the river by parties on large river craft. I readily agreed to do the commentary if I was free.

Apart from constant script meetings for *The Diamond Story* and the *Queen's Messenger* series, nothing much happened for the rest of the year, except my annual visit to the Isle of Arran to stay with Jean Fforde. I stalked for a couple of days and bagged eight hinds, which was all part of the yearly culling programme, and had a couple of days with her party shooting pheasants, the odd grouse, and wildfowl in the evenings. On one of these sorties I fell into a stream and got soaked. One of the guns, a rather large man, lent me his spare shooting trousers after lunch, so

I was at least dry again though the trousers were a bit tight under the arms!

It was a real white Christmas that year, and it was impossible to keep Haileywood's long drive clear, so the Land Rover was the only vehicle we could use. Even deliveries of mail and groceries had to be picked up from the gate lodge. Halucia excelled herself with a marvellous lunch, but it was the normally inscrutable Dunant who was the real star of the show.

He arrived in the dining room bearing a flaming Christmas pudding, wearing a Beatle wig on his bald head and singing, 'Yeah! Yeah! Yeah!' The children loved it.

New Year's Eve we spent quietly at home, hoping for better things next year.

26

All Work and No Pay

The New Year of 1963 started pleasantly enough for us, apart from the ghastly weather at home. Most of the local roads were almost impassable, and the train services were chaotic on the occasions when I had to get to and from London for some of my interminable script meetings and talks with George, Derry, Archie and Dick as we tried to make some headway with our film and TV projects.

Relief from this came when Dunant drove us to Heathrow for our flight to Geneva. Despite my worries, I had decided to take the family to Switzerland for our second holiday there, this time taking Fiona with us. Once there I shed my gloom and enjoyed an exciting and bracing couple of weeks. We had a delightful little flat at Montana, complete with a cheerful and efficient cook-housekeeper and a roaring log-fire in the sitting room. During the first week Kitty skated, the children tumbled about on the nursery slopes and I went off with a ski instructor. The second week Peter came down some of the higher pistes with me, and completely outshone my cautious efforts.

In the evenings we often dropped in at the main hotel in Montana-Crans for the *après-ski* warm-up, and early in our stay we met Peter Grosscurth and his wife. Peter was a property developer whose business was based in Reading only a few miles from Haileywood. We became great friends immediately and arranged to get together as soon as we were all back home. This was a chance meeting that was to add a new element to my daily activities in the near future.

We were sorry to leave, and sorrier still when our plane from Geneva was diverted to Manchester because Heathrow was fog-bound and iced-up. Manchester airport was a shambles that evening, with plane-loads of people cramming in from all over the world and seemingly no facilities to cope with them. It had never been like that when I was there doing my parachute-jumping training in 1943. At least in those days the WVS always had plenty of hot drinks and sandwiches to hand out! This time there was nothing – only hordes of people shivering, grumbling and trying to get some information. After some hours, batches of us miserable passengers were stuffed into buses and taken to the main railway station, where we were told that a special train had been organised to take us on to London. The 'special' train turned out to be the midnight mail train with a few extra old passenger carriages added on, and the whole rickety disaster rattled and clanked through the night, stopping at almost every station on the way. There was no heating and snow oozed through the cracks under the doors, forming slippery sheets of ice on the floor. The stewardesses from our Swissair flight did their best to look after those of us who had been on their flight, staying up all night, borrowing coats to cover children and trying to get some of the smaller ones to sleep. This was unlike a couple of BEA hostesses whom I found fast asleep in one compartment, each comfortably stretched full-length along a seat, covered in a mound of blankets.

Frozen, filthy and famished, we finally got to the flat, bathed, fed and took a hired car home. It had still been a lovely holiday . . .

So now, back to work!

For months my professional life had been fogged by uncertainty and the ever-present insecurities of almost every actor. I no longer had the shield of my Associated British contract or my close contact with Twentieth Century-Fox in America. And the major film offers were no longer rolling in. I began to wonder if perhaps I had not been sufficiently dedicated to my career; perhaps I should have devoted more effort to cultivating the right people; perhaps we should have filled Haileywood at weekends with producers, directors and visiting firemen; perhaps I should have changed our whole way of life when the first signs of recession appeared. Certainly perhaps I should not have given so much thought and time to my farms and now to the dairy company; nor perhaps should I have become so involved with local affairs, charities and organisations.

All these thoughts went through my mind as I counted the months between films. However, I decided to bumble on and hope for the best. I couldn't believe that something would not turn up – it always had before.

Week after week George Willoughby and I and our associates battled to bring our two projects to fruition, with little success. Perhaps we were not very good as salesmen! But in April John Davis, head of the Rank Organisation, suggested that we should speak to his director of productions at Pinewood, Earl St John, about *The Diamond Story*. This we did, and received a very enthusiastic and encouraging reaction from him. Thus fortified, we tried even harder to get our story line right.

One of my main problems, strangely enough, was the success of my cream venture. Still we simply could not produce enough of the stuff, though we had now invested in a larger van and employed a full-time delivery/salesman. Through my acquaintanceship with Garfield Weston I had added to our list of customers Fortnum and Mason itself and certain of the Fine Fare chain of supermarkets; while from John Cohen, chairman and founder of the Tesco supermarket chain, whom I also knew, I got permission to supply those of his stores within our reach. Harrods, too, became the lucky retailers of our product, as did Cranmer Court Stores opposite my flat in Nell Gwynn House. I was obviously better at selling my cream than my thespian services!

The need for expansion was crucial if I was to cash in on our potential: more buildings, more equipment, more land, more Jersey milk. I nearly got cold feet at the whole prospect. I was terrified of owing money to banks, yet all my available cash had already been invested in the land and the tide of my professional income had ebbed somewhat of late. Queenie told me that my living expenses, salaries and other outgoings amounted even then to about £40,000 a year, before any capital expenditure on the farms. That was a lot of money in 1963.

However at a couple of meetings with Paul Rosewarne, Basil Stebbings, Bill Evans (my bank manager) and Mr Partridge, the regional director of the Midland Bank, it was decided that I should go ahead and expand even if it meant bringing in a general manager to handle the dairy business.

Mr Keene agreed to let me have an option to buy the rest of Shiplake Rise Farm later in the year, and we started to draw up plans for a large new covered yard and milking parlour, with the old cow-byre to be converted into an improved dairy complex. In for a penny, in for a pound!

We solved our current supply problem when Colonel Phillimore agreed to sell his Jersey milk direct to me from his Coppid Hall herd, and we made the same arrangement with another Jersey farmer at Nettlebed. Both these herds were of excellent quality, hay-fed, and their milking conditions were very hygienic. We considered that silage feeding tended to taint the already strong-flavoured double Jersey cream.

While all this was going on, Tom Caden-Prescott and I were busily engaged in plans for the year's Henley Midnight Matinée. We had decided that the beneficiary should be Smith's Hospital in Henley, an institution entirely given over to the care and treatment of autistic children and apparently the first of its kind in the world. It was the brain-child of its founder, Dr Gerry O'Gorman, a really saintly child psychiatrist who was a consultant at the Borocourt Group of Hospitals.

Autism, it appears, can afflict a child in many forms, either from birth or as a later development. Basically it is a child's refusal or inability to use its powers of speech, or to control its limbs or sometimes any of the normal functions. The child is totally silent, helpless and occasionally inclined to be violent – they have simply opted out of life. Gerry devoted years to the study of this affliction, its causes and its cure. Years before, most of these children would have been locked away for life, but Gerry had found that what they needed most was love – physical, demonstrative love.

In the early days at Smith's Hospital – a grim, stone-passaged former fever hospital which had been bought and donated by Lord Hambleden, the head of the Smith family of bookshop fame – Gerry O'Gorman used to bring a bus-load of mentally-retarded women from one of his other hospitals to spend some hours each day with the children – his 'cuddle-machines', he called them. No matter that some of these women were pretty ugly – they would each gather up one of the little mites and hug, cuddle and rock them in sheer ecstasy at the chance of being given a child to love, and the children responded. To them the 'cuddle-machines' were all beautiful and warm.

Another thing that Gerry noted occurred in the early days when a group of the children were taken to the seaside. They had never seen the sea before, and when they were carried and seated on the sand by the water's edge as the wavelets splashed over them they emitted little shrieks of alarm or pleasure – they had involuntarily used their vocal cords. So a shallow pool was installed in the hospital and the children were urged into it. Again there were squeaks of alarm, but the voice-finding process had started.

The children were not malformed in any outward way. Indeed, they were mostly of more-than-average good looks. After Gerry's treatment and the work of a devoted staff, many of them went to local schools and did well, returning eventually to a normal life.

Gerry had now perceived that it was the parents who needed help and guidance, and for this reason it was decided to build some flatlets in the grounds where they could come and stay with their children during various stages of their treatment. It was towards this building that the proceeds of the Midnight Matinée would go.

Rex North, the *Daily Mirror* film critic, was Chief Barker of the

Variety Club that year, and at one of the lunches I mentioned Smith's Hospital and the Midnight Matinée to him. He immediately promised a Variety Club donation of £500, with further future help, and agreed to come to stay with us for the Matinée. Even more surprising was a donation of £1,000 from a local man, Mr Stapleton, after Tom Caden-Prescott and I had taken him to spend an afternoon at Smith's.

The Midnight Matinée that year was a great success. I had managed to secure the Royal Film for the occasion and we later handed over a cheque for £3,400 to the hospital. Not bad for a small-town effort!

When we took Rex and Lindy North round Smith's with Gerry O'Gorman they were enthralled. I am proud to say that I was voted to be Life President of the League of Friends of Smith's Hospital.

While I had been bemoaning the lack of movie offers coming my way, I was not exactly enraptured by those that *did* turn up. First MacGregor Scott, an Associated British executive and managing director of Warner-Pathé Distributors, called me to say that he had been approached by Harry Alan Towers to see if I would star for him in a film he was going to make in South Africa in April. Harry had been regarded as something of a whizz-kid during his early producing days a few years back, but had not fully realised that potential and had become a prolific churner-out of minor films, mostly co-productions financed from all manner of sources and not all getting major releases. A couple of years earlier I would not have given a second thought to such a project. However, Mac Scott assured me that this film was to be of reasonable quality and would get Warner-Pathé distribution if I were in it.

So I met them both, and heard from Harry that the film was to be a modernised version of *Sanders of the River* shot in Durban and Zululand. I was quite impressed with his obvious intelligence and enthusiasm and agreed to consider the idea, subject to reading the script and agreeing terms. He told me right then what the terms would be – a good deal less than I had been used to. Still, it was a job and the money would come in handy – and I wouldn't be the first actor to accept a deal for those reasons alone.

The very next day I flew to Rome with Michael Carreras, the independent producer son of James Carreras, founder and chairman of the famous Hammer Films. Michael had a subject, *The Devil Behind Me*, which he thought we could do together. The writer, Marc Brandell, was working in Rome, hence our brief visit for talks about the screenplay. At least I was leaving no stone unturned, and this could well be a follow-up to the Towers picture if I did it.

The *Sanders* script, written by Harry himself, was not bad, and certainly the locations sounded exciting. I agreed to make the film subject to certain alterations to the story and to my role. Subsequently I had a series of script meetings with Harry and his production manager, Bob Lynn, whom I already knew and liked. The movie was to be an Anglo-German co-production, with myself and Jeremy Lloyd as the leading English characters; the others would be German, including Marianne Koch, a very popular German star. Late April was to be the start date.

After one particularly long day of work with Harry Towers, I was glad to get to bed at the flat, only to be phoned early the next morning with the news that the film was off. The German finance had collapsed.

'Hell!' I thought. 'When is something going to go right?'

My depressed mood was not improved when Kitty collapsed that night. She was taken by ambulance to a Reading hospital and I followed by car. I returned home in the early hours, thoroughly alarmed and dispirited. After a couple of days she was allowed home, with instructions to take things very easy for a while.

For a time I seemed to be wallowing in a particularly dismal trough and feeling very down. I knew perfectly well what could lift me out of it: a film – *any* film. For the first time in fifteen years I was idle – not that I was sitting around doing nothing, but not doing what I wanted to do most and needed to do. Certainly I was busy nearly every day at some activity or other, but all the time I was fretting and beginning to be fearful. Even farming had become a business instead of a way of life. The plain fact was that I loved filming; it was not work to me, it was a pleasure.

Just as I was beginning to think that I had got into a deep and muddy rut, a new and totally unexpected prospect arose. I had been invited to attend a lunch at the Carlton Tower given by an acquaintance of mine, Fred Cumber, to what seemed to be a random collection of notable people including prominent industrialists, the historian Sir Arthur Bryant, Lord Swaythling, Lord Chesham, Sir Leonard Hutton, the great cricketer, and a very pleasant and chatty Member of Parliament, John Harvey, next to whom I was seated. John was a Conservative of some distinction, the member for Walthamstow East, a former member of the National Executive Committee of the Conservative Party and Chairman of the Woodford Conservative Association. Typical of his self-deprecating manner was his entry in *Who's Who*: under 'recreations' he had simply listed 'various in moderation'. John asked me if I was at all interested in politics and I replied, 'Of course – in moderation.' Then he asked if I had ever considered standing for parliament.

I replied, 'Good Lord, no!'

'Why not?'

'Well, I don't know enough about it for a start.'

'You'd soon learn.'

'Besides, I'm an actor. I never know where I might be.'

'You could make a career of it. And you could always be paired *in absentia*.'

'Anyway, I couldn't afford it.'

'You could easily get some directorships to augment your income.'

Then he came out with his suggestion. 'Look, we've got the by-election coming up for Woodford, Winston Churchill's old seat, and a very safe one. You'd make a perfect candidate, well-known and well-respected. Think about it seriously and I'll mention it to the party high-ups.'

I did think about it, very seriously. It was a tempting idea.

A few days later we met for lunch at the Carlton Club, that stronghold of Tory MPs. There I was introduced to various leading members who had obviously already been primed about John's idea. They all seemed very friendly.

John again asked me what I felt about his proposition. I reiterated my doubts, but told him that I would love to have a go if only I could feel sure that I would be a useful member. Worst of all, I said, I was likely to be off very soon to make a film abroad (*Sanders* was still in the air at the time), and I simply couldn't afford to turn it down.

Finally, after some days he phoned me. 'I'm afraid that perhaps you are right this time. The next election will probably be a close-run one, and long pairings would be difficult. However, keep it in mind for the future.'

So ended my unexpected flirtation with a political career. My friend Ronald Reagan would have thought me faint-hearted. He would have been right!

Back I went to the familiar routine of script meetings and dairy sales, enlivened by an evening on a Thames passenger boat with Brigadier Wieler and Field Marshal Lord Alexander of Tunis (amongest others) while we watched *A Fair White Tower*, the history of the Tower of London in *son et lumière* with commentary recorded by myself and Virginia Maskell, and directed by Val Gielgud. There followed the annual June Dairy Festival luncheon at the Mansion House, and then the Army Benevolent Fund show at the Palladium, which Harry Secombe and I had helped General 'Mat' White and Brigadier Wieler to organise. I was to do a comedy sketch in the show with Sharee Winton and others, but at the last moment she was ill. In desperation I phoned Liz Fraser and she agreed to step in; I delivered the script to her at her hairdressers in the afternoon, and with virtually no rehearsal she was terrific. Despite lots of fluffs, mistakes and inspired ad-libbing the sketch was a great success, and the more we floundered the more the audience loved it.

In June, just after I had once more made my annual duck in the President's match at Shiplake, and the farms had been opened to the public for the month, the unexpected happened again: Harry Alan Towers contacted me to say that *Sanders* was definitely going to be made, starting in August.

Once again I breathed a sigh of relief and crossed my fingers, and once again I started a series of script meetings at my flat with Towers and Laurence Huntington, the director.

I spent my birthday in Paris, dubbing my last French film into English, and followed this with a good Gold Cup day at Ascot, as usual with Boyd Gibbins.

In July I had lunch for the first time at the House of Commons with John Harvey, listened for a while from the gallery to Question Time, then spent a couple of hours with Laurie Huntington, followed by a meeting with Michael Carreras and Mark Brandell about *The Devil Behind Me* which was still possibly going to be shot in Spain later.

I was Bill Astor's guest at a meeting of the New Welcome Masonic Lodge of which he was Master; I was very impressed with his quietly authoritative working and his sure handling of the ceremony. Bill had just been through a dreadful time when the Stephen Ward scandal and trial had been in all the headlines.

When it first broke I asked him what he would do. 'Just try to maintain a dignified silence,' was his reply. The bizarre goings-on had been at a time when Bill was miserable after the break-up of his second marriage, but now he was very happily remarried to Bronwen, who adored him. Herself a great beauty and former Balmain model, she had created for Bill an idyllically happy family life at Cliveden where Bill's qualities as a good and kind family man were evident. The Bill that I knew as a friend was a good soul and a tireless worker for many charitable institutions, especially as a member of the board of the Great Ormond Street Hospital for Sick Children.

Born to great wealth and privilege, he had not been merely a rich layabout but had served his country in the RNVR during the 1939–45

war and twice as an MP, for some time as Parliamentary Private
Secretary to Sir Samuel Hoare. He had done a lot of good for a lot of
people, and I was sickened by the enthusiastic public muck-raking
which had shamed him.

Now he was just trying to carry on quietly with his public and private
interests.

Some of the others involved in the affair I knew slightly. John Profumo, who has since done everything possible to atone for his mistakes,
had been a very efficient Secretary of State for War whom I had met
a few times, and of course I had known and admired Valerie Hobson,
his wife, since we had filmed together in 1949.

Dr Stephen Ward, as mentioned, had once treated me for my neck
and shoulder trouble. There are all sorts of theories now concerning
some of his more sinister activities and certainly he seems to have
been involved in some lurid pastimes. Obviously I was too dull to be
introduced to them. My own estimation of him was that he was just an
amusing, talented, personable chap, who led a feckless bachelor life and
simply liked to enjoy himself, preferably amongst others of his kind. I
don't really believe that there was much genuine harm in him.

I did question his being allowed the use of the Spring Cottage, or
River Pavilion as Bill called it. However, Bill assured me that whatever
went on there was no concern of his, but that at weekends – when Bill
was more often than not giving one of his massive house-parties –
Stephen was on instant call if needed for his professional skills – Bill
suffered from frequent migraines, and Stephen was the only person who
could give him relief.

I and my family spent many hours at Cliveden in the house, in the
swimming pool and in the grounds (sometimes even when Bill and
Bronwen were not there), at parties, luncheons and dinner parties or
even just for a quick drink or cup of tea: we knew it only as a perfectly
normal, happy home, especially during Bronwen's time there. She and
Bill did their best to live quietly when they were not entertaining, and
even had a kitchen fitted up in their private suite upstairs where she
cooked their meals.

The end of July saw me once again in Johannesburg on my way to
work on the *Sanders* film. After a few days there I drove my hired Volvo
down to Durban, accompanied by my movie stand-in Dale Swanepoel,
a charming and quiet young South African. Arriving in the late evening,
I went straight to my hotel, the old Oyster Box, right on the beach a
few miles from the city. My rooms looked seawards across the sand and
the surf, frothing and dazzling in the bright African moonlight, the

waves giving a constant surge of sound as they crashed on to the beach. I loved it there.

The next day Jeremy Lloyd and I met our German colleagues – Albert Lieven, pretty, vivacious Vivi Bach and the strikingly beautiful and highly intelligent Marianne Koch – and did some publicity photography around Durban.

Work started in the Indian Market in Durban, a colourful open-air setting crammed with stalls and thousands of chattering, haggling Asians who are very numerous in and around the city. The sari-clad crowds seemed totally oblivious of the cameras as we threaded our way through them and played our scenes.

We had the Sunday off and enjoyed a lovely day of swimming, sunbathing and barbecuing at the beach cottage of my SA Films friend, Ernie Bisogno, before starting our filming in the Durban docks, then moving to a Zulu kraal in the Valley of a Thousand Hills. The children in this area were enchanting, with their huge black eyes and dazzling grins, and wherever we went they would dance an energetic version of the 'Twist'. The dome-shaped mud huts were immaculate, the earth floors kept free of any food garbage by cockroaches. I was told that when a Zulu family moved house, they took their cockroaches with them.

We then flew to M'Tuba'Tuba ('M'Tuba Twice' to us) to start our main location shooting in the St Lucia Estuary area, a wetland of lakes and swamps teeming with crocodiles and wildlife intersected by the St Lucia River. I may not have been making a blockbusting movie, but at least I was seeing places which otherwise I would never have visited!

Harry, Laurie and the leading actors all stayed at the Lakeview Hotel run by a friendly pair of Brits, Captain and Mrs Symonds. The main hotel consisted of a large bungalow in which was the dining room and lounge. We all slept in charming thatched rondavels, like large Zulu huts, but very cosy and well-furnished, and in the evenings we sat on the verandah watching the flashes of sheet lightning which were almost constant at that season in Africa.

Our main fear as we worked in the St Lucia area was of the snakes and we soon learned not to wander off the tracks except in single file. Marianne, married to a Munich doctor and herself a qualified doctor, was provided with anti-snakebite serum and acted as a voluntary medical orderly for the unit.

My old white-hunter friend Dawie from *The Hellions* days was in the area building a boma, or stockade, for another British film unit and acting as their wildlife adviser. Dawie soon got in touch and took me in his Land Rover to the nearby Umfalosi Game Park to see the herds of rhinoceros that abounded there. I had my movie-camera with me and got some good shots, but it was difficult to get a close-up of one of the beasts. Finally Dawie spotted one browsing alone in a large bush, only its rear end visible. 'I'll get this one for you,' said the intrepid hunter, wise in the ways of wild animals. He stopped the vehicle quite close by, told me to have my camera ready and walked up to the beast, giving it a whack on the backside. But as the animal turned to see what was taking such liberties with his nether parts, he revealed the unmistakable head of a black rhino, and the next moment Dawie was racing back into the driver's seat, starting up and roaring away in a cloud of dust. You don't stop to argue with one of those particularly tetchy pachyderms.

Dawie also lent me for a couple of days one of a pair of cheetahs that he had tamed. This beautiful young creature went everywhere with me – in the car, for walks and in my rondavel where he slept on the floor. He was really affectionate, and I soon had a red patch on my neck where he insisted on licking me as he sat beside me in the car.

We spent a fascinating month at St Lucia and our filming went well, except for a few crocodile scares which were nowhere near as bad as the experiences I had had years before on the Nile in Uganda. It was a happy time marred only by one incident that showed the stupidity of the apartheid system and the nastiness of some ex-British settlers.

The unit all lived at a nearby hotel run by another English expatriate couple. We had with us a delightful and fine-looking black actor, Simon; he had permission to eat at the hotel, but had to use a separate little room off the kitchen as the law forbade him to share the dining room with the whites. One evening the English proprietor set him a place in the dining room at a separate table and told him he could eat there. But it was a particularly malicious set-up; within minutes the local policeman walked in and arrested him.

As soon as I heard of this from our angry crew in the morning, I contacted a lawyer in M'Tuba'Tuba recommended to me by Captain Symonds. He came to interview Simon in his cell and then advised me that the best thing for him to do was to go to court that day in M'Tuba 'Tuba and plead guilty; he would then be fined and released at once, otherwise he would be held and tried later and probably imprisoned. This we did, and I paid the lawyer's very modest fee and also the fine.

It was my first and only personal experience of an evil system. Thank God things have changed since then in South Africa – not yet enough, but at least heading in the right direction.

I arrived home just in time for the Henley Agricultural Show, which was just as well as I was President of the Henley Agricultural Association that year. It was a lovely day and the show was a great success. As I knew so many of the show-jumping fraternity they turned out in force, including the great Alan Oliver.

Combining had just started on our corn crops, and Peter and I were in the fields till dusk. I had also agreed to buy the rest of Keene's farm, taking over at Michaelmas, after some hurried dealing with my bank, so adding another seventy-odd acres to my holding.

After we had finished post-synching *Sanders* I was back to the old routine of script meetings for *The Diamond Story*, the *Queen's Messenger* series and Michael Carreras' subject, touting for customers for our cream and going to the annual Horse of the Year Show.

The dogs also figured prominently in our lives at this time. While I had been in Africa Baron II had behaved very badly and been really wild, so I decided on a desperate remedy: to have him neutered. He soon recovered, seemed to bear me no grudge and was as good as gold and perfectly biddable and well-mannered from them on.

But there was nothing I could do for Trigger. Now thirteen years old, the pointer suffered the same helplessness which dear old Baron I had reached at the end. She was put to sleep and went very peacefully, joining the others by the tennis court. Poor old 'Smiler' left a great gap in our family, after being with us from 1951 to 1963. It was a very upsetting day.

At this time we lost old Joe Aggis, our vegetable gardener. It had worried me to see him cycling shakily to work and I felt that, in his seventies, the work was getting hard for him. When I told him, he agreed with all his customary courtesy, Within a month he was working at Shiplake School, nearer his cottage!

I had recently engaged a new head gardener, as Dykes wanted to leave and return to Scotland. Ernie Bigsby, an ex-Coldstream Guardsman, was the best gardener I ever had and his Scottish wife was also a great help.

During November I had a couple of awkward moments. The first was in connection with a reception given by the Queen Mother at St James's Palace to which we had for some reason been invited. We had driven up to the flat to change when I suddenly realised that I had forgotten to bring a white dress collar to go with my evening tails. Panic! Obviously I could not go to the Palace bare-throated, and all the shops were closed. The resourceful driver of our hire car saved the situation by dashing up to the Dorchester Hotel and borrowing a collar from one of the staff there.

Then a week later I had been invited by Lady Caroline Waterhouse, the Duke of Marlborough's daughter, to open a Red Cross bazaar at Oxford Town Hall and to lunch beforehand at Blenheim Palace, the Duke's great home at Woodstock. We arrived at the palace in good time and I drove into the forecourt of the enormous mansion. There were no other cars there except for one parked in a corner, so I left my Sapphire just near the steps leading up to the main entrance. We had scarcely reached the door before Caroline came rushing out saying, 'Terribly sorry – you can't park there. Only my father and Winston Churchill ever use that spot.' So I hurriedly moved my car to another corner more fitted to my humble status.

And so that winter passed. I managed to get a number of days' shooting, both with our Haileywood syndicate and at others such as Cliveden and Hambleden, and it was also the season for National Farmers' Union county balls. One of these took me to Blackpool as the guest of honour at the Lancashire County Ball where I stayed the night: then I went over to Ripon for the evening and a dinner party at Colin and Vera Barber's house.

Christmas Eve started with our annual staff get-together at Haileywood. In Joe Aggis's absence, Mr Wade proposed the toast to the household. Dick and Catherine Brandram joined us for our family Christmas lunch and in the evening, already stuffed with seasonal fare, we joined the Palmers. On the last day of the year we all went to Bertram Mills Circus, where I had my usual stomach-turning whirl-around at the fun-fair with the children.

27

A Farewell to Farms

1964 brought another dramatic turning-point in my life, and with hindsight I'm not sure that I didn't move in the wrong direction. The course that I took may have resulted from panic rather than from any firm, quick, logical decision.

The year started predictably: endless meetings with George Willoughby and our associates as we tried to get our film and TV subjects off the ground; several conferences at the Federation of British Filmmakers, one of them leading to a meeting at the Board of Trade with the President – at that time Mr Edward Heath, MP – at which the impending sale of the major film distribution company British Lion was discussed, along with the crisis looming over the British film industry; and my personal worries mounting ever higher and heavier.

Months had gone by since my last film and there was absolutely no sign of a lucrative offer coming up from English or American sources. But one consoling thought did enter my mind at that time: it was not entirely my fault that my film career was in the doldrums – the entire British movie industry was moving rapidly towards its nadir.

I did receive one exciting proposal near the end of January, but with my customary lack of diplomatic finesse I succeeded in talking myself out of the part. The great William Wyler gave me his script for *The Collector* and suggested that I should play the lead in it. Here was at last a chance for me to get back near to the front rank, especially in America, with the starring role in a picture based on a gripping story and directed by one of the world's greatest movie-makers.

As I read the script that same evening my heart sank as I realised that I was not right for the role: too old, and projecting the wrong image for the character. I had tea with Mr Wyler at Claridges a couple of days later and told him of my misgivings – and unfortunately he agreed with me! What a twit I was – I should have convinced myself and him that I could play *any* part within my physical scope, and anyway the character was in some ways similar to the role I had played in 1969 in Alfred Hitchcock's *Stage Fright*. It was not the first time that I had talked myself out of a picture – there had been *The Guns of Navarone, League of Gentlemen* and *Ice Cold in Alex* – but this latest stupidity of mine came when I desperately needed to make another important international film.

This was when I began to panic. I had never had a cool business head, especially when dealing with my own affairs. I had little fluid capital left available to me, although I had considerable asset value, and for several years I had been biting into my cash savings to finance land purchases and a costly way of life. I had recently taken out a bank loan to pay for Shiplake Rise Farm and, unless a lucrative film came soon, I was going to need more finance to expand the dairy company.

One morning Basil Stebbings spelled out the seriousness of my problems in no uncertain terms in a phone call to the flat. I was just about to leave for lunch with MP John Harvey and Lord Birkett and Peter de Sarigny, the film producers, when we would try to evaluate and suggest remedies for the cinema industry's plight, so it was not the most cheerful luncheon I ever attended!

Within a week I had contacted my neighbour Fred Doble, offering to sell him the last part of Keene's Shiplake Rise Farm that I had bought, less seven acres which I wanted to hold with a view to putting in a planning application for that one field.

Fred agreed to the deal at once, and within two days we had exchanged contracts. I had thus staved off most of my bank repayments, and felt that I could breathe easy for another few months if nothing else turned up. However, it was depressing that I had been forced to take a retrograde step, because the sale of this land also meant that I could not expand my herd much further.

About this time Kitty's parents decided to return to Scotland; they had never really been happy in the south. Kitty had never got on well with her father, and for the past few months had scarcely been on speaking terms with either of her parents.

At the end of February we made a trip which had no effect on the advancement of my career, but which I would not have missed for worlds. Along with several other showbiz luminaries, we had been invited by the Egyptian government to spend a week as their guests as part of their campaign to attract more tourism to the country in general, and to attend the gala opening of a new hotel in particular. The government had taken over several palaces formerly the property of the deposed King Fuad and had converted them into luxury hotels. I believe the one where we stayed and which was the subject of the gala had once been the home of the Empress Eugenie; it was an imposing mansion splendidly and luxuriously furnished with the original pieces and carpets – all very Empire in style. We were allotted a magnificent suite with our own maid and lady's maid to minister to us.

I think the newly-converted hotel was to be called the Omar Khayyam, and no effort was spared to make its opening a glittering occasion. The interior was immaculate, but the grounds had suffered from the builders' depredations and when we arrived they were virtually a sandy wasteland with a few palm trees dotted here and there. But amazingly, when we came down ready for the cocktail reception with the press that preceded the official dinner and ball, the inventive Egyptians had covered the bare ground with truck-loads of grass clippings from other lawns and had arranged hundreds of potted plants to simulate flower-beds. In the evening dusk it all looked very verdant and colourful.

At the ball that night, which ended after sunrise, Kitty lost her diamond bracelet, left to me by my grandmother and about the best piece of jewellery she had. We knew it had a defective catch, so could easily fall off the wrist, but even so had stupidly not insured it for this trip. Kitty only noticed its loss when we were undressing for bed, and had no idea when or where it had disappeared. We reported the matter next morning and gave a detailed description of the bracelet to the police, though with little hope of ever recovering it. After all, this was Cairo.

Yet as soon as we arrived home a few days later, we had a message that the bracelet had been found and was being flown to London. We never knew exactly where or how it had been discovered, but clearly the Cairo police had turned up trumps.

During our stay we had been given a marvellous time by the hospitable Ministry of Tourism. Early the morning after the ball we visited the Pyramids, which were closed to tourists for a few hours, then we were taken to lunch at a large tented night-club and restaurant some miles from the city called the Pearl of the Desert. It had been opened especially early for the government guests and we all sat on huge gold-threaded cushions, picking at exquisite Arab dishes while a troupe of belly-dancers kept up a non-stop performance.

We were then ushered out into the desert, where a group of beautiful Arab horses and some very supercilious camels were gathered for us to try out. Kitty opted for a camel ride, but after the richness of our luncheon I decided to play safe and chose a horse, picking out the one whose nostrils flared least and who looked the most docile.

That evening we attended the magnificent *son et lumière*, one of the most fascinating entertainments I have ever experienced. Its subject was the Sphinx, and in the darkness the statue's towering, flood-lit shape was almost hypnotic, and the narration of its history was extremely well-presented and spoken.

But more was to follow: the next day we spent in Cairo, visiting mosques and museums. The main National Museum was closed to the public for the day, so we were able to browse completely at our leisure through all the treasures on display from Tutankhamun's tomb. And the following morning we flew to Luxor to spend the day in the labyrinthine corridors and chambers of Tutankhamun's tomb itself.

The day before our return to London we drove to the Red Sea, where we swam and sunbathed, and returned to Cairo via Suez.

It had all been a most engrossing experience, but the euphoria was not to last for long: the day after my return I was back in Basil Stebbings' office signing the contract for the sale of Shiplake Rise to Doble. Later the same day I was marking out the exact areas at Haileywood for four housing plots with the County Planning Officer. I had been granted planning consent and reckoned that each half-acre plot would be pretty valuable. They were sited where they would least intrude on the privacy of our house, but required that I should cut off about two hundred yards of the drive and make a new entrance gate to join the drive nearer the house. The gate-lodge and Stables Cottage (Webb's house) would share the old entrance with the four new houses. I retained the right to veto any architectural plans which I felt were not in keeping with the area.

Our Henley Midnight Matinée guest list that March actually included a Beatle. George Harrison came with John and Mary Mills and their daughter Hayley. During the buffet supper at Haileywood I realised how disappointed Fiona would be to miss a chance to meet one of the famous four, so I asked George if he would slip upstairs with me for a few minutes to surprise my eight-year-old child. As we sat on her bed, one on each side of her, and she slowly woke up, her look of sleepy bleariness turned to ecstatic disbelief when she saw who was with me. It must have seemed like a dream to her.

I believe that George now lives in Friar Park at Henley, Peter's first school.

Our Swiss holiday friend, Peter Grosscurth, was the only big property developer whom I knew quite well, so I sought his advice regarding my four building plots. We had been meeting quite often since Switzerland over a year ago, especially when Mrs Grosscurth personally donated a new van to the Save the Children Fund, of which I was then President for the Thames Valley area; we had attended each other's dinner parties on several occasions too, so I knew Peter would not mind my seeking his advice. He did more than just advise me: he decided to take them into one of his companies and sketched out for me the type of house he intended to build – good-looking neo-Georgian-style properties. Our contract of sale to his company gave me a reasonable deposit immediately; the rest was to follow as each house was sold, the freehold to be vested in his company.

Meanwhile George Willoughby and I had made some progress with the *Diamond Story* project. Jon Cleary, a well-known novelist and screenwriter perhaps best known for his script for *The Sundowners*, had agreed to come into our planning and to write the screenplay; while Robert Parrish, an American director of some distinction, liked the subject and agreed to direct subject to a satisfactory script; he proposed to work alongside Jon Cleary on this. The Rank Organisation was prepared to fund a trip to South Africa and South-West Africa (now Namibia), so that the four could search for location sites that would form the framework within which the screenplay would be set. We would leave in May.

Before this, I had already made a couple of departures from my normal routine. I had been invited by Peter Grosscurth to join the board of one of his companies, Polyhomes; this was the service company to the property development and building companies, responsible for the sales force, publicity and public relations. I was to draw a very fair annual salary for my part-time attendance at meetings, conferences and sales drives, and to learn what I could about the property business in general; I would also have a full-time assistant and secretary, and an office at Belmont House in Reading, Peter's headquarters. I had already visited some of his developments scattered around Berkshire, Wiltshire, Somerset, Oxfordshire and Hampshire and had been impressed with the variety of his designs, which ranged from imposing Georgian-style houses on prime sites to neat little semis and terrace houses on crowded but well-planned estates. One of Peter's selling points was that the use of plastics and fibreglass was a large element in his designs, especially in the high-density estates where quite pretty little terrace houses all had decorative in-fill panels of ready-to-fit fibreglass; they were identical to wooden clapboard, but would never rot or need painting. Door porches and windows were similarly prefabricated and fixed into position as his building process progressed. Clip-on interior skirting boards were another of his innovative ideas; behind these ran the electric wiring which would be altered, inspected or added to merely by unclipping the skirtings, which could stand up to any amount of Hoover-bashing without needing to be repainted. He was even then working on designs and ideas for bathroom units to be set on to a fibreglass 'tray' or floor, then dropped into position by crane for connection to the plumbing.

I was fascinated by his forward-looking ideas and plans.

My other departure was to depict Sir Alexander Fleming in a TV documentary about the discoverer of penicillin. Strangely enough, this very British subject was made by a French TV company, but the subject was really interesting and after reading the script I agreed to do it. The filming in early May took only eight days, and was largely set in the tiny box-room at St Mary's Hospital where Fleming first noticed the strange effect of mould on some neglected culture-dishes which he had decided to clean up and wash. So once again, I played a Scotsman on the screen.

Bob Parrish and I flew to Johannesburg together and were met on arrival there by George and Jon Cleary (who had set out a day or two earlier) and Oscar and Ruth Hurwitz, my friends from *The Hellions* period. We spent the next couple of days in meetings with members of the SA Films group and with various government departmental officials, then flew in a hired Cessna aircraft to Nelspruit, close to the huge area of bush and savannah that included the Kruger National Park game reserve.

Our pilot was a massive white South African who, after giving us bone-crushing handshakes, showed us to our tidy-looking plane. With his bass voice, rugged build and air of competence, he was the sort to inspire confidence in the most nervous of light-aircraft passengers . . . until we taxied to the beginning of the runway prior to take-off, when I noticed that he was the victim of dreadful twitches and tics at moments of stress. Sitting right behind him I was perhaps more aware of this than the others, and wondered how he kept the Cessna on a straight line as we sped down the runway.

We had a perfectly comfortable and uneventful flight until we neared Nelspruit, when our pilot again went through convulsive spasms as we swooped down on the tiny landing-strip, which was humpbacked and ended with a cliff-edge. As we smacked into the upward leading slope with considerable force and then proceeded to kangaroo-hop over the hump and down the reverse slope, I'm sure we all had the same thought

– 'Please God, let the brakes work before we reach the edge.' Fortunately
they did, and our flier relaxed back into his rock-like *alter ego*.

The next morning we took off for M'Tuba'Tuba to show Jon and
Bob an area that I knew well. As we wound up to take-off speed, we
went through even more harrowing moments than we had on landing.
The pilot jerked and twitched, we roared up the slope, were catapulted
upwards by the hump and actually flew for a few yards before bouncing
down again and careering down to the cliff-edge, after which we lost
height for several stomach-turning seconds before gaining enough speed
to pull up and fly safely over the town.

During our two days in M'Tuba'Tuba I took our little group around
Hlehlui and Umfalozi Game Parks, and to the St Lucia Estuary where
we had lunch with Captain and Mrs Symonds at the Lakeview Hotel,
my home during the making of *Sanders*.

Then we spent a day in Jo'burg once more, where we again visited
various government departments at Pretoria, and Oscar Hurwitz drove
us back.

The next morning we flew to Windhoek in South-West Africa, where
so many of de Beers' diamond fields are located and where much of
The Diamond Story took place. The whole object of our tour had been to
give Jon and Bob – who had never before visited any part of Africa –
some feeling for the terrain in which the future script would be set, plus
a smidgin of knowledge of the atmosphere and way of life in those areas.

We did not have time to visit the surface mining in the diamondiferous
area along the Skeleton Coast, as this would have required all manner
of permits, but we had seen a documentary film made for the Anglo-
American Corporation and had a fair idea of what it would look like.
Our purpose in spending a short time in Windhoek was mainly to find
out what facilities we could expect if we were to film in Namibia, and
also to make contacts there.

We were met at Windhoek airport by a group of people including
Jack Levinson, the mayor, and his wife; the latter was an authority on
South-West Africa's history. They were extraordinarily helpful and
hospitable to us, and remained friends of mine from then on. Jack gave
a cocktail party for us in the evening, where we met many of the
government and civil officials, and he also arranged for us to have a
meeting next morning with the Administrator of SW Africa, Mr du
Plessis.

South-West Africa had been a German colony before the First World
War, and a large permanent military garrison was kept there. Beautiful
little 'Beau Geste' forts were dotted all over the Kalahari Desert and

along the borders, shimmering in the sun. In Windhoek, the country's capital and administrative centre, the military and civilian heads had built delightful little castles for themselves one of which – Heinitz Castle, built for the German C-in-C – was now the Levinsons' home.

After a fruitful meeting with the Administrator, we flew back to Johannesburg. The other three flew straight on to London, but I stayed an extra day for talks with Ernie Bisogno and others of the SA Films set-up. On the day of my departure I had lunch with Oscar and Ruth Hurwitz in Pretoria, watched the Welsh Rugby touring XV play Northern Transvaal and then was driven by Oscar to Jan Smuts airport.

Before going to South Africa I had been approached by Delmer Daves, a leading Hollywood director/producer/screenwriter, to see if I would co-star in a film he hoped to make shortly in England with Maureen O'Hara and Rosanno Brazzi. I read the script of *The Battle of Villa Fiorita*, which Delmer himself had written, liked it, and asked Bob Lennard of Associated British to negotiate on my behalf, since it was through him that Delmer had contacted me. This had all been some weeks past and, having heard nothing further since, I concluded that the project had fallen through.

On the day I returned home I was surprised and delighted to get an urgent phone call from Bob Lennard telling me that *Villa Fiorita* was on and arranging for me to meet Delmer Daves for lunch next day at Elstree, where the studio shooting would be done. I found Delmer to be a charming silver-haired, kindly and avuncular man ideally suited to the gentle and romantic story he had scripted, produced and was about to direct. He told me he had been a little anxious about my hopping around South Africa in a light plane, as filming was to start next week.

Briefly, *The Battle of the Villa Fiorita* is the story of a British couple with two young children whose married bliss comes to a halt when the wife falls in love with a smooth Italian charmer and decamps to Italy, taking her children with her. The unfortunate husband sets out to win her back, aided by the young boy and girl who conspire together to wreck their mother's relationship with her lover. All my scenes were with the wife, played by Maureen O'Hara, and the children, and I never actually met her lover in the film played by Rosanno Brazzi.

My last day on the film coincided with my birthday and Delmer, typically, had arranged an enormous cake which he unveiled on the set after my final shot, making a valedictory speech to the assembled unit.

While I was filming I spent several evenings with George, Jon and Bob. It seemed that Jon and Bob were collaborating happily and successfully over the screenplay for *The Diamond Story*, and that the Rank Organisation was still keen about the project.

Any spare days I had when not called on to film were mostly spent at Polyhomes, or visiting sites where building was in progress. I also met and had long discussions with John Pole, a leading estate agent whose firm handled a lot of the sales of Peter Grosscurth's properties. I had begun to enjoy my latest business activity, and spent more time than was really necessary in my Belmont House office or touring round some sites which were still only in the planning stages and others which were already selling. Looking back, I now realise that by keeping busy I was shutting out of my mind the implications of the dread decision I had just made: that I would sell all my farmland, stock and cottages, and just keep Haileywood House and about 25 acres of garden and parkland. Although this would be a terrible wrench for me, it would rid me of any debt, leave a nice fat bank balance and enable me to concentrate on my acting career.

Sadly, the plain fact of the matter was that I had, in panic, made a wrong decision. I should have sold the house (which with its indoor staff of five plus three gardeners, was always going to be a heavy drain on my income), kept the farms and moved into the converted Stable Cottage. This, with the adjoining gate-lodge added to it, would have made a very nice house. Then I would also have been able to expand the Shiplake Dairy Company without any borrowing and to build up an already viable business. With hindsight, that is what I *should* have done, but I had persuaded myself instead that I would quit farming and dairying, concentrate on salvaging my flagging fortunes as an actor, make pots of money and then retire and farm full-time. Little did I realise what inflation and other pressures would do to the value of land in the future 1970s, or that my fading movie career was but one of the casualties of an entire cinema industry which was going through a period of ever-increasing attenuation.

The decision taken, I set about implementing it and asked Paul Rosewarne, my land agent, to value the farms, farm buildings and cottages and put them on the market.

One of the saddest moments came when I collected Peter at Victoria Station for his half-term holiday and drove him home. When we were clear of London, I broke the news to him as he sat behind me in the car as gently as I could, and explained some of the reasons for the sale. He seemed to be taking it very sensibly and from time to time murmured, 'Yes, I see, Daddy'; 'No, of course not'; 'I understand, Daddy.' Then I stole a look at him in my rear-view mirror and saw the tears streaming down his face. I realised that parting with the farms and the Jerseys was as much a blow to him as it would be for me. For seven years, more than half his life, he had spent every possible moment either in the farmyards or in the fields.

The coming sale of the farms presented another problem for me: what to do with the Shiplake Dairy Company? I would have to find a buyer for it or simply let it disappear.

While all this was happening and I was feeling thoroughly depressed, my spirits were lifted briefly by the offer of roles in two films: a 'guest star' appearance in Michael Anderson's forthcoming *Operation Crossbow* and the leading part in the next Harry Alan Towers film *Coast of Skeletons*, to be made in South Africa. I wished that the relative importance of roles could have been reversed!

With so much going on at home and in London I would have preferred to avoid a commitment I had undertaken weeks before – to serve as a jury member at the Berlin Film Festival at the end of June. However, I had given my word and could think of no valid excuse for backing out.

When we first gathered as a jury we chose Anthony Mann as our president and proceeded to spend many hours watching films. God knows why some of the movies had even been nominated. The main British official entry was *Night Must Fall*, based on Emlyn Williams' play, and we didn't think much of it. The US entry, *The Pawnbroker* with Rod Steiger, came near the top of our list but was criticised for being rather sluggish and studied. Finally we gave the Golden Bear to an obscure Turkish film about peasants squabbling over their rights to sources of water in an arid mountain area. We found this picture totally engrossing, even though it was subtitled and the Turkish language was all Greek to us. Very funny in some parts and very moving in others, it was our unanimous choice, a decision which was not at all popular with the festival officials or with the droves of hard-nosed dealers who had flocked to this most commercial of all the annual film festivals. 'How the hell can we sell *that*?' they wailed. However, we had a brief to select what we considered to be the best picture, and that we had done.

Marianne Koch was at the festival for a few days and when I first saw her I was delighted to hear that she too had been sought by Harry Alan Towers to play in his next film. At least if I made the Towers film, I knew who my leading lady might be.

As soon as I returned home I had a meeting with Towers to discuss the deal for *Coast of Skeletons*, got his agreement to better terms than I'd had for *Sanders* and said that I would do the picture subject to certain script alterations and improvements. He himself had written the original screenplay, but he readily agreed that I and Tony Veitch, a screen-writer, should polish the final shooting script.

A few days later I had an offer for the dairy company from a business acquaintance. He had once before shown an interest in taking control of it, but had later backed out. Now he was saying that having given the matter a lot of thought he had come to the conclusion that the Shiplake Dairy Company had a good future, and he was prepared to take majority control provided I remained as chairman. I was at his house going into the details of all this when several hours of talk were abruptly ended by a phone call from Dunant telling me that Biscuit, our old, ugly pug, had been killed. I drove home immediately, knowing that Kitty and Fiona would be very upset.

Apparently Biscuit had been found dead but almost unmarked on the road outside the entrance to the home farm. What she had been doing there nearly a quarter of a mile from the house nobody knew, as she had never been a wanderer, but there had been a thunderstorm that afternoon and perhaps she was out in the garden, became frightened and simply ran blindly in panic.

Our little line of graves at the edge of the tennis court was gradually extending . . .

Towards the end of July and only a day before I started work on *Operation Crossbow*, Paul Rosewarne arrived to say that he had come from talks with Fred Doble, my neighbour, and that Fred had decided to buy my farms. A price had been agreed and it only remained for us to draw up a contract of sale with all the details.

I suppose I should have been delighted. After all, I had decided to sell anyway and at least my land – which we had improved and worked on for seven years – was going to someone I knew and respected as a splendid farmer, rather than to some stranger. In fact, I felt physically sick. From that moment one of my lifelong dreams was snuffed out.

That evening I had to drive up to the flat preparatory to a dinner meeting with Peter Grosscurth and a PR consultant about our Poly-homes publicity. I found that the flat had been burgled.

It was not my day . . .

My brief part in *Operation Crossbow* was not exactly onerous and only involved me for a few days spread over three weeks. However, I enjoyed every moment at the MGM Studios at Borehamwood (now, sadly, a giant cold-store or something of the kind). The leading men were George Peppard and Richard Johnson, while John Mills, Trevor Howard and

I were three old stalwarts who appeared in a briefing sequence. Amazing how difficult it is to come in on cue when you only have the odd line in a long scene!

It was lovely to be working again with Michael Anderson, and with Erwin Hillier who had lit and photographed *The Dam Busters* and other pictures I had done.

While not on call at MGM, I was still busily hopping from one script session to another: with George and the others on *The Diamond Story* or *Queen's Messenger*, and with Tony Veitch polishing the *Coast of Skeletons* screenplay.

The day after I finished work on *Operation Crossbow* Basil Stebbings and I met the group proposing to take over the operation of Shiplake Dairy Company; after a session at Haileywood that lasted from 10.30 am until 6.30 pm a deal was fixed and agreed. On that same day my pigs, which were the first of my livestock to be auctioned, fetched a healthy few thousand pounds. I was not sorry to have been absent from the sale; I can't claim to have had any special pets amongst my porkers, but we had all been very proud of our pig unit.

I soon had all my tropical kit and clothing bought for *Coast of Skeletons* and was preparing to fly out to South Africa in mid-August. Tony Veitch and I had completed work on the script and I was just waiting for the date of my flight to be confirmed.

However, there were several days of ominous silence from Towers. Knowing something of the intricacies of Harry's financial arrangements for his pictures, nothing would surprise me even at this stage, and sure enough I was in my office at Polyhomes when a phone call from South Africa informed me that the finances for *Coast of Skeletons* had collapsed.

Only two days later, as I was helping Bigsby and his wife to move into the garage flat which Kitty's parents had previously occupied, news came through that the film was on again and that I should book a flight for the next day. This Queenie did, and the next afternoon I was literally on the point of leaving the house for Heathrow when another call came through telling me to hold everything because the film looked like being cancelled after all. The whole situation had become something of a Keystone Cops comedy, but I was not exactly in the mood to appreciate the humour.

Then at 10.30 the following morning, Towers phoned from Johannesburg saying that all was OK, please come out at once. Queenie got me a seat on a BOAC flight that evening.

I spent the afternoon saying goodbye to Webb, my head herdsman for five years, and his family, and to the ploughman and his wife. I would not be seeing them again, as they would not be required once the Jersey herd had been sold. Then I took Peter down to the home farm to say goodbye to my lovely Jerseys at milking-time. Kitty told me later that it had been a mournful sight to watch two dejected figures walking side by side away from the house. In many ways I was glad that I would be abroad when the Harpslake Jersey herd was auctioned. Mr Wade and Michael would be staying on until the hand-over to Doble, then they were going to the Isle of Wight to run Peter Gross-curth's estate there.

And so I took my last, lingering look at so much which I had cherished.

I spent two days in Jo'burg with Towers going through the altered script, all of which he agreed, then flew down to Durban and the Oyster Box Hotel once more. Marianne Koch arrived soon after, and we were also joined by Derek Nimmo, who was to play my comic assistant in the film as Jeremy Lloyd had done in *Sanders*, the American actor, Dale Robertson (without his faithful Tonto) and Heinz Drache, a leading German actor.

Coast of Skeletons was a straightforward cops-and-robbers story involv-ing diamond smuggling and various other illegal activities; a journey-man subject that would gain interest from the locations where we would be filming.

For the first month filming took place in the Durban area, already familiar to some of us – on the beaches, in the docks and in the Valley of a Thousand Hills, barely an hour's drive from the Oyster Box.

Quite a few days were spent on a rusty old cargo ship that Harry had hired, probably from a shipbreaker. The ancient tub was in an appalling state, while her skeleton crew of lascars in the charge of a scruffy white skipper and an even scruffier red-nosed Scots engineer did little to inspire confidence in our ability to put to sea.

Nevertheless, soon after we had boarded on the first day, the engines wheezed and rattled into action and we were off – or, at least, we thought we were off. As we cast off from the harbour berth and the engines were set at 'full ahead', we turned left towards the harbour entrance . . . and kept on turning. The steering had jammed and we went round in ever-increasing circles until the sweaty, swearing Scots-man freed it with a series of hammer-blows and a large can of oil. When we straightened up and headed out to sea there was a salvo of relieved

The Grange at Bampton

Haileywood House

The War Movies

Left: They went that a-way! With Lord Lovat at Pegasus Bridge during the filming of *The Longest Day*.

Below: In *Danger Within* with William Franklyn, Richard Attenborough and Donald Houston.

Bottom: A knotty problem during *Operation Crossbow*, with John Fraser, Trevor Howard and John Mills.

bove: One of those steamy moments with Laurence Harvey in *The Long and the Short and the Tall*.
elow: A council of war on board H.M.S. *Amethyst* during *Yangtse Incident*.

Above: Elke Sommer: a pretty back number.

Left: The gorgeous Gina Lollobrigida.

From Small Beginnings: Peter and Fiona admire my first dairy company van.

Above: The *Chase a Crooked Shadow* Lagonda: talk about dodgy steering!

Left: A study in dignity: Agatha Rolls and Baron.

A stable relationship.

Virginia at our London house during the first year of our marriage.

Strolling in the Bride's Avenue at Glassenbury Park.

Right: Andrew and
umas beginning to
sprout.
elow right: Our two
rep-school boys at
home.

Joan Collins enjoys a small stimulant after breaking her arm.

The Business of Murder: Mr Stone gives Peter Byrne an earful.

cheers from other craft, mostly Japanese whalers who had scattered in alarm.

As we wallowed along a mile or two from the coast it was quite pleasant, especially when we were joined by a school of dolphins who smiled, squeaked, jumped and played around our bows for hours.

By the end of that day we had come to the conclusion that our old hulk was at least fairly watertight, but our return to harbour was as comic as our exit had been. All the vessels under power gave us a wide berth; grinning sailors lined the decks on those which were tied up, and went through the motions of diving overboard for safety. Heading for our berth, either the skipper was late in giving the order to go into reverse or the gears had jammed, because we just kept on going and rammed the stone jetty with a resounding crash.

I had been in Durban for ten days when Kitty and the children arrived for a three-week stay. The Oyster Box was an ideal base for them with its marvellous beaches, rock pools and curling surf where dolphins frolicked about most days. While these lovely creatures were around there was no fear of sharks. During their last week in Natal, the family had the added thrill of spending a couple of days and a night in the Umfalozi Game Reserve, being flown there and back in the private plane of an acquaintance of mine. Fiona would have a lot to talk about when she joined her new school in September: Great Oaks, the prep school to St Mary's, Wantage.

The most interesting part of our location work – and in some ways the most hazardous – was the short period we spent at the Skeleton Coast itself, following a day or two spent in Windhoek doing street scenes. In the city I was particularly intrigued by the sheer physical beauty and tall, stately bearing of the Herero people, and by the colourful, tight-bodiced Victorian dresses that their women wore, their hemlines sweeping the ground. Both the men and the women of the tribe have splendid, graceful physiques and fine-boned features, and are often extremely handsome.

Once finished in Windhoek we flew to Walvis Bay, a small, largely German-populated fishing centre on the extreme northern tip of the Skeleton Coast. I settled into a neat little hotel, the Mermaid, and that afternoon flew down to our location site with Marianne Koch. Our pilot – revered locally as a former Luftwaffe ace – was a grizzled, tough-looking but quiet-spoken man who certainly proved a splendid flier. We were in a Canadian-built Beaver aircraft especially adapted for landings and take-offs on beaches. After some thirty minutes following the coastline south we saw our unit, a scattering of human figures and equipment dotted on the long strip of hard beach bordering the Kalahari Desert. Some four or five hundred yards inland we could see the hulk of a ship sitting firmly upright on the sand, seemingly undamaged, as if it had been carefully dumped there by crane. It was an incongruous sight. The pilot explained to us that the Kalahari Desert was gradually encroaching on the South Atlantic and each year pushed its shoreline further seawards. The ship, which had probably run aground on a sandy shoal when hugging the coast during the First World War, was now beached well inland. Our special-effects men were busy wiring it up ready to be dynamited at the end of this particular film sequence, so I went to have a closer look. All the woodwork had long since rotted away but the metal framework and plates, and the engines, were rust-encrusted but complete, giving the wreck a skeletal appearance perfectly in accord with the reputation of her resting-place.

The Skeleton Coast lived up to its name: totally arid, bounded on one side by the salty ocean and on the other by the shifting, rippling dunes of the Kalahari. Nothing could survive there. It was also the boundary of a very sensitive region, jealously guarded by the mining company whose mineral rights along it were total and patrolled day and night by land, sea and air. In this region diamond stones lay close to the surface and even on it – hence our quickly-acquired habit of walking about with our heads bowed, hopeful of treading near the next Koh-i-noor.

We filmed there throughout the afternoon and early evening, and were glad to finish as it got bitterly cold when the sun began to sink.

When the day came for us to finish the *Skeleton Coast* sequence the final act was to be the blowing-up of the stranded ship. It had to work first time – there would be no second chance.

Harry and the crew had flown down early in successive flights and at midday Marianne and I boarded the Beaver aircraft. She was helped in first by our pilot and, before I climbed the steps, he held me back for a second, saying quietly, 'Sorry, you won't have much room in the back seat because of all those boxes. They hold the dynamite and detonators for the explosion – but don't tell Miss Koch, she might get nervous.'

She might get nervous! What about *me*? All went well, however, and the unmarked boxes were unloaded at the other end by the crew and used as seats as we all tucked into a box-lunch. I could not resist taking some snapshots of our unit as they contentedly puffed at their cigarettes, lolling amongst containers packed with high explosive. If only they had known!

Our scenes completed, the moment arrived for the destruction of the ship. Preparations would take some time, so I wandered off over the dunes to look at a salt-pan that the pilot told me he had used for landing with light aircraft without special sand-wheels or skis. I found the area easily enough: a saucer perhaps half-a-mile in diameter with a hard, dirty-white surface cobwebbed with a tracery of tiny cracks and fissures. But what really intrigued me was a find that I made behind some dunes near the pan. It was the remains of a crude shelter made of poles and galvanised iron sheets; inside it was bare and empty except for a little pile of food tins, obviously years old, and of all things an ancient sewing-machine. Who had been the loner who once used the sewing-machine, I wondered, and for what purpose here in the Kalahari? And what happened to him – did his skeleton lie bleached somewhere along that coast?

The explosion worked perfectly and we left that evening to fly back to Windhoek. The others left the next day in the early morning but I, mindful of possible future needs for *The Diamond Story* in SW Africa, stayed an extra day. I shopped for home-going presents in the morning, guided by Jack Levinson, went to an official garden party at the Administrator's house in the afternoon and dined at Heinitz Castle that evening.

A week later, our filming finished, I flew home.

My pleasure at being home again was clouded as I looked out of my dressing-room window and there was not a Jersey in sight.

Fiona's half-term holiday from Great Oaks coincided with Queenie's wedding, and she was one of the bridesmaids. It was an altogether happy occasion and a lovely day as Queenie married Geoffrey Saunders, a highly successful and likeable young farmer from nearby Faringdon. Geoff had waited for Queenie for a long time and had even built their future home on his father's land to his own plans and specifications – and with his own hands, aided by farm staff.

My pleasure at Queenie's happiness was matched by my sadness a few days later as I said goodbye to Mr and Mrs Wade and Michael, and wished them well. They had both done so much towards the improvement and prosperity of the Haileywood farms.

With the farming and the dairying gone, my sole livestock interest was vested in a small flock of laying hens that we kept, together with some table birds and the pheasants Bigsby was keen to continue rearing for next year – and of course, the dogs and old Winnie, the cat. Ann

Weil gave us Emma, a beautiful bull mastiff bitch who soon settled down with us, so that we now had a great Dane, a bull mastiff, a springer, a corgi and a pug and were back to full strength.

I think the loss of my farms has been one of the saddest experiences of my adult life. Although I was only a weekend farmer, it was an experience which I had always craved and one that went with my deeply felt love of the land. So I still hoped then that I would recoup my fortunes and return to agriculture in the not-too-distant future.

Meanwhile I had plenty to occupy me during the last weeks of that bleak year. George Willoughby and I were still battling to make headway in setting up *The Diamond Story* and *Queen's Messenger*, and had frequent sessions at Pinewood and in London, and I spent a lot of time at my Polyhomes office or touring round sites as far afield as Heywood, near Manchester.

And, of course, I still managed to spend most Saturdays and some week-days shooting. Apart from invitations to other shoots, I had kept two guns in the Haileywood syndicate. But sadly I no longer had the right to shoot whenever I wanted over my own land.

One interesting reminder of days gone by came when I was invited to open the Christmas Fair at Sandhurst Royal Military Academy. Kitty and I lunched first with the Commandant, General Mogg, and the Assistant Commandant, General Tony Deane-Drummond, with whom I had served in 6th Airborne Division. Sandhurst did not seem to have changed much since my days there in 1940/41.

Our annual visit to the Isle of Arran as shooting guests of Jean Fforde went somewhat amiss. On my first day on the hill with the new head stalker, Howard Walker, I felt quite dreadful and found climbing a difficult task, only managing to bag a couple of hinds. The next two days I had to stay indoors with a heavy cold and bronchitis, so missed the pheasant shoots. To make matters worse, Kitty had to take to her bed on doctor's orders.

We were not the most scintillating house-guests that year . . .

Our spirits had recovered by Christmas time and by year's end I felt quite optimistic about the future, especially as I looked at my soaring bank balance which was once again very comfortably in the black.

28

There Is Life After Debt

1965 was to mark another exciting turning-point in my life, though at the beginning of the year I had no reason to expect it. Despite the bleak prospect of the waning of my film star career, I still clung to the hope that something would turn up, either through my own efforts or, more likely, just out of the blue. In fact I was feeling quite jaunty as a result of my restored financial position and immediately set about looking for means of dispersing some cash – sensible investment never occurred to me, such is my incautious nature. Besides, years earlier I had once had quite a portfolio of shareholdings nearly all of which had ended in thumping losses, so I did not fancy repeating the process. I think that was partly the reason for my buying more land and cottages. Liquid capital had always burned holes in my pockets. While selling the farms had been a heartbreak, they had at least shown a healthy profit, though I am now aware that if I had held on to them for a few more years that profit would have been increased spectacularly. But that's with hindsight.

Nothing had changed in our rather extravagant life-style at Hailey-wood, except for those lovely days when we all wandered freely over the land or visited the calf-pens in the evening.

I bought two new cars, an estate model for Kitty and an Austin-Healey 3000 open sports car for myself. This very potent little wagon reminded me of my early days with the Railton, and the children loved their first wind-blown spin in it with me.

One thing did shock me that January. Peter and I had been invited to a shoot at Cliveden; when we joined the team of guns I noticed that Bill Astor himself looked very poorly and was not shooting. Instead he sat with us at some of the drives looking quite shrunken, huddled in his green Inverness cape, accompanied always by his devoted Bronwen. Clearly, he had never recovered from the devastating effects of the Stephen Ward affair.

I also had a mounting problem in my own private life. Kitty and I were not getting along too well together. We both had faults and failings – who hasn't? – and our natures were totally different. She was inclined to be something of an introvert and did not make friends easily, whilst I was just the opposite. Perhaps my protracted absences from home and her uncertain health and resultant depressive moods were a factor in the cooling of our relationship. We still felt a mutual affection and shared a devotion to our children and our home. She had many sterling qualities and I hope I was a caring husband and father, but things were not right between us. I have no intention of going into details but I believe that even Peter had begun to notice that there was a problem, and many of our friends told me in later years that they too had been aware of it, much to my surprise.

At the end of the month I spotted an advertisement in *Country Life* for flats for sale in a new block in Ibiza. Hoping that the relaxed atmosphere of a holiday home in a sunny climate might help to sort things out, I flew to the island with Kitty. We were enchanted with the place as it was in those pre-package tour days when there was a tiny airport capable of handling only small planes. We stayed at the Montesol Hotel in the town of Ibiza itself, a shabby old place that was very cheap and friendly, where the terrace was the daily meeting place for all the Brits who gathered there each morning for gigantic gins and tonic and used the Montesol as their *poste restante*. We were fortunate in meeting a charming young Frenchman, Daniel Carré, who was busily involved in building and development on the island: he agreed to accompany us to the apartment block to check on the quality of its construction, which he assured me was excellent.

I decided to buy two adjoining flats on the third floor and have them knocked into one, which would give us four bedrooms, a large living room, two bathrooms, two balconies with marvellous views out to sea and a good kitchen, the second kitchen being joined to the main bedroom as a boudoir for Kitty. I spoke to the splendid foreman of the builders who agreed to do all this reconstruction for us 'on the house' and to put in extra cupboards as well. Furthermore, when I asked him if he knew of a woman who would clean and cook for us while we were there, and act as caretaker when we were away, he said, 'Yes – my wife, who speaks English and French.' Next day Daniel Carré took us on a tour of the island in his jeep. It was quite glorious in those days with its wooded hills and valleys and dozens of totally secluded beaches and coves, deserted and hard to reach over the very rough farm tracks.

We couldn't wait for our flat to be completed and ready for our family holiday that summer.

After a lovely five days we flew home. The next day Kitty went into hospital for ten days for a rather painful operation on her feet and I returned to the house to watch on TV the very moving ceremony of Winston Churchill's state funeral.

Most of my time in that period was spent in Belmont House in Reading – headquarters of Polyhomes and Peter Grosscurth's associated property companies – learning as much as I could about the business of property development, or visiting various active or potential sites as far afield as Manchester, Crewkerne in Somerset, and Newbury in Berkshire. I became quite expert at dealing with planning officers, borough surveyors, council officials, estate agents and various finance houses. I had become seriously interested in the business and its prospects, and enjoyed a good relationship with Fletcher, my assistant at Belmont, and with my very efficient and protective secretary there. At least I felt that I was earning my salary, though my Star Sapphire was knocking up a prodigious mileage.

One break in routine came when I was invited by Charles Forté to be a guest at a luncheon to celebrate the centenary of the Café Royal. My neighbouring guests were Lord Lonsdale whose great-uncle, the famous 'Yellow Earl', had been a pillar of that famous London establishment; and J. Paul Getty, the American super-billionaire who had just bought Sutton Place, near Guildford. I got on very well with James Lonsdale and he promised to invite me to shoot at his great estate in Cumbria, but the taciturn, lugubrious Mr Getty was not so communicative – at least, not until I happened to touch on the subject of trees and discovered that he was an ardent silviculturalist. He waxed lyrical about the thousands of trees he had planted at Sutton Place and the many thousands that were now growing on his Californian estate. Apart from making and controlling vast sums of money, and some of the less enviable characteristics of his reputation, tree growing seemed to be the interest closest to his heart, together with his acquisition of fabulous art and antique treasures for his museum in America.

I had also been invited to join the board of a proposed local radio station, Thameside Radio, whose directors included John Counsell, the director of the Theatre Royal, Windsor, Roger Manvell, the author and pundit of films and radio, Dr Crowther, a local chemical and baby-food industrialist, and the Bishop of Reading. We were quite a mixed bag.

In March I flew out to Argentina for the Mar del Plata Film Festival, and enjoyed a pleasant mixture of press and other official engagements and some hours on the beach and in local restaurants. Admiral Sir Charles Evans, who had been my host on board his aircraft carrier a few years previously and who was now President of the British Film Producers Association – having retired from the Royal Navy – was the Flag Officer of our British delegation, and had lost none of his bonhomie. He and his charming Greek wife saw to it that we enjoyed ourselves as well as doing a good job in promoting the British film industry. In this he was again assisted by the support of the British Ambassador from Buenos Aires whose PA, Pat Chandler, arranged my return flight and dined with me on my last night in BA, when I tackled the largest, most succulent T-bone steak I had ever seen.

I was home just in time for our annual Henley Midnight Matinée, which was again a great success and raised a substantial sum for the Henley Housing Trust which was building homes for elderly people in need of help and supervision. Kitty and I got to bed at 5.30 a m when the last of our guests finally departed. At a subsequent meeting of the matinée committee, I asked them to accept my resignation as president. I had started to run out of celebrities willing to flog down to Henley, and had begun to feel the financial strain of our increasingly elaborate pre-show parties, to say nothing of the hours of preparation involved in the office with Queenie and the tiring effect it had on Kitty. I was invited to remain as Honorary Life President.

I was also worried about the state of the Shiplake Dairy Company. Under its new management it had expanded rapidly, with a fleet of new purpose-built refrigerated lorries plying over most of Southern England from London to Exeter and Southampton – a far cry from my little emergent enterprise operated from my own farm buildings with two small vans. The products, now made under contract with a company in Wantage, were still excellent, and the increased range of creams, yoghurts and sausages the best one could buy anywhere. However, I feared that the whole business was enlarging too rapidly on shaky foundations. I had been asked to remain as chairman, but had absolutely no control over the operations, and furthermore I was still responsible for a bank guarantee, which bothered me. Certain elements of the original agreement which involved my shareholding had not been adhered to, so Basil Stebbings and I asked for meetings to discuss the situation.

During her spring holidays, Fiona had to have her appendix removed at the London Clinic. I visited her every day and was amazed at her quick recovery; within a couple of days she was scooting round the corridors in a wheel-chair. I think she had become the darling of the staff and was given a lot of freedom. She was home within a week, perfectly comfortable and not hampered at all. On the days when I went to see her at the clinic, I filled in a lot of time with George Willoughby as we were still trying to get a deal for our *Diamond Story*.

Daniel Carré from Ibiza came to stay with us for a few days, bringing with him details of a tract of coastal land on the island which might be available for a large villa development. Peter Grosscurth and I decided to have a look at it as soon as possible. Meanwhile we had discussions about the project in London with Arnold Schlaepfer, a Swiss banker. At the end of May we flew to Ibiza, looked at the land – gently sloping terrain surrounding a narrow sea inlet, ideal for development provided we could find a ready supply of fresh water – and had meetings with local council officials and the mayor of St Eulalia to enquire about planning consent. A couple of weeks later we were in Barcelona for a day to negotiate a very good deal at a meeting with Arthur Boote, our company legal adviser, Arnold Schlaepfer, Carré and Pedro Luis Poch, an important Spanish businessman who was interested in joining with us.

When Peter arrived home for his half-term holiday he did not seem unduly worried about his approaching Common Entrance exam for Eton, although I suspected that it would be touch and go. Fiona meanwhile was struggling academically at Great Oaks, but had not lost any of her cheerfulness. Peter's brief holiday was further enhanced when I took him to Reading to see a beautiful new Rolls Bentley S3, to my mind one of the greatest cars of that great make. Only some 400 were made and it was a stunner, finished in a gleaming Astral Blue. Peter Grosscurth agreed that it should be my company car; within a few days the pretty Star Sapphire had gone, after a final affectionate pat on the bonnet from me.

The day after Peter's return to Wellesley House School James McConnell, his future housemaster at Eton, phoned to say that he had passed his Common Entrance exam. Jubilation! I phoned Peter at school to congratulate him.

The Bentley's first public appearance that year was at the Henley Regatta, where it drew many admiring looks; the Shrewsbury School crew had been knocked out of the Princess Elizabeth Cup, so they only spent one day with us at Haileywood.

Kitty and I spent a few days in Ibiza at the beginning of July busily furnishing our new apartment. We made it really comfortable and attractive, and at the same time I arranged for a lawyer, Mr Ballester, to be my agent and adviser on local legal matters. I also arranged to engage and pay a local drilling engineer to prospect for water at our proposed villa development site.

Because I had to attend a Save the Children Fund veteran car rally near Reading I was sadly unable to go to Peter's sports day at Wellesley House, but Kitty watched him do very well and become *victor ludorum*.

A few days later I was back in Ibiza with Grosscurth and others, including Pedro Poch, to visit our land site and start planning the layout. I stayed at the flat for the first time, looked after by Maria, our new daily housekeeper. Soon we were all back there *en famille* for our summer holiday, accompanied by Irene, our young housemaid at Haileywood. She had never been out of England before and was thrilled.

It was while I sat on the beach one glorious afternoon that I started to read Oscar Wilde's *An Ideal Husband*. It had been sent to me by Peter Bridge, one of England's leading theatrical impresarios, who had seen my inglorious but well-received sketch at the previous year's Army Benevolent Fund show at the Palladium. He was quite determined that I should come back into the live theatre and had sent me several subjects to consider, none of which had enthused me. Besides, I was apprehensive about what sort of a reception I would have from the sterner critics, who would almost certainly be pretty sceptical about a little film actor presuming to play a leading part in the West End. Or so I told myself . . .

After all, it was seventeen years since I had trodden a theatrical board and I knew that such stagecraft as I had once garnered during my repertory theatre days in Dundee must by now be thoroughly rusty, especially in the vocal department. All my speeches and dialogue had been assisted for years by microphones.

In other words, I was petrified. I felt that I would be a target sitting duck to be shot at.

However I also knew that something had to be done if I was to survive as a leading actor. With Associated British now virtually out of action as a producing company; with my supporters at Twentieth Century-Fox, Darryl Zanuck and Lew Schreiber, no longer in control; and with a new wave of kitchen-sink dramas filling the movie screens, it was going to be hard for me to break back into any kind of big-league position as a film actor. Nobody thought of me as a character actor with a decidedly quivery upper lip. Furthermore, I was now in my mid-forties and somewhat aged for conventional heroic roles.

Nevertheless, I was going to need a lot of persuasion to take the chance of a return to the theatre.

It was Oscar Wilde who finally persuaded me. As I sat reading that marvellously witty play I laughed out loud at frequent moments, especially at some of the epigrams given to Lord Goring, the part Peter Bridge wanted me to play. I was surprised that he had not seen me as the more priggish, pompous Sir Robert Chiltern.

Few actors could have resisted the opportunity to play Goring, despite any reservations that they might have had about their suitability for the part.

I sent a telegram to Peter and took the first available flight to London. During ten days in England, spent partly at home and partly at the flat, I had several meetings with Peter and James Roose-Evans, who was to direct the play, and we reached agreement on the terms I was to be offered and the cuts to be made in the original script. Rehearsals were to start in late September with a very distinguished cast.

I had taken the plunge into the deep end, straight into a classic role in a classic play, and was delighted. Whatever the result, I would at least have had a go.

I could not have embarked on my new venture with a more charming, thoughtful and affectionate soul than Peter Bridge as my employer, nor with a more skilled, detailed and accomplished director than James Roose-Evans.

You never know your luck . . .

Before I returned to Ibiza I packed in a lot of work with Queenie in our office and at Belmont House with Polyhomes, also with George Willoughby on *The Diamond Story*. During the week the Rank Organisation signed an option to buy and produce the subject, so it was still alive and beginning to kick a bit more lustily.

Our holiday continued in sunny bliss as we explored just about every beach and cove in the tiny Seat I hired: this was about the only vehicle apart from a jeep or Land Rover that could cope with the boulder-strewn tracks as we all bounced along, the five of us crammed in with rubber boats, parasols and beach gear. The day we left we handed over the flat and Maria to Basil Stebbings and his family, who were to use it for a couple of weeks.

On 15 September, Peter settled in very happily on his first day at Eton.

Then followed several days of crisis meetings at Belmont House, where a few financial clouds were beginning to gather, the precursor of the national credit squeeze which was soon to hit business and industry in the country.

At last, on 22 September, we began rehearsals for *An Ideal Husband* and I met the assembled company. What a cast! Such was his confidence in the production, Peter Bridge had brought together a veritable *Who's Who* of the theatre world. Our leading lady was Margaret Lockwood and my colleagues included Michael Denison, Dulcie Gray, Roger Livesey, Ursula Jeans, Perlita Neilson, Gillian Raine and Cyril Wheeler.

They were an inspiring group to be working with and I did everything I could to rise to their level. Maggie Lockwood, famous from her *Wicked Lady* days and now at the height of her theatrical powers, sailed confidently through the rehearsals, setting us all a great example with her concentration and attention to detail; Michael and Dulcie were as polite and charmingly helpful as always; Roger and Ursula were sweet; and little Perlita, who had merited such acclaim for her portrayal of Anne in *The Diary of Anne Frank*, and who was a stickler for perfection of diction and movement, kept a watchful eye on my progress and helped me enormously to improve my voice production.

Before we started on our first read-through together, James Roose-Evans gave us quite a lengthy lecture on late-Victorian mannerisms and speech characteristics. From the beginning he insisted that we should over-enunciate our words, hitting the consonants hard and pronouncing the vowels to perfection so that, as the rehearsals went on, we would naturally fall into the clarity and slight exaggeration of the way of talking in the era of Wilde's play. Even our walking, posture, sitting and rising, James detailed that we should perfect in exact period style. (The ladies all wore long, heavy rehearsal skirts in order to practise the manipulation of their costume trains, especially when turning, sitting or mounting stairs.) All this I managed to do with some extra help from James, but I realised that, though my speech was quite correct, I was still not projecting my voice properly. I felt that I was shouting, when in fact my volume was several decibels below that of the others. I had lost the knack of placing my voice, storing breath with my diaphragm and choosing the right moments to inhale during long speeches without interrupting the flow of dialogue. That would come in time, I hoped.

Apart from the actual work, two things I remember from those weeks: first, I began to realise that my arms were not long enough to hold my script so that I could read the lines, so at last I had to admit defeat and visit an eye specialist for spectacles; second, every day Margaret wore the same headgear, a curious little black kind of woollen balaclava helmet, which I suppose obviated the need to have her greying hair done frequently. Twelve years later, when I was again rehearsing a play with her, she still wore the little helmet.

Margaret was a very private person. Always friendly and ready to break into a ribald, uninhibited guffaw of laughter when something amused her, she yet kept herself very much to herself, and even after working with her for nearly eighteen months I never really knew her or could count her as a chum. Even on tour when we might occupy the same hotels, we never shared a table or even had coffee together. In a way I was glad of this since I too like my privacy, especially when I am doing my daily crossword puzzle. Margaret tackled *The Times*, while I did the slightly easier *Daily Telegraph* puzzle, but I reckoned that she cheated because she always had a dictionary with her.

Rehearsals completed, we opened our ten-week tour at The Opera House, Manchester, one of the biggest theatres in Britain. Every seat in the house had been sold out for the entire week, and at our dress rehearsal I realised what a glittering, sumptuous production we were in. Anthony Holland's sets were quite gorgeous, as were the costumes. The pre-production costs must have been enormous, and the weekly break-figure tremendous with that power-packed cast. Later I was to understand Peter Bridge's strategy and the underlying reasons for his confidence in the success of his brave venture. As the pre-London tour progressed I began to realise what the provincial theatre – then in a pretty parlous state – needed to bring back the public: good plays, whether revivals or new works, good sets and, above all, star players who could put bums on seats. By the mid-sixties, with the competition of television, provincial theatres had become pretty shabby and audiences had grown sick of a series of tatty touring companies. It was Peter Bridge's courage that helped to start the revitalisation of provincial theatre. Touring had become almost a dirty word in theatrical circles, and most plays destined for a West End opening played a maximum of two or three weeks outside London, just to run-in the production. If the play was a success in London, then it would probably go on a more extensive tour with a second-eleven cast. Thus the people of Newcastle, Leeds, Glasgow or Aberdeen, for example, rarely got the chance to view an original West End show.

In addition actors were not easily persuaded to leave London for longish periods. The senior players found the rigours of touring unattractive (wasn't it Dame Edith Evans who once grandly said, 'God has been kind to me. He never took me on tour'?) and the younger ones preferred to sit on their backsides in London hoping for a lucrative 'telly' to turn up.

Peter and his backers, Howard and Wyndham – owners of many of the theatres we visited and of the Strand Theatre which was to become our eventual home – staked a great deal on their long tour of the costly *An Ideal Husband.*

I shall never forget that first night in Manchester. As I stood absolutely terrified waiting for my first entrance, sweating profusely, my hands shaking and my throat and mouth parched, I involuntarily thought for a moment, Christ! What am I doing this for? I had heard the applause which had greeted all the others as they appeared before the packed house, but it never occurred to me that I would get any sort of prolonged ovation. As a result, when I walked across the stage and spoke my first line, it went totally unheard, so I had to repeat it. Not the classiest way to start my performance! However, as the play progressed I gradually unwound and managed to stagger through without any major disasters. True, I did sometimes tread on the huge volumes of laughter which greeted some of Lord Goring's famous witty lines. I was often surprised that I had done more than provoke a mild titter. But then, after my long lay-off from live theatre, I had totally lost my sense of timing and reaction. I just wanted to plough on and get through my first night as fast as I could. The refinements would, I hoped, follow later.

The reception at the end was staggering: the applause went on and on as curtain followed curtain. Our party at the Midland Hotel afterwards was a real celebration and Peter hugged each one of us delightedly. The press gave the show rave reviews and were even quite kind to me, rather to my surprise and much to my relief. The cool, self-confident Maggie was universally eulogised.

On the Saturday, when we had a gap of only half an hour between first and second houses, it proved quite impossible to get 2,000 people away from the theatre after the first performance and another 2,000 into their seats – plus 400 that the police allowed in to stand round the back of the stalls and circles – for the second show. We opened nearly an hour late.

As the tour progressed as far north as Aberdeen and down south to Bournemouth, I did improve my performance and timing and regained a lot of my confidence. I also worked hard on my voice production with the help and insistence of dear Perlita, who came to my dressing room every night for five minutes to put me through a series of voice and diaphragm exercises.

We all evolved our *modus vivendi* as we were on the road. The Denisons and the Liveseys played a lot of golf together, while Margaret kept herself very private as always. I played some golf occasionally and even got a day's deer-stalking near Braemar while we were in Aberdeen, but usually I went off by car and explored the countryside. I had a series of comfortable suites in the main hotels and habitually ate in the best restaurants – something I could not afford to do today. The best I could do now would be a single room and meals at some little Italian trattoria.

Finally, the big test arrived: we opened at the Strand Theatre in London on 16 December, after a tour which had been an enormous success: packed houses everywhere, with never a seat unsold, vociferous receptions and a lyrical press. Peter told me that when we opened in London we were already £50,000 in profit, a huge sum in those days, especially when most shows needed months in London before they even recovered their costs. Since I was on a very generous salary and royalty, it had also been a lucrative ten weeks for me.

But now at the Strand we were to enter the literary lions' den. The advance bookings were staggering and we were assured of a successful few months ahead, but still we craved what all impresarios, producers, directors and actors crave: good reviews. In the event we were not disappointed, for the press raved about the show and even I came in for a share of the eulogies.

To quote a few:

J. C. Trewin wrote: 'Wilde is himself, with his faults and his felicities; and in *An Ideal Husband*. as James Roose-Evans has directed it, with propriety, understanding, and care for the period rhythms, we get the true dramatist. I repeat, this is, in Anthony Holland's settings, full-scale theatre with a company to match . . . there are Richard Todd to propel the epigrams of Lord Goring, probably Wilde as he liked to be thought of himself . . .'

Harold Hobson said: '. . . and Richard Todd managed to reveal to us the evident truth that Lord Goring is one of the most dazzling roles in theatrical history.'

W. A. Darlington wrote in the *Daily Telegraph*: 'Quite apart from the story, the evening is full of delights. It is an orgy of style and elegance of which we have been too long starved. Anthony Holland's decor and dresses are magnificent and together with Wilde's language seem to inspire the whole company to speak well and be heard.

'There is a big cast, with no weak links in it that I discerned.'

Milton Shulman thought that 'Wilde's brittle, mocking, pungent wit has lost little of its sharpness over the years. Richard Todd, as the indolent Lord Goring, is handed most of these gems and he keeps them sparkling nicely.'

Most of the superlatives were reserved for Margaret Lockwood's performance, and Perlita Neilson came in for a lot of praise.

Mind you, I caught a few brickbats as well. The best, I believe, was in the *Jewish Chronicle*: 'Richard Todd has about as much grace as a gumboot.' Oscar Wilde would have been proud of that line!

So I had done it – I had taken the plunge and come up safely for air. Now all I wanted to do was to keep swimming. The smell of the greasepaint (I had bought myself an elaborate new make-up box) had hooked me again, and I was once more caught in the act.

How's that for mixed metaphors?

My relief knew no bounds. It seemed that a whole new world had been opened up for me, thanks to Peter Bridge and Oscar Wilde.

29

Moving Moments

An Ideal Husband steered a triumphant course at the Strand Theatre for seven months, greatly adding to its profits – and mine, too.

I had also improved my stagecraft and theatre technique. The longer the play ran, the more comfortable and confident I felt in my role as Lord Goring. I had taken a course of lessons in voice production from a well-known coach, Mrs Wilmer, and soon I was trumpeting loud and clear to the back of the circle without any effort or 'pushing'. Much of her teaching was based on relaxation, and the beginning of each session found me feeling faintly ridiculous as I lay flat on my back on the floor while being exhorted to let my back, arms and feet sink into the carpet.

By August I had worked for nearly a year without a break, including the rehearsal period, the tour and the London run, and I was not alone in feeling pretty jaded. To my surprise, Peter Bridge agreed that I should have a holiday, but he felt that he could not run the show for a couple of weeks with an understudy in my place. Therefore he decided to close the show for a fortnight and give everybody a much-needed rest. Holiday payments meant that no one would be a loser, except the theatre itself. Despite the substantial profits which the Strand had made over the seven-month period, the owners refused to agree that the theatre should go dark for two weeks. So, with his typical courage, confidence and thoughtfulness for others, Peter said in effect, 'Right! We'll close and find another theatre.' And this at the height of the London season!

Thus it was that *An Ideal Husband* became peripatetic. After a nice two-week holiday – mine spent in Ibiza with the family – we reassembled for a few days' rehearsal and then went to the Piccadilly Theatre for a three-month season. We opened on a Saturday to a sold-out house and continued to fill our new home for twelve weeks; the time limit was imposed because the Piccadilly was due to close while the stage was being rebuilt for a forthcoming production of *Man of La Mancha*.

Not in the least put out, Peter Bridge organised another short tour starting at the end of October – during which we even revisited some of our previous dates, including Liverpool, and were hugely successful – before bringing us back to the Garrick Theatre in London for another season.

For the reopening at the Piccadilly, Michael and Dulcie had decided to drop out, and their places were taken by Michael Goodliffe and the lovely, elegant Rachel Gurney; at the Garrick we opened with Raymond Huntley and Joyce Carey in place of Roger and Ursula. That sweet woman, Joyce, was a particular success as Lady Markby, her performance delivered in a ringing, beautifully spoken style that delighted her audiences.

While *An Ideal Husband* was on the move, so were the Todds.

The tensions between Kitty and myself had been increasing, so we decided to move home and try again on fresh ground. Peter was now entering his second year at Eton and Fiona had got used to her prep school, Great Oaks, so they were both well settled.

We spent weekends scouring around looking for suitable houses and put Haileywood on the market. Paul Rosewarne found a buyer almost immediately, a Mr van Zwannenberg, so we had to hurry our search.

Luckily, as we drove into the courtyard of a house in Bampton, a beautiful Cotswold stone village not far from Oxford, we both felt instinctively that we had found our ideal.

The Grange was one of the most beautiful houses I had ever seen. Approaching from the main Oxford road, as we did, one had only a back-to-front impression of the place. First, a long, high stone wall along the roadside shielded the grounds from view; then the house itself, with very few windows opening on to the main village street, presented a massive and almost gloomy rear elevation to the passer-by, its ashlar stone walls part-creepered. At the end of the house, a single-storey barrel-vaulted gatehouse archway with hefty wrought-iron gates gave a tantalising glimpse of the cobbled courtyard and more stone walling.

Once inside that courtyard, the full glory was revealed. To the left lay the west end of the house and the canopied front door. To the south was another stone wall with an iron gate leading to the garden, and a pretty two-storey garden house with stone steps leading up to the top floor. This in turn abutted on to the blank stone east end of a fair-sized dwelling which had once been the dower house, and another short length of very high wall which formed a back-drop to a large and beautiful magnolia tree. The fourth side of the square was completed by a low staff cottage building which ran from the archway entrance.

Against the walls on two sides were little fountains emptying into lovely old lead troughs, each surrounded by carved stone frames.

As we drove in one summer evening it was a place of peaceful enchantment, its creamy Cotswold stone bathed in golden light. I wanted it, and Kitty too was spellbound.

The owners, Major and Mrs Scott, made us charmingly welcome. He had recently retired from the mastership of the Old Berks Hunt after being severely injured in a car accident in London. They had also been badly hit by one of the Pacific hurricanes which, as members of Lloyds, had rather dented their income. Therefore they had decided to convert the stables and coach-houses, about two hundred yards from the house, into a home for themselves, and sell the main house and grounds.

The interior was as enchanting as the exterior, with some lovely ceiling plasterwork and a large main hall with great stone-framed windows looking on to the grounds. It was a largish house, with six main bedrooms and five bathrooms, plus a small second floor with three staff bedrooms and a bathroom, and I realised that once the sale agreement had been reached, there was a lot which would need to be done before we moved in.

Furthermore, if I was not to lose the sale of Haileywood there were only six weeks to get everything completed, including redecoration, total rewiring and some plumbing. Fortunately the main structure and the gorgeous tumble of Cotswold stone roofing were very sound.

For once in my life I had a really bright idea. I approached a firm of quantity surveyors who agreed to second one of their qualified juniors to me, part-time. The very next day this young man went over the house with us, transforming everything that we wanted done into builders' jargon. Advising us that no one firm could do all the work within the specified time limit, he then set about obtaining estimates for us from a number of building companies, plumbers and electricians. In a few days he had sifted these through and recommended those we should accept.

Soon the house was crawling with workmen and specialists, and a great spirit of friendly rivalry pervaded the place. Each week our surveyor spent a day inspecting the work done and approving the applications for stage-payments. Such was the air of competition that, if one firm appeared to be lagging, a cautionary word from the surveyor and the offending foreman was likely to say, 'Right! I'll have another couple of men here tomorrow.'

As a kind of clerk of works, that surveyor made the whole thing possible and probably saved me thousands. Unlike an architect, whose fees would have been based on the total costs, he worked for a very moderate set charge – in the hundreds. My Polyhomes training had certainly paid off in this cost- and time-cutting exercise!

The grounds of the Grange were really lovely, but had been neglected. However the great Bigsby, who was coming to join us at Bampton, reckoned that with part-time help he could restore them to their full beauty. I had bought the adjoining Briar Cottage for him and Mrs Bigsby.

There were some five acres of formal garden, with the main lawn sweeping from the house down to the remains of a lake and small spring-fed trout hatchery. The lake was choked with reeds and we only realised that there was a fair depth of water still there when Dash plunged in one day and put up a brace of mallard duck.

One side of the main lawn area was bordered by a nice mixed and colourful deciduous wood of varied trees, and the other by two interconnecting walled gardens enclosed by huge stone walls each with splendid wrought-iron gates between pillars capped by large ball finials. The first court contained a big swimming-pool with a charming Georgian garden room in one corner, and the second was the vegetable garden. This in turn opened on to a lawned square which had once been a bowling green, but which we were to use as a croquet lawn, and beyond this was the hard tennis court and then an orchard.

Beyond the lake lay a ten-acre paddock intersected by a trout-bearing stream along which I had some 400 yards of double-bank fishing.

I no longer had the farms, and our only stock would be the laying-hens which Bigsby insisted we should bring from Haileywood. He would no longer be a part-time keeper with pheasants to rear, but he enthusiastically proclaimed himself to be my water-bailiff, and kept us supplied with trout as he spent his evenings fishing our little stretch of water.

When the time came for us to move to Bampton I had few regrets about quitting Haileywood. My heart had gone out of the place when the farmland went – and we were taking over a really beautiful house in lovely mini-estate grounds.

The garden front of the house was glorious, and seen from the lake and lawns – with their lovely trees including a great cedar, some chestnuts and a huge, gorgeous magnolia – it sprawled in a series of asymmetrical heights and elevations part Jacobean, part Georgian and part with Victorian additions, including a loggia on the left around the drawing-room garden front. The Georgian wing was on the right, the whole of its ground floor containing a magnificent book-lined library with a fine plaster-decorated and coved ceiling, while above it was a spare bedroom suite. This ceiling presented a problem: originally painted in blues, reds, greens and golds by craftsmen reputedly brought over from Italy, it was now pretty faded and shabby. I felt that it needed lightening and repainting, but I certainly could not bring painters over from Italy. None of the building firms thought that they could cope with it, but I had another of my rare flashes of ingenuity: I contacted a firm of sign-writers and they agreed that they could do the job. So for a week two men lay on their backs on planks stretched between high step-ladders and picked out the delicate plaster mouldings in shades of brilliant white against a background of off-white, with here and there light touches of gold. The finished effect was very pretty and light.

While Haileywood was being stripped we kennelled all the dogs near Bampton, and I visited them whenever I could. The owner of the boarding kennel told me that she always knew when I was coming about twenty minutes before I got there. At these times, Baron II became very restless and excited and could hardly be handled. Somehow, some canine instinct told him that I was on the way.

The final move in late October went very smoothly and included several lorry-loads of garden machinery, hen housing and logs from our demolished Haileywood orchard. Dunant, Marcella and Irene came with us. Dunant had been loath to move so far from London (where his only close relative lived near Heathrow Airport), but he loyally agreed to stay with us for a year in our new home. Queenie's home at Faringdon was now only six miles away, so within a week or so the household routine was back to normal.

This had all been achieved during the second short tour of *An Ideal Husband* and just before we moved to the Garrick Theatre for our third London season. All I hoped now was that the children would enjoy a happy Christmas holiday in their new home. We had every reason to be happy there, despite the widening gulf between Kitty and myself. I am intrinsically a home-lover, and there could be no more idyllic home than The Grange.

It was quite a wrench for me when *An Ideal Husband* finally closed after its nomadic fifteen-month run. As a return to the live theatre I could not have dreamed of a more propitious re-entry than Peter Bridge's production. I had been very lucky indeed, and my cautious wait for the right vehicle had been amply justified.

Perhaps my treasured hand-written note from Peter Bridge on the last night at the Garrick best epitomises all that this period had done for me:

I will *never* tire of thanking you, my *dear* Dickie, for being such a really wonderful part of my life for this long and magnificent run. You have been *the* perfect star and I am so delighted that you have found that the Theatre is not so bad as all that!!
Longing to have you with us again. Bless you – as always.

Most affectionately,
Peter.

Within a week of *An Ideal Husband* closing at the Garrick Theatre on 21 January, 1967, I was lunching at the BBC to discuss a TV play with Peter Hammond, one of their brightest young directors. Since the mad scramble of *Wuthering Heights* years before, I had not been too keen to launch into another TV play, and in fact had done very little on the small screen.

However the subject we discussed – *Edmund Gurney and the Brighton Mesmerist*, part of a trilogy of subjects based on occult themes called *Men and Magic* by the author Ken Taylor – was alluring. It was based on the true story of a believer in occult spirits who became totally enslaved by his spiritual beliefs, only to discover that his colleagues were imposters bent on fraud. Gurney, an honest and sincere man who was a founder-member and secretary of the Psychical Research Society at the turn of the century, found his own spirit broken by the perfidious cynicism of his collaborators and the malpractices of those whom he had trusted, and committed suicide in the Royal Albion Hotel in Brighton. I found it a compelling and fascinating story, well-crafted by the author, and the complex character of Edmund Gurney was a challenge that I relished. I had never really considered spiritualism in any form before, but during the rehearsals and readings for the play, and with the documentation available, I caught myself thinking about it a great deal.

I agreed to do the play and joined a splendid cast which included Diana Napier as my wife, and my old friend Lynda Baron as one of the conspirators.

We started filming parts of the story at Lime Grove Studios, then went to Brighton for three days to do the exterior scenes. We did not stay at the Royal Albion Hotel, I might add, although years later I stayed there when on theatre tours which included Brighton. It gave me an eerie feeling, remembering Edmund Gurney.

Work on the *The Brighton Mesmerist* lasted a month, and culminated in the actual recording at the BBC TV Centre after a horrendous day of chaotic technical rehearsal, something which seemed the norm from my limited experience of TV dramas. At 11.30 pm we finally finished and guzzled a much-delayed supper meal.

However, I was glad I had done the show. I enjoyed working with Peter Hammond and found Gurney an absorbing, tortured character to play. When the programme was finally screened in October it received considerable critical acclaim.

At that time I had also found a new and very satisfying interest: Guide Dogs for the Blind. It all came about when I was driving home one evening and passed a blind man precariously fumbling and tapping his way along a narrow, high-banked country lane. I stopped and gave him a lift into Reading, where he told me he was taking train to the Guide Dog Training Centre at Leamington Spa to meet and work with his first guide dog. He was so excited at the prospect of a new, more mobile life.

About three weeks later I was travelling along that same road when I passed the same man, now stepping out confidently and briskly with his new 'eyes', a yellow Labrador. I stopped and had a word with him, and it was then that an idea came to me . . .

I had been the focal point of 'The Richard Todd Fan Club' for years, and I never ceased to be amazed at the enthusiasm and loyalty of its several thousand members, many of whom kept in touch with fellow fans all over Britain and America. When my contract with ABPC had ended, I no longer had the facilities to print and issue the club magazine, but still various members sent out little news-letters of their own accord. I reckoned I was by now past this sort of activity, and that it was a bit silly keeping up an association with people who had started as starstruck teenagers and now had families of their own. Then the thought occurred to me: why not have the club serve some useful purpose? So Queenie and I sent out sheaves of letters asking the various regional prime-movers to persuade their fellow-members, past and present, to collect for Guide Dogs for the Blind. The idea worked, and for the next couple of years donations arrived steadily. We were also helped by a contact of Queenie's who was a member of the Greyhound Racing Association. He organised special races at meetings as far apart as London, Reading and Portsmouth where collections were made and racing proceeds donated to the charity. Within two years the Richard Todd Fan Club had been able to pay for the purchase and training of five dogs. I spent a very moving day at Leamington Spa, seeing the dozens of dogs being trained and the joy on the faces of the recipients as they met their new friends, and to this day I have a little silver statuette of a guide dog with a plaque thanking the Club.

That spring my business affairs were in considerable disarray. The Dairy Company, which had been lavishly expanded and now had a fleet of purpose-built refrigerated lorries plying all over the south of England selling not only creams and sausages but cheese and yogurts, seemed to have outstretched its resources. At a time when its new controller was on some trade mission to China, I was suddenly and urgently requested to put up a bank guarantee to cover borrowings. Stebbings and I agreed that I should resign as chairman as I had really no say in the company's affairs and knew very little about its activities or financial stability. I subsequently discovered that my shareholding had been watered down to virtually nothing by deals of which I had no knowledge.

I was sadder still when the parent company of Polyhomes, Cityfield, and its associated companies went into receivership, caught by the sudden government-inspired credit squeeze which hit so many businesses in 1967.

To cap it all, investments I had made in 1966 and 1967 in timber plantations in Australia, which had promised rich dividends, turned out years later to have been a gigantic fraud. Obviously I was going to have to rely for my future security on the one thing over which I had some degree of control – acting. And even that had not proved to be the most rock-sound of professions in recent years.

With all this troubling me, and with my continuing marital problems, I was not in the most buoyant of moods in the spring of 1967, and was glad to get a welcome two-week break with the family in Ibiza for the Easter holidays.

A few days later I was a guest at a dinner of the Building Society Association in Reading when Kitty phoned to say that there had been a panic call from John Redway in Hollywood. John, who was temporarily my agent, had been approached by Sam Katzman, a leading independent American producer, to see if I would star in a controversial film, *The Love-Ins*, about to start almost immediately. I got home at about 2 am and immediately phoned John, who advised me that I might not like the subject but that he thought it was worth doing.

When Katzman himself called me a few minutes later, his description of the story absolutely flabbergasted me. It was all about the new cult of flower-power and hippiedom which had hit America in a big way, emanating mainly from the Haight-Asbury district of San Francisco.

Drug- and LSD-orientated, from what he told me, the whole movement seemed to me a ghastly sham which opted out of everything on the spurious trip-taking grounds of living at peace. I simply could not believe his descriptions of the flower-children and their mass love-ins, nor the dreadful effects on their minds and bodies. In Britain we had as yet only a hazy idea of this hideous cult.

'Right,' said Sam, 'I'm prepared to fly you up to San Francisco so that you can see for yourself what's going on. Or better still, come out to Hollywood, talk to the director and scriptwriter and look at the footage of film we have already shot in San Francisco. If you still don't want to make the film, we'll fly you home again.'

It was an agonising decision for me to take. I could only visualise the setting and content of the film as being vaguely pornographic and certainly sleazy, and this at a time when there was still some self-censorship practised by even the most sensational of movie-makers.

Nevertheless, from what John Redway and Sam Katzman had already told me, there was a useful message to be put over by *The Love-Ins*. Besides, I wanted to work in Hollywood again and the salary would compensate for some of the losses I had recently incurred.

In the event I was flying to Los Angeles within 48 hours, and went straight into day-long discussions with Katzman, the director Arthur Dreifuss and Hal Collins, the roly-poly screenwriter whom I immediately dubbed 'Twiggy'. I also saw some amazing documentary scenes shot in San Francisco, which convinced me that all that I had been told about hippies and flower-children was no myth. Straight away I agreed to make the film.

Perhaps my decision was justified by a subsequent quote from *The Hollywood Reporter*, the leading trade paper in America:

What distinguishes the film is not the budgetary resource of exploitation film-making, but the evidence of morally responsible and dramatically sound pre-planning. If the film does not accomplish its intentions with an important dramatic result, it is still a very good, possibly even valuable, film. Because Sam Katzman's films make money, because *The Love-Ins* will reach a large audience to whom the questions raised by the film are relevant, because it will not brutalise them by the kicks of violence, it is Katzman's best film. For that he is beholden to Arthur Dreifuss' exceptional direction and to Hal Collins, who collaborated with Dreifuss on the screenplay.

The Love-Ins was quite the most extraordinary and disturbing film I have ever been in. I played the part of a university professor who starts out as a champion of freedom, particularly among young people and especially his own students. Angered by the dismissal of two students who edit and publish an underground newspaper, he resigns his position and enters into their world, partly out of frustration with the ordinary values of life, partly because he is regarded as a hero. He becomes their leader, advocating the unrestricted use of LSD and marijuana as the way to achieve freedom of thought and behaviour. But no one can stand adulation for long, and the corrupting influences begin. He becomes corrupt himself, a prophet for profit.

The young actors in the picture were splendid, especially Susan Oliver of Peyton Place fame and James MacArthur, the son of the great Helen Hayes. Jimmy gave a solid performance as the dismissed editor who, after an earlier period as one of his professor's most ardent disciples, gradually begins to see through the sham of the leader's teachings, especially when his own girl-friend, Susan Oliver – by now besotted with her hero – becomes pregnant and is persuaded to get rid of the baby lest the affair should ruin his crusading image. Finally, he shoots the prophet of hedonism at a large rally, but instantly realises that he has provided the martyrdom needed to keep the movement alive.

Susan Oliver was agonisingly convincing during a sequence where she goes on a very far-out LSD trip and dances through an Alice in Wonderland fantasy accompanied by frenzied rock bands.

Katzman made the film for Columbia release but we shot it in the MGM Studios, then standing almost idle. Arthur Dreifuss, one of the old school of skilled director-writers, was splendid to work with; he had started life in Germany, graduated in music from Columbia University Conservatory of Music and had been a child prodigy as a pianist and conductor. He had then gone on to choreograph and produce Broadway musicals before going to Hollywood as a director/producer/writer.

Some sixty hippies had been brought from San Francisco to give an authentic atmosphere to many of the scenes. Filthy and constantly semi-dazed, they couldn't believe their luck at actually being paid to do their own particular thing. Arriving with their bedding rolls, they were perfectly happy to squat in an empty building provided for them. There was some police supervision, but in general the authorities turned a blind eye to the behaviour of our extras. The air was pervaded by the pungent fumes of pot.

The more the story unfolded and the more I saw of these hapless creatures, the more I was appalled by the destructive influence of this ghastly new cult. I was seeing at first hand the effects of these drugs, and they were terrifying. I was sure that our film was right in being an exposé of the whole dreadful movement, and that it would do some good in bringing it to the notice of the public, especially the young people. Certainly it would do nothing to attract anybody to flower-power.

I made a point of trying to talk to some of the young hippies, and some of the things I heard made my hackles rise. When they weren't just mumbling in a daze, they were mostly totally inarticulate. The only thing that seemed to bring a semblance of life into their features and their bodies was blaring pop music. A lot of the blame must lie with those little brats in the pop music world. They have a great following and a great responsibility – a moral obligation, in fact, because all the kids ape what they do, and if they don't set an example then they should be made an example of.

I lived at the Beverly Hills Hotel for six weeks while shooting *The Love-Ins* and was glad to get home to a clean atmosphere each evening and to revisit some of my old friends and haunts.

One such reunion was a sad one for me, however. Harry Baum, my old friend and stand-in, had phoned to say that he could not be with me on the film, but I did not realise why until he called to take me out to supper one evening. I had suggested one of my favourite restaurants, but he asked if I would mind if we went to one that he particularly liked.

At the due time I was waiting by the door when a sleek black Cadillac rolled up. Knowing Harry's predilection for owning one of the most eye-catching cars in town, I thought it might be his, but I did not recognise the driver – a distinguished-looking white-bearded old gentleman. Then the doorman opened the boot and took out a folding wheel-chair. With great difficulty the handicapped driver was gradually eased out of the car and transferred to the chair. As he propelled himself up the special ramp alongside the entrance steps, I suddenly realised it was Harry. Dreadfully crippled by an acute form of arthritis and with specially-made large, soft boots and white silk gloves covering cruelly swollen feet and hands, only his smiling, sweet face was recognisable to me, even with its camouflage of well-trimmed goatee beard. It was lovely to see him again, despite the agony of his affliction. I also realised why we were going to a particular restaurant of his choice – it, too, had a ramp for his wheelchair and widely-spaced tables. Sadly, Harry died the following year.

Although *The Love-Ins* had been fascinating to make, I was not sorry when my work on it was done. My return to England was delayed by a further two weeks because I had agreed to star with Olivia de Haviland in a TV film, *The Last Hunter*, the story of a British agent who is tracking down a Nazi war criminal and finally manages to discover the whereabouts of one of his victims, played by Olivia. The chance to work with this famous actress was more than I could resist, and she proved to be as charming and talented as I had always imagined. The only time we had met before was in 1950, when she presented me with my Hollywood Golden Globe Award. She was as beautiful as ever.

Finally I set out for London at the end of June. Things had been happening during my absence. Our poor little pug Crumpet, Biscuit's daughter, had died of a heart attack. And Peter had had an emergency operation for appendicitis in the sanatorium at Eton. All had gone well and he met me on my arrival at London Airport, looking fit.

Although *The Love-Ins* had a mixed critical reception in America, it did good business and caused a considerable stir amongst its audiences. But it was refused a certificate by the British Board of Film Censors, and so was never seen here. Nowadays it would be considered quite tame. When I spoke about it to John Trevelyan, the chairman of the Board, he explained that they had considered it to be a good film but were afraid that it might give rise to an unhealthy trend in this country, where people had never even heard of the flower children.

A month or so later, the first-ever British love-in was held at Woburn Abbey, and attracted thousands! Perhaps if they had seen the film they would have thought better of joining in the dangerous cult.

We soon had the children home for their summer holidays and enjoyed a couple of weeks at home during a spell of gorgeous weather swimming in the pool, playing tennis and whacking the croquet balls around by floodlight after dinner. This game became quite a fetish with Peter and me, and we played until well after his proper bed-time.

I still had to go to London for occasional meetings with George Willoughby as we struggled to get one or other of our projects off the ground.

Then Peter Bridge, good as his word, suddenly turned up with a proposition for another theatre production. This was to be Dodie Smith's *Dear Octopus*. I read and loved this gentle, nostalgic play which had been such a huge success in the late 1930s with Marie Tempest, Leon Quartermaine and John Gielgud. I at once agreed to play Nicholas, the Gielgud part, and it was arranged that Peter should cast the play ready for rehearsals in late August after I had spent my annual holiday in Ibiza with the family. Knowing him, I was sure that he would come up with something special in his casting – and he did.

Before I went off on holiday I bought a consignment of trout finger-lings for the lake, which Bigsby had by now cleaned out by hand and much hard work with the help of his young second gardener. He had left a couple of little islands where waterhen had brought off their clutches of chicks; I could sit for hours watching the busy little mothers shepherding their broods of squeakers.

Ibiza was as lovely as ever, though getting more and more commer-cialised. We were disturbed to see the foundations of another block of flats going up between us and the sea, and hoped that it would not affect our view. One evening I took Peter out by himself for supper, and as we walked back we became aware of the sound of marvellous flamenco guitar music coming from somewhere near our flat. Eventually we discovered that it was coming from inside the wooden palings sur-rounding the new building site, so we found an entrance in the darkness and were led by the sound to a little workmen's hut. When we peeped in through the bead curtaining we could see a group of some ten or twelve people, including three girls who were swirling around in a gypsy dance. They caught sight of us and we were invited in and each given a bottle of wine; then they continued their music and dancing. Three or four of the men took it in turns with the guitars, stopping every now and then when an older man seemed to find some fault in their playing; he would then demonstrate how the passage should be played. One of them, a handsome young Spaniard, spoke English and had been working in America until he came home to marry. He explained that they were all one family of brothers, sisters, husbands and wives; his wife was one of the three girls, all sisters and all extremely beautiful. Their mentor was Pepe Escudero, the most famous guitar *aficionado* on the island.

We sat there entranced by the music and dancing for hours, and managed to creep into our flat without waking anybody. It had been a memorable experience.

After three weeks I left Ibiza and the family to continue their holiday, and was met at Heathrow by Dunant. Rehearsals for *Dear Octopus* started the next day.

What a company Peter Bridge had gathered together! Our director was Frith Banbury; no finer or more sensitive and hugely experienced man of the theatre have I ever met, nor one better suited to direct this charming old play. And my colleagues were to include Cicely Courtneidge, Jack Hulbert, Lally Bowers, Dorothy Primrose, Ursula

Howells, Geoffrey Kenton, Janine Miller, Christopher Reynolds, Nicola Novello, Valerie White, Cyril Wheeler, Constance Lorne, Dorothy Batley and my dear Joyce Carey and Perlita Neilson. Even Dodie Smith could not have wished for a more notable ensemble for the revival of her play.

To those who have never seen *Dear Octopus* I would find it almost impossible to describe the play. There is no plot as such, no story line, simply the gathering of a wealthy family brought together in their childhood home – the sons, daughters and grandchildren of a couple celebrating their Golden Wedding. They have all gone their separate ways and now find themselves enveloped once more in the tentacles of the one thing they have in common: the family, with all its memories and nostalgia, some of which they have resented and some that they have missed. The setting is in a fine old house, full of good antiques, fine silver and cut glass, while in the nursery a rocking-horse, discarded teddy bears and toys litter a room undisturbed for years. It is all redolent of a past brought to life by the artistry of a writer who was a master of her craft, and who developed her characters with unerring insight.

The final scene is the lavish dinner party where the whole family are at table. Having laid bare their hopes, disappointments, bitterness or complacency in their conversation, they have ultimately come together to honour their parents. The toast which – as Nicholas, the bachelor eldest son – I had to deliver is to 'The Family', and sums up what the play is all about: the unifying force in all their lives. My final line is, 'Here's to the family, that dear octopus from whose tentacles we are never quite able to escape, nor, in our inmost hearts, do we wish to do so.'

One newspaper review described it thus:

Richard Todd, as the son, Nicholas Randolph, lived up to all expectations. The effervescence of his acting youth seems to be ever-present. And even for those who had seen the play many times, it was a heart-touching moment when he proposed to his mother's 'companion', pretty Grace Fenning, played by Perlita Neilson. Last night everyone gave a splendid performance. To single out various actors is like plucking out the best petals in a beautiful rose.

Such was the team-work of a marvellous cast.

Rehearsals were a joy to attend as Frith moulded us all together.

Even Dodie Smith expressed herself as being thrilled when she attended one of the run-throughs.

My spirits were further lifted by the news that Peter had passed nine O-levels at Eton.

During this period I lived alone at the flat, except at weekends, while Queenie and Dunant saw that all was well at the Grange for the return of the family from Ibiza.

We embarked on our twelve-week pre-London tour in Edinburgh in mid-September. Our opening night at the King's Theatre was greeted by a rapturous audience and splendid reviews, which set the pattern for the entire tour, with weeks in Glasgow, Aberdeen, Liverpool and Leeds. My spare time was mostly spent touring the Highlands and the Lake District in the glorious autumn weather and looking up various friends.

Then in Newcastle at the end of October near-tragedy struck. Cis and Jack were always meticulous in the care they took to be at the theatre hours in advance of curtain-up time, and on the final Saturday at the Theatre Royal they arrived to find the entire building still in darkness. Feeling their way through corridors to their dressing rooms, Jack stumbled down some steps and fell, breaking three ribs. Anyone who has suffered this kind of injury knows how intensely painful it can be, making movement and even breathing agonising. In any other profession the victim would have at once retired to bed and rested for at least a week, especially if he was a man in his seventies. But not so that great old trouper, Jack.

A doctor was called, Jack was strapped up and sedated, and went through the two Saturday performances in dreadful discomfort. He couldn't move and played all his scenes from a chair, speaking with great difficulty, while the rest of us adjusted our movements around him. But the show went on.

Following the final performance, an ambulance took him to the station where he was stretchered into a sleeping berth on the night train to London. After a day at home there, he duly turned up on the Monday at our next date in Oxford. He never missed a performance and within a couple of weeks was back to normal. During all this, Cis never faltered.

They were an exemplary pair of great professionals. I have never known their like. It had been an inspired piece of casting by Peter Bridge to engage Cicely Courtneidge to play the imperious, sharp-tongued but witty and warm matriarch of the family. This she did brilliantly, suppressing all her natural exuberance and proving what a superb actress she was, bringing to the part a great depth of sympathy and understanding of her varied brood, very touching and emotionally moving at moments and never overdoing her comedy lines.

One endearing little habit – born of years as the star of so many musical comedies – she was never quite able totally to discard: on her first entrance she could not resist acknowledging with a little nod of her head the loud applause that invariably greeted her – not the usual form in a straight play. Despite the excellence of the rest of the cast, Cis was the star of the play.

She was a glutton for work and hated to be idle. On tour she was always generous and motherly to all the younger members of the company, regularly taking them out for lunch or supper. Where most actors travelled with their theatre necessities in one suitcase, she shipped around a huge pannier stuffed with ornaments, photos and table-covers, so that her dressing room always looked like a cosy boudoir.

Both on tour and in London, a nightly ritual took place: within ten minutes of curtain-down she would appear at her dressing-room door and emit a stentorian bellow:

'Jack!'

'Yes, darling.'

'Taxi's here!'

'Coming, darling.'

We all knew that the easygoing Jack had not yet even got into his trousers.

We were playing at Bournemouth when Peter Bridge arrived with the great news that we were to open in London during the first week of December at the Theatre Royal, Haymarket. We were all thrilled, even though we would only be at the Haymarket for a short season until February, as the theatre was already booked for another production.

The play received universally marvellous reviews in London. Without going into detail, I quote some of the headlines in the national newspapers: ' "Dear Octopus": a golden wedding in a golden glow'; 'Sentimental – and irresistible'; 'Audiences will love this "Octopus" '; 'Take a hankie, Miss Smith'; 'Old-hat, but we loved it'; and 'Many Happy Returns'.

Christmas with Peter and Fiona at home at Bampton was peaceful, enlivened by a vigorous theatrical performance by the Bampton Mummers, who visited us that evening and enacted an age-old traditional country entertainment which entailed a lot of bucolic hamming fortified by frequent dips into the punch-bowl.

30

A Perfect Stranger

When our season at the Haymarket ended *Dear Octopus* was moved, first to the Piccadilly Theatre in February 1968, and then to the Strand Theatre in March. After another four months at the Strand we ended our London run, and I was once again on the market. It had been altogether nearly a year of happy experiences for me, working with such a fine group of actors.

For a time during our run I was doubly busy. I had accepted a leading role in a thriller film, *Subterfuge*, for which the gravelly-voiced star of American TV's *Burke's Law*, Gene Barry, had been brought to London. Also in the picture with me were Michael Rennie, Marius Goring and the ever-glamorous Joan Collins, whom I had last worked with in Hollywood on *The Virgin Queen* years before. I managed to do my double stint at theatre and film studio for some weeks without too much strain, though I remember little of the movie.

I also fitted in rehearsals and preparations for a big charity performance in aid of the RAF Benevolent Fund one Sunday in July, to be attended by the Queen and the Duke of Edinburgh. It followed the usual format of such shows – a string of variety comics and acts interspersed with singers and musicians, all to be introduced by well-known personalities one of whom on this occasion was Richard Burton, who evidently considered it unnecessary to rehearse and only turned up in time for the performance. An hour or so later, he may have regretted his cavalier attitude when, trembling with nerves, he stumbled through his lines in a rather less-than-glorious few moments of purgatory.

It was in April, while *Dear Octopus* was at the Strand, that I first met Virginia Mailer.

I had a close friend, Alex Sterling, who was a well-known fashion photographer and something of an avuncular figure in my life. We often used to sup or lunch together at a club which he ran as a side interest; he knew a good deal about my domestic problems and was always a

279

ready and sympathetic listener. He also knew that I was something of a loner when in London.

Several times he mentioned a young fashion model with whom he had done several photographic assignments. He seemed to admire her particularly and to respect her very professional attitude to her work – not to mention her beauty. More than once he tried to persuade me to meet her.

'She has just come back to London after living and working for some years in South Africa. You'd like her. She's just like you. Her work comes first with her and she certainly wouldn't want to be involved with anybody. Do come and meet her some time. I know you'd get on well together.'

And so it went on. But I had problems enough as it was and had no desire to add to them. He had apparently pursued the same line with the girl in question, and had received much the same response – 'Thanks – but no thanks!'

Finally, however, I agreed somewhat reluctantly to meet them both for drinks in the Chelsea Potter, and then lunch nearby at the Club del Arethuse.

Thus it was that I met Virginia Mailer. As I entered the crowded bar of the Chelsea Potter I looked round for Alex, but my attention was riveted by the appearance of the most beautiful girl I had ever seen. Mini-skirted, as was the fashion then, tallish, very slender, with long blonde hair framing a lovely, lively face, she was an absolute stunner. It took me several moments to realise that the man she was talking to was Alex. So *this* was the girl whom he had been so adamant that I should meet! I certainly approved his taste . . .

But once I had battled my way through to her and Alex and he had introduced me, I soon got the impression that our reactions were not exactly mutual. Her manner towards me was reserved if not downright unfriendly. Cool and self-possessed would, I think, be the best description of her attitude.

I got another view of her as she led the way up the stairs to the restaurant. What a marvellous pair of legs!

No sooner had we sat down at our table, even before looking at the menu, than Alex – in one of the oldest tricks in the world – looked at his watch, suddenly announced that he had forgotten an important appointment and simply bolted from the room.

So Virginia and I found ourselves dumped on each other, neither having sought such a situation and both embarrassed by Alex's obvious ploy.

I am seldom at a loss for words, but I must say I found the next few minutes pretty heavy going. Virginia seemed to find the whole thing quite funny, and it was her sense of humour that gradually put me at my ease.

What we talked about I can't remember, though I do recall that I tried to find out as much as I could about her and her interests. This ability to talk together became one of our greatest bonds, especially since our subsequent meetings were always over lunches or suppers when we were invariably the last people to leave.

At that first encounter I knew that I very much wanted to see her again, so a couple of days later I plucked up courage to phone and ask her to join me for supper after the theatre; to my delight, she agreed.

And so began the deepest and most enduring friendship I had ever known. We met often, but rarely stayed out late, because Virginia was always concerned about her looks and never knew when she might suddenly be called by her agency to do some photographic job. Many times when we had arranged to meet she would phone to break our date because she was going to be working next day, and I never took umbrage. I understood and admired her professionalism, and she appreciated that.

I had great reason to be grateful to Alex Sterling . . .

In May the garden of the Grange was opened to the public for charity and we had a surprisingly large crowd. Thanks to Bigsby's work the whole place looked lovely.

But I had begun to realise that the house was a heavy drain on my resources and needlessly large. The children were both away at school, I was only there on Sundays while I was working, and the sadly unchanging gulf between Kitty and me cast a pall upon the place. When the Dunants eventually left, having overstayed their promised year, and Kitty lost the caring Marcella who had watched over her so patiently, we had trouble in finding a couple remotely like them. We did employ a young Spanish couple for a few months, but they were pretty hopeless and seemed to spend all of their spare time in bed – not necessarily resting, I believe.

Thank God for Bigsby! Mrs Bigsby was now our full-time cook and we still had Irene with us.

The decision to move having been taken, we set out once again in search of a suitable house somewhere in the Cotswolds. I hoped, too, that a small, cosy house would suit Kitty better.

It seemed awful to be leaving such a lovely place after only two years there, but the Grange had not been a happy house except when the children were home.

We had our usual summer holiday in Ibiza, and soon after our return Fiona started her first term at St Mary's, Wantage, which was her final public school. Rather to my surprise and relief she had managed to get through her Common Entrance exam, and I was delighted that she had got into a school which I admired and liked. Staffed by dedicated Anglican nuns and scrupulously kept, it was an establishment which radiated kindly but firm discipline and warmth, and I was sure that Fiona would be happy there. As the Sister Superior at Great Oaks had said, 'We don't want Fiona to lose her gift of laughter.'

That same week we found the house we were looking for. Maidenwell Manor, in the charming hamlet of Broad Campden close to the glorious Cotswold town of Chipping Campden, was a lovely old place with about four acres of garden and paddock, and had a fine little cottage ideal for the Bigsbys who readily agreed to come with us. The manor was mainly of the Tudor period and had a Victorian wing. It was not large and had just enough beamed and stone-fireplaced rooms for all of us, including a small attic flatlet for Peter. There was also a magnificent Tudor barn larger than the house itself, L-shaped to form a courtyard and with wonderful beams and timbers, part of which I intended to convert to offices and store-rooms and later, hopefully, to flats for the children as they got older.

There was a lot of restoration and improvement work to be done at Maidenwell, including complete rewiring, replacement of most of the bedroom flooring and the provision of a third bathroom to be shared by Fiona and Irene.

A sale for the Grange was agreed quite soon. We were to have vacant possession of Maidenwell on 2 November and hand over the Grange on 30 November to a Mr and Mrs Baxter, so we had a lot to get done in a short time. But I was quite used to this kind of rush by now!

Just prior to leaving the Grange I walked the property with Mr Baxter one Sunday and pointed out as many helpful tips as I could, including local amenities. Amongst other things, I advised him about a certain butcher in the nearby market town of Faringdon, telling him how excellent his beef was compared with the local branch of Baxters the butchers. He seemed quite impressed and courteously thanked me for the advice. It was weeks later that I found out who he was: Derek Baxter, managing director of the extensive chain of Baxters the butchers!

Since the close of *Dear Octopus* in June I had been in only one other production, a try-out of *The Man with a Load of Mischief*, a musical play which had been a great success in America. For me to be in a musical was the last thing I could have imagined, since I can't hit a note vocally and my only other rendering of a song, in my first movie in Hollywood (*Lightning Strikes Twice*), had been so awful that it had to be cut from the film. However, in *Mischief* I had only one short ditty to deliver, and that in the maudlin yowl of a drunken philanderer. With me were David Kernan, the popular tenor, Roberta D'Esti, who had been so good in the leading part in the London production of *West Side Story*, and Dilys Laye, who was my favourite comedic actress. They and others provided all the singing.

After several weeks of rehearsal under the direction of a rather intense American, we opened at the Intimate Theatre, Palmers Green, in mid-August for a three-week period prior to transferring to the West End. Although I quite enjoyed my roistering role and especially liked working with Dilys, I didn't feel that the piece would work in London and gave notice that I would not wish to carry on in it after Palmers Green.

Virginia, who had been busily working in London, Germany and France all that summer, and who had stolen some of my movie thunder by playing the lead in a film shot mostly in Venice, managed to come to watch a performance. She agreed with me that *Mischief* was not right for me, even though she thought I had coped quite well and had been very funny – for a change!

The show subsequently opened in the West End but did not survive for long, so for once I had been right in my theatrical judgement.

Then, at the beginning of October, I had a most extraordinary encounter. I was in the flat one evening when there came a knock on the front door and when I opened it came face to face with a very weird individual. He was short, enveloped in a voluminous overcoat and peered up at me blearily through long, tangled hair that covered most of his face.

'I'm Peter Everett. I've got a script for you to read. Can I come in?' Whereupon he pushed past me, went into the sitting room, threw himself into a chair (coat and all), thrust a script at me and blurted out his tale of woe.

It appeared that he had found a production company ready to let him direct his first film based on this script, which he had written himself. It was to be a low-budget picture, shot entirely on location in just six weeks. He had wanted another actor to play the lead, but had been told that he was to try to get me instead. Perhaps this accounted for the malevolent looks he darted at me as he rambled on.

'*Please* read it. I'll phone you tomorrow.' And without further ado, he barged out as abruptly as he had come in.

Neither his odd behaviour nor what little he had told me inclined me to take this bizarre episode seriously, especially as his filming was due to start within a week, giving me no time to find out more about the project.

However, I decided to read the script in bed that night – or at least to skim through it.

I hardly slept at all. As soon as I began reading, I realised that this was a gripping, harrowing story, poetical and almost surreal in its treatment, about a man whom I could understand and sympathise with.

Called *The Last of the Long-Haired Boys*, it was the story of an ex-fighter pilot unable to adjust to the realities of post-war life. Obsessed with memories of his finest hours and of so many of his RAF colleagues who died in the Battle of Britain, he becomes more and more lost in a hideous dream-world, to the contempt of his son and the agony of his long-suffering wife. Soon after their marriage he had taken over a pub on the edge of an airfield in Kent, the scene of many a wartime binge, which he stuffed with pathetic souvenirs of the past: photographs of old comrades, bits of aeroplanes and propellers.

Finally, almost totally deranged, he dons his old uniform and wanders out in the mist to the former airfield, while ghosts of the past rise up before him. His son finds him there and, at last understanding his plight, talks him quietly into sense. In a touching scene between them, the generation gap is breached.

It was not a heroic story of war, but of the aftermath of war and its effect on some of those who suffered it. I was profoundly disturbed by the script. It was beautifully written. I subsequently learned that its author, Peter Everett, was an award-winning poet and novelist of a modern school about which I knew little.

I agonised for hours that night. It was a part that I – or any actor – would love to play. But could I risk my status as an actor by getting involved in something which had all the hallmarks of a cheap, semi-amateur production? I simply could not make up my mind whether to pursue the matter.

The next evening Everett phoned me. 'Can I come round?' Then after a brief pause, '*Please!*'

Half an hour later he was at the door, this time in a pitiful state. Scruffier even than before, he stood there swaying and almost incoherent, his jeans saturated. Somebody had spilt beer all over him, he said; at least, that was his story. I brought him in, told him to take off his trousers so that I could dry them on an electric heater and gave him a dressing-gown to cover his bedraggled underclothes and shirt.

To my horror, he started to cry and said that he had been told that if I would not play in it, the film would not be made. He actually went down on his knees and pleaded.

I had never handled a situation like this. Still, I was sorry for him, and ever in my mind was that wonderful script. In the end, I agreed to meet his producers next day.

At a subsequent meeting with Jay Webb and Iain Quarrier, who were to be in charge of the production for Cupid Productions – an embryo set-up financed by the wealthy young Michael Pearson – I found that quite a sound cast had already been assembled, including Patrick Barr, David Markham, Sonia Dresdel, Sue Jameson and Malcolm Tierney. I suggested Gillian Raine for the wife, and she was soon added to the list. In the end, with considerable misgivings, I agreed to start on the film in five days' time.

As soon as our location shooting started at Hawkinge in Kent, I began to doubt my wisdom. The first day was a nightmare of incompetence and chaos. Peter Everett obviously had little idea of how to get his story on to the cinema screen, and apparently no coherent schedule plan. He had somehow persuaded the producers to let the photography be put in the charge of a young fashion photographer who might have been good with still pictures but who could not handle tracking or panning shots. Between the two of them hours were wasted and tempers frayed, and a thoroughly fed-up crew of technicians became almost mutinous. I phoned Iain Quarrier that evening and he arrived the next day with a new lighting cameraman and a competent production manager.

From then on, things improved and the pace quickened. I had worked before with Ken Hodges, the new lighting cameraman, and between the two of us we managed to guide Peter into a workable series of set-ups, occasionally much to his fury. At one point he actually stomped off in a huff, so we just carried on shooting. Surrealism was all very well, but we were trying to make a cinema film for ordinary public viewing.

Scenes in a local pub that we had taken over at Paddlesworth went well, and I loved working with that splendid actress Gillian Raine. I even persuaded a group of friends – Stanford Tuck, Brian Kingcombe and Paddy Barthropp, all fabled and much-decorated heroes of the Battle of Britain – to come down and take part in an unscripted scene where we all swapped wartime reminiscences over beers at a table in the garden, adding a touch of verisimilitude to the yearning of Trigg (the part I played) to be back amongst some of his erstwhile comrades.

The other interiors were shot in sets built in an old hangar at Panshanger, a former RAF airfield near Welwyn.

We finished the film in November just in time for me to help with the move from the Grange. It had been a strange experience. I was a conventional film actor and I had found myself getting impatient, even angry sometimes, but never fed up. We had been reaching for something weird and intangible, and I felt we had nearly grasped it.

What happened to *The Last of the Long-Haired Boys* I don't know. I was out of the country when it was due for release. Certainly I never saw any of my percentage of profits. But at least one day I had a pleasant surprise: sitting in a restaurant I was suddenly and loudly set upon by Trevor Howard – 'Just seen your film, *The Last of the Long-Haired Boys*. Bloody marvellous, Dicky, old boy!' I could not have asked for a finer accolade than that from my screen hero.

While work was still going on at Maidenwell Manor – much more extensive and costly than I had bargained for – we moved into a cottage in the garden of the Cotswold House Hotel in Chipping Campden and all our belongings went into store for a period. Irene, who was with us still, pedalled off each day to the Manor to get on with the cleaning up. I had a feeling that some of her enthusiasm was not unconnected with one of the technicians working there who had obviously taken her fancy.

In mid-December we moved into Maidenwell and were more or less organised there by the time Peter and Fiona came home for their Christmas holidays. I was sorry to have missed his confirmation in the lovely Chapel of Eton College earlier that year, but looked forward to being with them both for a few weeks. It had been an unsettling year for all of us.

Once the Christmas holidays had ended, it was clear that the differences between Kitty and me were not healing. I thought that a trial separation might be the best thing, and towards the end of January I sought advice from a London solicitor who specialised in these matters.

I told him about all the circumstances which over a period of years had led up to the seemingly insoluble rift, but explained that there was nobody else involved. I mentioned my very close friendship with Virginia, but that I doubted if she would wish to be involved in any more intimate relationship. I realised that all this would affect the children, especially Fiona who was only fourteen, though Peter was verging on manhood. However, Fiona had not been especially close to her mother for some time.

His advice was to talk things over with Kitty and to see what could be arranged.

Some weeks later I brought the matter up while Kitty and I were dining at the nearby Lygon Arms Hotel at Broadway. Her reaction was that if *I* wanted a separation *she* wanted a divorce, and that was final. I agreed to give her grounds for divorce – adultery, which was the most reliable cause in those days – and also agreed to pay all her pre-court expenses.

It was a sickening moment for both of us who had shared so much, good and bad, for twenty years. I personally could hardly believe it was happening.

The children were told during their Easter holidays and seemed not unduly surprised or upset. Fiona had a few parties to attend locally and back at Bampton; Peter went off to stay for a week in Paris with friends whom we had met in Ibiza, returning just in time to take part in a public schools athletics meeting at Crystal Palace. He was quite a useful sprinter and was now Keeper of Athletics at Eton.

Meanwhile our routine remained outwardly much the same as usual. I did my usual bi-annual effort for the Army Benevolent Fund Show at the Palladium, nervously watched by Virginia and her mother as I fumbled for my spectacles when trying to read one of my introductions which I thought I had memorised, and in March I was invited to open the annual Chelsea Antiques Fair.

I also decided to sell the Ibiza flat, as I did not feel that we would have much use for it in the future. I let my land-development associate Pedro Luis Poch have it for exactly what I paid years before, and in return he promised to give me an interest in one of the villas he was building at Portinax. I never heard from him again. Property deals were obviously not destined to be my strong suit.

On a short visit to Ibiza, I arranged to have some of the contents of the flat shipped back to England, and also reserved rooms in a very nice beach hotel at Saint Eulalia for Kitty's summer holiday with the children.

During these months none of my local or London friends seemed to be surprised by the break-up of my marriage; I spent many pleasant days at their homes, and managed to get to all Fiona's visiting days at St Mary's. When she and Peter left to start the summer term they were in good spirits, despite the fact that they both knew that I was shortly going to South Africa for three months to do a play there.

Towards the end of April I had been approached by Pieter Toerian, South Africa's leading theatre impresario, asking if I would be interested in playing Lord Goring once again in a tour of Oscar Wilde's *An Ideal Husband*. I had filmed out there but never appeared on stage, and the idea intrigued me, especially as it would give me a chance to see more of that country at first hand. What's more, he had already assembled a very strong cast. Anthony Sharp was to be the director and the company included Jean Kent, Peter Graves, Vanessa Lee, Derek Bond, Elizabeth Knight, Joyce Grant and Peter Bevis. There was little to choose between it and our original London cast of 1965. I loved the prospect of playing Goring once more and working with such a distinguished group, so I readily accepted the offer.

We rehearsed for three weeks in London during which time I stayed continuously at the flat prior to flying to Johannesburg, only going to Maidenwell one day to collect my clothes for the trip. I felt almost a stranger there, and bade Kitty a rather strained goodbye. If I am reticent about that whole unhappy period, it is partly because I was bemused by the situation – one that I had never imagined possible, and in which my feelings would be hard to describe. Twenty years of marriage, even with a longish period of discord and unhappiness, form a bond that is not lightly broken.

I had of course told Virginia about all these happenings, even though I did not think that they directly concerned her. She and Queenie were the two people in whom I confided everything. When I told Virginia one day that I was going to give Kitty an easy uncontested divorce, she asked me what the grounds would be. 'Adultery,' I replied. 'I can arrange that easily enough.'

Her response, calm and quiet, staggered me. 'If anyone is to be named as the co-respondent it will be me.'

In that moment I knew that Virginia cared for me far beyond the friendship we had formed and beyond any hope that I had ever had that she might one day marry me, fond of me though I believed she was. Suddenly a whole new world lay before me, and I could scarce believe my good fortune.

She made one proviso: that I should talk to her parents and explain what was going to happen. This I did one day in their home in Totteridge, North London. I was as nervous as I had ever been at my first audition, but they were both absolutely sweet and understanding.

And so it was that Virginia and I became unofficially engaged, though it could not be official until all the legal proceedings of the next few months were completed. I had never dreamed that this could be possible, although I already knew that I loved Virginia and had hoped that some day in the future I could persuade this very independent bachelor girl to consider marriage. Once having found a perfect stranger I did not want to lose her.

The day after my fiftieth birthday I flew to Johannesburg, where Pieter Toerian met me at the airport. I was surprised by the youthfulness of this lean, courteous man who had established himself as the country's leading impresario. An ardent Anglophile, Pieter travelled the world regularly seeking plays and players and was mainly based on Cape Town, though he kept an elegant flat in Johannesburg. He took me to the comfortable apartment he had arranged for me at the new President Hotel, and also arranged a hired car for my use.

After a few days of further rehearsal, which included a special performance for Asians, we opened to a glittering first night at the vast Civic Theatre. South Africans took their theatre very seriously and audiences were nearly all in evening dress. The show was a huge success and probably the most spectacular production ever seen out there, rivalling in its setting and costumes our London production of 1965.

We were in Johannesburg five weeks altogether, playing to packed houses. Fortunately, within a few days I was contacted by Ken Palmer – like myself an old Wimburnian, who was then head of Norwich Union Insurance – and through him met many members of the local business community. I also spent time in Pretoria with my old friend Oscar Hurwitz, and visited Dawie van Heerden's military museum and wild animal sanctuary at Irene.

I had cards from Peter and Fiona, who were enjoying their holiday in Ibiza.

After a couple of weeks I phoned Virginia and persuaded her to come out for a month or so. I knew that the lure of seeing her old friends and revisiting the scenes of her youth would overcome her resistance to taking time away from her work in London. We had a week or so together in Jo'burg before we left for Durban, which she knew well and where she had many friends. Because I was still officially married, Virginia always insisted that she had her own room. We never gave interviews together and avoided any public comment about our relationship; only her closest friends knew about our future plans.

After two weeks in Durban we spent a very pleasant three weeks in Cape Town. I could well understand Virginia's affection for the place; it really is very beautiful in its setting on the coast, dominated by the massive, brooding Table Mountain and with all the hilly suburbs clothed in woodland – and everywhere an abundance of flowers in exotic gardens or neat street-beds, or simply growing wild.

Virginia still had many friends in the area, and we had a busy social programme keeping up with all her calls.

She showed me round Stellenbosch, the wine-growing area where we lunched extremely well at Lanzerac, a very beautiful old Cape Dutch wine-farm converted to a hotel and restaurant; and she took me to see Cape Point, the rocky tip of Africa where the Indian and South Atlantic Oceans meet. As she pointed out the pretty little house which she had shared with her great friend Jill at Higgovale, a suburb set amongst a magnificent stand of ancient oak trees, it was obvious that it compared only too well with her poky little mews flat in Kensington.

When the time came for me to leave South Africa, it was not in the least surprising that Virginia asked to stay on there for a while. Quite apart from the nostalgic feelings she had for the Cape area, I sensed that she was also suffering from a personal conflict now that she was in the midst of well-loved old scenes and meeting so many former close friends amongst whom she had led such a free, unfettered existence. In other words, she was having doubts about the constraints of marriage and was desperately looking for some excuse as a way out.

For me to have demurred would have been insensitive, if not downright stupid. To stay and get it all out of her system was the answer. I knew one thing would bring her hotfoot back to London: a cable from her agent saying that she was having to turn down important modelling jobs.

Meanwhile, the main purpose of my stay in Cape Town had been enormously successful. For nearly three weeks we had filled the very large and impressive old Alhambra Theatre, playing to packed and marvellously enthusiastic audiences. Pieter Toerian's season with *An Ideal Husband* had been a great success.

Virginia saw me off at the Cape Town airport. I stopped a couple of days in Johannesburg, spent a day in Pretoria with old friends, then flew on to Rome where I had decided to stay for a while.

It was oddly coincidental that, just as I was lunching in Rome with Marina Cicogna, now one of Italy's leading film producers, Harry Alan Towers was desperately trying to contact me in England from his Rome hotel, only a few streets away from mine. Eventually the muddle was sorted out (I had not told Queenie in advance that I intended stopping in Rome), and Harry made contact with me.

Would I play the leading supporting role in a new version of *The Story of Dorian Gray*? Helmut Berger was to star in Harry's Anglo-Italian co-production and work had already begun. If I accepted, I would start work in London in only two days' time. He rushed a script round to me, and it was quite readable. Since by then I had concluded that my professional future lay more with live theatre than in films, any occasional movie would come as a dessert to the main meal, so I was no longer greatly concerned with quality and set-up. I agreed the deal that Towers offered and set off back to London with only a day to spare to collect the wardrobe and make other preparations.

Towards the end of my filming in England we had several evenings of night locations in Kent, at a glorious old house called Glassenbury Park. Built entirely on an island surrounded by a wide, deep moat, the bulk of the house was Georgian, but nearly half was the original medieval manor house built in 1490 and still solidly intact and occupied. The owner was a member of the ancient local Roberts family, who had married a German, while her daughter and grand-daughter, Jane Sutcliffe, also lived there.

The house looked enchanting illuminated by the film lights, and I spent many interesting hours there chatting with Jane and her mother while I was not working. When we left Glassenbury, I invited Jane to join me two weeks later in London for the Horse of the Year Show.

My last week on *Dorian Gray* was spent in Rome working on the interiors.

Once back in London I decided that exactly a month in Cape Town should have been enough for Virginia, so I persuaded her agent to send an urgent cable.

She returned to London within two days, and everything was as before.

I had taken a Crown lease on a very charming little Regency house near the Tate Gallery and this I made available to Kitty. It was agreed that she should move there in November, taking with her all her own furniture which had been gifts to us from her parents and as much of the rest as she could manage to get into the new house.

Towards the end of October Virginia and I went to a memorable annual school play production at Eton – memorable perhaps not for the best of reasons. It was *War and Peace*, rather too grandiose a subject for their schoolboy talents, especially amongst the ladies of the cast who seemed singularly ill-at-ease in their period gowns. Peter did his best to look regal as the Tsar, quite a small part fortunately.

Fiona's and Peter's half-term breaks coincided and they both came to London to spend a couple of days with us, Fiona staying in Virginia's flat while Peter stayed with me. Both of them had immediately taken to Virginia and she to them, so we were a merry quartet wherever we went.

Kitty's suit was heard on 16 December and she was granted a decree nisi. I had visited her in her house the week before and we had parted for the last time as man and wife, neither of us saying much. At the weekend I had driven home alone and sad. A long chapter had ended.

Under the terms of the divorce settlement Fiona was to remain in her mother's custody until she was eighteen, but I was to have unlimited access to her, while Peter was a free agent. The financial terms were very fair, though not easy for me to meet, and Kitty was very understanding about the difficulties that I would face.

One of the happiest features of the whole sad sequence of events was the attitude of the Sister Superior at St Mary's. Months before, I had gone to tell her of the impending break-up in Fiona's home life and she had said, 'Don't worry, Mr Todd. We won't let her suffer.' In the event, on the day when the divorce was grabbed at by the press, all the newspapers were impounded and not distributed in the school; and, in the meantime, for that term Fiona had been given a double room to share with a happy young girl whose parents were divorced also. The school showed great sympathy and understanding.

Christmas at Maidenwell was warm and cheerful that year, with Virginia and her parents and her brother, Dallas, all coming to stay with Peter and me. Mrs Bigsby did a great job with all our fare, the local Mummers came and entertained us (led by a notorious local poacher who was a great character) and the dogs had a lovely time, utterly spoiled by the Mailers who doted on them.

As one door had closed, so another had opened.

31

A Triumphant Beginning

The first days of the New Year set my life off at a new tangent, heralded by the portly arrival on the scene of a theatrical impresario, one Duncan Weldon.

Duncan came to Maidenwell armed with the script of a play, *Four-Sided Triangle*, by Terence Kelly, a fairly successful TV and theatre writer. Duncan and his partner, Paul Elliott, wanted to know if I would be interested in doing the play for a short tour prior to a London opening. Adrienne Corri, Edward Judd and Amanda Reiss had already been contracted to appear.

Duncan I found fascinating. A short, fat, dark-bearded person, his mannerisms alone were quite mesmerising, two of them being particularly eye-catching: when excited or animatedly arguing a point, he would flap his hands as if they were fresh-washed and he was trying to dry them; and when puzzled or cogitating, he furiously scratched his beard with a curious over-arm movement. Above all, he lived and breathed theatre and had an encyclopaedic knowledge of its history and its players. His flat in Southport, his home town, was walled entirely with prints and photos and playbills.

He had launched his career as an impresario by booking a one-man tour for David Kossoff when almost fresh from school, and had since been very active with Paul Elliott and on his own account in promoting and managing touring productions. Like Paul, who had started with the presentation of summer seasons at small resorts such as Rhyl, he had battled his way up the theatrical ladder by sheer hard work and dedication. Together they were known affectionately if perhaps a little derisively in the business as 'The Boys'. When I checked I received conflicting opinions about them both from past employees and from their peers – opinions tinged, perhaps, with some grudging admiration. But then we all know that to start up a business with little or no backing requires frequent corner-cutting.

The more I began to see of him and Paul, it was not so much the play Duncan had brought that intrigued me as their partnership and their expertise in provincial theatre. They had come up the hard way and knew every facet of mounting and managing touring productions. If I could enthuse them with my ideas and hopes for a high-quality touring set-up as a means of revitalising British provincial theatre, perhaps they would fill in all the gaps in my knowledge and provide the know-how to make my dream materialise.

They were a likeable pair, complete opposites in many ways: Duncan dedicated, shrewd, cute and cautious; Paul much more overt and flamboyant, typically 'show-biz' and radiating bonhomie and cheerfulness. In other words, they seemed to be just what I had needed.

But first I wanted to know a lot more about them, so I decided to do *Four-Sided Triangle*. It was rather a flimsy story with just four in the cast playing out a matrimonial imbroglio involving lots of suspicions and acrid accusations between me and my wife (Adrienne Corri) and our supposed partners in infidelity (Edward Judd and Amanda Reiss), but it had sufficient wit and comedy in it, I hoped, to be made into an amusing piece if played by a very competent group.

We started rehearsals in London in early February, preparatory to opening in Liverpool on 1 March.

Meanwhile, much else had happened since the start of 1970 . . .

I had already decided to sell Maidenwell Manor months before, but had not felt unduly pressed to dispose of the house in any hurry. There had been few prospective buyers – this seemed to be a time when fair-sized houses with large gardens were hard to shift. Household staff and gardeners were becoming increasingly difficult to find, running costs were rising and maintenance charges were getting heavier every year. These were some of the reasons why I decided to live more economically – especially as the terms of my settlement on Kitty had drained much of my fluid cash.

I had also convinced myself that when Virginia and I eventually set up house together it should be in London, the source of both our careers, with eventually perhaps a country cottage as a weekend and leisure home. This was a weighty decision to take. From farmer to Londoner in five years was a big step, and I had never been fully based in a city before in my adult life. To sever my main tap root in the country would be a big wrench. And what about the dogs? Even though they were both well past middle age, Baron and Emma were devoted to me and had years ahead. My dear old springer spaniel was sadly near the end of her life anyway, at thirteen years, and could scarcely walk.

However, it would make sense to move, I told myself.

Before Christmas I warned Mr and Mrs Bigsby of my intention and told them that they should start looking for a suitable new post. The house might be sold at any time and I didn't want them to suffer for their loyalty by being left jobless. In mid-January they told me they had found ideal jobs in the north, nearer both their family homes, and it was with great regret and many tears from Mrs Bigsby that we all parted in early February.

As luck would have it, I had interviewed a Mrs Bishop over tea in Fortnum's one day and she seemed ideally suited as the cook-house-keeper I now needed. In very precise tones she told me of her life at a colonial station with her late husband, of her widowhood and of her rather straitened circumstances. She assured me that she was an excellent and experienced cook, that she loved dogs and that she would have no difficulty in running the house with the daily help that I already had. I liked her and engaged her on a monthly basis.

So that was the house organised. Now I needed temporary help with the garden. Hatherleigh, Bigsby's assistant, stayed on (complete with Basil, his peacock, who roamed the garden) and I engaged a professional gardening firm to do most of the work.

So far so good . . . and I knew that everything was under the competent and watchful eye of Queenie.

In January I had managed to fit in some rehearsals for my installation as Master of Masonic Lodge No. 21, and was installed in the chair on 18 January. I also became automatically a Steward of Grand Lodge, a privilege extended to a select group of old lodges such as No. 21. I had postponed acceptance of the Mastership for several years because of my inability to attend all meetings regularly, but my masonic colleagues had finally insisted that I take the chair while one of the Past Masters could stand in for me when necessary.

At about this time I had been approached by the BBC asking if I would do a TV programme about my early life in Northern Ireland. Why they thought that this would be of general interest I don't know, but as the filming was to be at the end of April when my tour would be finished, I agreed.

We opened *Four-Sided Triangle* in Liverpool on a sad day for me and a worse one for Queenie. Dear old Dash, my great little companion – and gun-dog for over ten years – had almost totally collapsed and it fell to poor Queenie to phone the vet and arrange to have her put to sleep.

Our opening at the Liverpool Royal Court Theatre was rather less than triumphant; the play itself got universally poor reviews, though critics absolved the cast from blame. The same was true at the Opera House Manchester the following week, and at Brighton a week later, followed by Birmingham.

During our Wimbledon week – the play's last – I called at Kitty's house to break the news that I was to remarry. She seemed neither surprised nor upset . . . or else she put on a very good face. The following day she and Fiona came to our matinée performance. Fiona and Peter spent most of their Easter holidays at Maidenwell and I was with them for a few days after the tour ended.

Virginia and I had found an ideal home in London backing on to Regent's Park. It was a recently restored listed Nash terrace house which had been lavishly rebuilt and decorated by the Crown, and I was fortunate in obtaining a Crown lease as a tenant of the Queen. It seemed perfect in every way, very conveniently positioned for the West End, with two particularly fine reception rooms and just three bedrooms. The mews cottage no longer belonged to the house, but there was a large garage still part of the property – unusual, and priceless for London. And Regent's Park was just across the road.

So now the race was on to find a buyer for Maidenwell. One day I returned home to be confronted by a jubilant Mrs Bishop: 'I've sold your house for you, Mr Todd.' She had, too. That day a couple named Elliott had looked over the place and, prompted by Mrs Bishop, had decided without further ado to buy it. I later wondered why. He seemed about seven feet tall, and even I had to duck to pass under some of the old beams and doorways in the Tudor section. But they do say that it is always the wife who decides which house to buy . . .

Now two more problems presented themselves.

First, Mrs Bishop, flushed with success and cooking sherry, decided to retire. Her culinary arts demanded a great deal of wine-flavouring, but she had been a godsend for a few months – a remarkably good if expensive cook, and devoted to Baron and Emma.

Having to think of some means of keeping the house going and myself fed until the final move, my mind immediately turned to my two devoted and eccentric Irish aunts, Amy and Dolly. I phoned them, and they arrived within 48 hours, complete with their charming and very competent friend, Sheila Bradley.

The second problem was what to do about Baron and Emma. It seemed inconceivable that I should have to part with them after all these years. Nevertheless they could not be taken to London, where there would be nobody to look after them when Virginia and I were away or working. Fortunately Michael Gaze, the gardening contractor, agreed to take them to his home. He already knew them well and had a nice farmhouse near Sherborne. It would be fine for them, but I suspected that we would all miss each other; some dogs, especially Danes, only ever belong to one person.

Virginia and I were now free to marry, and we sought a suitable date. We decided that a day in May would give us a week clear for a brief honeymoon but Queenie, her superstitious hackles roused, was adamant. 'Marry in May, rue the day,' she intoned . . . so we settled for the last day of April. This also coincided with my BBC filming in Northern Ireland for my early life story, so we would be spending our brief honeymoon working amongst the scenes of my childhood. At least Virginia would learn something about my background and formative years.

I had also by now spent a couple of months under the management of Duncan Weldon and Paul Elliott, and had had time to assess their capabilities and suitability to help me form a company to back high quality touring companies – bringing suitable productions into London only when they had done a preparatory stint in the provinces – and to try to open up the English-speaking world to exported British theatre shows. I reckoned that the UK had two products unparalleled anywhere in the world: Rolls-Royce cars and live theatre. Rolls-Royce had a healthy export business – so why not theatre?

Duncan, Paul and I had many talks about the scheme and both were enthusiastic about the idea. We all got on very well together, despite our differing backgrounds and natures. The great thing was that they were both real professionals. Each had his own production company, but on occasions they set up joint productions and they shared a small but devoted staff all squeezed into a tiny suite of rooms in Leicester Square.

They had recently taken a lease on the little Ashton Theatre at St Anne's-on-Sea near Blackpool and reckoned that it would be a good, profitable launching-site for our productions, breaking them in and polishing them well away from any major local or national press. I agreed with this latter advantage, but very much doubted their financial forecasts.

Paul and Duncan wanted our shared company to be concerned only with plays that I was in, but I could not agree to this. I felt that *all* the productions should come under one company to facilitate accounting, staff wages, rents, management fees and all the other infrastructure and expenses involved in putting on large numbers of productions concurrently. In the end, this was agreed.

Finally, on the very day of my marriage to Virginia, Duncan and Paul lunched with me and we agreed to form a company together, the shares to be equally divided between us. When we came to think of a name for our new firm, I suggested that it should have something to do with three or trio; then I hit upon the idea of Triumph Theatre Productions, which the others felt would be at least a hopeful start to our venture.

So Triumph was formed, at least in principle, on that never-to-be-forgotten day of 30 April 1970 – when at least two joint ventures came into being.

As one who had spent many years in the film industry I recognised that the company name Triumph should take precedence in all our advertising and playbills, so that the company and not the directors should become synonymous with quality and volume of production. Duncan and Paul agreed but with considerable reservations, since they didn't believe that the name of a company could possibly mean much either to playgoers, theatre managements or actors.

On the other hand, I was thinking of the great company names of the movie industry such as MGM, Paramount, Twentieth Century-Fox, Columbia, Associated British Pictures or Rank. These household names were remembered long after producers had been forgotten. And I was right. Within a year or two, everybody in the business talked of a 'Triumph production' and the name carried a cachet which meant high standards and easier-to-get guarantees. Even actors talked of 'working for Triumph'.

Theatres throughout Britain at that time, and new ones since built, have reason to revere and be grateful for Triumph and its team: principally at first Duncan and Paul who were its power-house, and later Duncan alone with some support from me and Louis Michaels, who joined us after some three years as a director and nominal chairman.

A spate of good, well-cast and well-produced shows came from our offices, soon removed to Ivor Novello's old suite of rooms in the Aldwych over the Strand Theatre. Before long other managements, and especially local authorities, began to sit up and take notice as our shows filled theatres which had been in the doldrums for years. Gradually also, more and more actors to whom touring had been a dirty word became only too glad to do a Triumph tour – whether or not it was intended eventually for London's West End. There was hardly a knight, dame or distinguished actor of British theatre who did not work for Triumph within the next ten years, either in the UK, America, Canada or Australia.

I sincerely believe that a whole new era of British theatre – especially in the major provincial cities and in theatres throughout America, Canada and Australasia – emanated from the activities of Triumph Theatre Productions, and I am proud to have been instrumental in the company's formation and objects.

Many British provincial theatres had become sadly run-down during the period since the Second World War, when product of any quality was scarce; and the new phenomenon of television, with its huge job opportunities, had made performers unwilling to budge far from London for any length of time for fear of missing out on some lucrative TV part.

Furthermore, the majority of major city theatres were either privately owned or part of a large chain operated by companies such as Howard and Wyndham. Due to poor business and falling audience numbers they had become in the main pretty dreadful – tatty, poorly run, lacking modern lighting equipment and sound systems and badly in need of a total face-lift. If the auditorium in most cases was scruffy, the dressing rooms and back-stage facilities were far worse.

The success of Triumph's initial tours soon made local authorities aware of the viability of live theatre of a high standard, and of the audience potential in their localities for productions housed in comfortable and well-equipped theatres. And so, over about the next five years, many a great theatre was bought by the local authority, refurbished, re-equipped and subsidised, to become one of the main attractions of its city. To name only a few, this happened in Newcastle, Edinburgh, Glasgow, Norwich, Birmingham, Nottingham and Bristol, while many new theatres were built in places such as Guildford, Weston-super-Mare, Torquay, Croydon, Bromley and Billingham. Moreover, civic theatres or arts centres have proliferated throughout the country, while charitable trusts have saved and glorified such beautiful places as the Theatre Royal, Bath.

Many new touring companies have since set out in recent years on much-vaunted campaigns to bring theatre to the people, but it was Triumph which started all this in 1970. Without our company's efforts, there would have been few theatres left in the land for these crusading groups to play in.

Quite apart from quality, theatres cannot live without continuity, and here again Triumph was unique. During our most prolific years we rarely had fewer than twenty productions running or in rehearsal at any one time, and our annual output of top-class shows – usually including two or three in London – was something like 40–50, plus perhaps a dozen annual pantomimes. At our peak, we were by far the

most active production company in the world, and we reckoned to
employ more actors than any organisation other than the BBC.

For all this, full credit must go to the expertise and tireless enthusiasm
of Duncan and Paul during our first three or four years, backed by a
good team of office staff, company managers and stage managements –
helped not a little by the loyalty and hard work of a dedicated string
of actors such as Sir Ralph Richardson, Sir John Clements, Dame Cicely
Courtneidge and Jack Hulbert, Sir John Mills, Kenneth More, Ingrid
Bergman, Janet Suzman, Glenda Jackson, Googie Withers, Sir Michael
Redgrave, Glynis Johns, Eartha Kitt, Phyllis Calvert, Margaret Lockwood, Michael Denison, Dulcie Gray, Evelyn Laye, Douglas Fairbanks
Jnr, and many, many others. In many ways I myself did the trail-
blazing for Triumph, leading the first major tours both in Britain
and to America and Canada. For nearly nine years I worked almost
exclusively for Triumph, full of pioneering zeal and joy as I saw my
dream being fulfilled, unmindful of the fact that I was almost totally
wrecking my career. 'Out of sight, out of mind' applied perfectly to
what I was doing. While I was breaking new ground and helping to
create a theatre following in Inverness, St John's, Newfoundland or
Cleveland, Ohio, producers, directors and taxi-drivers in London or
Hollywood thought I was retired or dead.

However, I was not to know this as Duncan, Paul and I finally shook
hands after our lengthy lunch and Triumph Theatre Productions came
into being. I was only too thrilled – in fact I was so carried away that
it was only as I noticed the restaurant was empty that I looked at my
watch.

'Christ! I've got to go. I'm getting married in an hour!'

It was Peter who saved the day for me. He had been given the day
off from Eton to be my best man, and had arrived at my flat in good
time. Worried by my absence and mounting tardiness, he had changed,
dashed out and bought us both carnation buttonholes and collected the
Bentley from the garage and had it standing ready by the door.

I flew in, changed in minutes and, with Peter to drive the car and
find parking space, I arrived at the Chelsea Register Office in good
time, breathless, nervous and relieved to be the first one there.

The Registrar had been very cooperative when I saw him some week
or two earlier. I had said that I did not wish for any publicity or press
presence, and he suggested that I should arrive to sign the register the
statutory two days before the ceremony late in the afternoon, just before
closing, by which time all the press reps would have left. This I did,
and when they returned the next day my name was submerged among

several others. The Registrar also arranged for our ceremony to be the last one of the day, by which time again the press would have left. I wanted only one paper – the *Daily Express*, who had always treated me very fairly – to have any pre-knowledge of the marriage, and it was arranged that the only photographer present would be our mutual friend Alex Sterling, who would make his own deal with the *Express*.

It was all very quiet. The only people present were Virginia's parents, her brother Dallas, and Peter.

At least, it *should* have been very quiet . . .

Unfortunately, Virginia, Peter and I all share one dreadful failing when assailed by nerves on solemn occasions: we are the most dreadful gigglers. We corpsed, all three of us, especially when Virginia, her voice quavering on near-hysterics, promised to take me as her 'awful wedded husband'. The very earnest Registrar was rightly most disapproving of our conduct, as was Mrs Mailer who at one point hissed, 'Virginia, *really!*' As we tried to control ourselves the Registrar, his patience beginning to ebb, said, 'Shall we begin again?' and his admonishing tone and pursed mouth set us off once more. Somehow we got through to the end, and Virginia and I were finally pronounced man and wife.

She always did look gorgeous, but I shall never forget my admiration for my beautiful bride that day. She wore a dark blue, close-fitting mini-dress under a magnificent white Arctic fox coat, her long slender legs encased in soft white leather boots. With her blonde hair cascading under the hood of her coat, she was the archetypal snow-maiden on that balmy spring evening.

Later that evening Queenie joined us for a celebration supper party at the restaurant where Virginia and I had first met through the machinations of Alex Sterling, some two years previously.

Northern Ireland in 1970 was not the most obvious choice for a honeymoon, but the day after the wedding saw Virginia and me ensconced in our sandbag-protected hotel in Belfast, prepared to do a five-day stint with a BBC film crew to which I had committed myself some weeks before.

We had a very pleasant and amusing dinner that first evening with Marjorie Wallace, the presenter of the programme, and the director and cameraman, during which they discussed their plans for the next few days. They were obviously going to be fun to work with, and I felt that our rather strange working honeymoon might not be so bad after all. We were to make an early start in the morning, so all went to our rooms very soon after dinner.

I eventually woke feeling rather chilly, only to find Virginia and most of the bedclothes missing. Bewildered, I went to the bathroom, where I found poor Virginia sleeping quite peacefully in the bath, propped up by pillows and bundled in blankets and the eiderdown, driven there to escape from my snoring. There could have been a more romantic start to our wedded bliss, and I was covered in shame.

Those five days that we spent around Toome, Brecart, Duneane Church and Moneyglass Castle – scenes so well-remembered from my early days – were both harrowing and hilarious: harrowing because of the awful changes which had taken place in the last 30 or 40 years, and hilarious because we all had such great fun.

The first shot in the morning was to be of me arriving at the gate entrance to Brecart, my grandfather's house and my early home. I was to be in a chauffeur-driven Rolls-Royce, and had to promise to keep my eyes closed until we swung into the gateway, whereupon the director would shout, 'Action, Richard!' and I would open the car door, step out and open my eyes. Not having any idea what was in store for me, I did all this quite faithfully and the camera and microphone caught a perfectly involuntary and natural reaction from me: 'Oh, *Christ!*'

All around me was desolation and devastation – I could never have anticipated such a melancholy scene. The park wall that ran alongside the road was breached and ruinous, the gate-lodge was a roofless, windowless wreck and, worst of all, the great iron double gates and the elliptical sweep of massive railings which led into them were all gone – taken, I suppose, as iron scrap for the war effort years before. The small park itself was scarred by cracked and weed-covered concrete tank-standings, and there was not a tree left. All the woodland as well as the park trees had been clear-felled and I could see in the distance the house itself, shrouded from view in the past by timber and laurel or rhododendron belts. Even the line of fifty great limes which had lined the river bank in front of the house was gone.

No wonder the BBC had been so keen to see my initial reaction to this depressing sight. Apparently when my two eccentric aunts, Amy and Dolly, had been lumbered with the place after my grandparents' deaths early during the Second World War, the house had been requisitioned by the Army as an Armoured Brigade HQ – hence the tank-standings – while the family went to live in the gate-lodge. A lot of amphibious river-crossings had also been practised there, which had demolished most of the stone-shored banks of the Bann River. Short of ready cash and not wanting to live alone in that remote region, my aunts had then sold the place. Different local tenants and farmers had bought it up piecemeal and the house itself and home farm and some of the land was now occupied by one such small farmer. Timber contractors had moved in and shorn the place of all its woodland.

Meanwhile the aunts – as mentioned earlier – had buzzed off to Australia for a few years on the proceeds.

While the vista on which I now gazed appalled me, worse was to come when they drove me up to the house. The gardens, tennis court and ornamental trees and hedgerows had all been obliterated and the grounds were nothing much more than scrubby fields; the old house itself was in a dreadful state – the occupier lived in just a small portion, while the rest had been left to rot or used as corn stores.

We went from room to room with the camera crew while I tried to describe what each had been like.

It was awful.

The remainder of our stay was on the lighter side. On the first morning we needed a young billy-goat, something which the props man was not entirely used to providing. However the problem was solved when we were advised to go to the little general store in the village – in my day it had been McMillan's. 'Sure, you can get anything there.' So there we went – and there we got our goat.

The village had changed and yet was much the same. The railway line had closed and no longer level-crossed the main street. The eel fishery once owned by friends of ours now belonged to a German company, but the little dock area was still busy with lighters and fishing boats – and the McErlaine family still operated the lock on the canal joining the Bann to Lough Neagh.

We also went to Moneyglass Castle, a mile or two from Brecart, a large house I remembered from days when I had been taken there to tea as a little boy. It was a total ruin. Most of what had not collapsed into the cavernous cellars had been looted. Only one feature remained: the front door portals and *porte cochère* were intact and stood out incongruously, almost pristine, fine and handsome. A local told me legend had it that somebody had been buried below the steps to the front door, and no one had had the courage to disturb his ghost.

We also hired a motor boat to go for a trip downriver past Brecart to Lough Beg and Church Island, my childhood fantasy world with its ruined priory, dank undergrowth and healing tree. The healing tree, now a very spindly blackthorn, still was festooned with bandages and sticking plasters and I dunked my only ailment, tennis elbow, in the water in the natural stone trough beside it. I've never had elbow trouble since . . .

Virginia appeared in many of the shots with me, and made quite an impact in a scene on the boat. They had me in the stern, looking over the waters of the Lough, while she sat on the cabin roof bundled up in Wellington boots and a fur coat. On a particular cue she launched herself off the cabin roof, landed on the floorboards with a resounding thump and then clumped noisily towards me, all smiles and wonder as she trilled, 'Darling – and you really rew all by yourself all over this lough?'

'Yes, darling' – I felt obliged to support her unorthodox syntax – 'I rew all by myself everywhere around here.'

One of our problems in the Toome area was to find anybody old enough to remember me. As a child I had not known too many youngsters round about, and all the old people like the cobbler, the tailor Mr McMillan, the lightermen and the Scotch lassies from the sweet-shop were long gone. However, we did find Brian Grant and his sister Sheila; their family had owned the O'Neill Arms Hotel where there was a tennis court, and we used to play there or at Brecart. We had plenty to reminisce about.

Very soon our honeymoon, unconventional as it was, came to an end. I had seen some sad sights, but at least we'd had lots of fun both in and around Toome and with Marjorie Wallace and her director at our hotel.

Now the time had arrived to return to our own home and to plan our lives together.

32

An Heir-Raising Experience

A few days after our return to Maidenwell from Ireland I had one of my saddest moments: I waved goodbye to Baron and Emma as they disappeared out of the courtyard for the last time in Michael Gaze's car. Two puzzled faces peered out of the back window, their eyes full of concern: my own eyes were too blurred to see them clearly. They had been devoted to me for years, especially Baron II, and it would be the first time in 22 years that I had been without a canine friend.

At least Baron II had left his mark on the place, a substantial dent in the wrought-iron gate that separated the lawn from a walled-in quarter-acre of rough ground known as the Angel Garden, apparently because a pub of that name had once stood there. Last thing every evening it had been my practice to let the dogs out through the French window leading into the garden from the sitting room and they always rushed out in a tumbling heap, usually with Baron treading the others into the ground, especially poor old Dash. They would race across the lawn and out through the gate, which was always left open at the end of the day. On this one particular evening, however, it had been left closed, perhaps by Hathaway, and after the dogs had bounded into the night I heard a sickening thud and then a moan. I ran with my torch to the gate, and there lay Baron, apparently dead. I felt his chest and there seemed to be a heartbeat, so I rushed to Bigsby's cottage and between us we rolled the great animal on to a blanket and carried him indoors. At least he was alive. Indeed, by the time the vet arrived he was twitching. The vet examined his head and neck, gave him some sort of stimulant and promised to arrange an X-ray in the morning. We carried him up to my bedside and I lay awake listening for any sign of movement. Presently he stirred and then tottered to the bedroom door, showing every sign of wanting to be let out. We stumbled downstairs and into the garden where he did all that was necessary before clambering back upstairs to his bed. Next morning when Irene brought my tea, Baron was out of the room like a shot, as was his wont, and was off outside, seemingly none the worse for wear. There was not a mark on his head – no bruising or swelling and no cuts. The vet later pronounced him perfectly fit apart, probably, from a nasty headache.

But for ever after there was a large bulge in the offending gate where Baron II had hit it. That gate was made of quite heavy-gauge metal. God knows what Baron's head was made of!

Emma, too, had left her mark – on my slippers. Christened by Virginia as 'ever-hopeful Emma', she had a habit of drooling copiously whenever she saw food, especially when my breakfast was brought to me each morning. She would sit there with her naturally-wrinkled forehead furrowed with expectancy, even though I never offered her a tit-bit, and if I had forgotten to put them well under the bed I would step into a very soggy pair of slippers.

I was going to miss those dogs dreadfully . . .

The aunts and Mrs Bradley had welcomed us home and had everything running smoothly for us. Aunts Amy and Dolly coped with the cooking and saw that the daily help kept the place in good order. They brought up our breakfast each morning and were thrilled to have something to do. One morning when they arrived with the trays Aunt Amy, full of good cheer, pulled back the curtains and asked if we had had a good night. A rather ratty Virginia said, 'No, awful. He kept me awake nearly all night with his snoring.' Whereupon Amy, without so much as a look of commiseration for Virginia, said solicitously, 'Oh, poor Toddles. You *must* have been tired!'

Our days at Maidenwell were now numbered. I had stupidly not taken up the new lease on my Nell Gwynne House flat, and as we had a London house soon to go to, I also persuaded Virginia to give up her St John's Wood flat. But she at least had the sense to sell her lease.

Duncan Weldon came down to lunch at Maidenwell one Sunday and we arranged our first Triumph tour. It was to be *Roar Like a Dove*, a popular comedy by Lesley Storm. We agreed that our first productions for Triumph should be revivals of tried and trusted successes which had probably not been seen in the provinces with top-class casts.

Soon we were in rehearsal with a very happy and effective cast. Derek Bond, Robert Beatty, Renée Houston, Patricia Noble and Michael Percival were amongst those who joined me.

While we were rehearsing it fell to Virginia and Queenie to organise our move from Maidenwell Manor to Regent's Park, and to see to the decoration and carpeting of the London house. First, there was a sale at Maidenwell of all the furniture and effects for which there would be no room in our new home. I was glad I wasn't there to see some of my favourite pieces go. The enormous sofa which I had had specially made for the dogs, and which had been prominent in my sitting rooms for twenty years, was given to Michael Gaze for Emma's and Baron II's continued use. And then, on my birthday, we moved to London.

Virginia had seldom cooked before and we had some rather strange meals at first but, armed with a shelf-full of cookery books, she soon became a splendid and imaginative *cuisinière*. We were also lucky to employ a marvellous young Portuguese daily maid, Fatima.

Roar Like a Dove was the story of a Scottish nobleman desperate to beget an heir to his title and estates, despite the clutch of daughters already presented to him by his attractive American-born wife. Rebelling at last, the wife appeals to her parents to come to Britain and support her refusal to continue her unproductive marathon.

We opened at the New Theatre, Oxford and did a tour lasting 21 weeks, during which we broke the post-war record at 14 of the theatres that we visited. To illustrate this success, I shall quote from a major press review:

ROAR LIKE A DOVE TOO GOOD TO MISS

So what makes a play a play-and-a-half? And what transforms a merry little laughter-romp into a sparkling Rolls-Royce comedy?

The play in question is Lesley Storm's hit comedy *Roar Like a Dove* . . .

A very funny play, cleverly constructed, cleverly written. An ideal vehicle, in fact, for playgoers in search of happy, laughing evenings.

But what increases the laughter value of this production by at least 50 per cent and gives it a super-quality label is, quite simply, the casting strength.

Richard Todd, Renée Houston, Robert Beatty, Derek Bond – now here's a star-studded line-up which shrieks its own story. And the result is a beautifully professional lesson in how to act and how to entertain.

The simple story of a landed Scottish laird in search of a son and heir is unfolded with meticulous precision. But such is the skill of Mr Todd and Co. that the entire exercise is presented with effortless, almost nonchalant ease.

Richard Todd's world fame as an actor was based on much sterner stuff than this Lesley Storm comedy. Laughter, however, is just as much his wee drop of highland honey as the war epics of yesteryear. His portrayal of the Scottish laird is a master example of how to do the right things superbly right.

And ditto for Robert Beatty's king-size American business giant who is the terror of Wall Street but scared to death of his wife. A delightful performance.

Renée Houston plays the wife with all the skill and aplomb which has made her a warm favourite with millions. Here is the prototype American mother-in-law. Very formidable.

Glamorous Patricia Noble gives the production a lot of beauty and a lot of talent as the laird's American wife, and there is a first-class performance by Derek Bond as the family's easy-going friend.

Michael Percival turns in a gem performance as the laird's London cousin.

So far, so good. Our first Triumph effort was a huge success.

While we were on the road with *Roar Like a Dove*, Duncan and Paul were busy mounting many other shows, including *Oh, Clarence!* with Cicely Courtneidge, Jack Hulbert, Robertson Hare, William Kendall, Austin Trevor, Roger Livesey and Ursula Jeans – whose total ages amounted to a grand total of 500 years; J. B. Priestley's *When We Are Married* with Peggy Mount, Fred Emney, Renée Asherson and Hugh Lloyd, a production which was later to be our first London presentation at the Strand Theatre; *Goodnight, Mrs Puffin* with Kathleen Harrison; *The Chalk Garden* with Gladys Cooper and Joan Greenwood, which we eventually brought into the Theatre Royal, Haymarket and then sent out to Canada; *His, Hers and Theirs*, the Hugh Williams play, with Irene Handl, Peter Graves and Vanessa Lee; *Treasure Island* for a thirteen-week tour with Sir Bernard Miles; and *Harvey* with Harry Worth – to say nothing of six pantomimes being prepared for the Christmas season. And that first year was probably our least productive season!

And now I was not on my Todd as the only member of my family involved with theatre. Peter had never given up his ambition to follow in his father's footsteps.

I was certain that he was far too nice a chap to be a good actor, so I persuaded him to learn about theatre from the bottom up, in order that he might eventually become a producer. On his last Easter holiday from school, therefore, while I was doing *Four-Sided Triangle* on tour, I engaged him as my dresser, one of the most lowly jobs in the theatre. He got a pitiful wage and had to find his own digs; I didn't subsidise him, except for one good meal a week just to make sure that he didn't starve. He was most efficient and conscientious, pressing my suits, polishing my shoes, bringing me my cups of tea and generally being very helpful. I'm afraid he loved it and I noticed that he hung around backstage at every possible moment, watching all that was going on. It was not going to be easy to curb his enthusiasm.

He left Eton that summer with nine O-levels and three A-levels, none of the latter good enough to guarantee him a place at Oxford or Cambridge. So the die was cast – he would enter the theatrical business. I spoke to Duncan and Paul about him and they agreed to take him on as an assistant stage manager. 'You hire him; you fire him,' I told them. 'But don't make it easy for him.' An ASM is the dogsbody in a theatre company, particularly on tour where he works with the scene-shifters and helps with any task that might be required of him, especially on the get-out on a Saturday night when he helps load the scenery, furniture and props on to the huge lorry that moves the company around, often having to sleep in the lorry that night on long hauls, ready to get-in on the Sunday. He revelled in this, even though he took quite a lot of stick from the stagehands who twitted him about his 'la-di-dah' upbringing.

His first assignment was to the rather geriatric *Oh, Clarence!* tour. His face fell at the prospect, but he soon got to love it and all the old dears loved him too. Cicely Courtneidge thought he was the nicest, politest young man she had ever known in the theatre. He was particularly devoted to dear old Robertson Hare, who was nearing 80 years of age and very vague and poor-sighted. Every evening he would pick him up at his hotel, see him to the theatre, ensure that he found his way round all right, get him on stage on cue and then ensure he got home safely.

Peter progressed quickly to deputy stage manager and ran the show from the prompt corner, in charge of all the lighting and effects cues. But still he itched with the acting bug and was only at his happiest when he had some small walk-on part to play. Such was his dedication that at one time he played the policeman who walks on stage in a complete black-out at the end of the play in *Wait Until Dark*, simply shining his torch around and saying something like, 'Now then, what's all this?' When Paul went to visit the production one evening, there was Peter running the book from the prompt corner wearing police uniform and complete stage make-up – as he said, 'After all, there *is* the curtain-call!'

He worked his way up from backstage to front-of-house, becoming a house manager at Louis Michael's Playhouse Theatre in Bournemouth; then he went as house manager to the Royal Court Theatre in London after a spell at Louis's Richmond Theatre, and finally, at 24, became manager of the Duke of York's Theatre, probably the youngest theatre manager in London. He rarely took a day off, except to watch motor racing at Brands Hatch on Sundays, his other great love since his schooldays.

Then came a great opportunity for him: he was offered the post of assistant to the general manager at Brands Hatch, later becoming circuit manager responsible for safety, marshalling and track maintenance and given a seat on the board which owned Brands and other circuits. He seemed to have found a niche with prospects.

Meanwhile our extensive tour of *Roar Like a Dove* carried on until the beginning of December. When we were in theatres near London I was able to stay in our London house and lead an almost normal existence. But mostly I stayed either in hotels or rented flats or houses. Frequently I thought, 'What the hell am I doing this for?' but my consolation was that I was doing what I had set out to do – bringing good theatre to people and areas that had been starved for years – so I couldn't grumble.

Virginia joined me as often as she could: with her new responsibilities as a housewife, she spent less and less time modelling and seemed quite content to devote her time to me. Peter visited her as often as he could and Fiona, who officially was supposed to live with her mother, came to stay whenever possible. They were both devoted to her, and she to them.

Virginia had adjusted marvellously to her new way of life. She was alone a lot, but she had married an actor and she made the best of it. I was always sorry that the heady days of glamorous film locations and star-studded parties were past, but we did eventually manage some exciting journeys where she was very much the centre of attraction. She took a lively interest in Triumph's activities and was a very discerning critic of plays and players; on occasions she even acted as the fashion adviser for some of our productions, and had a tremendous instinct for what suited the actresses and where to shop for them. In this she had a willing helper in Ron Lucas, who became my dresser for years and also acted as wardrobe master. An ex-New Zealand ballet dancer, his droll humour and occasional bitchy remarks met their match in Virginia.

It was not always easy for me, either. I had never before had to trail around on lengthy tours, often playing in theatres which had seen better days. The only trouble was that as Triumph increased its list of productions, all the available spare cash and profits from some shows were going into the pre-production costs of others. And for all the shows that made money, there were inevitably a few that lost. Our pantomimes were very often saviours, helping to keep our bank managers reasonably mollified.

Duncan and Paul very rightly took reasonable regular salaries and received their travel and entertaining expenses from the company. I drew no salary as a director, and in all the years I was on the board of Triumph I never took a penny in expenses other than my normal working salary, which frequently didn't amount to much. I had put a few thousand pounds into the company too, when first we formed it, and it appeared that I was very unlikely to see much of that again. When I was not working, I was not being paid, either.

Just before we finished the *Roar Like a Dove* tour, Duncan came to see me at the house bringing with him John Downing, a gifted writer and director. Between them they convinced me that I should play Scrooge in John's adaptation of *A Christmas Carol*. I had never seen myself as a full character actor, but I had never enjoyed myself on stage so much before. We rehearsed under John Downing's direction and the company included Robert Beatty and Derek Bond again, so we had almost formed a team of three like-minded musketeers and had a lot of fun together. We opened on Boxing Day for three weeks at the Ashcroft Theatre in Croydon, so I was able to be home for a working Christmas.

I spent a couple of hours before each performance on a grotesque make-up surmounted by a balding, straggly grey wig, developed a hollow-chested shuffle and made Scrooge as much of an old skinflint as I could while still trying to maintain some of the sadness which I felt was the key to the old man's character.

John's production was a great success. In fact, we repeated it the following year for a month's season at the Theatre Royal, Brighton, with dear old Mervyn Johns playing Bob Cratchit.

This all did my confidence a power of good. 'If I can do that, I can do anything,' I thought. One of the great benefits of my work with Triumph was that I was really honing my stage-craft and playing a wide variety of parts, something that I knew would stand me in good stead in the future.

What a topsy-turvy but triumphant year 1970 had been: new marriage, new home, new professional departure; some things lost, but many things gained . . .

33

By Road, Rail and Air

My weeks as Scrooge were to help broaden my scope as an actor. After all, the show was as much a pantomime romp for children to enjoy as it was an adult drama of avarice, pathos and reformation.

I loved every moment of each performance and was immensely glad that the canny Duncan had persuaded me to have a go at the role.

We had started casting and rehearsing my next play before we even finished at Croydon. This was a play of my own choice, *The Grass is Greener* by Hugh Williams, and we were soon to embark on another marathon British tour with a cast which again included Robert Beatty and Derek Bond, plus the gifted Dilys Laye amongst others. Virginia was again credited as fashion adviser; she and Dilys had a great time seeking out some suitably chic but outlandish wardrobe for the latter, aided and abetted by the ever-present Ron Lucas.

The Grass is Greener, rather like *Roar Like a Dove*, was the story of a stately-home owner struggling to maintain his huge house and to increase its attractions to the visiting public, aided by his attractive wife who catches the eye of a visiting wealthy American – Bob Beatty, of course – and his urbane and caring butler, Derek Bond.

As part of our PR and publicity, we were often photographed and lunched at some nearby stately home at each venue – good for us and also for the owners of the real show-places.

We opened at the Royal Shakespeare Theatre at Stratford-on-Avon in February, and Virginia and I stayed at my old haunt, the Cotswold House at Chipping Campden. Warwick Castle was the first of our PR visits. We managed to have Fiona with us for her half-term holiday from St Mary's.

The following weekend we stopped for lunch with my old friends the Stonors at Stonor Park. Virginia had not met them before and was startled when the front door was opened to us by Sherman himself, wearing a paratrooper's trappings. The eccentric Sherman, now Lord

Camoys, had joined a parachute club, and his apparel was meant as a compliment to me.

At lunch Virginia was seated next to the loquacious Sherman, while I was between Jeanne and their rather obese chaplain, who gorged heartily and only uttered one sentence the entire time to say, 'Pass the port, please.' Sherman meanwhile regaled Virginia with tales of his parachuting exploits, including one when he had attempted a practice jump from a first-floor window and broken his leg. 'But my best jump was from this table into the fireplace.'

It was a happy if surprising reunion.

At Bradford I was visited by Holmes, who had been my first batman at Strensall when I was commissioned to the KOYLI. He was now a thriving insurance salesman.

At Hull we were shown round the beautiful Elizabethan Burton Constable Hall by John Chichester-Constable, who subsequently became a friend of mine, and at Nottingham our visit was to Belvoir Castle where in later years we were to spend many memorable and happy times with Charles and Frances Rutland.

When in Glasgow I even managed to lunch on Arran with Jean Fforde.

I carted my golf clubs around with me and usually got in a round or two each week, playing increasingly badly but at least getting the theatre dust out of my system.

When in Leeds we stayed with one of my dearest and oldest friends, Vera Barber, whom I had met when staying at Inveraray Castle years before. Born in Skipton Castle, former stronghold of the Clifford family, where her father was agent to the vast estates of Lord Bolton, Vera was the archetypal Yorkshire *grande dame*. Whilst no longer affluent, she still lived in some style and loved nothing better than an excuse to throw a party.

As the years went by, every time I stayed at Quarry Moor the house got shabbier, the garden more overgrown and the staff that much older and slower, except for Robert the chef who simply grew plumper and more florid from his frequent sips of sherry. Robert was, shall we say, a confirmed bachelor and when the time came that Vera could not really afford to pay him properly, she let him take on the catering for lunches or dinner parties at other houses in the neighbourhood. He would come back to an eager and appreciative audience of Vera and Virginia as he recounted all that he had seen: 'But, m'lady, you should have *seen* Lady So-and-so – a *disaster* in mauve!'

Vera and Virginia had a similar sense of humour and thoroughly enjoyed their evenings together.

To Vera I could do no wrong. 'But, darling, you bring so much pleasure to people,' she would say. Whenever she knew we were coming, she would immediately arrange a lunch party at her house, and ring round her friends to announce that the Todds were visiting and could lunch with them on Thursday or Friday. A stay with Vera was always a constant round of social occasions.

During that first visit to Quarry Moor our social programme was packed. On the Tuesday Vera gave a luncheon to which half the county seemed to have been invited, including Brigadier Johnny Walker, my KOYLI CO in Iceland in 1942, and Margaret his wife, who had remained friends of mine since those far-off early wartime days; on Wednesday we lunched with Roger and Edna Ingham at their home near Ripon; on Thursday with the Wombwells at their historic Newburgh Abbey; on Friday at Burton Constable Hall with the Chichester-Constables and on Saturday with the Robin Hills at Clifton Castle.

Vera must have been in one of her most commanding moods . . .

One of the few hazards at Quarry Moor was Vera's pack of five Labradors, all charming but totally uncontrolled and led by the only dog amongst them – Alfie, a huge and very masterful example of his breed. As soon as a car reached the end of the gravel drive, they would all come hurtling out in greeting, scrabbling at the doors to see who was inside. Vera's visitors, including myself, soon learned to leap out of the car almost before it came to a standstill, so as to save the paintwork.

Vera doted on her dogs. Towards the end of that first luncheon, Alfie somehow arrived in the drawing room and created mayhem with the coffee cups. When all the guests had left, Vera said fondly, 'I thought Alfie *made* the party, didn't you?'

Staying with friends became more and more a practice of mine and relieved some of the misery of constant hotels or rented houses. However, the main consolation for my itinerant life was that Triumph was going from strength to strength.

One very astute move Duncan and Paul had worked out was to get in quickly whenever they knew that a London play was liable to come off after only a brief run, and to offer to buy the set. More often than not we got it merely for the cost of carting it away to our stores – one in Eastbourne and one in a disused church which we bought for a tiny sum near Duncan's home town of Southport.

These sets had cost thousands to design and build and had probably never been seen outside London, so with a bit of rejigging and very little cost we adapted them for our tours. For example, for *The Grass is Greener* we had a magnificent Georgian drawing-room set which had hardly been used and cost us next to nothing.

During two weeks in our own Ashton Theatre at St Anne's I luckily found a pleasant house to rent and Fiona spent two weeks of her holiday with us.

I had no sooner neared the end of that tour in August than I began work on a presentation for the Edinburgh Festival. John Carrol, a producer, had asked me to play Sir Walter Scott in a kind of potted history of the great Scottish bard that was being written by Royce Ryton, who at that time had not yet achieved fame with his play *Crown Matrimonial*. Royce spent quite a lot of time at our house working with me on the script. He was a most exuberant person and Virginia found him also to be an enthusiastic trencherman who waded through enormous meals as if each was the last he might get for a long while.

I was a bit apprehensive about my reception in Edinburgh as a Sassenach daring to depict the great Sir Walter, especially since I had to deliver some of his greatest poetry beginning with 'The Stag at Eve'. However, all went well and the reviews were kind. It was nevertheless a relief to get through that week, and I was able to see some of the other festival productions, including one of *King Lear* in the round – which I thought was terrible – and a marvellous Frank Dunlop production of *Comedy of Errors* in which James Fox was outstanding.

I was staying at the George Hotel and found that Lord Goodman, head of the Arts Council, was also there. One day I buttonholed him and asked if the Council would ever consider subsidising a commercial company presenting a classical play, such as a Chekhov, which would not normally be within its financial scope. I thought him grossly unattractive and rather rude, and he firmly dismissed the idea. Anyway, I had thought it worth a try – and years later the Arts Council did in fact underwrite a couple of Triumph productions.

We had a short rest with Virginia's parents at Frinton, where they had moved on Colin's retirement, and were fortunately able to attend the wedding of Virginia's brother Dallas, though I had already started to rehearse my next play, *The Winslow Boy*, with Patrick Barr, Elizabeth Sellars (my wife in the film *Never Let Go*) and Carol Mowlam. It was an excellent play by Terence Rattigan in which I played an eminent QC. The tour started in September and ended just in time for me to start work on four weeks at Brighton as Scrooge in our last year's

version of *A Christmas Carol* with much the same cast. At least I was
able to commute by train to Brighton and had Christmas at home.

It had been a non-stop year for Virginia and me, and I sometimes
wondered whether I had taken on too much. She had been very supportive and never complained, but we had barely spent any time together
in our house and I knew that being on her own so much in London
would have been pretty irksome if she had not had girl friends she could
entertain.

We also worried about Fiona. Her home was officially with her
mother in London, but I knew that the two did not get on all that well,
so we did everything possible to see her on visiting days at St Mary's.
Since she was due to leave school next summer, I enrolled her for a
year's course at the Lucie Clayton School in Knightsbridge, a sort of
secretarial-cum-finishing school to which a number of her schoolfriends
would also be going.

It had become increasingly clear to me that London was not an ideal
centre for us. During the summer when I phoned Virginia at home, as
I did every evening, I would ask what kind of a day she had had. More
often than not the answer would be, 'Well, it's been a lovely day, but
what do you do in London on a fine day?' I began to regret having
given up Maidenwell, and thought seriously about looking for another
country home.

At that stage I had a bright idea. I did not want to rush into anything,
and thought it preferable to rent a house so as to give us time to look
around. With all my commitments I would not have much time to go
house-hunting. It was then that I remembered Jane Sutcliffe's beautiful
place, Glassenbury Park in Kent. Her grandmother and mother had
both recently died, and death duties had been heavy; the estate and
Jane's trust were handled now by trustees, and her income barely kept
the place going. I recalled that she had previously lived with her boys
in the mediaeval fifteenth-century manor, but knew that she had moved
into the larger Georgian part of the house, joined to the old building
by passages. When I phoned her and offered to rent the old house for
a year or two, she was delighted and we came to an arrangement.

I asked Virginia if she would make a home for us there and, with
some qualms about the state of the place, she agreed. And she did a
marvellous job with it. I sold the lease of the London house to an
American couple, and on 11 January 1972 we moved into Glassenbury
Park, with ample room for all our furniture and even some rooms
unused. It was totally independent of the main house and even the huge

cellars were clean and bone-dry despite being below the level of the big moat which lapped against the walls of the old place on two sides.

That week I also finished Scrooge at Brighton, but had already started rehearsals for another play. This was *The Marquise* by Noël Coward, a costume comedy-drama written by him primarily for Marie Tempest. This time the role was to be played by my dear friend Glynis Johns and the other leading man was Barry Sinclair, a charming and elegant actor who had for years taken over all the Ivor Novello roles.

We opened the play at the Royal Shakespeare Theatre in Stratford-on-Avon, and one morning I saw in a show-room there a lovely little green Morris 1000 Traveller, one of the most useful and ubiquitous small estate cars ever made in Britain. I had already owned two of them in the past, and realised that this would be the ideal country run-about for Virginia. I bought it on the spot and had it delivered to Glassenbury. Virginia had never attempted to drive my Bentley, but now she needed a car of her own.

Our tour lasted twelve weeks and Virginia was able to join me a few times, especially when I was staying with friends such as the Milburns near Newcastle, Johanna Brookes at Prestbury House (when I was playing at Wilmslow) and of course with Vera Barber when I was at Bradford. Vera gave her usual lunch party for us, and also took us to lunch with old Sir William and Lady Worsley at Hovingham Hall. As we left the front door of the Hall, which opens on to what had been a large indoor riding school, Vera turned to the startled butler and said, 'I'll ask Mr Todd to give you his autograph. I'm sure he won't mind.'

Fiona's term at St Mary's ended on a day when I was commuting up to Wimbledon, so she came to stay at Glassenbury for a week and I was able to spend my days with her. Jane Sutcliffe became very fond of Fiona and a good friend to her. When Virginia and I were away Glassenbury became almost a second home for Fiona, where the lovely little tapestry bedroom overlooking the moat and the lake was set aside for her.

Within two weeks of finishing our tour Virginia and I and the rest of the company were on our way to Canada, where we were to play for two weeks at the beautiful Royal Alexandra Theatre in Toronto, recently restored by 'Honest Ed' Mervish. He had started life as a junk salesman, then opened a gigantic antique furniture repository known as the Warehouse, and had waxed rich. A true theatre buff, he had made the old Alexandra into perhaps the most beautiful theatre in all North America – and today he owns and has refurbished the Old Vic

Theatre in London. Triumph had formed a close rapport with 'Honest Ed' and subsequently sent several productions to him.

We had a splendid two weeks in Toronto, during which time Virginia and Glynis became firm friends.

After that we broke fresh ground once more and spent three weeks at the Eisenhower Theatre in the Kennedy Center in Washington DC, a gigantic new complex of theatre, concert hall and restaurants. Again we established a very friendly contact with the director of the Kennedy Center, and later sent several productions there.

British theatre was certainly exportable . . .

After Washington we played in Boston for a week before flying home. Paul Elliott had handled the tour and his wife, who was in the play, was also with us, so it was quite a family affair. The only black spot had been when Washington was hit by the tail-end of Hurricane Betsy. It all started during the show one evening and we had no inkling of how savage the storm had been until we found ourselves unable to open the stage door against the force of wind and rain. When we did manage to get out and battle our way to the Sheraton Hotel, it was only to find that our bedroom windows had been smashed and half the room was awash.

Once home, we spent some pleasant weeks at Glassenbury before I started a whole summer season with a play at Weston-super-Mare – not really one's ideal choice for part of July and August, but made enjoyable by the fact that I was lucky enough to rent a really nice house with a pleasant garden on the outskirts of town and we were able to have friends down to stay with us, including Bob and Rosie Beatty. Having now left St Mary's, Fiona also came to us, which delighted us all because we were not going to see her for months.

In August I had signed a contract to go to New Zealand and Australia to play Andrew Wyke in *Sleuth*, with Gary Waldhorn playing the other role. The play was to be presented by Harry Miller, then Australia's leading impresario.

What an exciting prospect for Virginia and me! Neither of us had been to the Antipodes before and it was to be a lucrative and challenging theatrical experience for me. *Sleuth* is a marvellous play by Anthony Shaffer, a very unusual two-hander thriller. We started rehearsals in London, directed by clever young Nick Renton. Gary Waldhorn was an ideal partner, who had done a period with the National Theatre under Olivier.

We sent off piles of advance luggage to Auckland, which was to be our eventual destination. We were to spend three months on tour in

New Zealand before opening in Tasmania and Australia for a further three months.

Fortunately everything would be in Jane's good care while we were away, so we had no worries. Perhaps it was providential that I had decided to rent the Glassenbury house.

On 10 October we flew to Los Angeles in a Pan-Am flight, thoughtfully scheduled by Harry Miller who reckoned that we might like a break there for a couple of days and had booked us into a suite at the Beverly Hills Hotel.

Our dinner on the Jumbo that night was memorable. At about 8 o'clock we were handed an invitation card by a stewardess: 'Pan American Airlines request the pleasure of Mr and Mrs Richard Todd to dinner at 9 pm.' In those days, before the need for maximum seating capacity became the priority, the comfortable little lounge on the upper deck of a Jumbo was reserved as a relaxing area for first-class passengers and had a couple of wash-rooms opening off it. As we climbed the stairs to this lounge we were amazed to see that it had been set up as a small intimate restaurant with four or five tables all laid out for dinner, each with a silver candelabrum, lacy napery and high-quality cutlery. We enjoyed the most amazing *haute cuisine* dinner complete with wines, liqueurs and coffee. None of your cramped trays and plastic dishes on *that* flight!

If the rest of our trip was to keep up to this standard we were going to enjoy ourselves, and it would make up for nearly two years' living economically on a succession of tours, often apart from each other. Our only worry was for Fiona, who had now started her course at Lucie Clayton's and would be living with her mother. However, we would keep as closely in touch with her as possible, and we knew that she could spend her weekends at Glassenbury with Jane, who was very fond of her.

We had a pleasant stop-over at the Beverly Hills Hotel, always one of my favourites, then flew on to Auckland where we were met by Freddie Gibson, Harry Miller's associate, and moved into the Intercontinental Hotel.

Harry Miller was kindness itself and joined us for dinner after our opening performance with his charming and pretty wife, Wendy. He also arranged for us and the Waldhorns to spend the following weekend at Rotarua, the fascinating volcanic area with its bubbling sulphur springs and all-pervading aroma of sulphur. Our hotel there even had a steaming outdoor pool to wallow in.

We had a grand time in Auckland and made lots of friends who

showed us round and gave pool-parties for us. One man we met and
spent a lot of time with was an American oil tycoon from Texas who
was in New Zealand buying up oil-drilling rights for his father's Hou-
ston-based company, Republic Oil. Quite the antithesis of *Dallas*'s
J. R. Ewing, Gregg Wallace was a charming man who became one of
our dearest and closest family friends.

After nearly a month in Auckland's His Majesty's Theatre, we moved
to Wellington for three weeks where we met many delightful and hospitable people. We had already met some of my Todd cousins who had
been in New Zealand for several generations and were people of some
eminence there, both as large estate owners and as bankers. One of
them had apparently in the past prudently married a beautiful Maori
princess who had brought considerable lands into the family. The then
senior member of the family, Bob Todd, was a retired banker happily
rearing exotic pheasants as a hobby. Another was his sister, Eve Gorringe, with whom we spent a few relaxing days at her pretty stud-farm
before we left New Zealand.

But Wellington will always be remembered by Virginia and me for
a very personal and totally unplanned reason: a local gynaecologist had
confirmed that Virginia was pregnant. During our second week in the
New Zealand capital she had felt all the classic symptoms, and scarcely
needed a professional medical examination to tell her what she already
knew by instinct.

Though this was something we had not planned for, we were both
really delighted and Virginia proved an exemplary mother-to-be.
Nature seemed to have prepared her for just such a moment: she did
not smoke anyway; she went right off even a modest glass of wine; and
she was always very careful about her diet – never too much of anything,
and invariably a sensible, healthy balance. Despite the early stages of
frequent queasy spells, she acquired a happy serenity and looked absolutely stunning.

We wrote home with the news to our family and friends. Peter wrote
back to say he had taken the precaution of going to Eton to enrol the
child in case it turned out to be a boy!

On our return to Sydney Harry Miller and Wendy invited us to
spend Christmas with their family party at Harry's 12,000-acre farm
near Manilla, in central New South Wales. So on 23 December we flew
in a scheduled flight to Manilla and were then picked up by Harry's
light plane and landed on the airstrip by his farmhouse – a large,
sprawling, verandahed bungalow in the midst of a vast grassy
wilderness.

It was the most unusual Christmas I had ever spent since a wartime one in a château in the Ardennes in the thick of the 1944 battle of the Bulge.

For one thing it was ferociously hot, and for another the air was clouded by hordes of even more ferocious flies. Outdoors one could scarcely open one's mouth to talk without swallowing a mouthful of the creatures. Even so we rode for hours each day on Harry's cow ponies, usually finishing with a plunge in the sizeable river that flowed through his property.

We were quite a large party and sat down fourteen to Christmas dinner, all very convivial and jolly. I thought that Virginia might feel the effects of the heat with her pregnancy, but she was in great spirits.

Pretty Wendy was a vet by profession, and a very efficient one. She had even perfected a means of detecting which cows in the huge herds were bulling and ready for service by a bull. Harry's spread was split into 1,000-acre units by fencing. Because of the incidence of bovine venereal disease caused by dirt and flies – leading in many cases to premature abortion – no active bulls were run with the cows but all fertilisation was done in the stockyard by artificial insemination. Ordinary stock bulls still with plenty of libido were run with the cows. But before these bulls were let out with the herds, Wendy had cut the sac containing the bull's reproductive organs and opened another channel to the side, so that the penis was skew-whiff, as it were, and the bull could not penetrate the cow. Each of these bulls then had a sponge impregnated with a colourant strapped to its brisket. As he detected a cow ready and willing for his attention he mounted her and left her colour-marked on her back, whereupon he had a few brief moments of physical euphoria, but no harm was done.

Each day the plane covered the property and spotted those cows so marked, radioing back to base her location so that she could be found and brought in for insemination.

As an ex-farmer I was fascinated by this clever little scheme!

Back once more in Sydney I was feeling rather dreary with a dreadful cold, but Virginia was out and about every day, swimming and sunbathing either at the hotel's roof pool or at the Yacht Club. She was enchanted with Sydney and its beautiful harbour and Opera House.

I did feel fit enough to join her with the Gibsons at a very lavish party on New Year's Eve in one of the many plush Sydneyside homes, and a day or so later we went with the Gibsons to see *Jesus Christ, Superstar*, a super, super show – we were enthralled by it.

After a day or two shopping and sightseeing, we flew to Hobart,

Tasmania. About the size of Wales, this must be one of the most idyllic and varied islands in the world. As verdant as Ireland, yet with impenetrable forest to the south-west, it is almost more British than England, both in its ex-Brit population and in its architecture. Since most of the principle buildings are of stone, there is almost a Cotswold atmosphere about the place.

Hobart itself is quite lovely and mainly based around the harbour which is pure late-Georgian. All around are the most marvellous beaches with hardly a soul to be seen on them. Perched on a knoll overlooking the town and the sea inlet stands Government House, the residence of the Governor-General, a perfect little stone castle originally built largely by convict labour.

Tasmania had been the centre for a number of the penal settlements, many of those incarcerated there later being released to become the early settlers and to carry on their previous trades and crafts. Hence the profusion of Georgian buildings and bridges made of hand-cut stone by trained masons and carpenters.

I hired a car and we covered as much as we could of the area, though spending a good deal of our spare time simply lolling and swimming at Seven Mile Beach where we were usually the only people to be found.

We also drove to Port Arthur through magnificent stands of forest and by lovely little sea inlets before visiting the large penal settlement there, built by the convicts themselves.

We opened at Hobart's Theatre Royal, a most beautiful early-Victorian building where we ran for over two weeks and were sold out for every performance, including matinées.

The day following the opening was Virginia's thirty-second birthday; the Governor, Sir Edric Bastyan, and his wife Victoria gave a special lunch party for her at Government House. They were extremely kind throughout our stay in Hobart and asked us to join them on their yacht for a day's coastal sailing, but the weather was bad so instead we went for a Devonshire cream tea at the Old Colony at New Norfolk. Although the day was a Sunday, we had squeezed in a special extra performance because of the demand for seats.

There were plenty of excellent little restaurants there, especially in converted warehouses at the docks, and when the time came to leave Tasmania we were sad to go.

We were now to spend two weeks in Melbourne, doing nothing but enjoying a very good hotel and its pool, giving press interviews which mostly concentrated on Virginia – her pregnancy having been announced (though there was no visible sign of it) – seeing shows and films and meeting old friends, including Robert Morley who was there in *How the Other Half Loves*, and Harry Secombe, who was absolutely terrific in his show. We also had supper with John Sumner, who had been with me in my Dundee rep days and now ran the Melbourne Theatre Company. He and his wife had also invited Googie Withers and Frank Thring, an outsize, outlandish and amusing law unto himself in Australia.

We also found some exciting little restaurants, Italian, Greek and Spanish. In Australia at that time the flow of Poms had slowed to a trickle, but there had been a huge upsurge in the influx of new Europeans in recent years, so that everywhere we went we found signs of new cultures, especially in cuisine. This had all been foreshadowed for me by Jonathan Aitken, the British MP. Following an official visit to Australia he had written a book, *Land of Promise*, a copy of which he had left for me at Heathrow. I read it during our flights and it became my bible. I carried it everywhere. All I had known about Australians before had emanated from chance meetings with a few rather brash characters I had encountered during the war. Actually we found them universally to be the most outgoing, friendly, polite and hospitable people we had ever encountered. If it were not so far away, we would love to have a second home there.

Our next stop was in Canberra, the administrative centre of government and a very impressive new city where we stayed at the Rex Hotel. We were to spend two and a half weeks in the theatre there and again the play was a sell-out, which was fine except that the air-conditioning had broken down and we were working in temperatures over 100°F. With a very actively physical play like *Sleuth*, Gary and I were drenched in sweat every night.

It was all pretty tiring, and the heat was very trying for Virginia. I had a lot of TV, radio and press interviews to do (Harry's PR was terrific) and even flew to Sydney and back one day for a TV show.

We had one unexpected and exciting day. Some years before I had invested in some forestry with a company who had planted a large area in New South Wales near Jervis Bay, and had high hopes of a nice substantial lump sum in about twenty years' time. I had contacted the forestry company when in Sydney, and while we were in Canberra the head of the firm invited me to come and see the trees for myself. His private plane picked us up one morning and flew us down. As we circled over the mile upon square mile of young forest, a dreadfully little-looking airstrip came into view. We were glad of our seat-belts as we thumped and bounced to a stop over its rocky surface.

We were given lunch in the local manager's house, shown the nurseries and equipment and then taken to see the trees themselves. I must say that what I saw looked pretty healthy and flourishing. We flew back to Canberra quite contented – and also glad to get safely off that airstrip.

Sad to relate, years later this forestry project turned out to be a total fraud and I and thousands of others were left with nothing whatever to show for our investment. That was to come as a nasty blow for me.

While the torrential rain and stifling heat continued, we still spent an enjoyable couple of weeks in Canberra. One evening we were invited to an Asian Ball at which most of the guests sported Eastern costumes, especially the British High Commissioner, Sir Morrice James, and his chic and elegant French-born wife. He had previously been High Commissioner in India, so they were able to be very suitably and handsomely garbed. He kindly sent his official car to pick us up, later driving us back to our hotel most solicitously when Virginia began to feel decidedly queasy after a surfeit of curry and humidity.

The following evening they invited us to dine alone with them in his official mansion, Canberra House. This was a delightful occasion in that cool and spacious residence where we were attended by a staff of Indian servants in their smart, high-collared white uniforms, obviously retained from Sir Morrice's previous post. The delicious menu was not, however, remotely Asian, and we had a charming, chatty evening.

The day before leaving Canberra we picnicked at the Tidbinbilla Game and Nature Reserve, where we saw our first kangaroos and a koala bear, besides lots of gorgeous birds. That was a feature of Australia – everywhere beautiful colourful birds, including parakeets by the thousand and lots of black swans. The only feathered creatures we steered clear of were the emus, which apparently were inclined to be very inquisitive and aggressive.

From Canberra we flew to Adelaide via Melbourne, a trip of several hundred miles over quite verdant territory. We had a flat waiting for us in Adelaide in the same complex as Gary and Christie Waldhorn and their little boy, Joshua, who was quite a handful. Christie, who was American, described him in her best Doctor Spock manner as 'having a behaviour problem'. Only a few days later Virginia had to dive in and fish him out of the pool when he was going down for the second time.

Having a flat meant that we could at last enjoy home cooking and Virginia was able to produce lovely meals from the profusion of excellent fish, meat, vegetables and fruit available.

Adelaide was memorable for us in many ways, first perhaps because every seat for every performance, including matinées, was sold out for the entire three and a half weeks in the large Victorian auditorium of Her Majesty's Theatre. A 100-per-cent attendance in such a big theatre for such a period was something of a record, and *Sleuth* certainly took the venerable and conservative city by storm.

Secondly, that wide-streeted city enthralled us with its fine buildings, lovely parks and gardens, beautifully converted and modernised old shops and cottages and very grand and spacious houses on the outskirts.

Thirdly, we were delighted when Virginia was given a very clean bill of health by a local gynaecologist. I had never seen her looking so well. She fairly bloomed, and in other ways too nature had wrought great changes in her. Neither of us had ever intended to have children. I already had Peter and Fiona, to whom she was devoted, and Virginia was not a mumsy type in any case, her attitude to other people's infants being rather: 'Very nice – but take it away.' But now, totally content, she began to show every sign of building a nest in her thinking and planning like a proud mother hen. Always a keen swimmer, she took lots of exercise in the sea or pool. Expectant motherhood was clearly something that agreed with her.

And fourthly, we soon had a large circle of charming and hospitable friends in Adelaide.

At the first night in Her Majesty's Theatre, Virginia was seated with the Governor of South Australia, Sir Mark Oliphant, and Lady Oliphant, and they later invited us to lunch at Government House. Sir Mark was a scientist and an acquaintance of Barnes Wallis, so we had plenty to talk about. We also spent a day with Mr and Mrs Byron McLachlan, friends of the Bastyans of Hobart, at their beautiful estate Springfield some 30 miles away. He had a marvellous cellar and nearly every year went to Europe to buy wines for himself and the Adelaide Club, the cathedral of conservatism and as British in its atmosphere as White's or Boodles in London. They took us around some of the wine-growing area for which South Australia is famous.

On another occasion Sir Norman and Lady Giles took us for the day to their beach house at Maslin's Beach, which from then on became our favourite get-away place.

Tom and June Porter, the Ian Haywards, the Andrew Tennants – the list of those who entertained us was endless. We were sad to leave Adelaide.

Finally, after a marvellous month, we took the long flight to Perth, Western Australia, overflying more than a thousand miles of ever-changing but mostly arid country, with a few green areas surrounding farmsteads hundreds of miles apart. We had seen only a part of it, but already we were amazed at the vastness of that country.

Perth was quite gorgeous, not as a well-laid-out city like Adelaide but for its unmatched position on the Swan River and the surrounding varied countryside.

Our suite at the Parmelia Hotel was very impressive and had a superb view from its balcony. It was on a floor of that large hotel entirely devoted to five or six suites, including the massive Royal Suite, and had its own kitchen and individual staff. We had a room-maid, a valet and a waiter who never ceased to enquire if we needed anything. Such luxury!

Again we were shown great hospitality and lunched with, among others, the Governor, General Sir Douglas Kendrew, and Lady Kendrew. I was particularly excited at meeting him, as he had been one of the heroes of my youth when he was the England Rugger captain.

Business at the theatre was again good, though not quite what it had been in Adelaide – more like 90 per cent!

Our routine now quietened down a bit and Virginia started buying material for maternity dresses – not that she needed them yet. She still looked stunning in her bikini on the beach which we went to every morning, having discovered that the famous Fremantle breeze always sprang up about lunchtime and blew lots of sand around.

Just before our stay ended we met Maharaja Fatesingh Gaekwad of Baroda, whom I knew slightly and whose mother, Sita Devi, had been a friend of mine in London and Paris; he suggested we should stop in India for a while on our way back, staying with him at his home in Baroda. We were sorely tempted – Virginia had never been to India – but I reckoned that a stay in India, even in a palace, might not be the wisest thing for a woman now six months pregnant.

Instead we decided to fly via Singapore, spend a few days there and then stop off in Rome for a couple of days.

By now we had acquired such a lot of clobber that we bought a couple of trunks and sent them home by sea, leaving us reasonably unencumbered for air travel.

It had been a truly memorable and wonderful six months for us and we had loved Australia – but now we were excited at the prospect of getting home and starting a family. Our thanks will always be due to Harry Miller and Freddie Gibson for taking such care of us.

Singapore proved to be the most fascinating place we had ever visited, and we were determined to go there again if we ever had the chance.

I had booked a small suite at the Hilton Hotel and, quite forgetting that I had made a last-minute change of flight plan from Perth, was somewhat miffed that there was nobody from the hotel to meet us at the airport – over the years one had got used to being coddled. My annoyance increased when we arrived at the Hilton, had to wait ages before being able to register and were finally shown to a rather poky and claustrophobic pair of rooms.

Before we had unpacked, the phone rang. It was the PRO, who said she had just returned from the airport where she had been told that I had already arrived on a different flight. To make up for the error – my fault, not hers – would we accept the Presidential Suite with the hotel's compliments? *Would* we! Within moments we were transferred to the biggest hotel suite I had ever seen.

There were three huge bedrooms, three bathrooms, a separate cloakroom, a dining room and an enormous sitting room. I also counted nine telephones. Had he then been president, I would have called Ronald Reagan to tell him that I now knew how the other half lived! We were only sorry that we knew nobody in Singapore so that we could give a party . . .

Singapore beguiled and thrilled us. The whole place seethed and bustled with activity and the array of goods on show in the shops at seemingly impossibly low prices was dazzling – crocodile shoes and bags, pearls and jewellery, materials and silk shirts. We visited the historic and charming Raffles Hotel and lunched there under the old electric fans which still swirled lazily from the ceiling, had supper at Fatty's – the most famous of the street-stall restaurants that moved into the street at night – and spent another day window-shopping when I had a pair of crocodile shoes (badly) made the same day. I could never wear them, they were so painful and cramped. Virginia thought the maker must have left the croc's teeth in!

Our last day was spent lazing at the hotel's pool-side, eating delicious food out of pineapples, before taking an Alitalia flight to Rome.

We had a ghastly, uncomfortable flight to Bombay, where we changed to a DC10. Although the plane was better, the service was dreadful and the back of the aircraft was packed with Italians celebrating noisily all night. What with that and the garlic-laden atmosphere we had little rest. Worse still, our first-class loos were invaded by queues anxious to unload their 'vino'. Virginia, as is the need with pregnant ladies, wanted to spend frequent pennies and had to line up every time. When I complained to the chief steward he merely said, 'Oh, well, *signor*, they are happy to be going home.'

Staying at my favourite Hotel Flora we had a couple of days sightseeing in Rome, then flew on to London – where Anne and Colin Mailer met us with Fiona – and soon we were back at Glassenbury. Once home we realised that, with a family addition on the way, we must seriously start looking for a permanent home of our own.

Meanwhile, within a day or so I was back attending meetings at Triumph where Duncan, Paul and I discussed our future plans for the company. Duncan had kept in touch with me in Australia, so I already knew most of what had happened during my absence. One day Duncan and I had lunch with a Rodgers and Hammerstein representative to discuss *The King and I*, which we were shortly to present in London.

Virginia and I spent a couple of days in London at Duncan's flat, during which time she visited her chosen gynaecologist and arranged to have a room at Guy's Hospital for the birth (due now in a few weeks) while I spent the days in the Triumph office reading scripts and planning what my next project for Triumph should be. She and I also celebrated our third wedding anniversary at San Lorenzo. Triumph was now going great guns, with productions in Canada and Australia as well as in London and on British tours, and had presented ten pantomimes and Christmas shows while I was abroad including *Goldilocks and the Three Bears* in Toronto, the first panto there since the 1930s. Also my last film, *Asylum*, which I had made just before leaving for Australia with Sylvia Sims, Herbert Lom and Charlotte Rampling, had had favourable reviews and was doing good business.

Andrew Richard Palethorpe Todd was born at Guy's Hospital on the morning of 29 June 1973, arriving a few days earlier than expected. The evening before we had consumed large amounts of strawberries after dinner and early next morning Virginia woke very early with pains which she attributed to over-indulgence with the fruit. However, as a precaution I phoned her gynaecologist at 8 o'clock and he told me to bring her straight to Guy's, where he would be waiting. She had no time even to pack a bag, because by now it was obvious that she was in labour.

I must have broken all records for the road journey from Cranbrook to London during the rush hour. She sat beside me having increasingly frequent contractions, and never having experienced this sort of emergency before – except years ago in a film about a billet in France during the war – I was at a loss to know what to tell her to do. All I could think of was, 'Hang on, love, just hang on,' which was probably not very helpful. Normally a nervous passenger, thankfully she didn't even notice that the Bentley was surging along at well over 100 mph in places. To my horror at one point road-works had held up a queue of vehicles in front of me, stopped by a temporary traffic light. I simply raced up alongside the queue and got to the front where a bus was in the lead. Opening the passenger window, I called to the driver, 'Can you let me through – wife in labour!' Cheerfully he shouted back, 'Go ahead, Mr Todd – and good luck!' That kindly act probably saved the day.

We screeched to a stop at the entrance to Guy's maternity wing, Virginia was helped into a wheelchair and only fifteen minutes later a beaming nurse dashed into the little waiting-room next to the delivery room. 'It's a boy! You can see him and your wife as soon as he's been washed and cleaned up.'

Virginia looked wonderful when I went into her room as she proudly cuddled the little wrinkled bundle whom we had already decided to call Andrew, after his grandfather, while she had insisted that his second name should be Richard. Within a couple of hours Anne and Colin Mailer hurried in bearing flowers and some of the clothing that Virginia needed. One of the nicest tributes later came from Peter in the form of flowers with a card simply saying, 'Thank you for the best twenty-first birthday present I could have asked for.' His birthday was the next day.

Within days of Virginia's return to Glassenbury I had set off on a fifteen-week tour, starting fortunately at Croydon, so for the first week I was able to work from home before staying with Vera Barber while we played the second week in Leeds. She, bless her, had every excuse to throw a celebratory party at which Robert excelled himself, Alfie behaved himself and all my Yorkshire friends turned up to congratulate me.

In September we were able to stay for a week as a family with one of Andrew's godmothers, Johanna Brookes, at Prestbury House. Virginia had refused to have a nurse or a nanny, and was determined to do everything for the baby herself. It meant that she was pretty well housebound, but she didn't mind that in the least, and as Andrew grew he went everywhere with us. Jane, also one of Andrew's godmothers – as was Queenie – was always there at Glassenbury to help if need be and Virginia managed with just a daily. The only other person ever allowed to take occasional care of Andrew was his grandmother Anne.

My tour ended at Torquay in October and I took the night train to London because I was leaving the very next day for ten days in Tunisia.

Some weeks previously I had been approached when in Leeds by Jess Yates, a producer with Yorkshire Television. I had known him for some time, and he was aware of the fact that I had no interest in being involved in a lengthy TV series. However, with YTV's approval, he had cleverly devised and scripted a series to be called *The Boy Dominic*, in which I would have top star billing although I would only appear in the first and last episodes and merely top-and-tail the other eleven with a minute or so at the beginning and end. The whole thing would involve me for about a month, and he was able to offer me a very lucrative financial inducement and a nice semi-holiday in Tunisia.

I had agreed to do it as soon as my tour ended, hence the rush.

The Boy Dominic was a good series and very well cast with, amongst others, Brian Blessed, Hildegard Neil and Mary Morris. Dominic was played by a nice youngster who was the son of Jim Dale, the actor. The story opened with a nineteenth-century sea captain (me) who is wrecked off the North African coast and manages to struggle ashore, where he is captured, chained and put to work by Arab brigands until he contrives to escape and return to England. During his captivity the eleven episodes were played out in Yorkshire where his wife (Hildegard) and son Dominic are beset by all sorts of skulduggery on the part of an unscrupulous suitor intent on securing their fortune for himself, although they are befriended by a rugged individual played by Brian Blessed – such a good actor and nice chap . . .

In Tunisia we all stayed in a very luxurious hotel on the island of Djerba and filming went apace, first of all shooting the entire first episode of my capture and then a series of snippets showing my progress in captivity for the other episodes. It was a most enjoyable location, and I spent my last free hours shopping in the local Houmpt Souk, or market, where an incredible range of goods was on display.

Immediately on my return home Virginia and I drove up to Lincolnshire to look at a house that was for sale. We had reckoned that Lincolnshire, anywhere between Grantham and Peterborough or around Stamford, would be ideal for us because of its excellent road and rail connections with both London and the rest of England. Besides, I had known the county before from shooting days there and loved its spaciousness and varied scenery, from wolds to fens. Furthermore, it was mostly a stone area, and reminded me of the Cotswolds and Bampton and Chipping Campden.

Unfortunately we didn't like the house we had come to see – perhaps luckily, as it turned out. On our way back we were passing through the attractive little stone-built town of Market Deeping when we noticed a charming Georgian house near the heart of the old village, close to the road but with a fair bit of garden and grounds behind it, plus a large barn and stable building. On one side was a date plaque which gave the year 1734, if I remember rightly. The place had mainly caught our attention because of a 'For Sale' sign outside.

I stopped the car and went to peer through the front windows. What I saw astonished me: though rather small, the two main front rooms had very fine and ornately plastered ceilings and splendid fireplaces. Virginia agreed that it was really interesting, and liked the look of the village. From a phone box I got through to the agents, who told me that there was already a prospective buyer who had had a survey done. I also asked about the price, which seemed reasonable. Next I contacted the surveyors' firm and went to their office to buy a copy of the survey, to which they agreed. I don't know whether this was ethical or not, but it certainly saved a lot of time.

The survey, which I read then and there, was good. The whole house had recently been restored and renovated following the death of the previous owner, and was now being put on the market by the builders. Back I went to the agents and arranged to view the property straight away.

It was a bit small but quite charming, though the grounds were very overgrown. There were only three main bedrooms and one bathroom, and Andrew's room would be an attic one, but with the addition of a shower-room for me we reckoned that the place would do very well as a base until we found something better in the area.

I agreed the price and contracts were exchanged within three days – something of a record. We now had nearly a month before completion of sale, and a further three weeks to get the decorations, alterations and additions done.

Over the next few weeks I had rehearsals in London for the last episode of *The Boy Dominic* and then did various location scenes in Yorkshire.

We left Glassenbury and moved into Elm House, Market Deeping, on 20 December, so with Fiona and the Mailers coming to stay with us we were able to celebrate Andrew's first Christmas as a family once more in our own house.

34

Oh, For a Quiet Life!

A homing pigeon would sympathise with my feelings in those days: being taken away to God knows where, yet always instinctively flying home as fast and as directly as possible to its loft.

This was especially so now that we had put down our roots, at least for the time being, at Elm House. There was so much to be tackled there, especially in the complete wilderness of the garden. We were fortunate enough to find straight away an excellent daily for the house-work and a splendid old pensioner, Mr Knight; a retired table steward who had worked on some of the great liners, he lustily set about clearing up outside and doing any odd jobs that were needed. Later, as we began to make friends and entertain a bit, he even buttled very efficiently as he had been trained to do in his ocean-going days, wearing white gloves to cover his gnarled and soil-stained hands!

Having started from scratch, Virginia had developed into a superb cook and now she turned her attention to the garden. To begin with she had not known the difference between an annual and a perennial but soon, with the help of books and weekly garden magazines, she was planting and digging merrily. By midsummer our wilderness had been transformed into an attractive garden with new flower-beds, lawn and a path leading through to an area of natural woodland dominated by some fine old trees from which the house had obviously taken its name.

I would love to have helped, but 1974 turned out to be a particularly peripatetic year for me. At first I had a month or so of comparative quiet, interrupted only by weekly visits to London for meetings with my fellow-directors of Triumph. We were soon to have a fourth member of the Board, Louis Michaels, who was eventually installed as chairman and financial controller. Louis was a man of considerable wealth who had sold most of his varied commercial interests and property but had retained his love of theatre, and saw Triumph as being the ideal vehicle through which to increase his influence in that field. He had paid court to us for some time but we had resisted his overtures, partly because he and Paul did not quite see eye to eye on some things. But what Louis wanted he usually got, and when he did take a fourth share in the company he brought with him not only a useful source of cash but a burgeoning chain of theatres. He already owned the Richmond Theatre and the Playhouse Theatre in Bournemouth – together with the Westover Ice Rink there, where I had taken my first shaky steps as a schoolboy – and was soon to add the lovely Theatre Royal, Brighton, the Theatre Royal in Bath and finally the jewel of them all, the Theatre Royal, Haymarket, probably London's loveliest theatre, followed eventually by the Strand Theatre. So through Louis, Triumph had access to quite a few playhouses.

A kindly man in many ways, with a terrific sense of humour – his wit and Virginia's matched so well that we had some hilarious times together – he could yet be a demon in business matters and he and Paul were often at loggerheads. A bachelor, he lived alone in a flat at Grosvenor House and didn't even bother to own a car but simply hired one when necessary. In many ways a lonely man, he threw himself wholeheartedly into the affairs of Triumph and was seldom far from the office in the Aldwych.

Sadly, in time Paul broke away from Triumph though he and Duncan still often worked on joint projects. So Triumph once more became a trio of equal partners.

My wanderings began in February. I had always wanted to do the stage version of John Patrick's *The Hasty Heart*, the film of which had brought me my first international acclaim as a screen actor, before I got too old to play the Scot. Although now in my fifties, I could still get away with the early forties on stage with the help of Mr Max Factor, and I felt that there was something even more touching about the dying soldier being still friendless and bellicose as a mature man than as the young lad I had played in the film.

So we set up a longish tour as a joint venture with the Forum Theatre in Billingham which, with Guildford, was a producing theatre with its own workshops where our sets could be built more cheaply than in London and where a share of the up-front costs could be obtained.

It would have been the usual dreary round of hotels had I not been able to stay twice with Vera Barber and also with other friends. Virginia and Andrew were able to join me on occasions, too. Anne Mailer came to look after Andrew when Virginia travelled up to Glasgow to stay with me at Patrick and Gina Telfer-Smollet's lovely Lomondside home, Cameron House, where they kindly gave us the use of their guest flat in the central tower, but he came with us to stay at Duncan's Southport flat while I played at Liverpool.

It could have been a nightmarish journey for him because my Bentley, now some ten years old, was in for repair after a fire in the engine, and I was having to hire cars or use Virginia's little Morris Traveller. This time we used the Traveller and it was piled high with cots, prams, play-pens and luggage, with the wee fellow perched on top in his carry-cot. But he was marvellous and either slept or chirruped away happily. Every hour or two we stopped in some quiet spot, laid out a rug on which he could have a fast crawl, changed his nappy and set off again.

For our week in Brighton I had rented a very cosy house at Little-hampton and again we were all together – with Peter as well, who took a week's holiday to be with us. He doted on Andrew and insisted on pushing him for long walks. Andrew was now standing and climbing on to everything and was very naughty, encouraged by his older half-brother. The following week we were in Bournemouth where we rented a flat with a nice garden overlooking the Hampshire County Cricket Ground.

My tour finished in May and, except for some ten days at Elstree recording a play for ATV, I had a month of comparative calm at home during which Virginia and I scoured around Lincolnshire seeking a house more suitable for our needs than Elm House which, despite the improvements we were making there, was too cramped for us.

My agent, Richard Stone, accepted for me the leading role in a film to be made in Spain. I had read the script, which was based on a rather bizarre and unlikely story which he assured me was about the norm for films nowadays. It was to be an Hispano-American co-production star-ring Shelley Winters in the main female part and Dennis Hopper, and directed by Sylvio Narizano who was known for some good, sensitive work on American movies; my wife in the film was to be played by Faith Brook, for whom I had great respect since we had worked together years before on *The Boys*. We knew nothing about the Spanish pro-duction company set-up and realised that there would be a pretty lean budget – but that again was not unusual for films made in Europe in the seventies, before the era of elaborate science-fiction and disaster epics came into vogue.

Richard Stone had secured quite a generous deal for me, and I looked forward to getting in front of a camera again after the two-year gap since my last picture, *Asylum*.

I flew to Madrid at the end of June and was due to spend a night in a hotel there before flying on to Almeria. My confidence in the whole project was not enhanced when I arrived at the hotel only to encounter a mountainous and very sozzled Shelley Winters storming out on her way to the airport. From her brief tirade I gathered she was going back to America, although I couldn't make out whether she had been sacked or had withdrawn her services as I tried to sort out the facts from the profanities.

My mind was put at rest that evening by a phone call from Sylvio Narizano who assured me that she had already been replaced by Carroll Baker, due to arrive the next day.

From Almeria I was driven some 50 or 60 miles across an arid, mountain-fringed plain which reminded me of parts of Arizona that I had seen, a likeness confirmed by the scattered remnants of film-set ranches and stockades. Evidently some paella-Westerns had been made in the area. Climbing at last through the rugged coastal hills we came to Mojacar, which was to be our base.

It was a fascinating town, little spoiled and little changed since its ancient beginnings, crowned by a tiny and beautiful fortress castle perched on a cliff-edge. This was in fact Sylvio's home, and we were to spend some enchanting evenings there on a terrace with endless views over the craggy terrain, all misty blue and gold in the late sunshine. I was quartered in a pleasant little hotel down on the beach, and within a few days was joined there by Virginia and later by Fiona who came to spend a week with us.

My first day's shooting was sheer chaos. Making an English-language film with an all-Spanish crew was not the easiest of tasks, and I could see that Sylvio had his hands full of problems – not least with the unpredictable weather, which had us scurrying between interior scenes and exterior set-ups. The film was appropriately titled *The Sky is Falling*, and at moments the heavens opened and fell upon us in torrential rain, followed by hours of blinding sunshine. However, we soon settled into a reasonable routine, working very fast.

Most of my scenes were with Faith and I also enjoyed working with Carroll Baker, still extremely attractive and a real professional, acting uncomplainingly in some atrocious conditions and the flimsiest of costumes. She was utterly charming and great fun to be with. I realised that our strange little picture was not going to gain any Oscar nominations, but we worked with a will. From the moment when Virginia arrived for a fortnight, we decided to regard the whole episode as a pleasant working holiday.

Virginia also found Mojacar enchanting. It was like being in a time-warp, dark and almost secretive, the local people friendly but reserved and showing their ancient Arabic origins in their garb, their black eyes and aquiline features. One day we should like to go back there, hoping it will not have become too spoiled like the rest of the Costa Blanca. Virginia and Fiona mostly spent their days on the lovely stretch of deserted beach, or playing tennis with Henry Higgins, the English bullfighter who lived in Mojacar with his stunning Spanish wife.

My last scenes were on night locations in a narrow-streeted little hamlet called Bedar, high in the mountains and approachable only by a single, awful winding road partly washed away by the recent rains. I sweated as we were driven down from there in the dawn light. Virginia had by then left for home.

I soon discovered why my last moment in the film had been saved for the last day of my stint – I was to be shot in the chest by a series of bullets! The gruesome scene took place on the beach, and I was prepared for death by a smiling little special-effects man who assured me that he had done this sort of thing before on Westerns. Next to my skin he strapped a metal plate, then under my jacket were placed some small explosive charges covered with blood capsules. This jolly little contrivance was to be electrically detonated by remote control.

Anyway, it worked – and I'm still here!

But that was not the last of my hair-raising experiences. The next morning I was due to be called at 5 am to catch an early flight from Almeria, but the hotel night porter failed to rouse me until 6.30 am. Fortunately I was all packed and ready and, not even bothering to shave, dressed and dashed down to the waiting car. The driver said we could not make it in time by the inland road, but that we would have to go by the much shorter but hazardous coast road, not much more than a narrow ledge cut along the cliff-edge. He drove like a fiend and the whole incident reminded me of my driving experiences on the film *Chase a Crooked Shadow* – only this time I was not doing the driving . . .

When we arrived at the airport with only moments to spare, I was happy to give him a damn good tip.

While I had been doing the rounds Duncan and Paul had been very active, and Triumph Theatre Productions had been established as a major force in world theatre. Amongst many other productions at home and abroad, in 1973 they had presented four shows in London including the rock musical *Grease* at the New London Theatre and a revival of *The King and I* at the Adelphi Theatre. In addition to *The Marquise* with Glynis Johns and me in Canada and America, they had presented seven productions which included *Brief Lives* with Roy Dotrice; *The Chalk Garden*, with Cathleen Nesbitt and Joan Greenwood; *Move Over, Mrs Markham* with Honor Blackman and Cicely Courtneidge; *A Voyage Round My Father*, starring Sir Michael Redgrave; *Secretary Bird*, with Patrick MacNee; and in January 1974, *Lloyd George Knew My Father* starring Sir Ralph Richardson.

From small beginnings . . .

Now they had succeeded in arranging a most exciting venture: by arrangement with the governors of the Royal Shakespeare Company, Triumph was to present on tour in Canada and America the Royal Shakespeare Theatre productions of *The Hollow Crown* and *Pleasure and Repentance*, both shows which had been in the Royal Shakespeare Company's repertoire for some time.

The Hollow Crown had been devised by John Barton, one of the RSC's leading directors, and is an entertainment of readings by and about the kings and queens of England: music, poetry, speeches, letters and other writings from the chronicles, from plays and in the monarchs' own words. It derives its title from a passage in Shakespeare's *Richard II*: '. . . for God's sake, let us sit upon the ground and tell sad stories of the death of kings . . . for within the hollow crown that rounds the mortal temples of a king keeps Death his court . . .'

Pleasure and Repentance had been devised by Terry Hands, presently the artistic director of the RSC, and consists of readings and songs giving a lighthearted look at love and ranging from 'A Description of Love' by Sir Walter Raleigh to the Rolling Stones' 'Satisfaction'.

The great news for me on my return from Spain was that the RSC had accepted me to lead these productions.

During the next five weeks I and my colleagues rehearsed with John Barton and Terry Hands, both in London and at Stratford-on-Avon. I learned a lot from these two great directors, especially from Terry who broke down my inhibitions about quoting romantic poetry with vigour and enjoyment. My companions and fellow-performers were Prunella Scales, Anne Firbank, Clifford Rose, Hugh Sullivan and the gifted singer and lutinist, Martin Best.

At the beginning of September we all sailed on the *QE II* to New York, part of a deal which Paul had struck with Cunard in return for which we gave two public rehearsal performances in the ship's theatre. We were a very happy bunch of strolling players!

After a couple of days in New York we flew to St John's, Newfoundland, where we were to open the shows at the splendid University Theatre before going on to Halifax, Nova Scotia.

To chronicle all the events, people and places we encountered on that unique tour would entail a book in itself. For twelve weeks, usually staying only two days in each venue, we travelled by air and road the whole of Eastern Canada, from St John's to Sault Sainte Marie, and the length and breadth of America from Pittsburgh through New Orleans to San Francisco, staying in everything from luxury hotels to lousy motels and playing in everything from the greatest theatres to university halls – and everywhere being received with great enthusiasm and a degree of awe.

Some memories I shall always retain: a marvellous Salvador Dali painting in the Beaverbrook Gallery at Fredericton, New Brunswick; the magnificent new theatre in Charlottetown on the lovely, fertile Prince Edward Island, where I rushed to visit Green Gables only to find the pretty old house closed for the day; a wobbly stomach-turning night trying to sleep on a waterbed in Waterloo, Ontario; being drenched by spray on a visit to Niagara Falls; the lovely Georgian town of Hanover, Vermont, with its handsome Dartmouth University and lots of bookshops; being swamped by the sheer size of the 4,600-seater Civic Center Auditorium in Atlanta, Georgia; the all-pervading sounds of swinging jazz from the happy honky-tonks of New Orleans; a moving anthem specially composed and sung for us by the massive choir of the Mormon Tabernacle in Salt Lake City; and, most of all, that unlikely venue for the RSC, Las Vegas, Nevada!

After a short flight from Austin, Texas, during which we were fascinated by the single-minded concentration of most of the passengers as they practised their dexterity with packs of cards, we arrived at Las Vegas. As I ascended to the main concourse of the airport on the escalator, there at the top to greet me was Virginia, looking radiant!

That must have been the most wonderful surprise I had ever had . . .

Andrew was at home in the loving care of Granny and Grandpa.

We didn't like the look of the hotel which we had been allocated, so I decided that Virginia and I would move to one of the top hotels; there by great good fortune we were given an excellent, roomy suite simply because the manager was married to the young girl who had exercised and groomed my horses, Damson and Gemini, at Haileywood years before.

Louis Michaels, Duncan and his wife Janet had flown out from London with Virginia, so between us all we made the most of Vegas for a few days and particularly enjoyed the spectacular show at the Lido.

We were performing at the University Theatre, probably the only sane place in that ghastly city devoted entirely to gambling and razzle-dazzle. On the Sunday night we gave our last performance and Virginia and I entertained the company to a farewell party in our suite.

Previously, while in Toronto, I had had a series of phone calls from Richard Stone and Duncan, and he now confirmed that the National Theatre Company of Australia had asked if I would join them to play the lead in their special forthcoming production of *Equus* for the annual Perth Festival of Music and Drama. I had provisionally accepted and left Richard to work out a suitable deal. So I already knew what my next task was to be, starting in January 1975.

We flew home from Las Vegas at the beginning of December and were met at London Airport by Peter, now working as the house manager at Louis's Richmond Theatre. We went straight home by train where we arrived to a joyous reunion with Andrew, now chattering excitedly and tottering busily about.

After a couple of weeks at Triumph meetings, work with Queenie in my office and making arrangements for our Australian trip, Christmas soon came, when we were joined by the Mailers and Fiona and gave Andrew his first presents from a real Christmas tree.

35

Home Is Where You Make It

During that family get-together at Christmas, when Elm House was packed tight with all of us and a surfeit of furniture and belongings, Virginia's father made a most generous and welcome suggestion.

If we could find a house in Lincolnshire which was suitable and large enough to provide a totally independent wing for them, he and Anne would be willing to share it with us. We could thus be all together but separate, as it were. Virginia would never be totally alone and Anne would be near her adored daughter and grandson, while Andrew would always have Granny to care for him during any of Virginia's absences. It seemed a splendid idea to Virginia and me. We all got on well with each other – though I was never up to Colin's standards as a golfer – and it certainly widened my field of affordable places. Now we must accelerate our search, but not until we got back from Australia.

We started our journey in early January, this time complete with Andrew – now a self-possessed toddler who showed nothing but lively interest in the proceedings as he took off on the first of his many flights. We spent a night at the Beverly Hills Hotel in Los Angeles before breaking the tedium of the trip with a couple of days in Honolulu, Hawaii, and arrived in a sweltering Sydney, staying a night at a hotel near the airport where Andrew had his first splash in a big pool.

A day later we flew to Perth, Andrew this time insisting on latching his own seat-belt for take-off. We were greeted at Perth airport in the scorching heat by Tony Youlden, the administrator of the National Theatre Company, and Aarne Neeme who was to direct *Equus*. To our delight, we had the same suite at the Parmelia Hotel which we had occupied two years before.

Then followed some three weeks of rehearsals at the National's own theatre, and I was tremendously impressed with the company, most of whom were Brits who had emigrated – good actors and actresses all of them. I had seen the English National Theatre Company's production of *Equus* in London, but unfortunately not with the entire original cast and, though enthralled by this stunning and unconventional play of Peter Shaffer's, had thought the production rather dreary and scrappy. Perhaps some of its original verve had worn off. I was soon to believe that this Australian version was going to be better than the one I had seen in London.

For those who have never seen the play or the film, I should try to describe it. Set on a bare stage surrounded by tiers of *bleachers*, seating occupied by a section of the audience, it is basically the story of a psychiatrist trying to probe the mind of and give aid to a disturbed teenage stable-boy who has been convicted of savagely blinding a stable of horses with a sharp instrument. By question and answer, the doctor gradually elucidates the fact that the boy has been in love with a particular horse and has had what amounted to a physical affair with the animal, riding it nude in the night. When the boy is seduced by a stable-girl, the pair of them totally nude, he is unable to complete their physical contact when he hears the angry stamping of nearby hooves and imagines the accusing look of his beloved horse. In a frenzy of guilt, he is led to carry out his maniacal attack on his equine friends. The setting is reminiscent of an operating theatre, with the audience like medical students in a teaching hospital. The members of the cast come and go for their scenes from wooden benches on side-stage, and thus in a sense are always part of the action. The 'horses' are all men wearing leather and metal horses' heads and heavy iron hooves.

Aarne Neeme, an immigrant from one of the Baltic states, directed most sensitively yet firmly, and we were soon seeing a tremendous show emerging.

Unlike the London production in which the 'horses' were a motley collection of young student actors, ours were all trained ballet dancers with matching physiques, choreographed and drilled by a ballet-master. Their movements were cohesive and the rhythms of their hoof-beats led up to a crescendo of pulsing, thunderous sound. Even in repose, their statuesque stances were quite beautiful.

I was thrilled to share in this electrifying production in the role of the psychiatrist. The show was a sell-out during the Festival, and we kept it on for a further period.

Virginia and I had found a charming large flat in a modern block in West Perth, on the other side of the Swan River, with marvellous views across to the city. It was on the fringe of a pretty little, almost Bohemian community of shops and restaurants, and our nights were enlivened by all kinds of screeches and roars from the zoo close by. The PRO at the theatre had arranged for me to have a very comfortable air-conditioned Australian-built General Motors car, and with Andrew we had some super jaunts to beaches and nature reserves. Andrew especially had a great time, and was perfectly happy when left in the care of an elderly Englishwoman who came to us as a baby-sitter on the evenings when we were out.

Once again Perth had been a happy experience for us, and once again we stopped for a couple of days in the Hilton Hotel in Singapore on our way home at the end of February.

Peter had written to say that I was not to be too alarmed by his appearance when he met us at Heathrow. He was there with Anne and Colin and our reunion was only marred by his very badly scarred face. Poor chap, he had been involved in a crash in his open sports car, and the impact had been so great that his safety-belt had broken his collarbone and the screen had shattered around his head. Cosmetic surgery had patched up his face, but the scars would take a while to heal. He was terribly anxious that I should not be upset. That same day we also heard that Auntie Dolly, the last of the Hunters, had died only months after Auntie Amy's death.

It seems incredible now that within a day of my return to Market Deeping I started rehearsals again, this time for a new play with Moira Lister. *Miss Adams Will Be Waiting* was a package that Richard Stone had put together with Duncan as a co-production with the Yvonne Arnaud Theatre at Guildford. It was a nice little four-handed comedy which we hoped might prove suitable for London after a longish tour.

Then, on our first weekend home, Virginia and I found it – the perfect house for us! It was a late-Georgian former rectory which belonged to the large Stoke Rochford estate near Grantham, completely surrounded by land of the estate and close to the tiny hamlet of Little Ponton, so that it was not isolated. Down the little road that passed by the house was the minute church, of Norman origin and without even a tower – little more than a charming stone barn as seen from the road – and beyond that the entrance to Little Ponton Hall where lived the estate owner, Major Turnor, with his daughter and son-in-law Rosemary and Alastair McCorquodale, though I did now know that at first. I had seen an advert in a local paper, phoned the estate agent and met him at Little Ponton House so that he could show us round that Saturday.

Despite its neglected condition – the last occupant had been the Major's sister, and the place had not been lived in since her death some time previously – Virginia and I knew at once that it had all the makings of exactly what we needed. With its attached stable block which also contained two garages, the house was quite large and had been much added-to during its history; being U-shaped, it lent itself ideally to being altered so as to provide almost the whole of one wing for Virginia's parents with minimal structural alteration and plenty of room for us as well. There was a lot which needed to be done, both inside and out, especially decoratively – for some reason a previous incumbent had painted the entire interior (walls, woodwork and all) in two tones of dingy light and dark green – but it had been splendidly built with fine period doors, shutters, fireplaces, ceiling coves and some massive cupboards and beautiful floors.

The garden was a mess. The main lawn, which had once included a tennis court, was now just a small, weedy field covered with molehills; the little walled garden was overgrown and something of a rubbish tip. And, sadly, only two of many lime trees had survived, as we could see from the remaining stumps.

But we loved the place and saw it as a perfect future family home. I spoke to Colin on the phone that night and the next day made an offer for the place. From then on I had to leave everything to him, as I was once more about to embark on another barn-storming tour.

The London rehearsal period once finished, we opened with a very good three weeks at Guildford. We closed there on 12 April and the very next day Moira Lister and I flew to New York!

London theatre was having a difficult time. Because of bomb scares Americans had not been arriving in their usual droves, and this was the start of the new tourist season essential to the health and wealth of the theatre world. The Society of West End Theatre Managements, the British Tourist Authority and Keith Prowse, the ticket agents, had banded together to fund a promotion to drum up interest in the United States, and Moira and I had been chosen to act as travelling ambassadors for their cause. We were asked to go on a series of one-night stands all over America, doing TV and radio interviews and having press conferences and meetings with groups of tour operators and travel agents.

I won't attempt to describe that hectic trip except to say that we covered 18 major cities in 28 days! We flew thousands of miles, squired everywhere by a very efficient BTA official whose head office had laid on a masterly though killing programme. I was shattered at the end of each day, but the indefatigable Moira would often pop out to see a theatre in the evening. She was the breeziest, most entertaining of companions, and never flagged. I would wake up in some strange hotel room each morning trying to remember where I was.

I needed the week's break that I got on my return home, before launching out on an eleven-week tour of *Miss Adams Will Be Waiting*. This tour went reasonably well, though we had come to the conclusion that the play was not London material. The tour was much the same as all the others, with me hiring cars to get home at weekends. At Wimbledon and at Richmond I was able to spend some time in the Triumph office and do some work with Queenie. At Richmond also I worked under the authority of Peter who was then the manager there, a fairly unusual situation for me!

At Croydon I was urgently asked to go to Leeds to do an extra shot for *The Boy Dominic*. I took the night train up there, did the work and was provided with YTV's helicopter to get me back in time for the show. We landed at a large nearby country hotel with a helipad, where I was greeted by an under-manager in black coat and striped trousers, accompanied by a waiter bearing a silver tray on which was a large glass of champagne for me. It was all like a TV commercial!

Virginia and Andrew were able to spend a week with me at Wilmslow in a bungalow that Johanna Brookes lent us. Andrew's godmother was delighted to see him again, especially as his second birthday came at the end of that week. All had apparently gone according to plan with Little Ponton House, and Colin and Anne moved in there in July.

Virginia also came to stay with me on the last week of the tour in Birmingham. She needed to – we were not going to see each other again for two months! I had accepted a plea from the Australian National Theatre Company to do a further stint with them on *Equus*, including a short tour. We arrived home from Birmingham on the Saturday night, I spent Sunday packing and on Monday was once more on my way to Perth, this time in a very good direct Qantas flight.

After rehearsals we embarked on a tour of parts of Western Australia and Northern Territory, the prime objective being to be the first major company to bring theatre entertainment to Darwin, the city which had been devastated by a recent terrible hurricane. An interesting tour included such beautiful places as Broome, with its harbour full of picturesque Japanese pearl-fishing boats; and unusual ones like Parraburdoo, a town entirely owned by and depending on the Hammersley Mining Company which was in the process of shaving the top off – and thus gradually reducing – an entire mountain of iron-bearing rock.

Darwin, as I expected, was a scene of utter wreckage and one wondered why people still persisted in rebuilding and remaining in such a remote and stifling place. Money, I suppose, was the key, since wages were very high as an inducement to live and work there. After a few years the inhabitants could retire and move to more agreeable areas, their fortunes made. The high-rise and quite luxurious hotel where I stayed seemed untouched by the storm, and we were all very heartened by the enthusiasm and size of our audiences in the school hall we used. It made sense of our visit, and the whole tour seemed worthwhile.

We finished with a few days at Alice Springs, where of course I rushed to see the notorious Todd River only to find that it didn't exist at that time of the year – just a few puddles in a sandy bed, which turned into a turbulent torrent only when the rains came.

After a few days in Adelaide staying with Tom and June Porter, I returned to Perth where I had arranged to rent a very convenient little flat near the Parmelia Hotel. Three weeks at the theatre in Perth soon passed and included the usual rounds of social activity, trips round the countryside in my hired car, lots more crayfish suppers and lunch one day with Sidney Box, the British film producer, who had retired to live in Perth with Sylvia, his charming wife.

While I was gadding about down under, Virginia – bless her – was performing miracles at home. Elm House had been put on the market in May but was still unsold – in fact, we did not find a buyer until the following year, when we eventually moved to Little Ponton. Meanwhile she was commuting almost daily to and fro between the two houses, carting with her in the Traveller our only motor-mower and with enormous energy reducing the lawns to some semblance of respectability. In addition she was supervising the carpenters, decorators, electricians and plumbers working at Little Ponton and doing a lot of the decorating herself. Certainly it was due to Virginia's energy and good taste that Little Ponton House gradually became a gracious and attractive home, with a garden that would be opened to the public several times for charities.

During the next two or three weeks of comparative quiet, Virginia and I set about buying and planting young trees for Ponton. She was already a familiar customer at a large garden centre near Spalding and soon we were ferrying trees and shrubs of all sorts, including enough birches to make a small quick-growing grove; we reckoned this was a priority and that roses and other flowers could follow. Virginia's eye for garden design – a latent talent that she could now exploit – led her to visualise a means of 'compartmentalising' the rather flat and boring oblong of our grounds, so we planted hundreds of leylandii to form hedges and others to form a diminutive 'forest' in one corner for Andrew to play in. Within a few years the place was transformed.

I had also got fed up with a shortage of spares for the Bentley and now sold it, buying instead a roomy 2.3 Vauxhall hatch-back estate which was to prove a good and reliable workhorse.

In addition I had been having talks with Duncan about my next source of gainful employment. While I appreciated having a few weeks at home, I didn't fancy 'resting' for too long, especially now with Elm House still unsold and new outgoings at Ponton being incurred. We decided that a mammoth British tour of *Sleuth* would pay dividends, and I loved the play anyway.

So towards the end of October I started rehearsals with Peter Byrne, who was excellent and with whom I had as good a relationship as I had enjoyed with Gary Waldhorn in Australia.

During that period I had dinner with Fiona, who had cabled me excitedly when I was in Perth to tell me that she had got a job with a major firm of estate agents in London. The change in her was wonderful. She was brimming with confidence, had passed her driving test at first attempt and was now sharing a flat with a couple of other girls near Sloane Square – one of the first of the so-called 'Sloane Rangers'!

The plan was for Peter Byrne and me to tour *Sleuth* through November and part of December, then to take a break for the Christmas period when most theatres were running pantomimes, and to start the tour proper at the end of January.

The first leg of the tour fortunately included York and Harrogate, so again I was able to stay with my Northern landlady, Vera Barber – where else! That time there was great excitement when Vera and I went to Wetherby Races and her horse won a good steeplechase. Virginia came up to be with me for the second week, leaving Andrew at Little Ponton with his grandparents. As usual, Vera excelled herself with a lunch party and numerous invitations to other houses. Nothing at Quarry Moor had changed, except from the ravages of time and the loss of two of the dogs.

During my break we went to London for the first night of a not-too-successful Triumph presentation of Frederick Lonsdale's marvellous old comedy, *On Approval*. I thought it somewhat miscast and did not enjoy it, except for the inherent wit and humour of the play. We also had lunch with our dear American friend Gregg Wallace, whom we had first met in New Zealand; he was on one of his frequent business trips to London.

Peter and Fiona both came to join us for Christmas, and once again we were able to enjoy a real family holiday. We gave a dinner party for Virginia's birthday in January at which we and our ten guests managed to squeeze into our two small main rooms, and I even got a couple of days' shooting at the second of which (with Nick Playne at Aswarby Park) a howling gale drove the pheasants like rockets – very testing for someone who had not shot for several years!

Andrew went to his first children's party with the Benton-Joneses at beautiful old Irnham Hall, but his great moment came a few days later when he was christened at last at St Guthlac's Church. We had never seemed to have time to organise the ceremony before, and here he was 2½ years old!

He was christened by the Rector, Canon David Davies, a charming bluff ex-Wales Rugby forward who had become a close friend. As our little group gathered near the font, David sat down beside Andrew and said in his most avuncular tone, 'Now, Andrew, I'm going to tell you a little story.'

'Is it the three bears?' was the bright retort . . .

36

Another Heir Apparent!

After the welcome six-week break over Christmas and the New Year, the marathon *Sleuth* tour recommenced at Richmond, again to tremendous business and fine reviews. A long stint in a good play – and *Sleuth* was a great one – is never a hardship or just a boring routine. *Sleuth* is too exciting for that: only two actors carry the whole show, and each night they face the challenge of holding the audience with extremely active and wordy parts.

The routine of the nightly performance hanging over one each day does get irksome at times, also the inability to go out in the evenings, or to fit in with other people's pattern of living – but never the actual performance itself. During the course of a long-running play I am often asked, 'Don't you get fed up with doing the same thing every day?' The answer has to be: 'Who does not do the same thing every day? A doctor? A housewife? A business man or banker? A schoolmaster or a politician? A painter or an architect?' At least we in the theatre play to different people every night and get different reactions. It is in fact an obsessive profession – I have never heard of a successful actor who has chosen to retire, unless through physical disability.

The tour criss-crossed the country until June, with a few free weeks out – which were timely, since I was able to help Virginia with her decorating at Little Ponton, where the only furniture at first had consisted of a lawn mower in the empty hall, kept there because it was more convenient than out in the stables.

Virginia spent many nights at Ponton, sleeping with Andrew in a spare room with half the ceiling down while our own bedroom was being worked on and a new bathroom installed. Fortunately she had her parents there, by now cosily established in their wing, and numerous friends to entertain her – especially the McCorquodales, who turned out to be old acquaintances of mine since the days when their son Neil was at prep school with Peter at Wellesley House. They lived just down the road at Little Ponton Hall.

Elm House was finally sold and we moved completely into Little Ponton House on 20 March. As luck would have it I was playing that week at Peterborough, only a few miles away from both Market Deeping and Ponton, so I was able to help with the removals and get-in, and a week later had one of my free breaks which enabled me to carry on with arranging the pictures and furniture. The mower was banished to the stables . . .

Virginia and I celebrated our sixth wedding anniversary with Fiona at Bolesworth Castle in Cheshire with our friends the Richard Barbours – again, fortunately, during one of my clear weeks. We were also able to spend a week at our old flat in Bournemouth together with Andrew.

One nice diversion during the touring routine was a visit by Anthony Shaffer, the author of *Sleuth*. He was fulsome in his praise for our performance and reckoned it was the best he had ever seen. He asked me to take the lead in his next play, and gave me the script to read some weeks later.

As it happened, I had unfortunately by then already committed myself to another production. Pieter Toerien, for whom I had played in *An Ideal Husband* in South Africa years before, had asked me to do *On Approval*, a sparkling 1920s comedy, for him, so a week after the *Sleuth* tour ended I began rehearsals in London.

My fellow-actors for *On Approval* were Moyra Fraser, Amanda Reiss and Barry Justice, and the piece was beautifully and wittily directed by Frith Banbury with whom I had worked on *Dear Octopus*. We opened at the vast Civic Theatre in Johannesburg in July, and the show was an instant success. The reviews were uniformly good, and a typical one read

> . . . This is the excuse for some sparkling, epigram-studded dialogue and not a little visual humour, too, as due regard is paid to the modes and mannerisms of the period. It would be invidious to single out any one performance as being more worthy of praise than another. Overall they constitute a team to keep the humour bubbling merrily along and reflect the polish and panache of the era to fine effect.

Frankly, it was a better production than the earlier Triumph revival in London.

When we moved to Cape Town the show was a complete sell-out for the entire two weeks, and Pieter decided that we should return there for a further period later on.

While in Cape Town I met and lunched with Vernon and Maggie Lilford at their glorious Cape Dutch house at Constantia. I had met Lord Lilford when at our St Anne's Theatre not far from his Lancashire estate, and discovered that he had bought the old Lancaster bomber in which I had once flown on a memorable and frightening trip years before, and had set it up near his house as an attraction for visitors. Vernon was South African-born and English-educated and had recently succeeded his kinsman to the title, estates and considerable wealth. He had decided to spend some time in the country of his birth, where his elderly mother still lived, and had bought this lovely house near Cape Town. Meanwhile I had been living in the old Mount Nelson Hotel and occupying the same suite I had used when staying there before my marriage to Virginia.

After visits to East London, Grahamstown, with its fantastic new Monument Theatre, and Port Elizabeth, we arrived for a longish stay in Durban, a place well-remembered by me from previous visits filming and playing at the Lyric Theatre. Oscar Hurwitz had lent me his large flat in a block which he had built right on the beachfront, and after a couple of days Virginia and Andrew flew out to join me. It was lovely for me and all very exciting for Andrew, who was now three and taking note of everything in this strange new environment. I took him several times to watch the sharks in the Durban shark research unit, and also to an exhibition of snakes.

We spent ten days or so at the enormous new Cabana Beach Hotel, where the nearby rock-pools at Umsloti Rocks were ideal for Andrew to play in, safe from surf or sharks.

Our month in Durban ended, we went to stay for a week with Tim and Rosemary Scott, charming young friends who farmed near Pietermaritzburg in Natal – a verdant and fertile area heavily populated with English people, mostly involved in farming. Their house, Haycroft, was surrounded by a lovely garden where Andrew and the little Scott girls played. On one occasion the Zulu gardener disturbed a deadly black mamba snake which slithered away across the lawn as Andrew scuttled off in the opposite direction. He had actually recognised the mamba.

Unfortunately, after three or four days he caught a really bad cold and the doctor advised against his flying to Cape Town for a while, so I went alone, to be met at the airport by Vernon and Maggie Lilford Virginia and Andrew joined me there later.

Towards the end of a happy stay with the Lilfords, we had another reason for always remembering our weeks together in South Africa: a gynaecologist confirmed that Virginia was pregnant! We were of course delighted, and the Lilfords demanded to be godparents to our next child.

In October they finally saw us off to Johannesburg on our way home. Oscar and Ruth Hurwitz met us there and drove us to their home in Pretoria for a night before our flight to England.

All was well at Little Ponton.

While I had been in South Africa, Richard Stone had sent me a film script to read. It was a spoof spy thriller called *008 of the Secret Service*, to be produced and directed by Lindsay Shonteff, an England-based independent producer. My leading role was as a rich international trickster, a man of many disguises and shady dealings; it read well, and I agreed to do it. Within four days of returning home I had started filming in London.

My first scene, for plot reasons which I cannot remember, required me to be dressed very shabbily, to carry a small collapsible rostrum and harangue a crowd at Speakers' Corner in Hyde Park on Sunday morning, the time when all manner of orators and rabble-rousers set up their stands and attract large numbers of curious, amused or offended onlookers.

My dialogue was not scripted. Instead for some fifteen minutes I had to deliver an extemporary speech about the wickedness of capitalism, drawing quite a big crowd which eventually outnumbered those around the other speakers – probably either because I could bawl louder than the others or because of the seditious content of my speech. Nobody recognised me through my disguise, the hand-held cameras were concealed from view and the audience there obviously thought I was a genuine anarchist – quite a feat for me.

Eventually, on a signal from Lindsay Shonteff, I packed up my props and shuffled away out of sight to a point where I boarded a waiting Rolls-Royce and removed my wig and disguise.

The film kept me busy for a month, during which I lived in London at the company flat in Red Lion Square. Also during that time I had supper one evening with Fiona and with Rollo Clifford, her very special boy-friend. For some time we had known that she was serious about him and now I could see why: he was a charming young man.

With the movie finished in early November, I at last had a long break at home until mid-January, when I had arranged to go to Hong Kong to oversee the production there of *On Approval*, with the same cast, as a presentation in one of Derek Nimmo's highly successful series of dinner-theatre shows in the Far East.

At last we finished the papering and painting of the drawing room and dining room and were in a position to give our first dinner party at Little Ponton.

Rollo and Fiona arrived the evening before the party. Fiona came first, Rollo having spent the day shooting with his aunt and uncle, Lord and Lady Fisher, in Norfolk. Fiona was particularly starry-eyed, so we knew something was afoot.

After supper that evening she and Virginia tactfully disappeared into the kitchen, leaving me and Rollo alone in the sitting room. He wasted no time, and announced, 'Sir, I have something to ask you.'

I nearly spoiled the whole proceedings by telling him I already knew what he had in mind, but fortunately shut up as he went on. 'May I have the honour of asking your daughter to marry me?'

Such a charming, old-fashioned approach – unusual in this informal age – totally beguiled me and I happily shook his hand and wished him luck, then rushed to get some champagne, and with hugs, tears of happiness and lots of laughter we took Rollo into our family.

He was a very large, delightful chap, inclined to be cherubically plump – and in fact, as neither he nor Fiona was exactly sylph-like, we called them our jelly babies. The second son of Lord Clifford of Chudleigh, the head of a distinguished and ancient Catholic family, Rollo was working at that time in the City. We soon grew exceedingly fond of him. The engagement was officially announced on 20 January 1977, and they set September as their wedding date. Fiona had been happily accepted into the Clifford family too and had been spending frequent weekends at their home, stately old Ugbrooke Park in Devon.

During the weeks that followed we had any number of invitations to parties in the area both from existing friends and from others we were now meeting – primarily through the McCorquodales, who were very kind to us. Furthermore, my gun was now seeing plenty of active service.

Christmas that year was a really jolly family occasion.

Then, on Boxing Day, disaster seemed to strike.

The dreaded Dutch Elm disease had killed a magnificent line of trees which fringed the field surrounding our house. One by one they had begun to topple or lose their branches, and I was given permission by the McCorquodales to start logging some of the fallen timber with a hired and rather heavy chain-saw. For days on end I had been hard at it – working, as is my wont, far too ferociously – and coming in each evening aching and stiff from the unaccustomed labour. I also began to get a fair amount of pain in my chest and shoulders, which I put down to the strain on my muscles.

In the early morning of Boxing Day, however, I woke in agony, unable to move or even speak properly, my chest, shoulders and arms in a searing vice of pain and sweat pouring from me. I roused Virginia with a feeble whisper, and she immediately phoned our doctor, who arrived in minutes clad only in a sheepskin jacket over his pyjamas. He took one look at me, gave me a shot of morphia and phoned for an ambulance. He told Virginia that I was showing the classic symptoms of a coronary.

In the heart unit of Grantham General Hospital, I began to realise the awfulness of the situation. If I didn't recover, what would happen to my career and my family?

By ill-luck, a newspaper man covering another story had been at the hospital reception desk when I was stretchered in. That day the papers, TV and radio all over the world carried the story.

The phone at home rang non-stop. Duncan, who was in Canada, saw the news there on TV and called Virginia; Louis Michaels on his way to Eastbourne by car heard it on the radio; Hong Kong phoned to ask if I was going to recover in time for January; a friend of mine in Canada, Joan Henningson, an ex-nurse, called to say that her bags were packed and that she would come over to look after me; family and friends from every corner of the world, including Australia, rang to ask how I was.

All I can say is that I felt a complete fraud. Each day I got better and better, fussed over by a wonderful hospital staff who brought a TV set to my room, asked if there was anything special I would like to eat and even provided me with copious glasses of whisky for my nightcap. A heart specialist carried out every conceivable test on me, including X-rays, and could find nothing wrong with me. Everything – blood pressure, heartbeat and breathing – was completely normal, and after four days he told me I could go home.

When I asked for my bill before leaving, a surprised nursing sister said, 'Nothing. This is a National Health hospital and everything is free. There's no private heart unit around here that you could have gone to.'

So much for criticisms of the National Health Service!

It had been a nasty fright for us all and it was much later that we discovered the cause of it all: I had damaged discs in my spine while chain-sawing.

*

My first impression of Hong Kong matched all the descriptions I had ever heard or read: exotic, exciting, bustling and very beautiful, with a busy social life for the British community there.

I arrived with a filthy cold, so a doctor was called to my suite at the Hilton. I also had a course of treatment called 'Kee' from a Korean physiotherapist on my damaged back. This consisted of finger-tip massage and pressure on various nerve centres, and was so soothing that I fell asleep each time.

I welcomed those relaxing moments because I had a very busy schedule. Before the rest of the company joined me I needed to check the stage and auditorium, which were in the enormous ballroom of the hotel and turned out to be very adequate. I also went several times to see the progress of the set-building. To my astonishment this was being done out in the open in a narrow street teeming with traders and shoppers. However, the carpentry was excellent and the Chinese craftsmen produced a perfect replica of the original.

I also had a chance to see Hong Kong from the air when the RAF gave me a helicopter trip over the area, including a hover over the stricken liner *Queen Elizabeth* lying at the bottom of the bay. This was all very interesting . . . until I was asked to sit on the edge of the doorway with my lower legs dangling in space for photographs – very much like my old parachuting days, except that I wasn't wearing a parachute!

The whole population, British, Chinese and foreign, appeared to be horse-racing mad and huge sums were wagered by the wealthy Chinese. I was lucky to be there, a guest in the chairman's box, at the time of the big annual International Cup, which was won by Lester Piggott as I watched. As the big race reached the half-way point, his wife Susan nudged me and exclaimed, 'He's going to win!'

'How do you know?'

'Because his bum's up!'

Lester and his wife Susan were staying at the Hilton and I had had supper with them the previous evening, when he remembered many years ago riding the first horse I ever owned, at Windsor Races.

While we were rehearsing I was invited to lunch at Government House by the governor, Sir Murray Maclehose; he later brought a large party to our first-night performance, which was a great success.

Once our two-week run had got under way I had plenty of time to tour the area in the Rolls courtesy car which the hotel had put at my disposal, also to take some fascinating boat trips to the islands and a hovercraft to faded, beautiful Macao, made memorable as the subject of so many of Chinnery's paintings. I lunched one day with the officers of the 1st Battalion Light Infantry Regiment, some of whom had served with my old regiment the KOYLI, and was also invited to open the annual Gurkha Great Fête, where I was presented with a magnificent silver-ornamented kukri which now hangs on my study wall.

I suppose the high spot of my stay came when I was asked to fire Jardine's legendary noonday gun, made famous by Noël Coward's *Mad Dogs and Englishmen*. Due to a misunderstanding with the Chinese custodian, who spoke no English, I actually pulled the cord too early and probably caused havoc with all the local timepieces.

Once home, I had a short break before starting rehearsals for yet another lengthy Triumph tour, this time of *Quadrille*, an old Noël Coward romance in which I would be partnering Margaret Lockwood and Anne Rogers – and Margaret still wore her old black woolly hat for rehearsals!

This tour was to last until August, with a few breaks for an occasional week at home, and with one exception followed the old familiar pattern of my strolling-player existence, including the obligatory couple of weeks staying with Vera Barber.

The exception came on 10 May when I was in Brighton. That evening, just before the play started, Colin Mailer phoned me to say that Virginia had been rushed to the City Hospital by ambulance and was in labour.

That morning she had been shopping in Grantham, then spent the afternoon digging in the garden until quite late. It was after teatime that she felt the familiar pangs, and phoned her gynaecologist in Nottingham. For one so slender, it was amazing how she produced her babies with minimum fuss, bless her, and at 8.20 that evening Seumas Alexander Palethorpe Todd made his slightly premature appearance in the outside world.

God know what kind of performance I gave that night. As the curtain fell and I returned to my dressing room I was greeted by an employee of the *Daily Mail*, who handed me a simply beautiful picture of Virginia and Seumas taken immediately after the birth. It had been wired to London, printed and rushed straight down to Brighton with the compliments of the editor, David English, with the explanation that he didn't want me to get my first glimpse of my new son on the pages of a newspaper the next day.

When I later phoned Mr English to thank him for this human and touching gesture, he simply said, 'A pleasure. It's nice to be able to pass on some good news once in a while!'

The rest of that week, from Tuesday onwards, I was yearning to get home and see Virginia and the baby. It was misery for me but I obviously couldn't just leave the show and rush away. I had to content myself with sending flowers and talking on the phone. On the Saturday night, by which time Virginia was already back in the house, I drove the long journey to Little Ponton, reaching home at three o'clock in the morning.

One whole day with them was not much, but it was thrilling enough. Seumas was certainly the most beautiful baby I had ever seen, smooth and pink and lusty, and Virginia looked wonderful as always.

The next morning I had to leave early and drive down to Bournemouth, another tedious journey.

We soon had one more addition to our family when we bought a black Labrador pup from Sir Hereward Wake in Northamptonshire. 'Andrew's Black Sambo' – Sam, of course, to us – had curiously enough been born on the same day as Seumas and was a present for Andrew's fourth birthday – and, hopefully, a future gun-dog for me. His trainer's report months later, however, was that 'he'll make a nice dog to go shopping with'. Useless as a working dog, Sam became a devoted, affectionate and loyal guard-dog instead.

After the tour I enjoyed a lovely three-week July break at home, during which I spent a lot of time with Andrew so that he should not feel that his nose had been put out of joint by his new baby brother; I also did some gardening with Virginia and our new-found gardener, a cheerful, blue-eyed pensioner also called Mr Knight. Barney Knight, though handicapped after a severe kick in the legs during his days as a stableman, could turn his hand to anything and got through more work in a day than most men half his age and twice his size. With his help and that of the Thacker family who lived in cottages across the field from the house, our place was really taking shape. Mrs Thacker became our daily help and also waited at table, along with her daughter Angela, daughter-in-law June and the redoubtable Mrs Philips from Grantham, a trained waitress; Tony Thacker cleaned the cars, did a good deal of painting and erected wire-netting all around the garden to keep out the bloody rabbits; and Mr Thacker, a gardener at the Hall, trapped and banished the bloody moles. So we had an invaluable bunch of stalwarts to call upon.

We had also engaged Sarah-Jane to look after Andrew while Virginia was busy with Seumas. We had met her in South Africa, where she had been the Lilfords' nanny.

I was living in a rented house in Brighton while trying out a new

Alfred Shaughnessy play at Worthing when came the great day of Fiona's wedding to Rollo on 2 September.

What a memorable day that was, a truly ecumenical occasion in a leading RC church in Chelsea. Half the service was conducted by the Abbot of Buckfast Abbey (the Cliffords of Chudleigh had given great help and support to the brothers, who had built the Abbey with their own hands) and half by our dear friend Canon David Davies from Market Deeping. Lord Clifford read the first lesson, and I read the second. Andrew was a page along with several Clifford children, Rollo's nieces and nephews, all prettily clad in Regency costume, and the church was packed with a horde of Clifford family members and as many friends as I could muster.

Fiona looked adorable as she stood beside her towering young husband, her lovely little face aglow.

The only participant who did not fully cooperate that day was the Clerk of the Weather – he let it rain outsize cats and dogs. Even so the reception afterwards in a large house in Kensington Palace Gardens was attended by Seumas in his Moses basket, guarded by Sarah-Jane.

The bride and groom once seen off to the start of their honeymoon, we took train back to Brighton for a week. A day or so later Gregg Wallace, newly arrived from America, phoned to say he was coming down to meet his new godson Seumas. Could we all have a picnic? When we met him at the station next morning he was bearing a case of champagne in his arms, and we set off for a hilarious day with Jasper and Moggie Booty in their garden at Littlehampton.

After this boozy break from routine, the touring pattern seemed pretty humdrum, and I was glad to take a long break towards the end of the year – not exactly 'resting' however, since Triumph was at the peak of its activity and our business meetings, theatre first nights and visits to productions became more and more frequent.

On the home front, too, things were not exactly idle, with a lot still to be done around the house and garden. I had a number of shooting days as well – almost like the old Haileywood period.

The house was crammed for Christmas 1977, with Rollo, Fiona, Peter and Pam Hooper from America with her daughter, all joining us and the Mailers.

The year ended in grand style with Virginia, Andrew, Peter and myself all being guests for a few days at Ugbrooke, the Cliffords' great old seat in Devon, where we joined a large house-party of Clifford children, grandchildren and friends in that warm and jolly household. It was easy to see why Rollo, and indeed all the Cliffords, were so attached to their family home, a sprawling, ancient pile refurbished and partly rebuilt by Robert Adam, who had also designed and added the splendid ornate family chapel where Hugh Clifford himself invited me to read a lesson at the New Year's Day service.

The park around the house had been laid out by Capability Brown and was riven by a long, narrow valley with a chain of lakes overlooked by steep, wooded hillsides which gave us some marvellous shooting as driven birds swept and curled at great speed down from the tops.

Rollo's father, Hugh Clifford, and I had a lot in common and always much to reminisce about. We were the same age and had similar wartime backgrounds and interests. He too had been a parachutist, and was actually an instructor at Sandhurst Royal Military College when I was there at the beginning of my service; he remembered the night in 1940 when a German bomb destroyed part of the buildings and damaged me a bit as well.

Those lively, happy days at Ugbrooke – the lakes are fed by a little stream called the Ug Brook – were a memorable start to the New Year.

37

Here Endeth the Second Volume

To chronicle my professional activities over the next three or four years would be to compile a saga about as interesting and varied as a laundry list.

The plays and the actors were different but the routine was the same, as were most of the theatres in Britain and abroad. My experiences and encounters were predictable and not greatly changed, and nothing much worth recording took place except perhaps two events.

One occurred when Virginia and I were in Perth, Western Australia. It so happened that the Triumph RSC co-production of *The Hollow Crown* and *Pleasure and Repentance*, which I had led in Canada and America for some months, had been revived and came to play at the University Theatre in Perth, so we were able to give a supper party for the whole company after the shows – theirs and mine – at a nice restaurant with a private room and a terrace right on the edge of the Swan River. This time Sir Michael Redgrave had taken over from me and Derek Jacobi replaced Clifford Rose. It was quite by chance but very agreeable that we should all meet up at a point on the other side of the world from home.

Sir Michael, whom I had only worked with once on *The Dam Busters*, but who had done a couple of plays for Triumph, was not at all well, but was being very efficiently and caringly nannied by my former dresser and wardrobe master, Ron Lucas. It was not then generally known that he had Parkinson's disease. Nevertheless, we all enjoyed our get-together.

The other event was far less enjoyable and took place at Ugbrooke. The play I was doing at the time visited Plymouth for a week, and I stayed with the Cliffords a few miles away. This was at a time when Lady Clifford had recruited the services of a monstrous rottweiler called

Oliver as a guard-dog for the house. He was a savage, snarling brute and we were all terrified of him, except Kay herself and Andrew – neither of whom seemed to mind his constant growling and bared teeth. Even an ex-police dog handler had declared him unmanageable.

The awful thing was that Oliver had taken an inexplicable and very embarrassing amorous shine to me, and never stopped trying to clasp me to him with his forelegs. I felt like the bride of Frankenstein when he turned his attentions on me . . .

For that week it was arranged that Oliver, who normally slept in the hall, should be shut at night in Kay's bedroom so that I could make a safe entry to the house when I returned from Plymouth.

One night in the middle of the week, when Hugh was in London for his weekly few days at the House of Lords where he was on a defence committee, I came in as usual, reset the burglar alarms and went for my habitual generous night-cap in the morning room. After a mellowing half-hour or so I set off to climb the main stairs to my room which opened off a galleried landing some distance from the stair head; the stairs were shallow-treaded, uncarpeted and quite a remarkable architectural feature of immensely broad, highly-polished wood.

As I reached the bottom flight I suddenly heard an ominous rumbling and looked around the curve of the staircase to see, to my horror, Oliver standing at the top, snarling and bristling. I scurried back to the morning room, shut the door and tried to work out a plan of campaign. Obviously I couldn't stay here all night, nor did I think that Kay or anyone else would hear me if I wailed for help from downstairs.

After another shot of Dutch courage, I decided to try my luck. I had decided that, if Oliver launched himself at me from his place on the landing, I would dodge to one side, he would hurtle his huge bulk over my shoulder and go slithering and tumbling down the shiny steps to land in a heap at the bottom, while I ran like a rabbit to my room.

Fine – all seemed well as I started my cautious ascent, giving a kind of running commentary of, 'Now, then, Oliver, be a good boy. Now don't be silly, Oliver. You know me, don't you? There's a good chap, I'm your friend, remember?'

I got to a point where I was about five or six steps below him and my sweaty face was on a level with those awful fangs. And still the bloody dog hadn't budged, but just stood there like some carved Chinese dragon breathing fire. There was nothing for it but to keep going, still babbling pally platitudes. I got to within about four feet of him and his jaws were now chest-high. Then I saw it; his stump of a docked tail was wagging uncertainly and I realised that the dog was confused, no re whether he should carry out his duties as a guard-dog or welcome e as a member of the household.

I walked right up to him, shoved him aside and strode steadily to y room, my bottom tight with fright; thankfully I reached sanctuary, ily to remember that I had left all the lights on. Not wishing to push y luck any further I scribbled a note which I hurriedly put on a chest eside my door: 'Dear Kay. Sorry! I have left all the lights on for asons I shall explain in the morning.'

My professional life apart, at home there was plenty of happy change nd progress.

In April 1978 Andrew started his first term at Dudley House, a narming little local private school, and at about the same time Virginia ecame an officer of the British Red Cross Society in support of her reat friend Lady Benton Jones, the dedicated and immensely hard-orking President of the Lincolnshire County Branch. Virginia took on ne duties of a vice-president of the county and president of the Gran-nam area, a voluntary activity into which she was to put much time nd travel for years to come, organising fund-raising committees and narity balls, chairing meetings almost weekly and driving about all ver the county with Maggie Benton Jones to promote the work of the ed Cross.

In November we were guests of the Rutlands at an awesomely mag-ificent ball at Belvoir Castle to celebrate the twenty-first birthday of neir eldest son, David, Marquess of Granby. It was an altogether olendid occasion – a real tiara-boom-diay.

Unusually, our annual New Year shooting weekend at Ugbrooke was nrouded in snow-storms of Alpine proportions which provided us all ith some extra diversions. The beautiful Devon countryside looked narvellous, and we had our own version of the Cresta Run on the steep opes above the lakes as we hurtled down lying on our backs on strong lastic fertiliser bags stuffed with straw. The second night there saw ess exciting but equally hectic activity as all the younger males in the ouse party, including Rollo, spent hours shovelling tons of snow off ne area of leaking flat roof, while the more mature ones such as myself cuttled about placing and emptying buckets under the drips in the orridors below.

The two outstanding family occasions in 1979 were Seumas's christen-ng and Peter's engagement. The christening was performed by Canon David Davies at a ceremony in our diminutive local church of St ruthlac. Gregg Wallace, one of the godfathers, had flown over for the ccasion from Texas and my dear old friend, Jeanne Camoys – who had phoned insisting that she should be a godmother – also came to stay with us.

On an evening stage-managed at their London house by Rollo and Fiona, Peter asked me if I approved of his choice of fiancée, Janet Wantling. Indeed I did – I thought she was charming. The question was popped, a few female tears were shed and Rollo opened the waiting champagne.

The year ended with our usual family shooting party at Ugbrooke, this time happily unaffected by blizzards, and when 1980 opened we were staying and shooting in Norfolk with Lord Fisher of Kilverstone, Kay Clifford's brother. John Fisher invited me back a few days later to be a gun with him at the National Spaniel Field Trial Championships, and I accepted with some qualms since the shooters on these occasions came under the scrutiny of a large and very critical gallery. Woe betide the gun who misses a shootable bird, drops one in an awkward place for the dog on test to hunt out and pick up, or 'pricks' one, leaving a strong runner for the dog to chase and retrieve.

I must have acquitted myself adequately, because I don't remember any irate handler setting his dog on me.

Later in January Virginia and I visited Maidwell Hall School in Northamptonshire, the future prep school for both Andrew and Seumas. We were delighted with the place and at once took to the headmaster, John Paul, and his charming wife Susan. Maidwell is as near to being the ideal prep school as one can get, in my opinion. Based in a magnificent, turreted Victorianised Jacobean mansion surrounded by splendid grounds, playing fields, a lake and its own farmland, Maidwell keeps its numbers down to about 80 boys and, in addition to its excellent academic record, is a real home from home for little boys starting there at seven years of age. Despite its small numbers, the school holds its own with much larger schools in games and sports, due largely to extremely efficient coaching. We were sure that our two boys would be very happy there.

The early summer of 1980 was a busy one for us all. I was touring with a lovely old Noël Coward play, *This Happy Breed*, for most of the time, but still managed to get down to Devon one May weekend for a ceremony declaring Ugbrooke open to the public. The old place had gone the way of so many of its kind and was forced to earn part of its keep by being put on display.

The next weekend had been selected for Peter and Janet's wedding in the lovely old church at Ludlow, Janet's home town – mainly because on that date I was playing in Birmingham, not far away. It also hap pened to be Seumas's third birthday and this time he joined Andrew as a page. Among the guests that day I was delighted to see Peter's former housemaster at Eton; James McConnell and his wife Meg had been so good to him during his years there.

During that *Happy Breed* tour, I had two very unexpected and welcome visitors to my dressing room after the show in Oxford: Patricia Neale, whom I had seen little of since *The Hasty Heart*, and Jimmy Lane-Fox, my old platoon commander at Sandhurst in 1940. Pat had recovered splendidly from her stroke.

One appointment which I hardly ever failed to keep – except when I was abroad – was my regular Monday-morning date with my hairdresser, Rupert Flowers. This remarkable old man was already an octogenarian when first recommended to me by one of his regular 'gents', Lord Brownlow, and was to continue to keep us in good trim until well into his nineties. A Dickensian figure in a Dickensian setting, with a prodigious memory and a list of customers going back over some 70 years, he was a veritable *Who's Who* of the local worthies and the county folk round about Grantham; he had a fund of anecdotes about the more eccentric of his past clients, including the blind Lord Dysart, who always brought his terrier with him and then went off for a pint with his chauffeur in the pub next door.

Mr Flowers' father had been head coachman to Earl Brownlow at the turn of the century, and offered the young Rupert two choices of career: to train either as a coachman or as a butcher. Since Rupert was scared of horses and sick at the sight of raw meat, he chose neither, but became instead an apprentice barber. Since then he had tended the locks of three generations of locals, one of his earliest customers being the present Duke of Rutland who first came to him as a little boy with his father. Charles Rutland planned to give a party for Mr Flowers at Belvoir Castle on the old man's hundredth birthday. Alas, he just missed his century but was still snipping away steady-handed right up to the last, dreadfully worried about me and his other customers – what would we do when he had to hang up his scissors?

On 29 June, Andrew's seventh birthday, we opened the garden at Little Ponton to the public for the first time in aid of the British Red Cross. We were amazed at the number of people who turned up, genuinely interested in the way Virginia had redesigned and planted what had been a pretty dreary patch. In subsequent years we were to open the garden several times, once or twice in conjunction with the McCorquodales at the Hall and with the little part-Norman church also open and flower-filled. With the help of Red Cross and St John

Ambulance Brigade volunteers with teas and car-parking, we learned to cope with the surprisingly large crowds of visitors.

Our holiday that summer was spent with Simon and Maggie Benton Jones near the Hampshire coast at Mudeford. Their four children and our two had a great time on the beach every day, while Simon and I organised barbecues or went pigeon-shooting on an estate he owns in the area.

I was particularly glad of the break, as I had not had a real rest for years. I also felt it was time to review my whole career situation, and the conclusions which I drew were not entirely comforting . . .

I had entered into the formation of Triumph Theatre Productions with Duncan and Paul in a spirit of almost missionary zeal in 1970, and by the mid-seventies our early aims and hopes had been achieved: Triumph had indeed brought quality theatre to every corner of the country and exported British theatre abroad; it had by then grown to be probably the most active and prolific theatre production company in the world, and was respected for its standards everywhere; we had had a string of successful London West End presentations, and the sheer volume of our productions as well as their quality had done much to revitalise provincial theatres throughout Britain. For this most credit must go to Duncan and Paul, who formed the engine-room of our organisation. I had simply been the trail-blazer.

But where had this left me? For years I had been blazoning Triumph's name far and wide, from Inverness to Plymouth and from St John's, Newfoundland to St Louis, Missouri. I had never taken a director's fee or any expenses from the company and had been content to receive quite a moderate salary as I trailed around. When I was 'resting' I naturally got nothing, and the few thousand I had originally put into the company on its formation somehow was never mentioned again. In consequence I had been eating into my own funds for my living expenses for years.

But worse perhaps was the gradual realisation of the damage being done to my professional acting career. Out of sight, out of mind is a saying as true in the theatre as anywhere else. Furthermore, even when I was remembered, no film producers offered me lengthy roles as I was almost constantly committed to long-running theatre productions, while no major theatrical impresarios offered me plays in the West End since I appeared to work almost exclusively for Triumph.

So I decided to resign from Triumph's board of directors. I would still remain on good terms with Duncan and Louis Michaels, and would work for the company if something suitable came up, but I would n longer be fettered professionally by any bonds of loyalty or duty to the company.

The next milestone in my life was nothing whatever to do with my career: I became a grandfather. On 6 February 1981, Elizabeth Alice was born to Fiona, to be followed by Christopher and Alasdair in succeeding years.

It was at about that time that Duncan and I started to discuss a play by Terence Feely, a prolific and successful author and playwright with an imposing list of credits for plays, film scripts and TV series. It was an intriguing thriller called *Murder in Mind* and the plan was for me to do it with Joan Collins, starting at Guildford, going on a short tour and then transferring to the West End. I had read the play and felt that it had definite possibilities, and although there were areas of it which were not quite right, these could probably be remedied by the author once we started rehearsal.

We began rehearsals for *Murder in Mind* in London in early May. Our pleasant company included Moira Redmond and Geoffrey Davies, and Joan Collins herself was, as always, very professional and wonderful to work with. On this occasion I got to know her better, and to talk with her more than I had done on the two earlier films we had made together.

I admire Joan immensely both as a true, dedicated professional and as a resilient and courageous woman. Since those days in London she has become something of a legend for her looks, for her behaviour, for her honesty and for what the public expect most of all from a star: glamour. She has taken some severe knocks in her time, but has come up smiling and enjoying life – *and* quite rich! She's a classic survivor, and has worked darned hard for her success.

There is little that I can reveal about her which is not already well known to the public, but during our chats together over rehearsal lunches and an occasional after-work drink I learned that there were sides to her character and elements of her life which had escaped the attentions of the popular press. She was always a cheerful and amusing companion, very witty and forthright, but equally kindly and compassionate, and willing to discuss her problems with refreshing candour.

The caring tenacity and love with which she had watched over the recovery of her little daughter from a severe injury was evidence of the warmth and determination that were part of her nature.

Her film career had also gone through some depressing periods and *The Stud* and *The Bitch* – while helping her financially – had not exactly advanced her professional reputation; though she was not the first star forced to turn to questionable material in the scramble for survival. I had had a taste of that myself. As part of her professional rehabilitation Joan had quite recently done a play for Triumph, *The Last Mrs Cheyney*, which had opened at the Chichester Festival and done very well on tour. It had then come into London at the Cambridge Theatre, with her and her (then) husband Ron Kass – at his insistence – being part of the management with Triumph, with a minor share of the production costs. The show was not an unqualified success in London, and closed with losses. So it was that, with tax problems looming – a situation not uncommon to members of our profession – Joan was as keen as I was to bring *Murder in Mind* into good shape.

We were due to open at the Yvonne Arnaud Theatre at Guildford on Monday 26 May, but at the dress rehearsal on the Sunday disaster struck. A small balcony which was part of the set continued off-stage on to an unguarded rostrum. During her final exit, going from the bright stage lighting into the backstage gloom, Joan fell from the rostrum and severely hurt her arm. With typical courage she insisted on carrying on to the end of rehearsal, and when later that evening she was X-rayed and found to have broken a bone in her forearm, she willingly played the first two weeks at Guildford encased in plaster. Some of her movements had to be modified, but she never faltered.

The play got good reviews at Guildford and played to packed houses. It was then decided that, after further script changes, *Murder in Mind* should start a provincial tour later that summer, and that Joan and I and most of the original cast would bring it into London.

I had meanwhile celebrated my sixty-second birthday, which that year coincided with the annual KOYLI Officers' Club luncheon at Claridges.

With most of the summer free, I had a longed-for chance to spend time at home with my family, knowing that for the latter half of the year I should be gainfully employed. The *Murder in Mind* tour, starting in September, had been booked, and everything seemed set for its eventual return to the West End. We all went to Rollo and Fiona's refurbished old home at Cannington, in Somerset, for Elizabeth Alice's christening; we made up for my many absences by giving and going to numerous dinner parties and garden parties; and we saw Seumas join Andrew at Dudley House School just before the latter was to start his years at Maidwell Hall.

In August I drove the family up to Scotland for a holiday, first staying with Jean Fforde on her wild and beautiful estate on the Isle of Arran then going on to Kincardineshire to spend a week with Peter Gladstone my old friend from the days when he coached the Shrewsbury Schoo crews at Henley. He was now the custodian of his older brother's enormous estate at Fasque, the Scottish seat of his illustrious forebear, William Ewart Gladstone. His castle home was an untouched relic of the great prime minister's days, not changed in any way and still containing a revealing example of Victorian plurality: a gaming table which, with a deft reversing twist, could be turned into a bible-bearing lectern for Sundays!

It was at Fasque, blissfully unaware of what was happening during my absence, that I received an urgent call back to London from Duncan. While on holiday in Spain, Joan had received an approach from the producers of *Dynasty*, the American TV series. Without hesitation she had flown straight to Hollywood – and the rest is soap history.

Louis Michaels was furious – a contract *is* a contract – and threatened all manner of legal reprisals. Furthermore, Triumph's own theatre contracts were in jeopardy unless in a very short space of time the company could engage another actress acceptable to those theatres. If not, then Triumph itself could face reprisals.

Still, with hindsight I can sympathise with Joan's hurried decision. I'm not sure what I would have done in similar circumstances – probably nothing, thereby losing a literally golden opportunity.

However a good replacement had been arranged, the attractive Nyree Dawn Porter, hence the need for me to rush back to London to start rehearsals with a new leading lady.

Perhaps everything had happened for the best. Nyree was very good in the part, which called for a degree of vulnerability not easily associated with her predecessor. We opened in Bristol towards the end of September and set off on a highly successful tour, the plan being to tour until the end of November and then bring the play into London.

But despite its reception in the provinces I still had misgivings about *Murder in Mind*. My contract so far was only for the tour, and I felt that I did not want to come back into the West End in a vehicle which I did not wholly believe in, so I asked Duncan not to consider me for the London presentation. And for once in my theatrical life, my instincts were to prove right.

Only a few days after the tour ended, while I was already beginning to question the wisdom of my decision, Bill Kenwright – one of Britain's most venturesome and successful impresarios – sent me a play to read. It was *The Business of Murder* by Richard Harris, a writer who had already enjoyed considerable success with his works in theatre, films and television.

As I read it I became more and more convinced that this was *IT*!

The play was a beautifully-written and devised mystery-thriller, the best of its genre that I had read since *Sleuth* – which it closely resembled in quality, treatment and style. I found it totally absorbing.

But, above all, the leading role was a gem – the kind of part that is an actor's dream. Mr Stone *was* the play. He was off-stage for only a minute during the entire three-handed performance, and completely dominated and manipulated the whole story which was all about him and contrived by him. A shabby, seedy, devious little man, he was an embittered soul hell-bent on the mental, moral and physical destruction of two other characters. While his relentless and cunning pursuit of his ends was almost fiendish, he yet managed to be strangely endearing with his sharp wit, moments of pathos and overt glee as the pieces of his carefully prepared plan fall into place. It was a very funny play in places.

I simply loved Mr Stone. Not since playing Scrooge years before had I attempted to portray a character so utterly – I fondly hoped – out of character for me. My immediate reaction was to say to Bill Kenwright, 'Yes, please, I'd love to do it.'

But there were snags . . .

The play had already been at the Duchess Theatre for nine months and while it had received universal critical acclaim, it had done relatively poor business and was, according to Bill, still in the red. The original cast had come to the end of their contracts and were leaving. Yet Bill, with true showman's instinct, still believed in the play's potential and was determined to give it another chance. Hence his approach to me.

I dithered for only a day or so. Did I want to take over from another actor in the West End? Did I want to risk my reappearance in London after so many years in what had so far proved to be a less-than-profitable production? After all, if I took on Mr Stone and we stumbled along for a few more fraught months and then closed, as the leading man I would bear the brunt of the blame.

Furthermore, Mr Stone was a veritable marathon of a part and the original director, Hugh Goldie, was no longer available to help me. Still, like Bill Kenwright, I too believed in the play and so I did indeed say, 'Yes, please, I'd love to do it.' I had still not seen it in performance and deliberately avoided doing so in order that my version should be my own and not a hurried copy.

There followed the most frightening weeks of my lengthy career.

We only had two weeks to rehearse owing to the imminent departure of the original cast and although I had had the script for over a week and learned much of it parrot-fashion, I still spent every minute of my daily train journey to and from London swotting my lines.

To make matters worse, during the last week of rehearsal I developed a particularly virulent form of bronchial 'flu, with all the usual aches and pains, nausea, cough, streaming nose and eyes and laryngitis.

To open in the West End after inadequate preparation and with no director was daunting enough, but to do so in this condition and with a voice reduced to a croak was a horrendous prospect.

Nevertheless Carole Mowlam, Derren Nesbitt and I contrived to get through our first performance at the Duchess Theatre a few days before Christmas to a surprisingly good and appreciative audience.

I didn't really enjoy Christmas 1981. I drove home after the show on Christmas Eve feeling ghastly, spent part of Christmas Day in bed with what had now turned to an even more unpleasant variety of gastric 'flu, then drove back to London to do two Boxing Day performances.

A few days later I moved into a pleasant rented flat in Fulham; this had been arranged for me by Queenie in a house belonging to her friend, Mrs Easton, whose late husband Bill had been so helpful to me at Maidenwell and Glassenbury Park. There I was able to suffer in silence and solitude as I gradually recovered my health and spirits.

What a traumatic end to the year! So much had happened in those last few weeks, including Louis Michaels' sad and unexpected death from cancer. I was later to deliver the eulogy at his thanksgiving service, held so appropriately in his beloved Theatre Royal, Haymarket.

During the first few weeks of 1982 business at the Duchess Theatre was steady but not spectacular, and once or twice we just scraped over the break-figure – a box office sum below which over a two-week period a theatre is entitled to give notice to its tenants. The change of casting had received very little publicity or advertisement, Bill's budget for the production now being somewhat restricted.

Then came a move which was to produce a complete transformation in our fortunes: the Mayfair Theatre became vacant, and Bill bravely decided to transfer *The Business of Murder* right into the heart of the West End. We went there in early May, at the beginning of the tourist season with its hordes of overseas visitors who are so crucial to the health of London theatreland, a very high percentage of them Americans whose main object is to see shows. Their priorities seem to be first, to take in the National Theatre and the RSC, then to get tickets for the current musical spectaculars, and then to shop around for those productions containing names familiar to them.

Almost immediately we began to coast along happily on this tourist band-wagon. Bless those ardent foreign visitors, especially the Americans! They sent us to the top of the table and were to keep us there, but some of their reactions were quite amusing. At almost every performance a puzzled American would approach one of the usherettes:

'Isn't Richard Todd appearing tonight?'

'Yes, that's him – Mr Stone.'

'Oh, my Gahd!'

The deterioration of Robin Hood, Peter Marshall, Sir Walter Raleigh and Guy Gibson into the shambling, shuffling, hunched and bespectacled Mr Stone really aroused sympathy for their erstwhile hero.

Within weeks the theatre was being filled nightly, and thereafter we never looked back for years and years until we eventually became the longest-running play in London's theatre history – with the exception of Agatha Christie's prodigious tale of a certain household rodent-catcher – and I believe I came to hold the record for the greatest number of consecutive performances by any leading actor.

So, for the foreseeable future, my professional life had become a comfortable routine: my working week spent in the Fulham flat and my short weekends at home after a long night drive on Saturdays to Lincolnshire, Sundays with my family and friends and Mondays back to work.

In all that time I have never been able to share a summer holiday with Virginia and the boys because this was our peak season at the theatre, though I have snatched a few weekends with them on the Isle of Wight in Richard Stone's idyllic flat overlooking the sea; appropriately named Seaview, this is a charming, uncrowded little backwater where the boys are able to swim, fish and water-ski to their hearts' content.

I have, however, managed to squeeze in a couple of guest star vignette roles in films such as *The House of the Long Shadows* where, almost in my dotage, I was the youngest leading member of a geriatric cast which included Vincent Price, Peter Cushing, Christopher Lee and John Carradine. And in February 1988 I even took a week off with Virginia to spend a fascinating few days in Athens filming a role which I was asked to take over as a replacement for my dear old chum and revered fellow-actor, Trevor Howard, who had died a few days before.

Other than those few departures, there is little to record as far as my work is concerned.

Only in my family life have there been any changes or developments worth mentioning.

Andrew started at Maidwell Hall and, after a tearful beginning when Susan Paul kept us constantly informed of his progress and well-being, he did well and became one of the stalwarts of the school teams. When he was eventually joined there by Seumas, before going on to Uppingham School, the two of them had a happy year together. Seumas, who has always had the challenge of an elder brother to keep up with, is developing into a remarkable all-round games player, as is Andrew much to my pride, and both boys are good, keen shots and trout fishers.

With both boys away at school, Virginia is able to spend more time with me in London, and Andrew and Seumas love to spend the odd few days with me as well.

After 1982, Bill Kenwright – by agreement with the Mayfair Theatre – agreed to close the show for a longish period over the Christmas season so that I could at least have an annual break. This has enabled me to fit in a few shooting days each year, including two which have become regular events: Christmas Eve at Belvoir Castle, when the Duke always has a shoot with guns that include his own family and closest friends; and Boxing Day at Irnham, when Simon Benton Jones does much the same thing. To my joy, after some tuition at a local shooting school, Andrew shot his first pheasant on the first drive at Belvoir in 1987. He was using a feeble .410 gun then but has now progressed to a smart little 20-bore, the .410 having been handed down to Seumas who used it very effectively on clays a few weeks ago at the shooting school.

Over the past few years many things have happened in my private life – some memorable, some, hopefully, forgettable; some sad, some joyous. There have been additions to and subtractions from my circle of family and friends and changes, good and bad, have occurred.

Dear Vera Barber and Jeanne Camoys have gone, and so has Mr Flowers. Peter has been divorced and happily remarried. Christopher and Alasdair have joined the Clifford family, but Hugh Clifford has died and is buried at Buckfast Abbey.

New friends have come into our lives too, among them Admiral of the Fleet Sir John Fieldhouse and his dear wife Midge. John, as C-in-C Fleet, commanded all our forces during the Falklands War and master-minded that brilliant campaign. In 1983 I took an evening off to dine with them and Virginia at his headquarters in north London, and a couple of years later – while he was First Sea Lord and living in his official flat over Admiralty Arch – they invited us to join a very august company at a private dinner party there. Their chief guests on that – for us – thrilling evening were the Prince and Princess of Wales. A more delightful, natural and charming pair could not be imagined. I was seated next to Princess Diana at dinner and was surprised when she said, 'Oh, I know your house well.' Then I realised why: her sister Sarah is married to Neil McCorquodale and the princess has been a frequent visitor to our little hamlet. In fact we had loaned our pram and high chair to Sarah for her babies, so our nursery equipment has seen some service: two Todds, three Cliffords and two McCorquodales.

Maybe more in the future – who knows . . .

In addition to new arrivals and new friends, old friends – many of whom have been mentioned in these pages – still continue to pop into my life from all quarters of the globe, often unexpectedly and always happily for me. Whilst my days are as busy and active as they have ever been – and, hopefully, will remain so for years to come – they have mostly shed their responsibilities and laid aside their workloads, or at least have shifted into a smoother form of long-distance overdrive. One such true and loyal old friend suddenly reappeared only a few days ago while I was penning these last pages:

To my great surprise and joy, Virginia and I were invited by the Prime Minister to a dinner party at 10, Downing Street, to be held in honour of ex-President and Mrs Reagan during their recent brief visit to London when he was deservedly invested with a knighthood by the Queen.

It was a never-to-be-forgotten evening for us, not only to be guests on those august premises and to be invited by Mrs Thatcher herself, but to be re-united for a while with my old chum from *The Hasty Heart* days, forty years past. Although we had kept in periodic touch by letter and telegram, I had not seen Ronald since the early fifties.

It was quite a small gathering of some twenty people which Mrs Thatcher described as 'a happy little family party'.

That amazing, tireless and redoubtable lady, after what had probably been a heavy official day in the House of Commons, was at the front door to meet us simply brimming with charm, friendliness and good cheer, and that whole evening simply bubbled with unaffected energy and humour.

When Ronald and Nancy Reagan arrived and were introduced to the guests – most of whom they knew well – he evidently had not heard my name and did not recognise me (I don't blame him, after all those years!). But a few moments later Mrs Thatcher briskly led him back across the room to where Virginia and I were chatting to Mrs Catto, the American Ambassador's wife. This time the penny dropped, a delighted grin lit up his face and, with arms outstretched, 'Lachie!' he exclaimed (my name in *The Hasty Heart*) and gave me a great bear-hug.

He had not changed: still the exuberant, humourous and totally natural Ronnie that I remembered, and we spent a long time together reminiscing and chatting about old times.

It goes without saying that the dinner itself was delicious – quite simple but faultless, and accompanied by a selection of distinguished wines.

When the Reagans had left I asked Mrs Thatcher if our presence had been Ronald's idea.

'No' she said. 'Whenever we have met he has always mentioned you and his first visit to London to make *The Hasty Heart*, his favourite picture. In fact, when we were last in America, I could not think of something suitable and different to give him, so I suddenly thought of *The Hasty Heart* and took him some still pictures from the film; he was delighted. So asking you to be here tonight was my idea. I knew it would please him.'

As she bade us goodbye on that famous doorstep my hired car hove in sight. The firm had found me a limousine with a very appropriate registration plate, 666 TOD.

'There you are, Mr Todd. There's your car, 666 TOD,' said our very perceptive hostess.

What an evening to remember . . .

And so the water continues to run inexorably under the bridges for me and mine.

Whatever the future may hold for us, I only know one thing for sure:
The show must go on.
And on . . .
And on . . .

Index

Adelaide, 324–5, 326
Affair in Monte Carlo see 24 Hours of a Woman's Life
Africa, 120–29, 330
Aga Khan, 99
Aggis, Joe, 131–2, 137, 140, 158, 189, 232
Aitken, Jonathan, 323
Alexander, Terence, 145
Allen, Irving, 140, 182, 183
Allen, Ken, 203
Aman, Leigh (Lord Marley), 180
Ambler, Eric, 101
Amethyst, HMS, 100, 104, 145
Anderson, Judith, 178
Anderson, Michael, 62, 66, 67, 84, 90, 101, 105–6, 111, 116, 130, 243
Anderssen, Kaare and Mabel, 74
Andrews, Eamonn, 170
Annakin, Ken, 22, 28, 91, 186–7, 189, 194
Annakin, Pauline, 194
Argyll, Ian, Duke of, 47, 143
Argyll, Margaret, Duchess of, 143
Argyll and Sutherland Highlanders, 43–4
Armstrong, Bob, 49, 135, 140
Army Benevolent Fund Show, 227–8, 287
Arne, Peter, 145, 146
Asherson, Renée, 167
Assassin, The see Venetian Bird
Associated British Picture Corporation, 9, 11, 13, 30, 82, 145, 151, 163, 215–16, 256; contracts, 70, 89–90, 119–20, 204–5
Astor, Lord William, 108–9, 118, 141, 189, 228–9, 251
Astor, Lady Bronwen, 228, 251
Astor, Lady Nancy, 167
Asylum, 328
Attenborough, Richard, 39, 145, 148, 172
Attenborough, Sheila, 39, 172

Auckland, 319, 320
Australia, 318, 320–26, 340–42, 344–5, 359
Aylmer, Felix, 110

Bach, Vivi, 230
Baker, Carroll, 335
Ballymalis Castle, 212–13
Bampton Grange, 264–7, 281–2
Banbury, Frith, 275, 349
Barber, General Sir Colin, 143–4
Barber, Lady Vera, 143, 313–14, 317, 329, 346, 371
Barbour, Richard, 349
Bardot, Brigitte, 99, 108
Barfleur, HMS, 144
Barker, Felix, 114
Baroda, Maharaja Fatesingh, Gaekwad of, 326
Baron, Lynda, 268
Barr, Elsie, 48, 50
Barr, Patrick, 285, 315
Barrie, Amanda, 179
Barry, Gene, 279
Barry, Michael, 55, 56
Barthropp, Paddy, 285
Bartok, Eva, 10, 14–15
Barton, John, 337
Bastyan, Sir Edric and Victoria, 322
Batley, Dorothy, 276
Battaglia, Rik, 178
Battle of Villa Fiorita, The, 241
Baum, Harry, 80–81, 85, 88, 91, 97, 273
Baxter, Anne, 113, 116–17, 118, 138
Baxter, Derek, 282
Baylis, Derek, 205
Beatty, Robert, 306–8, 311, 312, 318
Beatty, Rosie, 318
Belfast, 192, 301

Ben-Gurion, David, 204
Benton Jones, Lady Maggie, 364
Benton Jones, Simon, 364, 371
Beret, Dawn, 180
Berger, Helmut, 290
Bergman, Ingrid, 300
Berlin Film Festival, 103, 243
Berman, Monty, 170
Berney, Sir Thomas, 22
Bernhard of the Netherlands, Prince, 73
Bertram Mills Circus, 84, 111
Best, Martin, 337
Bevis, Peter, 288
Bigsby, Ernie, 232, 266, 275, 281, 295, 305
Bigsby, Mrs Ernie, 266, 281, 295
Bille-Brahe, Count, 174
Bira, Prince, 100
Birendra, Prince of Nepal, 175
Birkett, Lord, 235
Birmingham, HMS, 115
Bishop, Mrs, 295, 296
Bisogno, Ernesto, 210, 216, 241
Blakeley, Colin, 186
Blessed, Brian, 330
Bolton, Peter, 28
Bond, Derek, 288, 306, 308, 311, 312
Boote, Arthur, 255
Booth, James, 186, 187
Booty, Jasper and Moggie, 357
Bowers, Lally, 275
Box, Betty, 9, 10
Box, Sidney and Sylvia, 345
Boy Dominic, The, 330, 331, 344
Boys, The, 198, 201, 202
Brackett, Charles, 85, 92, 96
Bradley, Sheila, 296, 306
Brand, Dick, 216, 221
Brandell, Mark, 225, 228
Brandram, Dick and Catherine, 179, 233
Bratby, John, 154
Brazzi, Rosanno, 241
Brecart, 131, 218–19, 302–3
Brett, Major, 212
Brett, Jeremy, 212
Brickhill, Paul, 8, 62
Bridge, Peter, 256–7, 261, 263, 267–8, 274
Broccoli, 'Cubby', 182
Brook, Faith, 118, 202, 334
Brookes, Johanna, 317, 329, 344
Brunius, Jacques, 4
Bryant, Sir Arthur, 226

Bryce, Alex, 37, 42
Buchanan Arms, Drymen, 42, 163
Buckingham, Frank, 182
Burton, Richard, 279
Business of Murder, The, 367–71
Bute, Lord and Lady 177
Buxton, Aubrey, 182
Byrne, John, 214
Byrne, Peter, 346

Caden-Prescott, Tom, 166, 223
Caine, Michael, 145
Cairo, 235–7
Calvert, Phyllis, 300
Camoys, Lady Jeanne, 361–2, 371; *see also* Stonor, Jeanne
Canada, 91, 139, 317–18, 338
Cannes Film Festival, 64, 99–100, 115–16, 156, 189, 210
Canning, Victor, 9
Cannon, Dennis, 162, 163, 173
Cape Town, 289–90, 349–50
Cardiff, Jack, 138
Carey, Joyce, 264, 276
Carpenter, Frances, 16–17
Carradine, John, 370
Carré, Daniel, 252, 255
Carreras, Michael, 225, 228
Carrington V.C., 166–7
Carrol, John, 315
Cartier, Rudolph, 55, 56
Castleman's Stud Farm, 36, 41, 140
Cervera, Carmen, 197–8
Chaffee, Don, 146
Chambord, Pierre, 27
Chandler, Pat, 254
Chard, Fiona, 126–7
Chase a Crooked Shadow, 113, 114–15, 116–18, 119, 130, 138
Chatwin, Clara, 64
Chelita, Princess, 100
Chichester-Constable, John, 313, 314
Christmas Carol, A, 311, 315–16
Churchill, Lady Clementina, 156
Churchill, Sir Winston, 92, 129, 156
Cicogna, Contessa Anna-Maria, 15
Cicogna, Bino, 15, 28–9
Cicogna, Marina, 15, 28–9, 101, 290
Ciné Cita, Rome, 59
Clark, May, 149

Clark, Robert, 8, 9, 11,13, 27–8, 61–2, 70, 82, 89–90, 92, 101, 114–15, 149, 196
Cleary, Jon, 238, 239, 241
Cleaver, Tony, 140
Clements, Sir John, 300
Clifford, Alasdair (grandson), 365, 371
Clifford, Christopher (grandson), 365, 371
Clifford, Elizabeth Alice (grand-daughter), 365, 366
Clifford, Lord Hugh, 352, 357, 371
Clifford, Lady Kay, 359–60
Clifford, Rollo (son-in-law), 351, 352, 357
Clifford-Turner, Jill, 3
Cliveden, 108, 118, 167, 229
Clyde, Tommy, 113, 114, 118
Coast of Skeletons, 243–4, 245–9
Coates, Eric, 72
Collector, The, 234–5
Collins, Hal, 271
Collins, Joan, 32, 85, 279, 365–6, 367
Colouris, George, 15
Columbia Pictures, 184, 272
Comrie, Pat, 91
Connery, Sean, 196
Cooper, Gary, 181
Coppel, Alec and Myra, 97
Corri, Adrienne, 293, 294
Cotton, Henry, 3, 6
Cotton, Jack, 211
Counsell, John, 253
Courcel, Nicole, 65, 73
Courtneidge, Dame Cicely, 277–8, 300, 309
Cowan, Theo, 103
Coward, Noël, 317, 362
Coyne, Harold, 145
Crichton-Stuart, Charles, 177
Crimes Does Not Pay see Gentle Art of Murder, The
Cripps, Miss, 162, 200, 217
Cullinan, Anne, 26, 35, 98
Cumber, Fred, 226
Currie, Finlay, 110, 128
Cushing, Peter, 370
Cuthbertson, Allan, 166

D-Day, the Sixth of June, 95–7, 112
Daily Express, 301
Daily Mail, 355
Daily Telegraph, 261
Dale, Jim, 330

Dam Busters, The, 8, 61–3, 66–70, 85, 90, 91, 92
Danger Within, 143, 145–7, 148, 155
Darlington, W. A., 261
Darrieux, Danielle, 198
Darvi, Bella, 99
Darwin, 344–5
Daves, Delmer, 241
Davies, Canon David, 347, 357, 361
Davies, Geoffrey, 365
Davis, Bette, 82, 86–7, 141
Davis, John, 103, 222
Dayan, General Moshe, 204
Dayan, Yael, 208, 209
De Havilland, Olivia, 274
De Sarigny, Peter, 164, 167, 172, 235, 255
De Sica, Vittorio, 59
De Villiers Graff, Sir, 188
De Woolf, Francis, 110
Dean, Vaughan, 177
Deane-Drummond, General Tony, 250
Dear Octopus, 274–9
Delannois, Jean, 92, 94
Decoin, Henri, 53, 56, 73
Denison, Michael, 258, 264, 300
Denmark, 173–4
'Desert Island Discs', 41
D'Esti, Roberta, 283
Devil Behind Me, The, 225–6
Diamond Story, The, 205, 210, 215, 222–3, 238, 249, 257
Dietrich, Marlene, 73
Dillon, Carmen, 22
Disney, Lillian, 79
Disney, Walt, 51–2, 79, 171
Disney Company, 12–13, 26, 28, 41
Doble, Fred, 148, 235, 244
Dobson, Arlette, 147
Docklands Settlements Dinner, 202
dogs, 6, 7, 19–20, 42, 43, 48, 63, 98, 128, 129, 137, 142, 147–8, 149, 150, 152–4, 157, 167, 172, 190, 195, 196–7, 232, 244, 249–50, 267, 294, 295, 296–7, 305–6, 307, 356
Don't Bother to Knock, 177–9, 180–82, 189–90; see also *Love From Everybody*
Douglas, Angela, 179
Douglas, Robert, 85, 97
Douglas, Sue, 97
Douglas-Hamilton, Lord Malcolm, 61
Douro, Lady Diana, 141, 154

Douro, Lord Valerian, 141, 153, 154, 167
Downing, John, 311
Drache, Heinz, 246
Drake, Betsy, 139
Dreifuss, Arthur, 271, 272
Dresdel, Sonia, 285
Dublin, 112, 156, 211–12
Dunant, Harold, 133, 153, 218, 220, 267, 281
Dunant, Marcella, 133, 267, 281
Duncan, Archie, 41
Dunfee, Jack, 10
Dunlop, Frank, 315
Durban, 187, 229–30, 246–7, 350
Duryea, Dan, 8
Dykes, Mr, 198, 232
Dymchurch Redoubt, 203

Easton, Mrs, 369
Ed Sullivan Show, 92
Edinburgh, 180, 277
Edinburgh, Duke of, 102, 114, 118, 279
Edinburgh Festival, 315
Edmund Gurney and the Brighton Mesmerist, 268–9
Elizabeth, Queen, 102, 118, 279
Elizabeth, Queen, the Queen Mother, 154, 156, 232
Elizabeth, Princess of Yugoslavia, 179–80
Elliott, Paul, 293–4, 297–8, 300, 311, 333, 364
Elm House, Market Deeping, 330–1, 332, 340, 345, 349
Elson, Cliff, 192
Elstree Studios, 30, 31–2, 34, 109, 129–30, 139, 176, 182, 204
Engel, Ruth, 75
Engel, Sam, 71–2, 75–6, 77, 82, 92
English, David, 355
Equus, 339, 340–41, 344
Esmond, Jill, 72
Evans, Admiral Sir Charles, 163, 254
Evans, Rupert, 23, 41
Everett, Peter, 283–5
Ewing-Crawford, Brigadier and Mrs, 47

Fair White Tower, A (son et lumiére), 227
Fairbanks Jnr, Douglas, 112, 114, 118, 130, 300
Faith, Adam, 169, 172
Fan Club, 11–12, 166, 204–5, 269–70

Farmer, Tommy, 24
farming, 73, 84, 99, 119, 130–31, 140, 244; *see also* Shiplake Dairy Company
Federation of British Film Makers, 157, 234
Feely, Terence, 365
Fellows, Hugh, 91
Ferreira, Mario, 155, 198
Fforde, Lady Jean, 151–2, 219, 250, 366
Fick, Ben, 21, 133
Field, Shirley Ann, 183
Fieldhouse, Sir John, 371
Film Finance Corporation, 145
Firbank, Ann, 337
Fisher, Lord John, 362
FitzPatrick, Eileen (aunt), 37, 156, 212
FitzPatrick, Fintan (uncle), 37, 156, 212
Fleming, Ian, 205
Flesh and Blood, 6
Fletcher, Eric, 158
Flowers, Rupert, 363
Fonda, Henry, 196
Forbes, Bryan, 148
Foreman, Carl, 188
Forres, Lord and Lady, 152
Forté, Charles, 253
Four Sided Triangle, 293, 295–6
Fox, James, 315
Foxwell, Ivan, 2, 3, 5, 6
Francis, Michael, 41
Frankel, Cyril, 174, 177, 181, 209
Franklyn, William, 146
Frankovitch, Mike, 219
Fraser, Liz, 179, 228
Fraser, Moyra, 349
Fraser, Ronald, 176, 178–9, 186
Freddie, King of Bugunda, 129
French, Harold, 40, 41
French, Valerie, 97
Frewin, Leslie, 7, 8, 64, 73, 139
Furie, Sidney, 198, 199, 201
Furze, Roger, 109

Gale, General Sir Richard, 171
Gardiner, Nadia, 97
Gardiner, Reggie, 97
Gardner, Ava, 20, 21
Gayton, Freddie, 48
Gaze, Michael, 296–7, 305, 307
Genn, Leo, 3
Gentle Art of Murder, The, 198, 201, 210
Getty, J. Paul, 253

Gibbins, Boyd, 190, 211
Gibson, Eve, 62
Gibson, Freddie, 319
Gibson, Wing Commander Guy, 8, 62, 67, 68; dog 'Nigger', 67–8
Gielgud, Sir John, 109, 110
Gielgud, Val, 227
Giles, Sir Norman and Lady, 325
Gladstone, Peter, 118–19, 175, 192, 367
Glasgow, 163–4
Glassenbury Park, 291, 316–17, 331
Gloucester, Duke and Duchess of, 90
Godwin, Frank, 145, 163, 174, 178, 181, 183
Goldie, Hugh, 368
Gollins, Franklin, 114
Gondrée family, 194
Goodlatte, Jack, 158
Goodliffe, Michael, 264
Goodman, Lord, 315
Gordon, Colin, 179
Goring, Marius, 279
Gorringe, Eve, 320
Gotfurt, Fritz, 7, 11, 91, 173
Gough, Michael, 27, 41
Grant, Brian, 304
Grant, Joyce, 288
Grant, Sheila, 304
Grant-Bogle Mr and Mrs, 192–3, 201–2, 235
Grass is Greener, The, 312
Graves, Peter, 288
Gray, Dulcie, 258, 264, 300
Greco, Juliette, 125, 127–9, 130, 154
Green, Guy, 41
Greene, Graham, 90, 91
Gregson, John, 15
Grinsell, Sergeant, 171
Grosscurth, Mrs, 238
Grosscurth, Peter, 221, 237–9, 255
Grunwald, Anatole de, 10
Guide Dogs for the Blind Association, 269–70
Guinness, Alec, 211
Gurney, Rachel, 262
Guy, Charles, 42

Haileywood, 99, 119, 130–5, 172, 181, 202, 203, 237, 242, 264, 267
Haileywood Films, 163
Hakim, André and Susan, 84
Hall-Caine, Derek and Maggie, 3, 8, 73, 74

Hammond, Peter, 268, 269
Hancock, Kate, 171
Hands, Terry, 337
Hanson, Robert, 214
Happy Breed, This, 362
Harbottle, Lt. Colonel, 198
Harbottle, Laurence, 98, 114, 120, 216
Hare, Robertson, 309
Harper, Ken, 10
Harris, Richard (actor), 176, 177
Harris, Richard (writer), 367
Harrison, George, 237
Harvey, John, 226–7, 228, 235
Harvey, Laurence, 173, 176–7
Hasty Heart, The, 176, 333, 373
Havelock-Allan, Anthony, 212
Hayward, Ian, 325
Heath, Edward, 234
Hedley, Jack, 212
Helen, ex-Queen of Rumania, 179–80
Hellions, The, 182, 184, 186–7
Henderson, Miss, 132, 138
Henley Midnight Matinée, 172–3, 189, 203, 204, 223, 225, 237, 254
Henley Regatta, 118–19, 175, 192, 255
Henningson, Joan, 353
Herbst, Willi, 184–5
Heywood, Anne, 209, 212
Higgins, Henry, 336
Hill, Bertie, 90, 102
Hillier, Erwin, 70, 245
Hobson, Harold, 261
Hobson, Valerie, 212, 229
Hodges, Ken, 285
Holland, Anthony, 259, 261
Hollow Crown, The, 337
Hollywood, 30–31, 74–6, 79–83
Hollywood Reporter, 271
Honey, Aldine, 154
Hong Kong, 351, 354–5
Hopper, Dennis, 334
Horse of the Year Show, 53, 73, 217
horse-racing, 12, 21, 23–4, 41, 140–41, 203
Horstig-Primuz, Olga, 8
House of the Long Shadows, The, 370
Houston, Renée, 306, 307, 308
Howard, John and Joy, 194
Howard, Trevor, 97, 244, 286, 370
Howells, Ursula, 275–6
Hughes, Howard, 78, 79
Hughes, Ken, 135

Hulbert, Jack, 275, 277, 300
Hunter, Amy and Dolly (aunts), 218–19, 296, 302, 306, 342
Hunter, Colin, 148
Huntington, Laurence, 228, 230
Huntley, Raymond, 264
Hurst, Veronica, 23
Hurwitz, Oscar, 187, 217, 239, 350, 351
Hurwitz, Ruth, 239, 351
Huth, Harold, 183, 187
Hutton, Sir Leonard, 226

Ibiza (holiday home), 252, 255–6, 257, 275, 287
Ideal Husband, An, 256–64, 267–8, 290
Innes, Hammond, 196
Intent to Kill, 136, 138–9
International Horse Show, 73, 144
Israel, 203–4

Jackson, Glenda, 300
Jackson, Hal, 149, 151
Jackson, Peter, 149
Jacobi, Derek, 359
James, Sir Morrice, 324
Jameson, Sue, 285
Jeans, Ursula, 258
Jeffries, Lionel, 186
Jersey, 144–5
Johannesburg, 184, 216, 229, 239, 246, 349
Johns, Glynis, 20, 28, 36–7, 41, 48, 300, 317, 318
Johns, Mervyn, 169, 311
Johnson, Richard, 244
Johnson, Van, 8
Jones, David, 170
Joyce, Eileen, 93
Judd, Edward, 293, 294
Justice, Barry, 349
Justice, James Robertson, 20, 28, 41

Kass, Ron, 366
Katzman, Sam, 270
Keene, Mr, 144, 223, 235
Kelly, Terence, 293
Kendrew, General Sir Douglas, 326
Kent, Jean, 288
Kenton, Geoffrey, 276
Kenwright, Bill, 367, 368, 371
Kerans, Commander John, 100, 104–5
Kernan, David, 283

King, Sir Alexander, 163
Kingcombe, Brian, 285
Kitt, Eartha, 60, 207–8, 300
Kitzmiller, John, 125, 130
Knight, Mr, 332
Knight, Barney, 356
Knight, Elizabeth, 288
Koch, Marianne, 226, 230, 243, 247, 248
Koernitz, Harry, 9
Kolek, Teddy, 204
Kortner, Peter, 219
Koster, Henry (Bobby), 75, 85, 86, 96

Lancaster, Burt, 8
Land God Gave to Cain, The, 196
Lane-Fox, Jimmy, 363
Langley, Lee, 160
Las Vegas, 338–9
Last Hunter, The, 274
Last of the Long Haired Boys, The, 284–6
Latta, C. J., 11, 21, 158, 182
Laurie, John, 179
Laye, Dilys, 283, 312
Laye, Evelyn, 300
Lazar, Irving, 20
Le Mesurier, John, 169, 179
Leahy, Fred, 28
Lee, Bernard, 145
Lee, Christopher, 370
Lee, Vanessa, 288
Lennard, Robert, 7, 11, 13, 61, 70, 171, 182, 204, 241
Lesley, Carole, 158
Lesslie, Colin, 143, 146, 148
Levinson, Jack, 240, 249
Levy, Charlie, 50
Lieven, Albert, 230
Lightning Strikes Twice, 6
Lilford, Vernon and Maggie, 350–51
Lime Grove Studios, 57
Lister, Moira, 342, 343
Lit, Le, 53, 56–7, 59, 73
Litchfield, Basil, 70
Little Ponton House, 342–3, 345, 348–9, 363
Livesey, Roger, 258
Lloyd, Jeremy, 226, 230
Lockwood, Margaret, 258–9, 300, 355
Lollobrigida, Gina, 4, 10, 23, 163
Lom, Herbert, 118, 328
Long and the Short and the Tall, The, 155, 162, 173, 176–7, 183, 203

Longest Day, The, 141–2, 191, 193–6, 204, 219
Lonsdale, Frederick, 4
Lonsdale, Lord James, 253
Lorne, Constance, 276
Loser Takes All, 90–91
Love From Everybody, 157, 162, 173, 174–5, 177; *see also Don't Bother to Knock*
Love-ins, The, 270–74
Lucas, Ron, 310, 312, 359
Lynn, Bob, 226

MacArthur, James, 272
McCallum, David, 176
McConnell, James and Mary, 363
McCorquodale, Alastair, 342
McCorquodale, Neil, 348–9, 372
McCorquodale, Rosemary, 342
McCorquodale, Sarah, 372
MacGregor, Sir Malcolm, 47
Mackay, Fulton, 179
McLachlan, Byron, 325
Maclehose, Sir Murray, 354
MacMurray, Fred, 8
Maddern, Victor, 110
Magee, Patrick, 212
Magpie, HMS, 104
Maidenwell Manor, 282, 286, 294, 296, 306
Mailer, Anne (mother-in-law), 301, 340, 344
Mailer, Colin (father-in-law), 301, 315, 340, 344
Mailer, Dallas (brother-in-law), 301, 315
Mailer, Virginia (wife), 238, 304, 306, 310, 320, 333, 338, 345, 359; first meeting with future husband, 279–81; engagement, 288–9; marriage, 297, 300–301; birth of children, 328–9, 355
Man Called Peter, A, 70–72, 76–9, 81–2, 87–8
Man with a Load of Mischief, The, 282–3
Man Who Could Find Things, The, 167
Man Who Never Was, The, 84
Mann, Anthony, 243
Mann, Christopher, 93
Mann, Roderick, 139–40
Manning, Hugh, 166
Manvell, Roger, 253
Mar del Plata Film Festival, 183, 253–4
Marais, Mr, 210, 215
Margaret, Princess, 90, 157
Marie Antoinette, 90, 92, 94–5, 99

Markham, David, 285
Marmstadt, Laurenz, 53
Marquise, The, 317
Marriott, Mr, 132
Martinez de Hos family, 183
Marshall, Catherine, 70, 79
Marshall, Herbert, 85
Martin, Mickey, 8, 62
Martins, Orlando, 128
Maskell, Virginia, 227
Mason, Diana, 90
Masonry, 107, 139, 228, 295
Maurey, Nicole, 178, 180
Member of the Family, 207–8, 209–10
Men and Magic, 268
Men from Moscow, The, 135
Menday, Colonel Ronald, 203
Merrow, Jane, 179
Mervish, 'Honest Ed', 317–18
Metro-Goldwyn-Mayer (MGM), 20, 30, 244, 272
Michaels, Louis, 298, 332–3, 338, 353, 367, 369
Michelmore, Cliff, 170
Miller, Harry, 318, 319, 320–21
Miller, Janine, 276
Miller, Wendy, 319, 320–1
Mills, Hayley, 237
Mills, Sir John, 237, 244, 300
Mills, Lady (Mary Hayley-Bell), 237
Miss Adams Will Be Waiting, 342, 344
Miss World contest, 37, 197, 219
Mr Blessington's Imperialist Plot, 7–8, 9
Mitchell, Warren, 179
Mitchell, Yvonne, 55
Mitchum, Robert, 64
Mitford, Nancy, 92
Mogg, General, 250
Moment of Truth, 164–5, 167, 168 *see also Never Let Go*
Monroe, Marilyn, 76
Monte Carlo, 2–6
Montrose, Duke of, 47, 60
Moore, Kieron, 3
More, Kenneth, 300
More O'Ferrall, George, 72, 166, 167
Moreau, Jeanne, 53, 56, 60
Moreland, Mr, 131, 198
Morgan, Michèle, 92, 94, 99, 198
Morley, Robert, 201, 202, 323
Morris, Mary, 330

Moscow, 158–62
Mountbatten of Burma, Earl, 163, 217
Mowlam, Carol, 315, 369
Murder in Mind, 365–6, 367
Murray, Stephen, 4
Murray-Hamilton, Miss, 58, 132

Naismith, Laurence, 128
Naked Earth, The, 112, 119, 124–30
Napier, Diana, 268
Narizano, Sylvio, 334
National Film Finance Corporation 163
Neal, Patricia, 363
Neame, Ronald, 84
Neeme, Aarne, 340, 341
Neil, Hildegard, 330
Neilson, Perlita, 258, 260, 276
Nell Gwynn House, 41, 155, 215, 306
Nesbitt, Derren, 369
Never Let Go, 168–70, 172, 175 *see also Moment of Truth*
New Zealand, 318–20
Newton, Robert, 97
Nimmo, Derek, 246, 352
Noble, Patricia, 306, 308
Norman, Leslie, 173, 177
Normandy, 194–6
North, Lindy, 225
North, Rex, 224
Northwood, Nanny, 113, 136
Norway, 73–4
Novello, Nicola, 276

008 of the Secret Service, 351
Oberammergau Passion Play, 165–6, 172
Oberon, Merle, 2–4, 6
O'Brien, Colonel Tuonig, 215
Ockenden Venture, 141, 145, 173, 218
O'Connor, Christy, 212
Ogden, Archie, 216
O'Gorman, Dr Gerry, 224
O'Hara, Maureen, 241
O'Herlihy, Dan, 85
Oliphant, Sir Mark, 325
Oliver, Alan, 73, 232
Oliver, Susan, 272
On Approval, 349–50, 351–2
Operation Crossbow, 243, 244–5
O'Reilly, Tony, 24
O'Toole, Peter, 155
Oxley, David, 110

Palmer, Carol, 111
Palmer, Ken, 289
Palmer, Lord Raymond, 110, 182
Palmer, Lady Tory, 101, 110, 182
Pampel, Queenie (later Mrs Saunders), 154–5, 191, 245, 249, 267, 269, 288, 295, 297, 329, 369
Paris, 24–5, 93–5, 198–9, 204
Parker, Al, 89, 98
Parrish, Robert, 238, 239
Parsons, John, 24, 25
Paul, Jill, 7, 26, 40, 42, 93–4, 100, 112
Paul, Susan, 371
Pearce, Joyce, 141, 171, 217–18
Pearce, Perce, 12, 20, 23, 28
Pearson, Michael, 285
Pegasus Café (Caen), 194
Peppard, George, 244
Percival, Michael, 306, 308
Perth, 325–6, 345, 359
Peters, Jean, 76, 77–79, 82
Phillimore, Colonel, 223
Pickman, Kay, 75, 79
Pickman, Milton, 9, 20, 75, 79, 83, 87, 101, 135, 165, 215, 219
Piercey, Bridget, 7, 36
Piggott, Lester, 23–4, 354
Piggott, Susan, 354
Pine-Coffin, Colonel Geoffrey, 171
Pinewood Studios, 32, 33–4
Pitcher, Nanny, 49–50, 60, 79, 93, 106–7
Playne, Nick, 347
Pleasure and Repentance, 337
Plomley, Roy, 41
Poch, Pedro Luis, 255, 287
Pole, John, 242
Polyhomes Company, 238, 270
Porter, Nyree Dawn, 367
Porter, Tom and June, 325, 345
Preisinger, Anton, 165
Preminger, Mary, 97
Preminger, Otto, 109–10, 111
Prescott Affair, The, see Chase a Crooked Shadow
Prevett, Mr, 131, 135, 137, 147, 184
Prevett, Mrs, 131, 135, 138
Prevett, Tom, 131
Price, Vincent, 370
Primrose, Dorothy, 275
Profumo, John, 229

Quadrille, 355

Quarrier, Iain, 285
Queen's Messenger, 215–16, 232, 245, 250
Quigley, Sarah, 75
Quinn, Derry, 210, 215

Raine, Gillian, 258, 285
Rambeau, Marjorie, 77
Rampling, Charlotte, 328
Rank Organisation, 9, 11,30, 238, 257
Ratner, Dr Victor, 201, 217
Ratoff, Gregory, 88
Rattigan, Terence, 315
Reagan, Ronald and Nancy, 372–3
Redgrave, Sir Michael, 66, 300, 359
Redmond, Moira, 365
Redway, John, 270
Reeve, George, 7, 37, 107
Reeve, Tim, 26, 35
Reeves, Kynaston, 179
Reiss, Amanda, 293, 294, 349
Rénaud, Line, 24
Rennie, Michael, 279
Renton, Nick, 318
Reynolds, Christopher, 276
Richards, Dick, 129
Richards, Sir Gordon, 24
Richardson, Sir Ralph, 300
Rilla, Walter, 15
Roar Like a Dove, 306, 307–8, 310
Rob Roy, 26, 28, 42–6, 49, 53, 54, 61, 74
Robertson, Dale, 240
Robin Hood, 16
Rogers, Anne, 355
Rollo, John, 61, 163
Rome, 59, 225
Ronaldshay, Lord, 157
Rooke, Laurence, 90
Roose-Evans, James, 257, 258, 261
Rose, Clifford, 337
Rosewarne, Paul, 84, 130, 131, 217, 223, 242, 264
Royal Film Performances, 53, 54–5, 154
Royal Shakespeare Company, 337
Russell, Jane, 8
Russell-Flint, Sir William, 140
Rutland, Mr and Mrs, 7, 40
Rutland, Charles, Duke of, 313, 361, 363
Rutland, Frances, Duchess of, 313
Ryan, Cornelius, 141–2, 191
Ryan, Paddy, 23, 41
Ryton, Royce, 315

St Joan, 109–13, 118
St John, Earl, 223
Sanders of the River, 225–6, 229–32
Sanguinet, Paul, 139
Saunders, Geoffrey, 249
Save the Children Fund, 238, 256
Saville, Victor, 2
Scaife, Ted, 181
Scales, Prunella, 337
Schlaepfer, Arnold, 255
Schock, Rudolf, 103
Schreiber, Lew, 70, 71, 83, 91, 92, 95
Scott, Major and Mrs, 265
Scott, Tim and Rosemary, 350
Screen Gems, 219
Seberg, Jean, 109–10, 111, 118
Secombe, Harry, 227–8, 323
Secrets d'Alcove see Lit, Le
Sellars, Elizabeth, 168, 169, 315
Sellers, Peter, 165, 169, 172, 175
Shaffer, Anthony, 318, 349
Sharp, Anthony, 288
Shaughnessy, Alfred, 357
Shaw, Robert, 70, 155
Shepperton Studios, 32–3
Sheridan, Dinah, 103
Sherman, Vincent, 112, 119, 124, 125, 127, 130
Sherriff, Robert, 61, 62
Sherwood, John, 7, 8
Shiplake Dairy Company, 205–6, 210, 217, 242, 243, 244, 254, 270
Shonteff, Lindsay, 351
Shrewsbury School, 118–19, 175, 192, 255
Sievewright, Eric, 91
Simmons, Bob, 23, 186
Sims, Sylvia, 328
Sinclair, Barry, 317
Singapore, 326–7
Sitting Duck, 100–101; *see also Yangtse Incident*
Skeleton Coast (SW Africa), 248–9
Skofic, Milko, 163
Skouras, Spyros, 88, 136
Sky is Falling, The, 334–6
Sleath, Alan, 165, 170, 172
Sleeping Mountain, The, 140, 142, 145, 151, 157
Sleuth, 318, 325, 346, 348
Smith, Dodie, 274, 277
Smith's Hospital, 223–5
Solon, Ewen, 41

Sommer, Elke, 179, 181, 182
South Africa, 184–8, 229–31, 239–40, 245–7, 349–51
Spain, 116–17, 334–6
Speakman, George, 157, 192
Spector, Maud, 20
Stafford, John, 91
Stebbings, Basil, 84, 89, 98, 217, 223, 235
Steele, Tommy, 158
Sterling, Alex, 279–80, 281, 301
Stevens, Warren and Lydia, 139, 140
Stockdale, Sir Edmund, 153
Stokes, Sister, 113
Stone, Richard, 334, 339, 342, 351
Stonor, Jeanne (later Lady Camoys), 119, 132, 313, 361–2, 371
Stonor, Julia, 132, 154
Stonor, Sherman (later Lord Camoys), 119, 132, 312–13
Storm, Lesley, 306
Story of Dorian Gray, The, 290
Stross, Raymond, 208, 212, 215
Subterfuge, 279
Sullivan, Hugh, 337
Summer, John, 323
Summerfield, Eleanor, 179, 180
Sutcliffe, Jane, 291, 316, 319, 329
Suzman, Janet, 300
Swanepoel, Dale, 229
Switzerland, 113–14, 221
Sword and the Rose, The, 12–13, 20, 22–3, 26, 27–8, 50, 52
Symonds, Captain and Mrs, 230, 240

Tasmania, 321–2
Taylor, Elizabeth, 97
Taylor, Ken, 268
Taylor, Robert, 95, 96
Teaser, HMS, 105
television productions, 165, 172, 216, 274, 295, 301; *see also Boy Dominic, The, Carrington V.C., Edmund Gurney and the Brighton Mesmerist, Member of the Family, Wuthering Heights*
Telfer-Smollet, Patrick and Gina, 333
Tennant, Andrew, 325
Terry, John, 173
Tesler, Brian, 216
Thacker family, 356
Thameside Radio, 253
Thatcher, Margaret, 372–3

theatre productions *see Business of Murder, The, Dear Octopus, Four Sided Triangle, Ideal Husband, An, Man with a Load of Mischief, The, Murder in Mind*, Triumph Theatre Productions
'This Is Your Life', 170–72
Thomas, Ralph, 9, 10, 21
Thompson, Alan, 166
Thorburn, June, 174, 180
Thring, Frank, 323
Tierney, Malcolm, 285
Todd, Granny, 64
Todd, Andrew Richard Palethorpe (son), 328–9, 334, 339, 347, 361, 371
Todd, Major Andrew William Palethorpe (father), 60–61
Todd, Bob, 320
Todd, Fiona Margaret Palethorpe (daughter), 97, 101, 157, 191–2, 217, 237, 254–5, 264, 282, 292, 296, 316, 317, 346, 351; engagement, 352; marriage, 357; children, 365
Todd, Kitty (Catherine) (wife) 2, 3, 4, 6–7, 35, 41, 59, 64, 73, 93, 135, 141, 155, 171–2, 236, 264, 296; birth of children, 25, 97–8; illnesses, 50, 56, 106, 109, 114; death of grandmother, 60; divorce, 286–7, 288, 292
Todd, Peter Grant Palethorpe (son), 25, 35, 39, 95, 113, 142, 211, 242–3, 275, 296, 300, 308–10, 342, 346, 362, 371; schooldays, 138, 175, 184, 203, 255, 287; engagement, 361–2; marriage, 362–3
Todd, Seumas Alexander Palethorpe (son), 355, 361, 366, 371
Toerian, Pieter, 288, 289, 349
Towers, Harry Alan, 225, 226, 243, 245, 246, 290
Trevelyan, John, 274
Trewin, J. C., 261
Trier, Peter, 134, 135
Trimmer, Colonel, 121–2, 124
Triumph Theatre Productions, 297–300, 308, 310–11, 315, 328, 332–3, 336–7, 355 364–5; *see also Christmas Carol, A, Equus, Grass is Greener, The, Happy Breed, This, Miss Adams Will Be Waiting, On Approval, Roar like a Dove, Sleuth*, theatre productions
Tuck, Stanford, 285

Tunis, Field Marshal Lord Alexander of, 227
Tunisia, 330
Turner's Court, 203, 204
Turnor, Major, 342
Tutin, Dorothy, 152, 166
Twentieth Century-Fox, 30–31, 70, 75, 79, 119, 136, 256
24 hours of a Woman's Life, 2–6, 35

Uganda, 126–9
Unsworth, Geoffrey, 22, 174, 181
Uys, Jamie, 186

Van Heerden, Dawie, 289
Variety Club, 21, 170, 172, 224–5
Vaughan, Ivan and Maureen, 156, 212
Veitch, Tony, 244
Venetian Bird, 9, 10, 14–16, 20, 35
Venice, 14–17, 28–9
Very Edge, The, 210, 211
Victorious, HMS, 163
Virgin Queen, The, 82, 84, 85–7
Voisey, Peter, 207, 208
Vorster, Norma, 185, 187
Vow, The, 172

Wade, Mr, 184, 188, 189, 192, 206, 246, 249
Wade, Michael, 184, 210, 246, 249
Walbrook, Anton, 110
Waldhorn, Christie, 324
Waldhorn, Gary, 318, 323, 324
Waldhorn, Joshua, 324
Wales, Prince and Princess of, 372
Walker, Brigadier Johnny and Margaret, 314
Wallace, Gregg, 320, 346, 357, 361
Wallace, Marjorie, 301
Wallis, Dr Barnes, 62–3
Wallis, Jimmy, 92, 115, 151, 171, 173, 205, 215
Wantling, Janet, 362
Ward, Stephen, 188–9, 229
Varner Brothers, 11, 30
Warrington, John, 207
Varter, Sir Philip, 11
Warwick Films, 182
Washington DC, 78
Waterhouse, Lady Caroline, 233
Watkin, Larry, 22
Watkins, Arthur, 156

Waugh, Ann, 147, 155, 182
Wayside House, 6–7, 36–7, 84, 98, 99, 119, 133
Webb, Bob, 170
Webb, Jay, 285
Webb, Peter, 155, 184, 189, 206, 245
Weil, Ann, 8, 35, 249–50
Weil, Colonel Freddie, 8, 12, 39, 73, 140
Weldon, Duncan, 293–4, 297, 298, 300, 306, 311, 336, 346, 353, 365
Weldon, Colonel Frank, 90, 101, 102
Weldon, Janet, 338
Wellington, New Zealand, 320
Wells 'Bombardier' Billy, 145
Weston, Garfield, 196, 223
Wheeler, Cyril, 258, 276
When Kinghtood was in Flower see Sword and the Rose, The
White, Mr, 112, 132–3
White, Carol, 202
White, General 'Mat', 228
White, Valerie, 276
Whittaker, Bill, 67
Whittaker, Michael, 154
Widmark, Richard, 110
Wiehann, Barry, 188
Wieler, Brigadier Leslie, 219, 227
Wilcox, Herbert, 100, 106, 111, 114, 115
Wilde, Marty, 186
Wilde, Oscar, 256, 262
Wilding, Michael, 60, 97, 145
Wilkie, Pat, 100, 109, 141, 147
Williams, Elmo, 193
Williams, Hugh, 312
Willis, Ted, 151
Willoughby, George, 205, 210, 215, 216, 238, 255, 274
Willoughby, Stanie, 205
Windhoek (SW Africa), 241, 247, 249
Windle, John, 149, 167
Windsor, Duke and Duchess of, 16
Winestone, Julius, 7
Winslow Boy, The, 315
Winters, Shelley, 334, 335
Winton, Sharon, 228
Withers, Googie, 300, 323
Wolff, John, 3, 166
Woolf, Bob, 21
Worker, Andy, 138, 139
Wuthering Heights, 55, 57–8

Wyler, William, 234
Wynter, Dana, 88, 92, 95, 112

Yangtse Incident, 101, 104–6, 111, 114,
   115–16; *see also Sitting Duck*
Yates, Jess, 329

Youlden, Tony, 340
Young, Terence, 10

Zampi, Mario, 177
Zanuck, Darryl, 70, 82–3, 92, 128–9, 130,
   191, 194, 219